Anticapitalism and the Emergence of Antisemitism

This book is part of the Peter Lang Political Science, Economics, and Law list.
Every volume is peer reviewed and meets
the highest quality standards for content and production.

PETER LANG
New York • Bern • Berlin
Brussels • Vienna • Oxford • Warsaw

Stephanie M. Chasin

Anticapitalism and the Emergence of Antisemitism

PETER LANG
New York • Bern • Berlin
Brussels • Vienna • Oxford • Warsaw

Library of Congress Cataloging-in-Publication Data

Names: Chasin, Stephanie M., author.
Title: Anticapitalism and the emergence of antisemitism / Stephanie M. Chasin.
Description: New York: Peter Lang Publishing, Inc., 2020.
Includes bibliographical references and index.
Identifiers: LCCN 2019022449 | ISBN 978-1-4331-7087-4 (hardback: alk. paper)
ISBN 978-1-4331-7084-3 (ebook pdf)
ISBN 978-1-4331-7085-0 (epub) | ISBN 978-1-4331-7086-7 (mobi)
Subjects: LCSH: Antisemitism—Europe, Western—History. |
Antisemitism—Europe—History. | Capitalism—Europe—History.
Classification: LCC DS146.E85 C427 | DDC 305.892/404—dc23
LC record available at https://lccn.loc.gov/2019022449
DOI 10.3726/b15877

Bibliographic information published by **Die Deutsche Nationalbibliothek.**
Die Deutsche Nationalbibliothek lists this publication in the "Deutsche Nationalbibliografie"; detailed bibliographic data are available on the Internet at http://dnb.d-nb.de/.

The paper in this book meets the guidelines for permanence and durability of the Committee on Production Guidelines for Book Longevity of the Council of Library Resources.

Printed in the United States of America

Contents

Contents

Introduction

A 1933 definition of the word "Jew" in the *Oxford English Dictionary* reads: "As a name of opprobrium: spec. applied to a grasping or extortionate person." Even as late as the 1970s, the term "Jew" was commonly used to refer to a greedy person. The link between Jews and money is, as one writer noted, a "terribly durable myth," that has ebbed, halted, lay dormant, and flowed again through history. A recent upswing in antisemitism in Europe and the US includes comments made by public officials about Jews and finance that some years ago would have ended in a resignation. In February 2019, Ilhan Omar, the Democratic representative for Minnesota, tweeted that the relationship between the US and Israel was "all about the Benjamins." In France, Yellow Vest protesters (*Gilet Jaune*) protested outside the Rothschilds bank in Paris, holding signs referring to "Banksters" and condemning "slavery by usury" (*l'esclavage par l'usure*). In England, the Labour party is rife with antisemitism, and one slogan used by some supporters twisted Jeremy Corbyn's mantra, "For the many, not the few," replacing the last word with "Jew." In 2018, Corbyn defended a 2012 mural by the American artist Mear One which depicts hook-nosed Jewish bankers sitting at a large Monopoly table stacked with money. The table rests on the backs of faceless black men. In March 2019, a carnival float by the group Vismooiln in the Belgian city of Aalst, Belgium, featured a grotesque version of two Orthodox Jews. While their hands grabbed moneybags, a rat sat on top of another sack filled with cash. The float was decorated with gold and silver coins. The response by the float makers was that it was a piece of satire, no different to the polemical cartoons put out by the magazine *Charlie Hebdo* in Paris.[1]

This idea that Jews are money-driven and that capitalism is Jewish has a long history. This longstanding myth is the subject of this book. It explores the interconnection that ran, and still runs, across the political and social spectrum and was constructed over centuries by critics of capitalism. From medieval usury (lending at interest) to modern capitalism, Jews were depicted as the bearers of this economic system that has been denounced as everything from extortionate to evil. In the modern era, German economists Karl Marx and Werner Sombart were two of the leading proponents to claim that capitalism was a Jewish invention and formed what was called the "Jewish spirit," in their respective books *Zur Judenfrage* (1843) and *Die Juden und das Wirtschaftsleben* (1911).[2]

Notwithstanding the enduring stereotype, as Julie L. Mell points out in *The Myth of the Medieval Jewish Moneylender*, the number of Jews who took up usury as a profession was small and, by the late twelfth century, Christians, mainly Italians, had entered into moneylending in significant numbers and, in many places, dominated the profession. That said, even though it is true that most Jews were not financiers, this does not negate the ones who were. It does not erase them from history, nor should they be. Individual Jewish moneylenders, however small a number, were not inconsequential. Some were high profile figures and extremely wealthy and influential; most were small to medium-scale financiers, as Mell documents, who helped people start small businesses, buy their merchandize, supply their daughters with dowries, pay taxes and other bills, and just get by during bad harvests and hard times. To argue their insignificance simply because they were not numerically dominant, as Mell does, suggests an unease with this link between any Jews and capitalism along with a desire to put a great distance between the two. It is not the case that Jewish moneylenders were virtually non-existent. The myth lies in the transference of that professional identity of a relatively small number of Jewish individuals onto Jews collectively. This myth is compounded by others, suggesting that Jews have an inherent ability for finance and that the love of money is an innate trait.[3]

The association between Jews and capitalism would be meaningless, or harmless, if the capital-based profit economy and its institutions were not widely seen as a vice. It is not enough to try and distance Jews from capitalism as that would not undo this centuries-old stereotype. The myth of the inherent evil of capitalism has to be attacked as well. To its harshest critics, capitalism is exploitative and oppressive, and the people who practice it were, and are, naturally motivated by "the greed of gold," as Sombart described it, rather than the common good. Financiers have long been cast as society's villains, whatever their religion, and that continues today with groups such as Occupy Wall Street and Extinction. Rebellion. Whether it is a thirteenth-century preacher denouncing usury as uncharitable, Karl Marx's comment that money is the Jews' god, the alt-right White Nationalists who chant "The Jews will not replace us," and disparage free trade and global markets, or an American actor retweeting a cartoon of an arm bearing the Star of David while its hand crushes a multitude of people and has a tag line that reads, "Follow the money," there is a consistent and enduring connection made between a mythical "vampiric" capitalism and a mythical "vampiric" Jews. Ulrike Meinhof, a member of the anticapitalist terror organization, the Red Army Faction, stated that, "Antisemitism is really a hatred of capitalism." It might be more correct to say that antisemitism and anticapitalism feed off each other.[4]

In his book *The Ascent of Money*, Niall Ferguson notes that debtors have always been more numerous than creditors and financial scandals and crises have always caught people's attention. So much so, that the myth evolved whereby capitalism was the cause of all financial problems, the source of poverty and financial volatility, instead of prosperity and stability. Financial innovations, such as credit and deposit banks, were imperative for the move from a subsistence existence (which was at the mercy of the weather, a person's health, or warfare) to a surplus economy destined for the local and overseas markets. Ferguson rightly argues that a democratic state that implements an economy that has banks, bond markets, stock exchanges, and a property-owning populace—all made possible by credit—is generally in better fiscal state than those that do not have these institutions. That is the case whether they are medieval feudal or modern-day economies. It was the creation and evolution of banking that was the necessary first step in the "ascent of money." As Ferguson writes, poverty is not caused by "rapacious financiers exploiting the poor," but has "more to do with the lack of financial institutions" and access to credit. And that development of banking began at the moneylender's bench (*banci*) in the market square.[5]

To say that it is a myth that capitalism was the source of poverty and all financial problems is not to deny corruption and failures on the part of individuals or groups. The temptation towards greed, a human weakness on which medieval critics based their anti-usury campaigns, led some to extort, defraud, and commit other acts of dishonesty, but no more than in any other business. Capital can, of course, be recklessly or deceitfully employed, but that is human folly and personal corruption. Capital has funded profitable businesses, turned ideas into inventions, patronized culture, and created a better standard of living for the majority. As William H. Goetzmann claims, the emergence of interest (along with the invention of debt) were "the most significant of all innovations in the history of finance." Where Ferguson is mistaken, however, is in declaring that financial services were disproportionately provided by members of ethnic or religious minorities, excluded from land or public office and that their success in finance was due to their network of kinship and trust. Not only were Jews not the majority of moneylenders historically, it is yet another myth to claim that all Jewish moneylenders were forced into the profession due to lack of opportunities. Contrary to the idea that they were left with no other livelihood but moneylending, Jews were involved in all kinds of employment, at all economic levels. Nevertheless, this remains a common contention in histories of antisemitism and Jewish history. [6]

Despite the ongoing efforts to depict the Jews as "the Other" in the history of antisemitism, Jews were not eternal pariahs, living apart from Western European society. There were brutal attacks in various places at various times and this book documents the consistent efforts to taint Jews as immoral because of their presence in moneylending. Yet, Jews also had business contacts, friendships, and sexual relationships with Christians. They were not a "bloc" standing around, generation after generation, waiting for the next expulsion or violent event, frozen in anticipation. People traded, delivered babies, healed the sick or hastened their death, sold bread, cut diamonds, harvested their grapes, and collected coral, among many other things. And those other things included lending money at the *banci* in medieval Europe, speculating at the early stock exchanges in Amsterdam and London, or, today, trading on Wall Street.

* * *

This book is a broad inquiry into why, when, and how this connection emerged in Western Europe and became the most enduring stereotype underpinning antisemitism. How did the attitudes towards a market economy based on capital intersect with, influence, and affect the image of the Jewish moneylender? The fact that only a small number of Jews were ever involved in finance leaves the questions as to why usury was considered corrupt and immoral in the first place and why money/usury/capitalism/banking become bestowed collectively on all Jews? Why and how did this stereotype endure for so long and why didn't it dissipate when Christians entered the field of usury or over the many centuries that followed? And were there places or times that it was not as virulent as other regions at other periods?

To grapple with these questions, the book's geographical scope begins with Western Europe and ends with the United States and Israel. It is in early twelfth-century Europe that we find a marked upturn of anti-Jewish rhetoric concerning Jews and usury. It is the contention of this book that this negative connection between Jews and money was forged during this time. That is not to say that objections about Jewish moneylenders were not heard in earlier times. But it was the confluence of three major developments during the late medieval period that sparked the idea that the capital-based economy was "Jewish." First, a small number of Jews held a virtual, but brief, monopoly in moneylending. Second, this came at a time of immense economic change and, for political and economic reasons, the demand for capital greatly increased. Third, this prompted a reaction by those who were against the proliferation of interest-bearing loans, which they regarded as immoral.

For its critics, usury was not just a bad thing; it was a dreadful sin and harmful to the common good. It went against the idea of *caritas* (charity) which was a critical issue for members of a Church often attacked as too worldly, because it is uncharitable to profit off your neighbor's financial distress. It devoured the poor and ruptured society. In contrast, the highest mark of virtue was to own nothing and to give everything freely. The idea that a component of an economic system, and the economic system itself, had a moral character encouraged critics to term the profession of moneylending as "Jewish" and those who were not Jewish but who practiced it, as "Judaizers." It was circular reasoning: Jews were immoral because they practiced usury and they practiced usury because they were immoral.

The spur for this widespread concern over usury was the significant economic expansion in Western Europe that went hand-in-hand with the long and uneven transformation of the economy from feudalism to capitalism. As many historians have pointed out, this was not a neat transition from a so-called "natural economy" to a market economy. Barter continued, especially between families in rural areas, even as markets and fairs expanded. But more people desired products that could not be obtained from their family and neighbors, and so the need for coinage and capital grew. Stability after a period of Viking and Hungarian raids, combined with Western Europe's greater fragmentation after the cessation of the Carolingian empire, and the desire of secular rulers to enhance their power and fill their treasuries, encouraged a greater reliance on capital in an increasingly global market. With the development of insurance, mortgages, limited regulations, legislation and policing for merchants' safety, along with a vigorous circulation of credit, commerce and trade prospered over the centuries. Old ways of life were not automatically dispensed in favor of new. Instead, the economy evolved over time with news ways and institutions side by side with past customs and sometimes in conflict with them.[7]

The debate over usury was never static. It shifted over time and was dependent on the personal views and needs of the authorities and the various members of the population, as well as social, political, and economic conditions. Usury was therefore defined and redefined to accommodate the changes in economic and political society. Once interest loans were accepted, the debate changed to other aspects of the market system, such as "excessive" interest, luxury, and speculation. What is consistent is that, despite the small percentage of Jews involved in finance, regardless of the presence of Christians, and blind to the benefits the expanding commercial world brought to generation after generation, critics over the centuries derided Jews for money-hungry exploitation of the poor.

The issue of Jews and usury, banking, and capitalism, thus took place within this larger contest between those who claimed, at one end of the spectrum, that virtue and the common good rejected the pursuit of money and profit and, at the other end, those who understood that credit was an essential component in the growth of the economy. Some critics maintained that if Jews extricated themselves from the financial professions, they would be better subjects or citizens. Rather than making money off money, which was "parasitical," they should take up "honest" and "real" occupations that were physical, such as agriculture and manufacturing. This was an argument regularly used by anti-usury critics against Jews, which led to discussions about the "regeneration" of Jews by physical labor. With the rise of national identities and racial categorization in the nineteenth century, the notion of inherently unmalleable traits altered the debate. By the modern era, the belief on the part of anticapitalists that those in finance were corrupt and corrupting, because capitalism itself was innately immoral and exploitative, was deeply entrenched in wide sectors of modern society. Even though bankers came from all different backgrounds, the myth endured that it was a "Jewish spirit" that pervaded capitalism.

Given the long history that forged the myths that Jews pursued gold at the expense of others and that capitalism is an immoral system, the two figures on the float in 2019 Belgium or the cabal around the Monopoly table needed no explanation to their audience.

* * *

There are some major terms that need explanation. Antisemitism is a word first popularized by the radical journalist Wilhelm Marr in 1879. His purpose in using this new term to describe his ideology about Jews in Germany was to distance his point of view from other anti-Jewish perspectives. His was not a religious animus, and he had no time for that sort of anti-Jewishness. The term emanated from the racial studies of the nineteenth century which described and categorized human beings into races and then attributed to those categorized races various characteristics. The categories into which humans were caged, were based on skin color and ethnicity. There were the Whites, the Blacks, the Yellows, and the Semites. The latter comprised Jews and Arabs but as Europe was home to a significant number of Jews and few Arabs, the term became synonymous with Jews. The term antisemitism was therefore racially charged and part of the modern world. Racial theorists contemplated the temperament of the various groups, giving the Whites the most favorable attributes, the Blacks the least. Jews were middling, given both good and bad attributes. But what is critical is that there was a significant shift in how Jews were regarded. Race was something finite and unchangeable. Character was set at birth. The term antisemitism, therefore, is more suited to describing the hostility to Jews from the late nineteenth century on rather than in earlier centuries. It is for this reason why the title speaks of the "emergence of antisemitism." People in the medieval period or the early modern era did not share Marr's outlook or generally think about Jews in a "racial" sense.

The words "moneylender" and "banker" are used interchangeably with the understanding that until the modern era, the lines of a banking profession were blurred. Most medieval bankers combined that profession with other, often related, occupations, such as goldsmith and moneychanger. The term capitalism, first coined in the mid-nineteenth century, is used in the broadest sense to refer to an economy based on capital as opposed to a service-in-kind or state-run economy. There is no sharp divide between a feudal system and a capitalist one—they overlap for centuries. I have therefore used the term capitalism throughout the book to describe a market profit economy based on capital and coinage and it is understood as a system without moral character. There was, and is, always potential for human economic dishonesty and exploitation, whatever the system, but this is not the focus of the book. There is no assessment as to whether some moneylenders were exploitative or not, as assessing each individual would be an impossible and fruitless task. Instead, capitalism is identified as a morally indifferent economic system that can be used well and productively by the honest and diligent, or poorly and unjustly by the inept, the reckless, and the dishonest.

There is a tendency in books and in popular culture to relate antisemitism to political views that are contrary to the author's political stance. The terms "leftwing" and "rightwing" are generally unhelpful in the history of antisemitism, or, indeed, history in general, although they are frequently employed. Antisemitism is often labeled "right-wing," but this is clearly erroneous. The stereotype about Jews and money comes from a wide array of people—from peasants and townspeople, from aristocrats to blue collar workers, from the educated and non-educated, from Liberals, Socialists, Conservatives, Communists, Anarchists, Utopians and populists. It is found in strikingly different countries. If the "Jews/money/capitalism" construction was not rooted in a wide range of people, then it would have endured as it has. Nor would it have any troubling effect if there had been no Jews in moneylending at a time that usury was a critical issue in society. The fact that so many people for so long connected Jews with capitalism, and capitalism with greed, made it a powerful weapon for antisemites in the modern era, as well a cause for antisemitism.

To argue that the stereotype of Jews and money has lasted throughout centuries while other stereotypes have decayed under reasoned argument is not to say that antisemitism is inevitable and certainly not to argue that it led inevitably to the Holocaust. But, once this historical construct of the greedy and exploitative Jewish moneylender was created, anticapitalist views made fertile ground for antisemitism to grow. And continues to do so. Let us, though, consider the contrary situation. It is clear that there were some places and periods of time in the pre-modern period where Jewish moneylenders did not suffer, or, at least, not as badly or not worse than their fellow subjects or citizens. In the modern era, antisemitism has never been a dangerous issue in a number of western countries (which is not the same as saying it is absent). This is particularly true of the United States, but the same could be argued for Australia, South Africa, Canada, and England (notwithstanding the Labour party's recent embrace of antisemitism). We now see a disquieting rise in antisemitism in Europe and the US, a type that is outside of Islamic antisemitism but overlaps insofar that many activists hold views that merge anticapitalism with anti-Zionism. In places such as the US and the UK, once known as their commitment to Enlightenment values such as free speech, free trade, the freedom to worship, and tolerance, an increase in both antisemitism and anticapitalism is surely not coincidental just as, in the past, it was surely not coincidental that countries with a strong commercial economy were relatively more tolerant towards Jews.

Finally, this book does not take a classical approach to economic history with flow charts and mathematical equations. Instead, it grounds the history of antisemitism within a larger critique of an evolving economy based on capital and the overarching question about the common good versus individual liberty. There are, of course, other facets of antisemitism, but the economic stereotype is the more insidious due to its longevity and its ability to hide under the mantel of "social justice." This approach, and the time span involved, involves large questions which I hope offers something new in the history of antisemitism. It does not treat Jews as apart from society nor does it assume that all negative action or rhetoric towards Jews—individual or collectively—is irrational, "the chimerical fantasie of the "mysterious" Jew, or antisemitic. And it rejects any idea that the history of antisemitism is a long-connected chain of lachrymose events that ends at the gates of Auschwitz. In presenting a cacophony of voices in their historical context, I have attempted to avoid such a teleological account. Instead, the focus is on understanding how, when, and why certain people crafted and promoted the view that a mythical collective—"the Jews"—was the chief exponent of a an economic system they believed was based on theft, greed, corruption, and went against the common good. It is this book's contention, in the strongest possible terms, that in both cases they were wrong. And so, too are the modern secular critics, of any political and social stripe, who took up this mantel, disrobed it of the religious garb, and promoted the same ideas for different purposes.[8]

Notes

1. Sara Lipton, "A Terribly Durable Myth," *The New York Times Review of Books*, June 27, 2019; *Reuters*, May 1, 2019, https://www.reuters.com/article/us-israel-antisemitism/anti-semitic-attacks-rise-worldwide-in-2018-led-by-us-west-europe-study-idUSKCN1S73M1; *VOA*, May 30, 2019, https://www.voanews.com/europe/un-condemns-rising-antisemitism-europe-us; *The Wall Street Journal*, July 15, 2019, https://www.wsj.com/articles/the-new-anti-semitism-11562944476; Eliot A. Cohen, "Socially Acceptable Anti-Semitism," *The Atlantic*, March 6, 2019, https://www.theatlantic.com/ideas/archive/2019/03/belgian-carnival-float-shows-virus-anti-semitism/584251/; Jennifer Rubin, "Opinions: Occupy Wall Street: Does Anyone Care about the Anti-Semitism?" *Washington Post*, October 17, 2011, https://www.washingtonpost.com/blogs/right-turn/post/occupy-wall-street-does-anyone-care-about-the-anti-semitism/2011/03/29/gIQA43p8rL_blog.html?utm_term=.09e778eedf40; Gilet Jaunes devant la banque Rothschild: l'esclavage par l'usure, https://www.youtube.com/watch?v=U76_JoZ2Ul4.
2. Werner Sombart, *The Jews and Modern Capitalism* (Glencoe IL: Free Press, 1951); Karl Marx, *On the Jewish Question* (Cincinnati OH: Hebrew Union College-Jewish Institute of Religion, 1958.
3. Julie L. Mell, *The Myth of the Medieval Jewish Moneylender*, vol. I and II (New York: Palgrave MacMillan, 2017).

4. Werner Sombart, *The Quintessence of Capitalism* (Miami: Hardpress, 2017), Kindle ed., chap. 2; *Washington Examiner*, June 17, 2019, https://www.washingtonexaminer.com/news/follow-the-money-john-cusack-apologizes-for-tweeting-anti-semitic-meme; Jillian Becker, "The Red Army Faction: Another Final Battle on the Stage of History," *Libertarian Alliance*, http://www.libertarian.co.uk/lapubs/cultn/cultn012.pdf.
5. Niall Ferguson, *Ascent of Money: A Financial History of the World* (New York: Penguin Press, 2008), Kindle, Introduction and "Evolution," and Afterword.
6. William N. Goetzmann, *Money Changes Everything: How Finance Made Civilization Possible* (Princeton NJ: Princeton University Press, 2016), Kindle ed., chap. 12; Ferguson, *Ascent of Money*, introduction.
7. R. H. Britnell, *The Commercialisation of English Society 1000-1500* (Cambridge: CUP, 1993), 1–2, 10; Goetzmann, *Money Changes Everything,* chap. 27.
8. Gavin I. Langmuir, *Towards a Definition of Anti-Semitism* (Berkeley and Los Angeles, University of California Press, 1990), 14. For books that treat antisemitism as an unceasingly tragic history of victim/oppressor, in varying degrees, see, for example, Anthony Julius, *Trials of the Diaspora: A History of Antisemitism in England* (Oxford: OUP, 2012); S.W. Wistrich, *A Lethal Obsession: Anti-semitism from Antiquity to the Global Jihad* (New York: Random House, 2010 and *Anti-semitism: The Longest Hatred* (New York: Pantheon, 1982); David Nirenberg, *Anti-Judaism: The Western Tradition* (New York: W.W. Norton, 2014); Phyllis Goldstein, *A Convenient Hatred: A History of Antisemitism* (Los Angeles: Facing History and Ourselves, 2011).

1

"The Shadowy Realm of Usury"

From the eleventh to the thirteenth century, new towns sprung up over Europe along the high roads and coastlines, subject to royal or seigniorial authority. They became centers for tax collecting, the trading of surplus goods, and the circulation of money. A multitude of newly-constructed monumental cathedrals and abbeys in the contemporary Gothic style soared towards the heavens, built at great expense for the good of the soul. Bridges, canals, and roads were constructed, all of which aided the transport of people and goods. As pilgrims made their often arduous journeys to view the body parts of saints in cathedrals, and theologians anxiously contemplated the omens in the skies, amber, honey, beeswax, glassware, basalt, metal jewelry, pottery, wool, and wine were carried across Europe. Tastes grew for more exotic items, and so spices (cumin, ginger, cardamom, and saffron) and luxurious textiles, such as silk and toile, arrived at ports from the Mediterranean, Africa, and the Levant. Aristocrats filled their drafty castles with tapestries, lit them with tallow candles, and decorated them with ever more comfortable furniture. They adorned themselves with more colorful and sumptuous textiles and jewels and bought armor to protect themselves in war.[1]

The late medieval world was one of hierarchy, privilege, servitude, and dependency. Private fortunes were concentrated in the hands of the monarchs and nobility and would continue to be for centuries to come. Up to the tenth century, the region was covered by forests and marshes, moors and heaths, and much of it was woefully unproductive. Life consisted of a network of obligations and duties with everyone born into their place in life as part of a feudal society. The economy was based on self-sufficiency, barter, and service-in-kind, that gave the individual little, if any, ability to sell their labor freely. Founded on vassalage and inherited land held by the king and his favored nobles, fiefdoms were granted from lords to their vassals in return for personal service and allegiance. These self-sufficient manorial estates were worked by the villeins—peasants who were subject to the lords—and serfs (a term that came from the Latin *servus* meaning slave) who were bonded to the feudal estate. But between the twelfth and early fourteenth centuries, those feudal ties would be weakened. Even by the late eleventh century, many goods were being exchanged not by barter but according to the law of the market.[2]

In France, the unsystematic Carolingian *villa* economy evolved into a loosely structured type of manorial estate called a *seigneurie.* The small royal domain centered around Paris was surrounded by powerful lords who ruled, among other regions, Toulouse, Normandy, Champagne, Anjou, Brittany, Burgundy, and Aquitaine who were vassals of the king of France. In Italy, councils of prelates or nobles ruled over its patchwork land of independent duchies, kingdoms, and republics. England's power, from the time of the Norman invasion in 1066, was more concentrated in the hands of its kings, although the weakness of a particular monarch was often the opportunity for powerful barons to exert their strength and demand certain rights and liberties. At the pinnacle of every society was the Church, the wealth of which lay in the extensive demesnes that had been transferred or bequeathed to monasteries and abbeys. Within the Church, there was a vast difference between the archbishops at the top and the poor rural priests who had more in common with the peasants. Nobles were equally varied with the highest lords in control of vast estates and holding immense power while, at the other end of the scale, were poor, low-status knights. Among the peasants, there were those who were wealthy enough to rent land out to tenants while others were landless and barely survived from day to day. But in a world of hierarchy, where status trumped wealth, it was more advantageous to be a poor priest or lowly knight than a rich peasant.[3]

Subsistence farming left the population at the mercy of the weather. If a crop failed, it could mean famine, which, in turn, often brought disease, malnutrition, plague and death, especially for the young, old, and weak. Feudalism reached its height in the eleventh century, but the economy was transforming. Change varied from manor to manor, town to town, and country to country and, as many historians have noted, there was no sudden divide between the manorial economy and the earliest stages of capitalism. Even as the instruments and methods of a capital-based economy were being implemented, it remained a highly structured economy that was "embedded in a system of mutual social responsibility." Even so, in the middle of the eleventh century deeds of gift, including land, started to give way to title deeds contingent on money payment and coinage became a more common method of payment.[4]

Economic developments are perhaps best viewed as a continuum with distinct periods of expansion and decline. The eleventh to the beginning of the fourteenth century was a time of expansion. A milder, drier climate fostered more bountiful harvests and led to surplus produce that was sold at local, and increasingly, overseas markets. More coins were minted on a more regular basis and in larger amounts. Monasteries such as the one at Cluny increased their use of money and a larger number of peasants were paid in coinage. This greater circulation of cash prompted capital formation and paid for new and improved agricultural techniques and machinery, metal working, and new settlements. With more money available, nobles hired better craftsmen and day workers, and instituted farming on a bigger scale which yielded more surplus. The population grew and people demanded a greater amount of goods—whether meat, wool, timber, or leather—as well as a wider variety as overseas traders began to channel exotic spices and new textiles into Western Europe.[5]

As one historian observed, the economy of Western Europe experienced a "broad, sustained, and rapid development." After centuries of brutal invasions by Vikings, Hungarians, and the Slavic Wends, European society enjoyed relative peace and sufficiently stable conditions to allow for sustained economic expansion until the early part of the fourteenth century. Western Europe, the once poor relation of the glittering Eastern Byzantium Empire, was on the threshold of a significant and life-changing economic boom. Land was cleared, forests felled, and marshes drained to create more agricultural land to feed its growing population and create surplus produce to sell in domestic markets and, increasingly, overseas. New buildings altered the landscape, and ever larger number of people trudged over more and better roads and bridges. Castles and churches began to dominate the towns and cities—symbols of power, culture, wealth, and, on the other hand, the World to Come. Construction was often crude, but there was a lot of it.[6]

There was no power without wealth. Those with power—the monarch, the Church, and the nobility—were usually exempt from taxation and the economic burden in the form of taxation and fines generally fell on the rest of society. In the eleventh century, tallages, or *tailles*, tended to be imposed spasmodically in response to a particular need or event. As expenses grew, rulers looked at all possibilities to replenish their coffers to pay for their wars, household expenses, hospitality, building projects, and the daily running of the kingdom. By the thirteenth century, tallages were usually annual and fixed and yet it was a constant battle to garner more funds without incurring flight, protest, and revolt on the part of the tax-burdened populace. Anxious to avoid rebellion, and aware that taxation was an unpopular method of financing the realm, kings often turned to creditors for loans. But this had one major disadvantage. Moneylenders expected a profit on their cash advance and that, in the eyes of the Church and hence society, was usury.

* * *

"One went furtively to visit the money lender as one went to visit a whore," the French historian Fernand Braudel wrote, "but one went all the same." Except that not everyone went furtively. Credit revitalized the economy of Western Europe from the eleventh century and made Europe the center of trade, commerce, and cultural innovation. It was credit, as the modern economist Joseph A. Schumpeter later observed, that was the basis of Western Europe's economic growth from the eleventh century and the foundation of the capitalist system that developed over the following centuries. It removed the necessity of wealth from free enterprise by allowing those without much money to fund projects and buy merchandise. And it was a network of moneylenders that provided that crucial credit to everyone from the monarch to the peasant.[7]

When William of Normandy made the crossing to England, landing at Pevensey on September 28, 1066, he met his rival for the English crown, Harold Godwinson, on the battlefield. The Norman soldiers charged against the defensive shield wall erected by the English troops, and amid the grisly carnage Harold was hacked to death (according to the 1067 poem *Carmen de Hastingae Proelio*), perhaps after receiving an arrow in the eye (according to the Bayeaux tapestry). William the Bastard, as the English called him, was crowned king of England at Westminster Abbey on Christmas Day. It was said that a comet appeared but whether that was interpreted as a good sign or an evil omen is unknown.[8]

Accompanying the Norman conquerors on their successful invasion were a number of Jewish merchants, who initially settled in London. Exorbitant taxes, the source of much protest throughout Europe, were exacted upon them for the privilege of settlement, economic opportunity, and protection. This was not unique to Jews. New tenants on a lord's land paid entry fines, sometimes fixed and sometimes dependent upon the quality of land and the length of the tenancy, and all foreigners paid settlement fees. London was a city full of migrants attracted by its vibrant trading and financial activity. It was the main center of both local and long-distance trade with many craftsmen. It was generally self-governing, its inhabitants electing their own mayors and sheriffs. Merchants ebbed and flowed from many countries, ships laden with merchandise seemed to arrive from every nation, and horses and carts filled with goods clogged the narrow streets. All cities built walls to control the flow of people and good and London's city walls, erected by the Romans, were secured by seven gates: Aldgate, Aldersgate, Bishopsgate, Cripplegate, Ludgate, Moorgate, and Newgate. Street names reflected the goods sold: Cheapside and East Cheap (the name came from the Saxon word "chepe" meaning market), Poultry, Cornhill, Old Fish Street, Ermine Street, Honey Lane, and Milk Street. Two miles outside of the city, the palace of Westminster sat on the banks of the River Thames. Just outside the city walls, between Fleet Street and the River Thames, stood the New Temple, the English headquarters of the Knights Templars (the Poor Fellow-Soldiers of Christ and of the Temple of Solomon, to give them their full title), which served as the royal treasury during the reign of King John and where the wealthy deposited their money for safekeeping. To the north lay fields and meadows through which ran streams. Beyond the pastures, there was a great forest full of wild animals and thick foliage. The attractions of this bustling city went unappreciated by Richard of Devizes, a monk at Winchester. He objected to London as a place of "actors, jesters, smooth-skinned lads, Moors, flatterers, pretty boys, effeminates, pederasts, singing and dancing girls, quacks, belly-dancers, soceresses, extortioners, night-wanderers, magicians, mimes, beggars, buffoon." His advice? "Do not live in London."[9]

If Richard's description was only a little correct, it is not surprising that Jews gathered in their own communities. We regard ghettoism today as a problem to be eradicated but the medieval world built on hierarchy, with the monarch at the pinnacle, was far removed from modern ideals of integrated "race," "ethnicity" or "class." Such segregation was often a privilege that was sought; it was expected that each group would live, and want to live, in their own sectors of town. Old Jewry was situated in the shadow of the ancient Saxon royal palace with another Jewry situated close to the White Tower built in 1078, which would become the most inner ward of the Tower of London. Jews newly-arrived in the city gravitated towards these Jewries where it was easier for Jewish leaders to control and maintain Jewish traditions and religious law and prevent interaction with non-Jews that might lead to undesirable liasons or even apostasy. It also gave them protection, when necessary, against those who were hostile towards them.

Despite efforts by the most orthodox to keep the Jewish community isolated, however, interaction was common in the markets, in the streets, and in private homes. This was especially true for those who were involved in business and those who were less inclined toward strict religious observance. Soon Jews ventured to other market towns throughout England, settling in Oxford, Cambridge, York, Winchester, Lincoln, and Norwich. They preferred towns with mints, which suggests that they may have handled coinage for the Crown.[10]

Many of these Jews traded precious metals, which were in high demand from the eleventh century as gold and silver mining was revitalized, along with other commodities such as copper, tin, and alum, which was used to bind dye to cloth. As competition increased in these trades, the Jews in England began to narrow their professions and specialize in moneychanging and usury, although people at this time rarely stuck to one trade and most of these early bankers also worked as merchants, mint workers, and goldsmiths. As moneychangers, they calculated the values of the different currencies in circulation and, as moneylenders they lent capital at variable rates of interest. Their capital was a service, a product, to be sold like any other. Yet, the addition of an interest rate onto the principal loan amount made the transaction usurious. The practice of accepting valuable items as collateral, if the loan was large, or as insurance against default, if the sum was small, set some Jews up in pawnbroking. By the end of the twelfth century, pawnbroking, like usury itself, had become synonymous with Jews.[11]

To most people in the twelfth century, and for centuries after, this form of profit was wickedly immoral. Those who were against usury did not necessarily believe that money was immoral in and of itself nor was all profit considered illegitimate. Clerics such as Thomas, the rector of Chobham (c.1160–c.1236), Alexander of Hales (1185–1245), and Peter Olivi (1248–1298) took into account risk and uncertainty as well as theft, fire and other possible losses a merchant might encounter. Wealth could be put to good use, for the betterment of the common weal and the poor, or it could be put to ill use. It could aid those in need, or it could drive people to greed, corruption, and all sorts of deviancy. If used unjustly, riches were antithetical to piety, the twelfth-century Parisian theologian Peter Comestor asserted. This stood in opposition to *caritas*, or charity, which was deemed to be the love of God as expressed through the love of oneself and one's neighbors. The centrality of the poor (however they were defined) and mercy (from the Latin *misericordia* meaning "poor heart") in Christian theology was in place by the fifth century and molded this twelfth-century virtue of charity. For the archbishop of Canterbury, Stephen Langton (c.1150–1228) faith and charity were interwoven and it was a traditional view that the rich had an obligation to help the poor. For most religions, and for most people to this day, caring little about material goods is indicative of the truly spiritual. Renunciation of all material wealth had once been the mark of the virtuous, and it remained the pinnacle of sanctity. But by the late medieval period, it was sufficient for the rich to give up only as much of their wealth to fulfil their societal obligation but still retain enough to maintain their social standing. Charity not only benefited the recipient of that act of altruism, it was also morally beneficial to the giver, rewarding men and women with salvation in the World to Come. It was the source of virtue for the individual and society. That meant surplus goods should be distributed to those in need and money should be lent freely without interest for the common good.[12]

By demanding a profit off a loan, the usurer was committing a sin against *caritas*, according to the Church. A neighbor in need should be helped without the expectation of financial gain. Whether it involved simple or compound interest, usury was therefore inherently extortive, exploitative, and deceitful. Money was said to be conjured up "in the shadowy realm of usury, an unnatural vice." It was "an instrument of exchange that [had,] devil-like, magical powers of luring people and then corrupting them." It stood to reason, from this perspective, that if person A made money off a loan it was inevitably at the expense of person B, the borrower. A virtuous authority was therefore obliged to protect person B from the exploitative and sinister business dealings of person A.[13]

That assessment was not new as usurers had long been criminalized and its association with Jews stretched back to ancient times. In antiquity, Aristotle had denounced usury because he regarded money to be "barren" and unable to breed. It was therefore "unnatural" for money to beget money. In addition to agreeing with Aristotle's misgivings, medieval theologians objected to usury on biblical grounds. One vague comment by Luke, that said a person should not lend expecting more in return, was bolstered by many admonitions in the Hebrew Bible about the evils of usury. Jews were not to engage in moneylending, except with "strangers." So while Christians interpreted the text to mean usury was forbidden to all Christians, Jews censured usury only between Jews and not between Jews and non-Jews, so long as the Jew was the creditor. In practise, however, Jews were not only creditors but borrowers, too, from both Jews and Christians.[14]

The connection between Jews and moneylending was notable in the early Church. To the fourth-century archbishop of Constantinople John Chrysostom, moneylenders and Jews were synonymous, and he denounced them as plundering, covetous thieves who cheated in trade. He also complained about the aristocrats "jacking up of prices," and decorating their villas than doing "anything with some sense in it." The influential fifth-century Syrian bishop, Theodoretos of Kyross, accused Jewish moneylenders of accumulating wealth at the expense of Christians while Isaac of Antioch cautioned Christians not to imitate the Jews who "fast, and devour profits . . . pray, and absorb the usurers . . . and devour the flesh of the poor." To such critics, making a profit off moneylending was simply financial exploitation; whether the particular transaction was amicable and honest or coercive and extortionate was irrelevant.[15]

The Council of Nicea, in 325, had issued an edict banning usury (labeling it "filthy lucre"), but this applied only to the clergy. It was not until the early twelfth century, as towns grew and the capital market expanded, that the subject of usury became urgent and members of the Church pushed for a complete ban. It was nothing less than a sin against God, said the Cistercian abbot Bernard of Clairvaux (1090–1153), and he rejected any attempt by lay and religious rulers to come to some sort of accommodation with it. Cardinal Robert of Courcon (c.1160–1219), who became the formative chancellor at the University of Paris, thought usury was "universally infecting society," and called for an unequivocal ban. Not only was usury unneighborly and anti-social, not only was it motivated by greed and was against charity, it was nothing less than theft. The Italian monk Anselm of Canterbury (1033–1109) warned people not to become rich by "theft and usury and fraud." His pupil, Anselm of Lucca, continued with this analogy, calling for the return of usuries to the borrower because they were stolen goods. Their countryman, theologian Peter Lombard (1100–1160), quoted Aristotle when he placed usury under "furtum" (civic, but not criminal, theft) in his influential *Book of Sentences*. The French scholastic theologian, William of Auxerre (1145–1231), acknowledged profit as legitimate if it was gained with moral honesty but he was disgusted by the way in which moneylending was conducted as if it was a legitimate profession. In his mind, usury was the theft of time. As time was God's possession, so the usurer who added future interest onto a loan was charging for the use of time and, in essence, stealing from God. The twelfth-century poem *Les Vers de la Mort* (Verses of Death) was written by the minstrel-turned-monk Hélinand de Froidmont and he, too, equated usury with theft.

> The usurer says: I know very well
> That what I have stolen is not mine
> I am a dishonorable sinner
> Because I keep, against the law
> That which belongs to another, in which I have no part.

Accepting a profit from a loan was no different to breaking into a home and taking someone's money or goods. It was the same as stealing livestock from your neighbor. With money in greater circulation and more interest loans transacted, usury became a matter of social justice for its critics.[16]

In 1139, usury was officially pronounced a sin for every Christian by the Second Lateran Council. According to the Church, usury tainted not only the moneylender but anyone who benefited from the profits of usury, a stance at odds with most secular authorities. Even alms were not allowed if the money had been made from usury, although how much this rule was followed is impossible to know.[17]

Interest loans were a thorny issue for the Church and it was clear that monasteries and clergymen indulged in usury in contradiction of edicts forbidding the practice. There were those in the Church who believed they had to adapt to the new financial world and urged compromise, such as regulating a lower interest rate. Given the fact that the Church was both a creditor and borrower, buying and selling land and goods, collecting tithes and other revenue from its properties and agriculture, which provided the money for its parish services, this was a pragmatic and self-preserving concession. The papacy therefore sought to redefine usury with clear instructions on what was legal and moral and what crossed the line and became sinful and harmful to the common good.

Up until the Third Lateran Council in 1179, Luke's curt admonition about usury had been negligible in the discussion of it, and it was debatable whether or not it was a command to ban usury completely and forever. The council guided by Pope Alexander III made Luke's brief utterance the reference point for the Church, and the definition of usury was broadened to include credit that was sold at a higher price than cash sales. While acknowledging that usury was ubiquitous in spite of moral outrage, the Church now employed the weapon of denying usurers a Christian burial. Of course, this only concerned Christians but that was the main concern of the Church. Jewish moneylending was a matter of Church policy only insofar as it affected Christians.[18]

In 1185, when Uberto Crivelli became pope, taking the name Urban III, he went further than his predecessors by claiming that usury was simply the "intention to gain." Nearly two decades later, Pope Innocent III, in a letter to the French bishops entitled *On Usury*, wrote:

> We believe that you know how pernicious the vice of usury is, since, in addition to the ecclesiastical laws which have been issued against it, the prophet says that those who put their money out at interest are to be excluded from the

> tabernacle of the Lord [Psalms 15:5] And the New Testament, as well as the Old, forbids the taking of interest, since the Truth [Christ] himself says: "Lend, hoping for nothing again." [Luke 6:35] . . . . We command you all by this apostolic writing not to permit those who are known as usurers to clear themselves by any subterfuge or trick when they are charged with the crime.

Usury was trickery and deception practiced upon the desperate and uninformed. Yet, despite his condemnation, Innocent understood the important role moneylending played in the Church's and the wider society's economic life. He therefore advised a cautious enforcement of the Lateran Council decrees, concerned that if the numerous usurers were forbidden their profession "many churches would have to be shut down."[19]

Innocent presided over the Fourth Lateran Council in 1215 which prohibited Jews from charging exorbitant interest. Ostensibly, this was to guard Christians against the dangers of moneylending, but it begged the question: What was considered exorbitant? And why were risk and availability of capital not taken into consideration, as they were in other economic transactions, such as the sale of goods? Profits were not guaranteed but dependent upon a multitude of factors—changes in coinage or the circulation of money, debasement of currency, unforeseen political events including war, bankruptcies, changes in the balance of payments, manipulation of the exchange rate, and many other things. But in the case of interest loans, risk was not valued. Canon 67 of the Council stated:

> The more the Christian religion is restrained from usurious practices, so much the more does the perfidity of the Jews grow in these matters, so that within a short time they are exhausting the resources of Christians. Wishing, therefore, to see that Christians are not savagely oppressed by Jews in this matter, we ordain by this synodal decree that if Jews in future, on any pretext, extort oppressive and excessive interest from Christians, then they are to be removed from contact with Christians until they have made adequate satisfaction for the immediate burden. The Christians also . . . shall be compelled by ecclesiastical censure to abstain from commerce with them. We enjoin upon princes not to be hostile to Christians on this account, but rather to be zealous in restraining Jews from so great oppression.

One of those "cruel oppressions" condemned by the council was licensed pawnbroking carried out by Jews, especially in France and Flanders.[20]

To opponents of usury, charging a profit on loans corrupted society and consumed its victims as viciously as the wolf ripped apart its prey. It savaged the simple, devout people in their lust for wealth or pleasure, like "beasts of the forest [ways of the flesh]. . .which devour the Church and the faithful soul." With a small number of Jews prominent in the moneylending business in Western Europe and Christians forbidden to enter into it, usury was labeled a Jewish profession. It was considered an "immoral" profession, only suitable to people who had denied Christ. We cannot know if there were Christians at this time who, on a non-professional and clandestine basis, lent money at interest to their friends and neighbors. If there were, then they would simply be labeled as "judaizers." Every usurer was, for all intents and purposes, a Jew.[21]

* * *

Demand for credit was growing and it would not be long before Christians would clamor to enter into the field of moneylending, even if it was officially prohibited to practice usury by religious and secular authorities. But, until that time, this meant that for a brief time at the end of the eleventh and early-twelfth century Jews were dominant in the field of moneylending in Western Europe. This is one reason why, despite the long and hostile association between Jews and usury that stretched back to antiquity, it was not until the twelfth century that serious debates about interest loans occurred in Western Europe. It was not until that time that the Lateran councils began to proscribe usury and issue punishment for those involved.

The reason for these changes in policy towards moneylending was the great economic change and expansion in Western Europe, whereby money in the form of coinage was more abundant and a larger number of interest loans were conducted as the demand for capital increased. In a short space of time, interest loans were to become an integral part of Western European societies that were slowly and unevenly adopting a surplus-rich, capital-based economy. Weekly markets linked the urban areas to the isolated rural villages, offering local everyday necessities to the townspeople and peasants. On a grander scale, fairs were annual or biannual events that became the hub of international finance and trade, with important fairs arranged in Troyes, Provins, Bar-sur-Aube, Lagny, Aix-la-Chapelle (Aachen), Geneva, Cologne, Frankfurt, Bruges, Stourbridge and the hilly French province of Champagne. By the thirteenth century, an initiative by the authorities was needed to get markets and fairs recognized, with the time and place regulated, and these authorities also had the right to close down any market or fair if they were unlicensed. Feast days and trade were intertwined as people flocked to the fairs, often held on saints' days, to buy and sell goods and make other deals. They were entertained by jongleurs who performed acrobatics, magic tricks, and juggling, as well as strolling players and musicians, while vendors sold food and drinks. These trading venues not only benefitted the merchants and traders. They became a vital source of revenue for the local authorities, who profited from taxes, rents, and other fees, as well as the religious houses, which were given the right to weigh and tax the goods. So crucial were these events that great effort was taken to prevent any disruption of the market and fair so that those conducting business could do so in peace.[22]

Many people today would agree with the French theologian and philosopher Peter Abelard (1079–1142) that Jews took up the "immoral" trade of moneylending because they had little or no choice. Yet it was often the case that Jewish moneylenders fought to retain their privileges and position as bankers, which does not indicate a forced profession that Jews were driven into due to a lack of other choices. Throughout Europe, Jews worked in a variety of professions, including as metal workers, vintners, dyers, glass workers, miners, smiths, tailors, butchers, bakers, sailors, and physicians. Only a small number of Jews ever sat at the banker's bench and an even smaller number *only* sat at the banker's bench as people commonly held two or more overlapping occupations. In addition, this monopoly was short-lived, which dispels the myth that only Jews were moneylenders. During the twelfth century, Christians, particularly Italians, entered into moneylending in significant numbers including the Riccardi of Lucca, Betti of Lucca, Ballardi of Lucca, Frescobaldi, and Spini. Italians who lent money to monarchs generally took their profits in the form of commercial advantages rather than a cash return on the principal. Cahors from southern France were so influential in banking that the Benedictine monk of St. Albans and chronicler Matthew Paris (c.1200–1259) equated the word "Caursines" (Cahors) with moneylender. They cloaked "their usury under the show of trade," Paris wrote, plying their "horrible-nuisance" with "heavy rates of interest." Paris had no love for any usurer, who, with the help of "the extortions of the pope and the cheating of the king" had enslaved England in a sea of debt. Criticism was also directed at the the Lombards, although there seems to be little difference between Cahors and Lombards and the two words appear to be used interchangeably. The Lombards had control over the moneylending trade in many lands and, like the Jews and the Cahors, they were reviled for their "ill-gotten gains."[23]

With the growth in trade and commerce boosting the need for more bankers and their ready money, the ranks of usurers were swelled by these Christians who eagerly entered the financial trade in defiance of papal and royal prohibitions. This again suggests that moneylending was not a forced occupation but one that many Jews and Christians expected would provide them with a good living. So long as people paid their debts, moneylending could indeed be a highly profitable business. Interest rates were set at an average of 40 to 45 percent and could reach as high as 60 percent. The steep rates were determined by the high taxes imposed on foreigners for settlement and other tallages, and the risk involved in lending money—the possibility of default as well as the chance that the currency would be debased and inflation would make each coin less valuable on repayment. On the other hand, debased coinage benefited the debtor, who received the loan at a higher value and repaid his debt with devalued coins.[24]

In sum, Jews were not solely moneylenders nor were they unique players in the business of moneylending even if they were dominant for a short period of time. They did not, as traditional accounts often claim, invent banking or capitalism single-handedly and there was nothing to link the religion of Judaism and moneylending, as the nineteenth-century economist Werner Sombart claimed. At the same time, the fact that the number of Jews involved in moneylending was small in comparison to the Jewish population, does not make the presence of those individual Jewish moneylenders a "myth," or irrelevant.[25]

In the Church's efforts to keep Christians free from the sin of usury, an effort doomed to failure after the Italian Christians took up usury, the Jewish moneylenders played a key role. Theoretically, they provided the capital necessary for economic growth while ensuring that Christians kept their souls pure and their hands clean, spiritually untainted by the "immoral" profession. Christians could benefit from the results of usury, but they could not be seen to be practicing it. They could take loans off Jews while condemning them for immoral practices. They could assure themselves that participation in such a vile profession substantiated claims that Jews were spiritually bereft. It was a grand deceit. Because almost everyone—directly or indirectly—was involved in usury.

* * *

Roman law was in the early stages of being rediscovered and being taught in the universities at Bologna and Paris. The Romans had ruled that the cost of a transaction was determined by the agreement between the buyer and the seller, and it had allowed usury so long as it was under 12 percent. This only referred to simple interest—a single payment of a set percentage. Compound interest had been forbidden in the Roman Empire as an immoral, unprincipled, and ruthless practice, which was how the Church defined all usury. Until written contracts became commonplace, loan agreements were based on a man's word and disputes were settled by witnesses willing (or bribed) to testify to the truthfulness or mendacity of the creditor and debtor.[26]

Mutuum contracts were loans of fungibles—items that could be returned to the creditor in the same state, such as jewelry or clothing. A commodatum contract was one that dealt with non-fungibles (such as houses) that had a return in excess of the principal because it was a loan for use. Although coins were categorized as fungibles, interest-bearing loans were fast becoming necessities in business transactions. To get around charges of usury that might land a moneylender in prison or with hefty fines, profits from interest payments were disguised in a variety of ways, and increasingly convoluted loan charters were devised in order to hide the payment of interest from the authorities. Late charges were added to time dated contracts, which, though legal, were seen as ploys to gain usurious profit, which, of course, they were. Damages were assessed, deposit charges issued, and a myriad of complicated contracts were drawn up that included partnerships, mortgages, sea loans, loans on exchange, dry exchange, and forward contracts, all with the aim of concealing the fact that interest was charged and paid. Other ways to mask interest payment and escape the usury laws was to execute a fake sale at an inflated value and then resell at a lower price, a practice called *chevisance* (meaning an unlawful agreement or contract). While the legal system was still rudimentary, it was relatively easy for the usurer to avoid detection. As the law became more sophisticated, contracts had to become even more complicated in order to avoid the lender's possible prosecution for usury.[27]

As trade increased, new banking methods were developed to fit a changing and more dynamic economy that was spreading further afield. It became standard for business at markets and fairs to be conducted within a chain of credit transactions as buyers bought goods on credit and then sold to a merchant who also needed credit for his purchase. One of the earliest and most revolutionary developments in early pre-industrial capitalism was the bill of exchange. These new promissory notes included the terms of the loan, the repayment schedule, and the hidden interest rate. With these bills, merchants could make cash-free transactions. Credit notes offered the merchant-moneylenders another way to disguise interest payments as they could be easily concealed in the exchange rate, with the lender simply inflating the exchange rate to his benefit. In addition to the bills of exchange, other innovations shaped the rudimentary capitalist world. The emergence of Christian Humanism that used and assimilated Greek and Roman texts that were now rediscovered and translated, contributed to the late medieval changes in commerce and finance. Despite Aristotle's distaste for usury, it was the mid-twelfth century translation of the first three logical texts of his *Organon* that encouraged the questioning, systematization, and categorization that aided loan transaction by reformulating bookkeeping and finance. Merchants began to specialize in various industries and commodities, markets were organized, weights, measures, and exchange began to be standardized, and transportation was improved both on roads and seas. With these changes, the new money economy flourished, that is, coinage, whether gold, silver, or copper, as money can equally be bits of paper, shells, stones, or, in today's world, virtual cryptocurrency. Laws were introduced and action taken to protect buyers against unscrupulous traders who sold them short of a product, gave them inferior or fake goods, or deceived the customer in countless other ways, such as engrossing (hoarding). There were always fears that the unscrupulous would manipulate supplies either individually or in collusion with others, to fix prices or hoard goods until the price was driven up by scarcity. It was a concern that never disappeared and resurfaced time and again, particularly during times of dearth or for political gain. On the books, the penalty for such frauds was imprisonment and the confiscation of all the convict's goods to the Crown, although the law was more stringently imposed when harvests were bad.[28]

Everyone—kings, queens, nobles, clergymen, tradesmen, and peasants—borrowed money. The papacy may have called usury a sin, Jewish trickery, and detrimental to the common good, but the Church needed money, and lots of it. In the eleventh century, Godfrey of Bouillon pledged an allodial property to Bishop Otbert of Liège in return for a loan of 1,300 silver marks and 3,000 gold marks, while the archbishop of Cologne secured credit from Jewish moneylenders. Thirty years after William's landing in England, the first crusade was called by Pope Urban II (Odo of Châtillon) to retake the Holy Land from the Muslims who had conquered the Levant in the seventh century. What was supposed to be a mission for God did not always attract people for that cause alone. With wages intermittent, some of the crusaders were more intent on enriching themselves than on pleasing God and looting was rife. The attacks on Jews mainly in towns along the Rhine were violent plunders. To what degree the attack was motivated by religious animosity and how much was due to greed is impossible to say. It seems safe to assume that the two were often mingled to a greater or lesser degree.

All orders of society were expected to support the crusade both morally and financially, but this costly expedition could not be undertaken without recourse to loans. Knights often had to mortgage their estates in order to obtain the money necessary to fight and maintain their families during the time they were away. When the second crusade loomed in 1147, after the fall of Edessa to the Muslim armies, there was a pressing need to help people in debt so that they could embark on the crusade. Pope Eugenius III (Bernardo da Pisa) had already issued a bull in 1145 which included the plight of crusaders who were "oppressed by debt." While crusaders should not be concerned with "precious clothes or elegant appearance or dogs or hawks or other things that are signs of lasciviousness . . . multicoloured clothes or minivers or gilded or silvered arms . . ." they should be able to could begin their "holy . . . journey with a pure heart" and free -from usury on past loans. If a crusader or someone acting on their behalf was bound to a usurious contract by an oath or pledge then he was absolved of that debt by apostolic authority. Peter the Venerable (1092–1156), the abbot of Benedictine abbey of Cluny and the first to translate the Quran into Latin, had another idea about how to raise funds for the campaign. He urged Louis VII of France (r. 1137–1180) to make the Jews contribute to the campaign expenses. Peter despised moneylenders who, he said, preyed on the poor and desperate. For that reason, they were no better than thieves. "Robbers as they are," he implored, "this is the very occasion to compel them to disgorge!"[29]

Peter's hatred for moneylenders may have resulted from his own need for loans. He pawned valuable items from the sacristy at Cluny, to both Jewish and Christian creditors. In 1147, while he derided moneylenders for filling their storage bins and wine cellars and reaping significant riches at the expense of the weak and impoverished, he sought aid from the Jewish moneylenders of Mâcon. When his monastery fell short of funds again, he turned to Henry of Blois, the bishop of Winchester and younger brother of England's King Stephen, who gave the monastery 2,000 marks to pay their debts and another 7,000 marks six years later. Even the cross donated to Cluny by Henry was stripped of its gold.[30]

Over the course of the twelfth century, it became standard for the economy of the abbey of Cluny to be run on credit. Monks were supposed to live comfortably in accordance with their status and churches and monasteries were to be richly adorned to honor God. The Cistercian monasteries were also well immersed in the everyday world of moneylending. Bishops and other clerics all over Europe pledged chalices, statues, crosses, rings, robes, bells, books, lamps, and altar panels, among many other items, as collateral in return for much needed funds. In one case, William, the sacristan of a monastery, secretly took out a compound interest loan for forty marks from Benedict, a Jewish moneylender. When the debt came due, Benedict returned to the monastery for the 100 pounds now owed and it was only at that point that the other monks and the abbot learned of the sacristan's debt. More borrowing was needed to cover the loan amount with the result that, after some years, the debt owing to Benedict was a staggering 1200 pounds.[31]

Trading in sacred pawns was commonplace but some Jews feared and despised it. Rumors were spread that once in the custody of the Jews, the pawned Christian objects were used sacrilegiously. Although he traded pawns for money, Peter the Venerable lamented the holy vessels "held captive" by Jewish pawnbrokers, which, he claimed, were used for despicable and unspeakable purposes. And it was not only Christians who deplored the pawning of religious items as security for a loan. Rabbi Jacob Tam, a Jewish community leader in twelfth-century northern France, was also hostile to the practice and forbade the commerce of "Prayer books of the Church." In Tam's case, possessing Christian items was an act of idolatry and the trade of "cult" artifacts was a sin punishable by God. Not only did he rage against the pawnbrokers who traded in Christian sacred objects, he also reviled usury as a sin against God and urged moneylenders and pawnbrokers to turn away from such an ungodly trade. Rabbi Eliezer ben Nathan of Mainz looked at the issue with a different perspective. He thought so little of the pledged Christian sacred items that taking a Christian religious item as a pawn was of no importance. To Eliezer, the items so sacred to Christians were not intrinsically holy to Jews, but, rather, goods attached to a "cult." Taking a cross as a pawn was the same as taking a necklace or a set of cutlery. In his eyes, to suggest otherwise was to give credence to Christian beliefs.[32]

Within a century, in many areas of Western Europe, people were becoming used to a credit-based economy. A thirteenth-century Jewish scholar from southern France, Meir ben Simeon of Narbonne, expressed his astonishment at the ongoing Christian opposition to usury:

> who can imagine society without loans? .... Since your wealthy [Christians] refrain from lending free of interest, how will the common people and the needy make a living? Or isn't true that many [of these less privileged people] bring livelihood to their households through a loan of money to purchase one single [cow] for plowing or a bit of cereal or wheat for sowing and [also] for the protection of their families?

Technical innovations, such as the mechanical clock, the spinning wheel, and the astronomical compass were possible thanks to capital, as was entrepreneurship, the growing knowledge of foreign trade, strategies, calculations, better record keeping, and the learning of other languages so as to better participate in that trade. The credit economy fostered alliances as the exchange of a greater array of goods interconnected the new European nations that had been forming since the eleventh century. Greater economic interdependence was seen as a possible path to peaceful relations between the nations that so often were at war.[33]

Monarchs, in particular, took out vast loans. The costly construction of Notre Dame began in 1160 under one French king, Louis VII, while another, Louis IX (1214–1270), redeemed the Crown of Thorns, which was deposited in Notre Dame during the nineteenth century. Before it was offered to the French king by Baldwin II, the emperor of Constantinople, it had been a pledge in the hands of the Venetians against an enormous loan. Rulers spent vast sums of money on military campaigns, running their households, wages, ever more luxurious clothing that marked a person's status, buildings, gifts, and hospitality. The two main sources of governmental income were taxes, which were unpopular, and loans, which made the rulers debtors. As they took on larger loans more frequently, the subject of usury became a battlefield over which popes and secular rulers tested their power and a subject for popular protest.

The idea that usury was a form of theft was not picked up by secular governments and there is no indication that secular authorities punished usurers as thieves. Nor did the secular authorities regard those who gained from usury in a secondary fashion—that is, not the usurer but someone who benefited from the profits of usury—as a criminal. Given the pressing need for capital, monarchs and other authorities were not always willing to give in to the anti-usury faction's call for strict adherence to the laws forbidding interest loans. But this conflict of opinion was complicated by the blurred lines between royal jurisdiction and clerical jurisdiction. It was difficult to know exactly where each began, ended, or overlapped and these discrepancies led to intermittent conflict between the pope, determined to retain his power over kings, and rulers, who were eager to wrest free from the tight grip of Rome.[34]

Any economic activity on the part of monarchs—whether borrowing or imposing taxes—was usually an *ad hoc* response to political events rather than consistent policy. If it suited their financial or political needs, or if they were pious, monarchs gladly towed the ecclesiastical line by upholding anti-usury laws and sometimes officiating usury law cases. The benefits of this tactic were the monarch's ability to confiscate property and issue fines to proven usurers which added much needed revenue to the treasury. For foreigners, and that included Jews, conviction of usury might also mean expulsion as well as the appropriation of property. In general, monarchs followed canon law, depending on their relationship with the pope. But in comparison to the benefits of loans, there is no evidence that kings made a substantial enough profit when they banned usury. In late twelfth-century England, the property and debt contracts of a dead usurer came within the jurisdiction of the king, but there is no indication that kings actively appropriated the land of the deceased moneylender. The impetus to disrupt and prohibit usury generally came not from the kings but from sectors of society that were adversely affected by moneylending—those in debt they could not repay their loans, other moneylenders eager to gain a monopoly and push out competition, and those in the Church who objected to what they claimed were its harmful moral, social, and economic effects.[35]

If their need for funds was not met, monarchs tended to turn a blind eye to usury laws and customs, as did nobles, clergymen, and the peasantry. When protests over more tax demands grew dangerous, the monarchs turned instead to the moneylender to borrow the capital necessary to fund their battles, lavish banquets, briberies, and gifts. While they paid lip service to the papacy's anti-usury regulations and even their own anti-usury laws, monarchs throughout Europe were holding out their hand for an interest-bearing loan. That is, until the moneylender was more trouble than they were worth.

Notes

1. Britnell, *The Commercialisation of English Society*, 72; Michel Mollat and Philippe Wolff, *The Popular Revolutions of the Late Middle Ages* (London: Allen & Unwin, 1973), 34; Georges Duby, *The Early Growth of the European Economy* (Ithaca, NY: Cornell University Press, 1974), 235.
2. Britnell, *The Commercialisation of English Society*, 7, 128.
3. Francois Louis Ganshot and Adriaan Verhulst, "France, The Low Countries, and Western Germany" in *Cambridge Economic History of Europe, I: The Agrarian Life of the Middle Ages* (Cambridge: CUP, 1966), ed. M.M. Postan, 332–33; Adriaan Verhulst, *The Carolingian Economy* (Cambridge: CUP, 2002), 128; Duby, *The Early Growth of the European Economy*, 157–59, 161, 165–67, 169, 229; Merry E. Wiesner-Hanks, *Early Modern Europe* (Cambridge: CUP, 2006), Kindle ed., chap.1.
4. James Davis, "The Ethics of Arbitrage and Forestalling Across the Late Medieval World," in Simon and James E. Shaw, eds., *Market Ethics and Practices, c. 1300–1850* (Abingdon UK & New York: Routledge 2018), Kindle ed., chap. 1
5. Charlemagne's empire Middleton had used silver coins but with a silver shortage there was less demand for coins in Western Europe than in more developed regions. Ferguson, *The Ascent of Money*, chapter 1; Raymond de Roover, "The Concept of the Just Price: Theory and Economic Policy," *The Journal of Economic History* 18.4 (1958): 428; Roy C. Cave and Herbert H. Coulson, *A Source Book for Medieval Economic History* (New York: Biblo and Tannen, 1965), 70, 148; David Herlihy, "The Economy of Traditional Europe," *The Journal of Economic History* 31.1 (1971): 155,

162; Martyn Whittock, *A Brief History of Life in the Middle Ages* (London: Robinson Publishing, 2009), 186; Andrew Cowell, *At Play in the Tavern: Signs, Coins, and Bodies in the Middle Ages* (Ann Arbor: University of Michigan Press, 1999), 60

6. Duby, *The Early Growth of the European Economy*, 170, 180–81, 194–96, 205, 217, 255–257; M. M. Postan, "England," in *Cambridge Economic History of Europe*, ed. Poston, 576, 581.
7. Fernand Braudel, *The Wheels of Commerce: Civilization and Capitalism 15th–18th Century*, vol. 2, quoted in Shael Herman, *Medieval Usury and the Commercialization of Feudal Bonds* (Berlin: Duncker & Humblot, 1993), 77; Goetzmann, *Money Changes Everything*, chap.11.
8. *The Chronicles of Melrose*, "A.D. 1066," Ebook, https://archive.org/stream/thechurchhistor104fiskuoft/thechurchhistor104fiskuoft_djvu.txt
9. Morris, *A Great and Terrible King*, chapters 1 and 6; William Fitzstephen's description in Dan Jones, *The Plantagenets: The Warrior Kings and Queens Who Made England* (London: Harper Press, 2012), Kindle ed., "Births and Rebirths."; William of Malmesbury and the *Chronicle of Richard of Devizes* (late twelfth century), in Borer, *The City of London*, 76, 89; L. Blanchard, *Documents Inédits sur le Commerce de Marseille au Moyen Age*, vol. I (Marseille, 1884), 361, in Cave and Coulson, *Sourcebook for Medieval Economic History*, 99, 112, 144; Postan, *Cambridge Economic History of Europe*, 553; Britnell, *The Commercialisation of English Society*, 8.
10. Postan, *Cambridge Economic History of Europe*, 556, 561, 564; Ivan G. Marcus, "Jews and Christians Imagining the Other in Medieval Europe," *Prooftexts* 15.3: 209.
11. Robert C. Stacey, "Jewish Lending and the Medieval English Economy," in *Commercialising Economy: England 1086 to c.1300*, ed., R. H. Britnell (Manchester: Manchester University Press, 1995), 78–79.
12. Davis, "The Ethics of Arbitrage"; Miri Rubin, *Charity and Community in Medieval Cambridge* (Cambridge: CUP, 1987), 1, 58–59, 63, 289.
13. Lester K. Little, *Religious Poverty and the Profit Economy in Medieval Europe* (Ithaca, NY: Cornell University Press, 1978), 34–35, 53; David Hawkes, *The Culture of Usury in Renaissance England* (New York: Palgrave Macmillan, 2010), 17; Cave and Coulson, *A Source Book for Medieval Economic History*, 169.
14. Goetzmann, *Money Changes Everything*, chap. 4; Odd Langholm, *The Aristotelian Analysis of Usury* (Bergen: Universitetsforlaget, 1984).
15. Anthony of Padua, "A Sermon for a Bishop" (Palm Sunday Sermons); "Fourth Sunday after Pentecost Sermon," www.franciscan-sfo.org/.../St.%20Anthony%20of%20Padua-.
16. Hawkes, *The Culture of Usury*, 65; Charles R. Geisst, *Beggar Thy Neighbor* (Philadelphia: University of Pennsylvania Press, 2013), chap. 2; Norman Golb, *The Jews in Medieval Normandy: A Social and Intellectual History* (Cambridge: CUP, 2012), 201; John W. Baldwin, *Masters, Princes, and Merchants: The Social Views of Peter the Chanter and His Circle* (Princeton: Princeton University Press, 1970); Mary

E. O'Carroll, *A Thirteenth-Century Preacher's Handbook* (Toronto: Pontifical Institute of Mediaeval Studies, 1997), 5; Peter Abelard, Letter 130, LPV, I, 32730; *The Letters of Peter the Venerable*, ed. G. Constable, 2 vols., *Harvard Historical Studies*, LXXVIII (Cambridge, MA: Harvard University Press, 1967); Little, *Religious Poverty*, 39.
17. Mirin, *Charity and Community*, 66.
18. Third Lateran Council, 1179, *Papal Encyclicals Online*, https://www.papalencyclicals.net/councils/ecum11.htm
19. Innocent III, *On Usury: Letter to the French Bishops* (1198), *Medieval Sourcebook: Innocent III* (r.1198–1216): *Letters on Papal Policy*, http://www.fordham.edu/halsall/source/innIII-policies.asp and Innocent III to the bishop of Arras, quoted in Mark Koyama, "Evading the 'Taint of Usury': The Usury Prohibition as a Barrier to Entry," *Explorations in Economic History* 47.4 (2010): 14.
20. Britnell, *The Commercialisation of English Society*, 91; Joseph Shatzmiller, *Cultural Exchange: Jews, Christians, and Art in the Medieval Market Place* (Princeton: Princeton University Press, 2013), 80–81, 91; Jean Dunbabin, *Charles of Anjou: Power, Kingship, and State* (London and New York: Longman, 2014), Kindle ed., chap. 3; Raymond de Roover, *Money, Banking, and Credit in Mediaeval Bruges—Italian Merchant Bankers, Lombards and Money Changers—A Study in the Origins of Banking* (Cambridge MA: Harvard University Press, 1948), 63; John H. Munro, "The Medieval Origins of the 'Financial Revolution': Usury, *Rentes*, and Negotiability," *The International History Review* 3.25 (2003): 507, 518, 521; Matthew Paris, *English History from the Year 1235 to 1273*, trans. J. A. Giles (London: H.G. Bohn, 1852), http://legacy.fordham.edu/halsall/source/1235cahorsins.asp and also, p. 100, http://babel.hathitrust.org/cgi/pt?id=uc1.32106006150517;seq=108;view=1up;num=100; Fourth Lateran Council (1215), Canon 67, http://history.hanover.edu/courses/excerpts/344latj.html; Edwin S. Hunt and James M. Murray, *A History of Business in Medieval Europe 1200–1550* (Cambridge: Cambridge University Press, 1999), 72; Hawkes, *The Culture of Usury*, 65.
21. Anthony of Padua, "A Sermon for a Bishop" (Palm Sunday Sermons); "Fourth Sunday after Pentecost Sermon," www.franciscan-sfo.org/.../St.%20Anthony%20of%20Padua-.
22. Britnell, *The Commercialisation of English Society*, 11, 15, 19; Hunt and Murray, *A History of Business in Medieval Europe*, 24, 26; Cave and Coulson, *A Source Book for Medieval Economic History*, 76, 112–13,119, 125, 151.
23. Juliette Sibon, "Peut-on croire en la parole du juif?" in *Croire ou ne pas croire*, eds., Monique Cottret and Caroline Galland (Paris: Éditions Kimé, 2013), 242.
24. Johannes Fried, *The Middle Ages*, trans. Peter Lewis (Cambridge MA: Harvard University Press, 2015), Kindle ed., chapters 1 and 2; Geisst, *Beggar Thy Neighbor*, intro. and chap. 1; Michael Prestwich, *Edward I: War, Politics, and Finance* (Endeavour Media 2018), Kindle ed., chap.9.
25. Mell, *The Myth of the Medieval Jewish Moneylender*.

26. June 1273, *Calendar of the Close Rolls: Edward I A.D. 1272–1279*, Public Records Office (London, 1900), 50, https://play.google.com/books/reader?printsec=frontcover&output=reader&id=snQnAQAAMAAJ&pg=GBS.PP1; Mary Cathcart Borer, *The City of London* (New York: McKay, 1978), 54, 55; George G. Perry, *The Life and Times of Robert Grosseteste, Bishop of Lincoln* (London: Forgotten Books, 2012), 10; R. B. Dobson, *The Jewish Communities of Medieval England: The Collected Essays of R. B. Dobson*, ed. Helen Birkett (York: The Borthwick Institute, 2010), 2, 5; Christopher Dyer, *Making a Living in the Middle Ages: The People of Britain 850–1520* (New Haven: Yale University Press, 2002), 101.
27. Koyama, "Evading," 4, 17; Gwen Seabourne, *Royal Regulation of Loans and Sales* (Woodbridge, Suffolk, UK: Boydell Press, 2003), 35; Humbert de Romans, *In Merchatis* (London 1926), 562, quoted in Cave and Coulson, *Sourcebook for Medieval Economic History*, 113.
28. Ferguson, *Ascent of Money*, Introduction; Roger *of Wendover's Flowers of History*, trans. J. A. Giles, vol. II (London, 1849), 169 quoted in Cave and Coulson, *A Sourcebook for Medieval Economic History*, 89; Koyama, "Evading," 2; Shatzmiller, *Cultural Exchange*, 8, 9; Sophus Reinert and Robert Fredona, "Merchants and the Origins of Capitalism," Working Paper, Harvard Business School, https://www.hbs.edu/faculty/Publication%20Files/18-021_b3b67ba8-2fc9-4a9b-8955-670d5f491939.pdf; Davis, "The Ethics of Arbitrage."
29. Marc Morris, *A Great and Terrible King: Edward I and the. Forging of Britain* (New York and London: Pegasus Books, nd), Kindle ed., chapters 1 and 3; Davis, "The Ethics of Arbitrage."; Baldwin, *Masters, Princes, and Merchants*; O'Carroll, *A Thirteenth-Century Preacher's Handbook*, 5; Little, *Religious Poverty*, 69; Hunt and Murray, *The History of Business in Medieval Europe*, 72; Eugene III, *Quantum praedecessores*, Dec. 1. 1145 reprinted in Jonathan Phillips, *The Second Crusade: Extending the Frontiers of Christendom* (New Haven: Yale University Press, 2007), Appendix I; Introduction to Peter the Venerable, *Against the Inveterate Obduracy of the Jews* in *The Fathers of the Church: Medieval Continuation*, trans. Irven M. Resnick (Washington, DC: The Catholic University of America Press, 2013), https://books.google.com/books?id=-TmKvbusGjkC&pg=PA23&lpg=PA23&dq=peter+the+venerable+to+king+louis&source=bl&ots=zsr32tmJQ7&sig=9U2bkLKzoDP7DDrrj9ls40DAUbk&hl=en&sa=X&ei=eO3oVIS6M4qUNrLDg_AE&ved=0CCEQ6AEwAQ#v=onepage&q=peter%20the%20venerable%20to%20king%20louis&f=false; Duby, *The Early Expansion of the European Economy*, 231.
30. Priscilla Heath Barnum, *Dives and Pauper*, vol. II (Oxford: OUP, 2004), 262; Cowell, *At Play in the Tavern*, 60; Golb, *The Jews of Medieval Normandy*, 201; Introduction to Peter the Venerable, *Against the Inveterate Obduracy of the Jews*; Little, *Religious Poverty*, 69.
31. Koyama, "Evading," 2; Shatzmiller, *Cultural Exchange*, 8, 9; *Chronica Jocelini de Brakelonda*, ed. J. G. Rokewode (London 1840), 2, in Cave and Coulson, *Sourcebook*

for Medieval Economic History, 175–76; Duby, *The Early Growth of the European Economy*, 218.

32. Shatzmiller, *Cultural Exchange*, 27, 28, 31, 33–36, 71; Gavin I. Langmuir, *Towards a Definition of Antisemitism* (Berkeley and Los Angeles: University of California Press, 1996), 200–201; Fried, *The Middle Ages*, Chap. 1; Jürgen Kocka, *Capitalism: A Short History* (Princeton: Princeton University Press, 2016); Robin R. Mundill, "Christian and Jewish Lending Patterns and Financial Dealings During the Twelfth and Thirteenth Centuries," in *Credit and Debit in Medieval England c. 1180-c. 1350*, eds., P. R. Schofield and N. J. Mayhew (Oxford: Oxbow, 2002), 45, 211; Koyama, "Evading," 2; Borer, *The City of London*, 54, 93; Paul Rapin de Thoyras, *An Abridgement of the History of England* (London: John and Paul Knapton, 1747), 217; William Stubbs, *Select Charters of English Constitutional History*, ed. H. W. C. Davis (Oxford, 1923), 256 in Cave and Coulson, *Sourcebook for Medieval Economic History*, 176-77; Hans F. Sennholz, *Age of Inflation* (Belmont, MA: Western Islands, 1979), 21.
33. The quote in the original reads:. . .Povertá, alto sapere,/a nulla cosa soiacere,/en desprezo possedere/tutte le cose create./. . .Chi desia è posseduto,/a quel ch'ama s'è venduto;/s'egli pensa que n'ha 'vuto,/'han avute rei derrate./. . . .La richeza el tempo tolle,/la scienzia en vento estolle,/la fama alberga ed acolle/l'ipocresia d'onne contrate./Jacopone da Todi, "De la Santa Povertá e Suo Triplice Cielo" (On Holy Poverty and Her Threefold Heaven) Laude 60, reprinted in Evelyn Underhill, *Jacopone da Todi: Poet and Mystic 1228–1306, A Spiritual Biography* (London, Toronto: J.M. Dent & Sons, 1919), 421–27; Fried, *The Middle Ages*, chap. 9.
34. Mollat and Wolff, *The Popular Revolutions of the Late Middle Ages*, 25; Seabourne, *Royal Regulation of Loans and Sales*, 40, 44, 62, 68.
35. William Chester Jordan, *The Great Famine: Northern Europe in the Early Fourteenth Century* (Princeton: Princeton University Press, 1998), 44–45, 62; Whittock, *Brief History*, 141; Seabourne, *Royal Regulation of Loans and Sales*, 45, 51.

2

"The Purses and Leeches of Princes"

By the twelfth century, merchants and trade were viewed as potentially good for society and in the thirteenth century, trade was regularized with the aim of reducing risk and increasing exports for greater profit. The rise in tenants paying cash rents pushed them to produce surplus for markets, while increased commercialization prompted greater control over law and order by the authorities as well as significant capital. This was acceptable so long as merchants remained within the perimeters of moral integrity. Usury remained outside those borderlines but, nevertheless, the practice was expanding, not contracting. In England, at the end of the twelfth century, loan charters (*Chartae* or *Chirographa*), written in Hebrew, Latin, or French, were kept not in the Jews' homes but in "a publick Chest provided for that purpose, called the Chest of the Chirographi, or of the Chirographers." This step was taken in order to prevent mobs from destroying the debt records by burning down Jews' houses. One part of the chirograph was kept by the Jewish moneylender, signed with the borrowers seal. There were three locks on the chest where the other part of the chirograph was put and keys were given to two Christians and two Jews, as well as clerks of the place in which the chest was housed. When it came time to open the chests, the chirographers, both Jews and Christians, along with the sheriff, cofferers, and, in London, the barons of the

Exchequer were all present. Copies of the receipts of any payments made to the Jews were likewise given to the Christians, the Jews, and the keeper of the rolls.[1]

Peter the Chanter (d. 1197), head cantor at Notre Dame in Paris, protested that "the detestable usurers are now the bosom companions of princes and prelates, who surrender to the blandishments of the moneybags and promote their sons to the highest posts in Church and State." Usurers were "the purses and leeches of princes" who by vomiting cash, sucked everyone dry and avarice was their daughter. Along with this charge, he added the rebuke that the creditor made a profit without physical exertion. This was an accusation that was to endure over the centuries; work meant physical labor and if financial gain by usury could happen even as the moneylender slept, then it was not honest work or any kind of work.[2]

Peter's vicious attack on moneylenders was correct in one aspect. Money became more necessary in the twelfth and thirteenth centuries in transactions between the king and his subjects, landlords and their tenants, and in fairs and markets. If between 1160s and 1170s, the currency in circulation in England was less than one million pennies, by the 1250s, it was fifteen million, due in large part to the wool trade and an increase in silver mining. The appearance of smaller denominations in the thirteenth century made it possible for many more people to use coins for everday purchases. As R.H. Britnell writes, the "commercial development of the twelfth and thirteenth centuries permitted a growth in population . . . and greatly enriched the resources of knowledge and experience which future generations had at their disposal." In 1202, Leonardo of Pisa, who was later became known as Fibonacci, wrote *Liber Abaci* (The Book of Calculation) in which he used the Hindu-Arabic numerical system to cover fractions and their application to commercial bookkeeping, currency conversion, and calculation of interest. It was the first time that mathematics was tied to profit making and moneylending and offered in terms that were comprehensible for the general public. According to some historians, this book signaled the beginning of modern finance.[3]

Ruling authorities may have accumulated a lot of money but they also spent vast amounts and found themselves almost constantly in need of funds. Wars were not only bloody affairs, they were costly and the price of waging a war often far exceeded the financial rewards gained by the victor. In addition to military endeavors, rulers had many other expenditures and were left with little option but to take out large loans to cover their expenses. Taxes may have been the obvious choice to increase revenue but it was an unpopular one that could lead to civil unrest and worse. The taxes demanded by the archbishop of Mainz were so exacting that he was murdered in 1160 in front of the monastery of St. Jakob. Rulers in need of funds were, therefore, forced to look for a variety of financial sources.[4]

Throughout Europe, Jews were, effectively, the "king's Jews," a status formally recognized in the thirteenth century. Everything they owned, effectively was the monarch's property. For this reason, rulers had a vested interest in the Jews not only thriving but in their debtors paying their loans fully and in a timely manner. Jewish moneylenders, after all, could not pay their substantial tithes to the king if their loans went unpaid. But this relationship between moneylenders and monarchs—based on protection by the ruler and a thriving and steady banking business by the Jews—had the potential to breed serious resentment on the part of debtors and critics who were far removed from the seats of power. This was especially true if the king exacted heavy taxes or fines, impelling people to take out loans, and then forcing them to repay their loans under duress.

After nineteen winters of "chaos, anarchy, and suffering" under King Stephen, the reign of Henry II (1154–1189) was fortuitous for Jewish moneylenders in England. Henry had inherited a disatrous economy and, with war against France approaching, he needed to right the financial ship as quickly as possible. In 1177, at Henry's request, the Bishop of London and the treasurer of the exchequer Richard FitzNeal wrote *Dialogue Concerning the Exchequer*. The purpose of his book was to explain the auditing and registration of the sheriff's accounts. In the process, he tackled the subject of usury. Unlike the depiction of it as theft and injustice, usury was not an evil in Fitzneal's estimation. Far from it. Capital was vital for a strong kingdom and those without it would always find themselves at the mercy of their enemies. Henry certainly knew this. When he amassed his tremendous army in the summer of 1159 for the invasion of France, he had to cover the cost of the mercenaries which amounted to nine thousand pounds. That sum exceeded the king's revenue for the entire previous year. With war and daily expenses draining the treasury, Henry spent much of his time trying to find ways to fill the coffers, as well as asserting his control over wayward nobles. He grabbed what he could from his subjects in the way of taxes, including between a quarter and a third of the Jews' property. As a number of England's Jewry helped to supply the capital he needed, either by loans or taxes, he also protected them so that they could collect their debts without the overreaching arm of the Church interfering.[5]

Even with high taxation levied on them, by the mid-twelfth century certain Jews profited from moneylending, enabling them to purchase land, the main source of wealth in the medieval world. Men such as Isaac and Abraham of London, Jurnet and Benedict of Norwich, Brun and Josc Quatrebuch of London, and Aaron of York, and especially Aaron of Lincoln (c.1125–1186) amassed great fortunes. In fact, his wealth was so immense, Aaron of Lincoln warranted his own exchequer (*Scaccarium Aaronis*), which led to the recording of all debts owed to Jews in the Exchequer of the Jews (*Scaccarium Judaeorum*), a detailed account of all financial transactions concerning the Jews of England. During his lifetime, Aaron was said to have lived in great splendor in his father's London house that he rebuilt, and he reportedly helped to fund multiple ecclesiastical buildings, including St. Albans Abbey, Lincoln Minster, and Peterborough Cathedral. Aaron's income came from lending money at interest to the higher echelons of society, including the monarchy, leading to criticism of the Jews being the "king's usurers." It was commonly said that he was the richest man in England, with more money than even the king. After Aaron's death, Henry confiscated his entire estate and his outstanding debts were collected in a more thorough and harsh manner.[6]

In 1187, after Jerusalem fell to Salah ad-Din, Henry imposed the largest tax ever experienced in England. Everyone, with the exception of crusaders, was responsible for a 10 percent tithe on his revenue and movable goods. This Saladin Tithe was to fund the third crusade and those who tried to avoid the payment risked imprisonment or excommunication. The chronicler Gervase of Canterbury assessed the amount given by the small minority of Jews to be £60,000, while the Christians gave £70,000. These numbers have since been revised downward with the amount for which the Jews were responsible being £10,000 initially, with a further £2,000 the following year, although the actual amount demanded and the amound paid are unknown.[7]

Two years after Jerusalem's capture, the thirty-two-year-old son of Henry and his wife Eleanor of Aquitaine was crowned King Richard I of England. According to Raphael Holinshed's chronicle, Jews from London and other counties gathered at Westminster palace to present the new monarch with a gift to show their loyalty. They also wanted to assure themselves that Richard would retain the privileges and liberties that had been given to them by previous monarchs. Richard, however, was not inclined to give the Jews an audience. A rumor quickly spread that the king had ordered the destruction of the Jews. Crowds tried to force their way into the Jews' homes, and when this proved unsuccessful, their houses were set on fire. The flames not only consumed Jewish buildings but those of their Christian neighbors "so hideous was the rage of the fire."[8]

Informed about the riot, the king sent some of his councilors and officers to quell the violence. Not only did he want to maintain law and order, Richard wanted to make sure revenue from the Jews was not interrupted or damaged. The crowd, however, was in no mood to listen to Richard's advisors. Intent on robbing the homes and shops of the Jews, the ransackers turned on the councilors who fled for their lives. As the fire blazed, lighting up the night, Jews inside the homes were either smothered to death with the smoke or burned. Those who tried to escape, were butchered by "the furious and disordered people" with spears, swords, and bills (a type of polearm with a hooked, chopping blade and protruding spikes). The massacre continued until the afternoon of the following day, when, exhausted, the crowd dispersed.[9]

Shortly after the riot, Richard departed English shores to join the third crusade leaving England without a monarch. His crusade was costly. The ships being readied for the campaign were stocked with silver, furs, food and spices, weapons, and much more. Funding came from taxes that were exacted from all quarters of society. Heretics' property was confiscated, donations were expected from all towns, and tariffs were imposed on the Jews. Richard's need for military campaign funds prompted him not only to tax Jews in England but also to levy a special tax on the Jews in Normandy, which was part of the Angevin empire under English rule during the twelfth and early thirteenth centuries. As usual, non-payment of government taxes meant fines, confiscation of property, and imprisonment.[10]

It was not only heavy taxation that was a problem. With the king absent and his troops assembled as they prepared to follow him, lawlessness increased. More attacks on Jews spread throughout England in spite of Richard's command that the Jews should be left unmolested. The reason for the violence, in Holinshed's opinion, was the "unmercifull usurie practised [by the Jews] to the undooing of manie an honest man." In Lincoln and Norfolk, Jews were slaughtered while in other towns they were beaten and robbed. The worst attack occurred in York on the sabbath before Passover, March 16, 1190 which was also the eve of Palm Sunday. According to the chronicler Ephraim of Bonn, the houses of the richest Jews were looted and burned. As the Jewish community sought protection at the royal castle keep, a decision was apparently made to either die by their own hand or that of their family rather than by infidels. Those who ignored this command and fled from the fire were slaughtered by the mob storming the castle.

The exact details of the story are lost to us but it is clear that the issue of usury was a critical factor. Bonds owned by the Jews were often left in churches for safekeeping, and in York they were kept at the Minster. With the Jews massacred, people swarmed into the Minster, broke into the chests where the promissory notes were kept, and, in the middle of the church, the bonds were burned. With this action, all debt was erased. William of Newburgh one of the contemporary chroniclers of the disturbances, evaluated the source of the violent riot:

> Of the Jews of York . . . the principal were Benedict and Joceus, men who were rich, and who lent on usury far and wide. Besides, with profuse expense they had built houses of the largest extent in the midst of the city, which might be compared to royal palaces; and there they lived in abundance and luxury almost regal, like two princes of their own people, and tyrants to the Christians, exercising cruel tyranny towards those whom they had oppressed by usury . . . when the king was afterwards resident in the parts beyond sea, many people in the county of York took an oath together against the Jews, being unable to endure their opulence while they themselves were in want; and, without any scruple of Christian conscientiousness, thirsted for their perfidious blood, through the desire of plunder. Those who urged them on to venture upon these measures were certain persons of higher rank, who owed large sums to those impious usurers. Some of these, who had pledged their own estates to them for money, which they had received, were oppressed with great poverty; and others who were under obligations, on account or their own bonds, were oppressed by the tax-gatherers to satisfy the usurers who had dealings with the king.

The killings, the theft, the destruction, were all justified by Newburgh as a legitimate response to the illegitimate and vile practice of moneylending on the part of the Jews. There was only one Christian account, by Ralph of Diss, that condemned the killings outright and without equivocation. In general, even those who despised the aims of the murderers understood the hatred of moneylenders. William of Newburgh did not condone the massacre, which he believed to be motivated by avarice and conducted with immense cruelty. The carnage, in his assessment, was less a spontaneous outburst of anti-Jewish hatred and more a well concerted and organized murder of men to whom some highly ranked Christians owed considerable sums of money. Nevertheless, he placed most of the blame not on the murderers but on the usurious and rich Jews.[11]

Like all chronicles of the time, Ephraim's account of the massacre needs to be handled with caution. He had no interest in history; he was, after all, writing a martyrology, the important message of which was the holiness of dying for God. Nevertheless, the end result was without doubt: York's Jewish community was brutally butchered, their money and goods stolen, and the debts owed to the Jewish moneylenders in the city were wiped clean.

Noblemen such as Richard Malebisse owned large estates—in his case, in Lincolnshire and Yorkshire—and actively sought to harness royal power, which he believed was encroaching on the rights of the barons. He was also in debt to Aaron of Lincoln, whose estate had fallen into the hands of the king after the moneylender's death in 1186. Malebisse's aggrievement led him to join the conspiracy headed by the future King John against his absentee brother Richard. He was further accused of joining forces with members of the Percy family, to whom he was related, to plot the attack on the Jews of York. Other leaders accused of the riot were similarly indebted to Jews, including Robert of Ghent and Robert de Turnaham, who both owed money to Aaron of York. In addition, Robert of Ghent was in debt to another Jewish creditor, Brun of Stamford.[12]

When news of the assault on the Jews reached him in Normandy, Richard I took action against his rebellious lords and ordered his chancellor, the bishop of Ely William de Longchamp, to travel to York. Once there, he removed the sheriff and the constable of the castle. Most of those culpable for the riot had already escaped to Scotland or had joined the crusade. In their absence, the bishop confiscated a considerable amount of land. Fines were attributed to some of the richest subjects regardless of whether they were the most liable for the massacre or not. The estates of Malebisse were also taken and his esquires imprisoned.[13]

The attack in York was not only an assault against Jews as moneylenders. It was an attack on the king and his power. In the spring of 1199, on campaign at the Château of Châlus-Chabrol in the duchy of Aquitaine, forty-one-year-old Richard I succumbed to gangrene caused by a crossbow arrow wound. His rule had lasted ten-years, most of which time was spent outside of England on crusade, in captivity until ransomed, or, as at Châlus-Chabrol, devastating the lands of his rebellious vassals in France. His successor was his short, fat brother John and it was during his reign that the instigator of the riots against the Jews, Malebisse, had his estates restored to him. It was a case of one bad man being rewarded by another, for John was "a very bad man" who was "brim-ful of evil qualities," in the words of a contemporary. He was treacherous, lecherous, and cruel. "Nature's enemy" is how William of Newburgh described him. Starving his enemies to death was one of his favorite methods of execution and, fearful of his teenage nephew Arthur's popularity, he had him imprisoned and then murdered.

With high taxes, bad harvests, unsuccessful business ventures, and any other of the multitude of reasons debt is accumulated, the nobles' challenge to the monarch and talk of civil war led to the signing of Magna Carta by King John in 1215. An early form of political representation between the king and his barons, Magna Carta included, as one of its provisions, a proscription against the continuation of usury on Jewish debts after the death of the debtor if the heir was a minor. John's signature on that celebrated treaty failed, however, to suppress the tyranny of kings and the demands of hostile barons.[14]

Within five years of the York massacre, Jews resumed their moneylending activities, providing financial services even more prominently than before. The

Crown supplied closer supervision, as it was determined to prevent any repeat of 1190. These measures were taken not for the sake of the Jews but for the benefit of King John's finances which were greatly diminished after the loss of Normandy to the French and his costly military campaign in Ireland. In late 1209 and early 1210, after plundering the Cistercians and provoking Pope Innocent III to excommunicate him, John turned his attention again to the small community of Jewish moneylenders. Holding them captive, he had their income assessed and then exacted a tax of sixty-six thousand marks. If not voluntarily paid, the money was forcibly taken by means of torture and imprisonment. According to one chronicler, John "pillaged them out of nearly everything they possessed and drove them out of their houses." The chronicler wrote how the king had the eyes of some captives gouged out, or their teeth pulled, while others were starved, reduced to knocking on the doors of Christians to beg for food. Even if these accounts are exaggerations, when it came to filling his war chest and punishing his enemies, John was odious, craven, and remarkably cruel, even for such brutal times. No one can trust him, sang the troubadour Bertran de Born, for he was man with a "soft and cowardly" heart.[15]

When Henry III took the throne in 1216 as a boy of nine, the country was still riven with baronial discontent and rebellion. In royal tradition, he continued the demands for money and loans, burdening his population with heavy taxation and running roughshod over Magna Carta much to the barons' alarm. Henry's reign was initially a fruitful time for the Jewish communities, however, which numbered around two thousand living in around fifteen towns. By 1241, English Jews held around 200,000 marks in liquid assets, making it Europe's most affluent Jewish community.[16]

Wealthy Jewish moneylenders enjoyed close commercial relations with similarly well-to-do Christians. One of most successful Jewish moneylending family in the thirteenth century was the le Blunds and when Aaron II le Blunds married, Christians attended the wedding, mingling with his relatives who were sumptuously "clothed in silk and gold." Such was their wealth that in 1221 and 1223, Leo I and his son Aaron I together paid around 40 percent of the tallage—the tax levied in times of special needs—due to the king from London's entire Jewish community. In 1220, Aaron I and his brother Elias I were granted a property in London stretching from Colechurch Lane to St. Thomas Hospital on the other side of the Thames to the Palace of Westminster. Their benefactor was Peter fitz Aluf, whose relative Constantine, a former sheriff of London, had attempted an insurrection against the king and was hanged without trial, his property confiscated. The land belonging to the le Blunds brothers was also appropriated by Henry III but returned to them on one condition: that no Jew should reside there due to its proximity to the hospital that commemorated the sainted Thomas Becket. Aaron duly sold the land to St. Thomas's and purchased another property east of Colechurch Lane which was near to land owned by his brother Elias and his business colleague Aaron of York.[17]

The le Blunds' clients included some of the most powerful merchants and families in England. In the close role of 1236 Aaron was given the nickname "the rich," although the le Blunds' wealth paled in comparison to other moneylenders such as Aaron of York, David of Oxford, and Leo of York. Leading members of the Jewish community tried to negotiate, sometimes successfully, the amount of tax they owed to the king. Aaron, son of Abraham of London, for example, came to an agreement with Henry III to reduce the tallage owed by the Jews. In general, though, taxes increased as the king's financial needs grew. Those who did not pay their taxes had the misfortune to be imprisoned until payment was received, as in the case of Sampson Bunting, a Jew from Lincoln, who was locked up in the Tower of London for nonpayment of his part of the tallage. His release came only when Solomon, "the king's Jew of London," settled Bunting's debt. It was not only Jews that the king targeted. Christians such as William Cade, a wealthy Flemish cloth trader and moneylender in London and fellow merchant Walter de Cheriton were financially ruined by the king's demands and died penniless. Reginald de Conduit was imprisoned and William de la Pole, a wealthy wool merchant who lent huge sums of money to the Crown at the start of the Hundred Years' War and organized further loans from merchants in London and York, was held at Devizes Castle on charges of wool smuggling. His lands were seized until the charges were eventually dropped.[18]

It was during Henry III's reign that one of the wealthiest women in England, Licoricia of Winchester, lived and worked as a moneylender. From around 1230, she lent money in association with other Jews or alone, assisted by an attorney, becoming one of the most prominent moneylenders in Winchester. After the death of her first husband, Abraham, she married one of those richest Jewish moneylenders in England, David of Oxford. Their marriage was a complicated affair as David's first wife refused to agree to a divorce until the intervention of Henry, the Archbishop of York, Walter de Grey, and the Jewish courts (*bet din*) in England and Paris. Upon David's death in 1244, Licoricia was incarcerated in the Tower of London while the Jewish Exchequer scrutinized the official debts that were owed to her late husband. As the process dragged on, Licoricia languished in prison for months. Finally, the audit was completed and, as was usual with the king, there was a financial deal to be struck. In return for her freedom and the debts owed to her deceased husband, Licoricia was charged five thousand marks. A portion of that amount was earmarked for a project close to Henry's heart. A fervent devotee of the cult of Edward the Confessor, the king intended to build a chapel to house a shrine dedicated to the former king.

Even after paying this large fine, Licoricia remained an extremely wealthy woman. She quickly returned to her life in Winchester and to the business of moneylending, providing loans to royalty, the nobility, and the clergy. Through her financial business, Licoricia developed a good relationship with Henry and members of his court and it was a friendship that proved beneficial. When the heir of Sir Thomas of Charlecote brought a court case against her over his estate, the king intervened on her behalf. In spite of her conviction by the court for unlawfully retaining Thomas's late father's estate, her penalty was a miniscule fine. Licoricia's good fortune, however, was tragically cut short in 1277 when her daughter Belia found her lifeless body alongside that of her Christian maid, Alice of Bicton. Both women had been stabbed to death and an unknown sum of money was taken from her house. No one was apprehended or charged with either crime of robbery or murder, which was not an unusual occurrence. It was not until Henry's son, Edward, became king that the justice system began to take shape.[19]

* * *

In France, there were multiple efforts to curb usury. In 1182, King Philip II of France (r. 1180–1223) decided to help fill his treasure chests by expulsion and confiscation. This was a common practice for many reasons, used by authorities to rid themselves of a political foe or for religious reasons. In Philip's case, it was for financial need and it was at the expense of the Jews, who were expelled from the French realm and their property and goods appropriated by the Crown. The king then restored to his knights lands and title deeds, without interest, which had been pledged to Jewish moneylenders. Philip's son, Louis VIII, issued the *Establissement sur les Juifs* in 1223, which erased the interest off existing loans and stated that the principal sum had to be repaid to the Jews within three years. Nobles were given control over the loans with the power to collect the debt. But it was a change of policy that was not happily accepted by nobles who, like their English counterparts, were keen to challenge the king's authority. They may have legally been the "king's Jews," but that did not stop powerful nobles from regarding Jews in their lands as "theirs." Thibaut IV of Champagne baulked at these new regulations. He had a customary arrangement with the Jews of his region that in return for a high tax payment, they would be neither expelled nor have their property confiscated. Any property belonging to a Jew who died or left the region was to go to the Jewish community and not the count, who also agreed not to seize private goods, including horses, from the Jews. Thibaut's reluctance to spoil this agreement to accommodate the king's new laws led to conflict between the two men. Thibaut continued to vouch for Jewish moneylenders, including foreign merchants, such as Palmerius of Siena who lent money to Walter of Arzillières. The noble pledged his estate to the count if he failed to repay the loan. The property would be held by the count until Palmerius had his money returned by the deadline imposed by Thibaut. Another lord, Geoffroy of Deuilly transferred his fief to Thibaut, which again was held until he had repaid the debt he owned to "his [Thibaut's] Jews."[20]

Louis' brother, Alfonse, count of Poitiers and Toulouse, had his own deals with merchants and Jewish moneylenders. His property tax on the burghers of Poitou (the *fouage*) was accepted on one condition. In exchange for the tax, the count promised to expel the Jews, to whom many were in debt. Alfonse played both sides, benefiting from the tax while accepting money from the Jews for his promise *not* to expel them. As they were not expelled, the payment from the Jews seems to have outweighed the revenue from the *fouage*. Yet, this financial double-dealing was not sufficient and Alfonse still found himself asking his brother for loans.[21]

In 1234, Louis VIII's heir, the gaunt-faced Louis IX (known as St. Louis for his piety), created a new constitution, which demanded that the Jews abandoned usury or leave France "completely in order that it shall be no longer polluted with their filth," that is, usury. Following suit, the duke of Brittany, John I, gave way to popular resentment against Jewish moneylending, and exiled the Jews in 1239. Simon de Montfort and Eleanor of Provence, wife of Henry III of England, both expelled the Jews from their French estates, as did Louis IX's nephew, Charles of Salerno, who expelled Jewish usurers from Maine and Anjou for their "devious deceits." In most cases, the deficit that was incurred with the loss of capital was to be made up by a new set of taxes, readily agreed to by a populace thankful to be rid of Jewish moneylenders and the debts they owed. Moreover, the monarchs and nobles had the blessing of Pope Gregory IX, who, in 1234, urged rulers to expel usurers from their lands and never readmit them.[22]

To help the crusade he launched in 1248, Louis IX freed Christian borrowers and potential crusaders from a third of the registered amount of money owed to Jews if and while they were imprisoned. The new decree also forbade bailiffs to incarcerate Christians for unpaid debts to Jewish moneylenders or to force them to sell property to pay these debts, although the king's authorities continued to try and collect the debts owed to Jews. A court returned to Lady Catherine of Cadros property which her husband had given to a Jewish moneylender as collateral for a loan. It was ruled that her husband had no right to give away the property without his family's consent. In 1239, debtors were informed that, with some exceptions, they did not have to respond to Jewish demands for repayments. That the issue was usury and not religious antipathy is suggested by Louis' expulsion of the Lombards, Cahors, and other foreign moneylenders from his kingdom in 1268, although this was a short-lived departure. By the end of the thirteenth century, Lombards had become the most influential moneylenders in France, as well as England, with the Crown receiving twice as much in revenue from the Italians than from Jewish usurers.[23]

* * *

The southern port city of Marseille was a wealthy, free republic headed by merchants, and part of the independent county of Provence. It had the good fortune to be located on the crossroads of trade routes running from northern France to the Mediterranean and be in possession of a deep natural harbor. Merchants from many kingdoms, duchies, and republics traded and made contracts in this sun-drenched European center of commercial activity—traveling, in particular, from Tuscany, Toulouse, Lombardy, and the Rhone delta. Marseille was a place made wealthy during the crusades by profiting from the crusaders who boarded ships in its harbor and from the export of goods to the Levant. Cloths from Flanders arrived at the port ready to be shipped on to Sicily and Acre. Spices (such as cumin, ginger, cardamom, and cinnamon), herbs (such as myrrh and scammony), sugar, dyes, Brazil wood, medicinals, alum cordwain, and wax passed through Marseille before reaching their final destination. By the mid-thirteenth century, trade from Marseille stretched to Arras, Paris, Champagne, Ypres, Barcelona, Valencia, the Maghreb, Egypt, Pisa, Genoa, and Rome. The only routes from which the Marseille merchants were excluded were those under Venetian control in the Adriatic, Aegean, and Black Sea.[24]

Jews had settled in Marseille since the Merovingian period. During the thirteenth century they obtained the status of citizen, with the same privileges as Christians, such as the right to worship freely, and owned property in the city and on the outskirts. They had quarters in both the upper and lower part of the city, two synagogues, a hospital, schools, and their own market. Contrary to some studies that portray Jews as perennial "outcasts," the business activity of Jews in places such as Marseille suggests there was a great deal of interaction with Christians and that integration was not unusual. There were restrictions, as there were for all citizens. Jews could not give evidence in court against a Christian, openly working on Sunday or a religious feast day was not allowed, and some sort of insignia indicating that they were Jewish was to be worn, a regulation that was regularly exempted, avoided, or ignored.[25]

Located on the north-east corner of the port was Carreria Portus, the hub of Marseille's maritime and commercial business. Here, moneychangers sat at tables in front of the Isla dels Cambis building, rubbing shoulders with notaries, oar makers and caulkers. All merchants took an oath to trade honestly. They promised not to form monopolies, cheat, inflate the cost of goods, take bribes, steal, or contaminate produce. Some Jews participated in Mediterranean commerce, including Léon Passapayre, Abraham Bonehore, Abraham and Gardet de Bédarride, but, as most historians agree, the majority of these traders were of "middling status" and made up only a small percentage of Jews in the city. Unlike medieval England and France, the Jews of Marseille were not known for moneylending and chose instead the professions of physician, artisans, or worked in the coral, wool, almond, and tartar trades. What is difficult to know, however, is whether Jews and Christians offered loans to family, friends, neighbors, and others without formal contracts. To avoid the charge of usury or the grasping hands of government, it may be the case that some, maybe considerable, moneylending was on a more furtive level but, obviously, if this was the case we will never know.[26]

In the spring of 1248, the same year Louis IX began his crusade, fifty-four ships set sail from Marseille loaded with goods for other markets. On board some of these ships were seven Jews who were agents for investors and who, in partnership, had entered into a contract called a commenda, which allowed merchants to share risks and rewards. The use of this kind of contract illustrated how much Jews were involved in commerce and interacted with Christians in business enterprises. The commenda was a medieval commercial loan that involved a sedentary partner (commendator) and a tractator, who was the active partner. The first supplied capital to the active partner who might add their own capital to the amount, which made the commenda a bilateral rather than a unilateral one. The Jewish commendators in Marseille were either merchants who were, at various times, either commendator or tractator, investors in many commendae in a condensed time period, or investors in only one commenda, and they were usually low-level investors. Once formulated, the commenda was notarized with witnesses to sign it, which gave the commercial enterprise a legal standing. The tractator then took the capital, usually overseas, and used it in whatever way was agreed. When the particular venture had been completed, the tractator returned to report on the proceedings. This could occur even without the physical presence of the tractator. After deducting expenses and investment capital, the profits were split in whatever way had been agreed.[27]

The most important items traded in Jewish commenda contracts were saffron and cloves, followed by toile, silk, finished capes, and coins. After these came foods, dyes, and chemicals. These were items easily handled by low-level financiers, as they did not require extremely large sums of capital. Of 466 commenda contracts in the cartulary of Almaric, 11 percent had Jewish agents as either active partners or investors and out of the two contracts that had commendator partnerships, one of these was between a Jew and a Christian. The Jewish agent Bonanatus judeus filius Bonifilii and the Christian moneychanger Dulcianus de Sancto Victore gave a commenda contract for sulfur to three Jewish tractators in partnership. Bonanatus was also a tractator while Dulcianus was a witness to a contract, the commendator of which was a witness for Dulcianus and Bonanatus. Another Jewish merchant Mosse d'Accone entered into a contract with Petrus Cresteng, a Christian, in April 1248. From Mosse, Petrus took 40 capes from Metz worth £142.10d monete miscue, which were then transported to Sicily. Mosse then took 150 besants of millares from Petrus at a value of £45 monete miscue, which sailed to Bougie in the Maghreb. Mosse's sons, Salomon and Joseph were also involved in commendae as both tractators and commendators.[28]

These were clearly fluid professions and most of the partnerships were devised on an informal rather than a permanent basis, with partnerships formed and dispensed with as needed. It was also the case that tractators, once they had accumulated enough capital, became commendators for a more settled existence. The Jewish tractators were, as Julie Mell points out, professional commercial agents but the values of the contracts they executed were moderate, "ranging from £100 to 10 shillings." In Amalric's cartulary, the contracts associated only with Jews averaged £17.4s per commenda, which was far below the entire average of £62, when Christians are included. As Mell concludes, Jewish tractators were active professionals in this business but they were of "modest means."[29]

As shown, Jews and Christians interacted as partners and witnesses in commenda contracts. What is even more indicative of the business relationships between Jews and Christians is that Jewish commendators and tractators often chose Christian notaries and Latin contracts rather than a rabbinic contract (*Heter Iska*), which had stricter stipulations to avoid usury. The Jewish partners then had them drawn up in a municipal court instead of a rabbinic court (*bet din*). As a Christian court was used, Christians were witnesses and, in the case of a disagreement between the Jewish partners, they could be called on to give evidence. The experience of the Jews in Marseille is an important contrast to the experience of the Jews under Louis IX. If usury led to expulsion in the kingdom of France, there were other regions, such as Marseille, that were more amenable to anyone with capital to lend and invest.[30]

Before he left to head another costly crusade in 1270, Louis IX ordered the property of Jews to be seized if it had been gained through usury. This had a two-fold purpose. It satisfied the resentment and anger that many people held against moneylenders, especially those who charged high rates of interest, and it added to the king's treasure, helping to fund his crusade campaign. The crusade never made it to the Holy Land but was instead diverted to North Africa by Charles of Anjou, the king's brother, for his own political purposes. It was in Tunis that Louis died from dysentery at the age of fifty-six. When Louis' son, Philip III (the Bold) took the throne in 1270, there was an easing of these anti-usury ordinances, although they continued to exist on the books. Contrary to his father, Philip acknowledged pawnbroking as a valid profession for Jews, bestowing the pawnbroker with legal rights. He was also lax in applying Louis' stringent laws. Therefore, despite the prohibitions, by 1273, Jews were engaged in regular moneylending in the Ile-de-France due to the non-enforcement of anti-usury laws. Philip, it seems, was more concerned with the economic health of France than with the moral rights and wrongs of usury.[31]

Philip was not the only French ruler keen to harness capital for their own purposes. In the 1270s, Marseille was forced to recognize the suzerainty of Charles of Anjou, along with Arles, and Avignon. Under Charles, the city was incorporated into Provence and usurious transactions were restricted to twice a month with a general interest rate of 12 percent. After a revolt, he enacted harsh penalties against moneylenders but, in general, Charles' lands were hospitable to their profession. Intrigued by the idea of profit, he set about encouraging trade and commerce, creating a royal monopoly on salt, mining for precious metals, and collecting fees for exempting people from the onerous Sicilian *subventio generalis* tax. Those exemptions, however, meant that the tax pool was smaller and so those left paying tax paid a greater amount. To promote trade and commerce, he gave protection to merchants attending fairs in Anjou and encouraged Jews and Italian Christians to develop credit. He also stipulated that Jews did not have to wear the insignia that had been ordered by the French king. With such policies, Florentines settled in his dominions as moneylenders and merchants under his protection so that by 1274, Italians had a monopoly in the profession of moneylending in his realm, lending Charles large sums of money in exchange for privileges.

Jews under Charles' control were particularly involved in the economy of the Regno, which was comprised of the Kingdom of Sicily and parts of southern Italy. Sicilian Jews had a near monopoly on the dyeing trade while others acted as moneylenders under his protection like the Italians. Between Charles' large number of indirect taxes and the monopolization of industries, the economic benefits fell on the few rather than the many. Still, he brought his expanding state under one administration operating with one set of laws. With this more competent and consistent government, the presence of Lombards to provide credit, and new connections in the Mediterranean, profits were robust, even though Charles' expenditure was steep. This acceptance of usury was halted during the reign of his grandson, Robert I, who, in 1322, issued an edict against usurers. But by the middle of the century, the economic needs for loans outweighed moral concerns. Robert's successor was his granddaughter Jeanne (Joanna or Giovanna) of Naples, who permitted a maximum interest payment of 10 percent. It was not an overwhelming victory for moneylenders, who valued their risk at rather more than 10–12 percent, but it was an indication that the tide was turning in the attitude towards usury.

* * *

In England, the tallaging of Jews increased during the twelfth century but became a less profitable form of revenue for the Crown as the community's wealth declined, either because of the heavy taxation or loans that went unpaid. It may also be the case that income was hidden from the financially voracious monarch. Repeatedly denied taxes from parliament, Henry had become reliant on his sheriffs, foresters, and justices to bring in the necessary revenue and fines which were collected with growing oppression. In 1241–42, a massive tallage of 20,000 marks was imposed on the Jewish community. About half of the paid amount was provided by Aaron of York, David of Oxford, and Leo of York. This was followed up by a 60,000 tallage in 1244–45. In an effort to comply with the king's demands for taxes, moneylenders called in their debts, such as the one contracted between John de Carun of Sherington and Elias le Eveske. In the early 1240s, John de Carun was in need of money after joining Henry III's military expedition to Gascony. With the expense of his knighthood, the cost of military equipment, and the upkeep of his estate while he was overseas, he sought a loan from Elias, one of the most influential Jewish moneylenders in the thirteenth century. When Henry imposed his enormous tallage on the Jews, Elias, like other moneylenders, was obliged to seek repayment. After a judicial inquiry, that assessed his lands, John of Carun was ordered to pay an annual instalment of six marks to his creditor in repayment, much to the dissatisfaction of Elias. The debt was paid after the sale of thirty acres of John de Carun's land. Some Jews sold off their loans with deep discounts. These were eagerly bought by wealther courtiers such as William de Valence and Richard of Cornwall who had their eyes on the land on which the loan was pledged. In this way, the estates of vulnerable landowners fell into the hands of the wealthy elite, causing resentment and hostility on the part of the debtors towards the Jewish moneylenders and the courtiers who benefitted from their distress.[32]

The discontent of the barons and knights of the shire over the transfer of land from debt-ridden nobility to their creditors, who were often Jews but sometimes the Cistercian monks of Meaux, and then into the hands of wealthy Christian courtiers, forced a solution to the issue of usury. Having already rebelled against King John at the beginning of the century, action that led to the signing of Magna Carta, kings were well aware that the barons and knights had the ability to rebel successfully.[33]

A series of statutes in the 1250s promulgated that no Jew was permitted to reside in England unless he was in service to the king. These laws, combined with the tallages and the downturn in profits, convinced some Jews that there was no future for themselves as moneylenders in England. This included Aaron I le Blunds who, along with his son Samuel, his brother Elias, and their wives, attempted to leave England in 1252 with their realisable assets. They were apprehended before they departed, their houses and property held until they had paid their fine in full, and ordered to give a security bond to ensure that they would not attempt to flee again. These hefty communal taxes effectively destroyed the capital of these magnates. By 1255, Aaron of York was bankrupt.[34]

Violence and revolt surfaced once more after disease and torrential storms moved through the kingdom, bringing famine and plague and leaving the dead in the streets, their stomachs swollen with hunger. In 1260, the Jewish Exchequer that kept a record of the debts owed to Jewish moneylenders was ransacked and the rolls were stolen. A number of attacks on Jews followed a revolt against King Henry by his brother-in-law and friend-turned-enemy, the French nobleman and crusader, Simon de Montfort, the earl of Leicester and one-time ally of the king's son, Edward. Simon had expelled the Jews from Leicester, accusing them of causing Christians to suffer because of their usury. In leading the Second Baron's War (1263–64), Montfort ousted the king, removed his authority, and included ordinary townsmen in the parliament. With the country in chaos, an incident in

London in which a Jew supposedly wounded a Christian with a knife resulted in a mob-hunt for the Jewish culprit.[35]

As night fell and the crowd turned to looting, the local mayor and sheriffs drove "away those offenders by force of arms." A murderous riot by Londoners who welcomed Montfort's anti-royalist troops broke out a week before Palm Sunday in 1263. *The Annals of Thomas Wykes* that describes the rampage gives a simple reason for the violence: greed. According to one chronicler, the rioters pillaged the property of Jews who were "stripped naked, despoiled and afterwards murdered by night in sections." Authorities loyal to the king stepped in to stop the slaughter, although London's Jewry was "destroyed." They did, however, manage to save the chest of chirographs that held the debts to Jewish moneylenders, which had been put in the Tower of London for safekeeping.[36]

A year later, Henry III had regained the throne and Simon de Montfort lay dead on the battlefield of Evesham, his body mutilated with his head cut off and his testicles hung either side of his nose, his hands and feet severed and sent to different parts of the country. Property in London was redistributed as a means of punishment for the city's support of Montfort and a 20,000 mark fine was assessed in return for a pardon. All of Montfort's lands and the title of Earl of Leicester were transferred to Henry's son Edmund. The surviving rebels were able to regain their lands only by paying a hefty fine, which was in accordance with their culpability in the revolt.[37]

In 1264, Henry appointed the "twenty-four," a "self-perpetuating" group of "trustworthy and wise" men to act as guardians to the Jewish community of Winchester. Among the most prominent of the Jews of Winchester was Licoricia's son, Benedict, who, by 1280, owned nine properties in Winchester, Southampton, Bristol, York, and London. Like Elias of London and Benedict of Lincoln, Benedict of Winchester must have felt sufficiently secure to choose to make his home outside of the Jewish quarter. This is also borne out by the close commercial relationship between the Jews and the wealthy Christians of the town. Tension arose between the twenty-four and the general population when the group's members made Benedict a guild member. As the "twenty-four" were wool merchants, the credit that the Jews provided was vital to their business but to those outside the business Benedict's admittance was "a manifest scandal to Christian men." In an attempt to restore the economic wellbeing of the Jews, Henry took the Winchester Jews under his special protection and appointed a further twenty-five men as "guardians and protectors" of the Jews. These included Simon le Draper, a wool merchant and mayor, and a convert, Henry de Winchester, an exporter of wool. The twenty-five were to inform the public that no one "do the Jews harm, on pain of life and limbs, and protect them and their households, lands, rents and possessions, and if harm be done to them to have it amended at once."[38]

In order to rein in the abuses by courtiers who were buying up Jewish debt in the hope of grabbing the pledged land, legal restrictions were placed on Jewish moneylenders. Debts to Jews were no longer allowed to be sold without the king's permission and, if he permitted the sale, there was to be no interest added. But there was little effort made to implement this restriction and so the practice and the resentment continued to fester as the power passed from Henry to his eldest son in 1272.[39]

Henry's son and successor was Edward I, a tall, broad chested, blonde, imposing figure who was the first king to be crowned in Westminster Abbey, the building of which had been overseen by his father. He had a reputation for courage, exceptional ferocity, and spending his subjects' money. The biggest armies, the largest parliaments, and the greatest chain of castles were built during his reign in Britain. Military campaigns in France, Wales, and Scotland and crusades demanded vast sums of money. His palaces, such as Windsor, as well as his castles were sumptuously decorated with elegant floor tiles, sculpted marble pillars, wall paintings, tapestries, and courtyard gardens. To meet these expenditures, Edward pressed parliament to approve taxes, while shire knights insisted the king confirm the tenets of Magna Carta and enforce the restrictions on Jewish moneylending.

It was said that Edward's kingdom was "awash" in moneylending. But it was the Christian Riccardi bankers of Lucca, not Jews, who monopolized international finance and upon whom the king had become reliant to keep him in credit in the form of short-term loans that supplemented the king's existing funds. These Lombardi moneylenders had the benefit of a well-developed Italian economy behind them and in the first seven years of Edward's reign, he had received over £200,000 from them. As Edward's bankers, they financed his military campaigns and provided for the construction of castles, in return for control over the new custom system for the wool trade. To raise more reliable sources of income, as opposed to his father's irregular tallages, Edward introduced custom duties on England's most profitable export which he placed in the hands of the Italian bankers. The Riccardis thus handled thousands and tens of thousands of pounds, infinitely more than the amounts handled by the majority of Jewish moneylenders.[40]

Edward's deal with knights in 1270 for a crusader tax was in exchange for a renewal of Magna Carta. This bargain included a restriction on Jewish usury that allowed debtors more time to repay their loans. Curbing the ability of Jewish moneylenders to insist on prompt repayment was a popular demand by the barons, who were eager to delay settling their debts or willing to default on them. His debts from his crusade led him once again to ask parliament for another tax. In return, the knights of the shire demanded that he end the Jewish debt issue, which had led to smallholders losing their lands, once and for all. Resentment on the part of knights and the general population prompted Edward to take harsher action against Jewish moneylenders. As conflict continued in Winchester between the twenty-four and the community, Edward personally intervened, bringing the town under his control and destroying the power of the twenty-four. Benedict had already decamped to London, and by 1274, many other Jews left Winchester for other cities. In the fall of 1274, Edward ordered the mayor and sheriffs of London to issue a proclamation demanding that, "all merchant-usurers shall depart thence within twenty days from the date of these letters, and shall leave the kingdom, under pain of forfeiture of their bodies and goods, and if they be found in the city after that date, to cause them to be arrested and kept safely until otherwise ordered . . . ." This was not aimed specifically at Jews, but at all merchant usurers, including the Lombards who practiced the "vice" of usury over the "virtue" of charity. It is unclear whether the order was enforced or to what degree, but it did not eradicate moneylending as the Riccardi still contracted usurious loans after the proclamation.[41]

In the following year, legislation was written specifically against Jewish moneylenders, which was a concession to the knights in return for yet another tax. In October 1275, the Statute of the Jewry was sealed and sent to the Justices of the Jews before being widely circulated. It acknowledged that Edward and his ancestors had "received great benefit from the Jewish people in the past" and in return they had been "safely preserved and defended by his sheriffs and other bailiffs and faithful me" so that no harm should come to them "in their bodies or in their goods." Nonetheless, the statute stated, Jewish usury pushed Christians into debt and destitution. The new legislation prohibited loans being secured on rents and limited the amount of money and goods that could be seized by a Jew from a Christian. The larger aim was to turn Jews away from moneylending and into other employment. The Statute ordered all Jews to "gain their living by lawful merchandise and their labour . . . by selling and buying." This meant as "legal merchants" who traded cereal and wool. Lending money at interest was once more pitted against "honest" work that was physical in nature. Jews were only permitted to live in towns with an *archa* (chest), the repository where the contracts and deeds were kept recording loans, mortgages, vifgages, other pledges, lands, rents, houses, and chattels belonging to Jews. They were not to mingle with

Christians and, just so there was no chance of mistaking a Jew for a Christian and vice versa, Jews were to wear a yellow felt badge so they were easily identified. Being separated from Christians it was thought unlikely that usury could continue. This was, as has been recently pointed out, a functional regulation, not akin to the Nazi yellow star of David. Jews did petition Edward to protest but their pleas fell on deaf ears, although it is not known whether Jews evaded wearing the badge or whether any effort went into enforcing the law.[42]

While Edward was trying to stamp out Jewish moneylending, his wife, Eleanor of Castile, was eagerly acquiring land and estates with the help of Jewish moneylenders. Eleanor, therefore, was complicit in the issue that was paramount in the knight's argument for restricting Jewish usury. In particular, Aaron, son of Vives, acted as an intermediary in her transactions under the authority of Eleanor's brother-in-law, Edmund, the new Earl of Leicester who had been granted all of Simon de Montfort's estate. In 1276, Licoricia's son, Benedict (who had married into the le Blunds family) was nominated to be the new keeper of the queen's gold at the Exchequer of the Jews. He was to "receive her gold at the exchequer and to act in all matters to her benefit." Benedict had little choice in the matter. Like her husband, Eleanor had use of the Jews' loan debt and also seized the property of condemned Jews. Agreements drawn up between debtors and creditors, such as the one between Stephen Cheindut and Manasser, son of Aaron, were often withdrawn from the chest of the chirographers and sent to Eleanor. With a debt owed to a Jewish creditor in her possession, she was able to appropriate Leeds castle, which had been used as security. Resentment towards Eleanor swelled, especially on the part of the knights and the Archbishop of Canterbury, John Pecham, denounced her purchase of land which was possible only through usury by Jews "under the protection of the royal court." Not only was she admonished for committing the sin of usury, Walter of Guisborough composed a poem that complained of her, and her husband's, greed: "The king desires to get our gold/the queen, our manors fair to hold."[43]

It has been argued that the heavy taxation on the Jews by Henry III had depleted the wealth of the Jews to such an extent that Jewish moneylending had greatly diminished by Edward's reign. Edward was therefore led by "a usury discourse disconnected with the historical reality of Jewish economic occupations." It is certainly the case that Jewish moneylenders were poorer, but it is hard to know how many loans were made off the books between neighbors, friends, and business associates. What is recorded in ledgers does not necessarily give us the full picture. Certainly, the complaint over the loss of pledged land indicates usury was still being practiced by some Jews. Whatever the extent of usury, the

Statute was either redundant and would have no real consequences for the Jewish community or Jews were still engaged primarily in moneylending and the new regulations were an attempt to eradicate that completely. Regardless, the upshot of Edward's new law was a restriction on Jewish occupational freedom in return for new taxes and peace from potentially rebellious lords. In this increasingly hostile environment, Jewish moneylenders had roughly three options: move into a different occupation, leave the country to find a community that welcomed moneylenders and their services, or carry on lending money furtively. But it was not only the Jews that the Statute affected; it had unintended consequences for some of the Christian poor. Usurers may not have been loved, but they were necessary in the new economy. Fewer moneylenders meant less competition in the loan business and that enabled Italian moneylenders to increase their rates of interest, "causing great suffering to the people."[44]

* * *

After the military campaign against the Welsh, who were described as lazy, savage barbarians, Edward was once more in the red. The war had cost £23,000, which had been borrowed from the Riccardi bankers. In addition to the debt, money was needed for road clearance, canals, and castle building. Further loans from the Riccardi did not cover all the expenses, nor did the money he received by forcing all landowners with property worth £20 annually to become knights. As knighthood was an expensive affair, many opted to pay a fine for exemption, which went straight into Edward's treasury. Eager not to go cap in hand to parliament again, he soon found another source of revenue. The coins in circulation were in a bad state, due to natural deterioration of everyday use of coinage. One escheator complained that the inferior coinage made it next to impossible to collect taxes. With the coins devalued, the price of livestock and grain rose, making everyday living more expensive and poor-quality coinage also discouraged foreign merchants. With reminting, the king profited from the fees charged to his subjects and from the small changes in weight and silver content.

One of the biggest problems with coinage was counterfeiting and coin clipping, which was the most widespread monetary crime and the one with which financiers were most often charged. Before mill marks were introduced during Edward's reminting, it was relatively easy to clip slivers of silver from the metal's edge without it being detected. The charge of coin clipping dovetailed with the ongoing debate over usury. A loan transacted with clipped coins and repaid in unclipped coin was a way to disguise usury and circumvent usury laws. Rabbi

Meir, son of Baruch of Rothenburg, denounced coin clipping and "currency falsifiers who have led to the destruction of our brethren, the inhabitants of France and the island [England]." Matthew Paris wrote that English coinage was "so intolerably debased by money-clippers and forgers, that neither natives nor foreigners could look upon it with other than angry eyes and disturbed feelings." The guilty, he continued, included "certain Jews and notorious Caursins [Cahors], and also some Flemish wool-merchants." Yet, it was not only financiers and merchants who debased coins. Monarchs who controlled the mint intervened in the economy to bolster the amount of currency in circulation to meet their spending needs, thus debasing it and causing a cycle of inflation. Whoever had a monopoly over the money supply were the only ones to benefit from this greater increase in currency.[45]

A sound currency was a key element in regulating the money economy and debasement the source of much misery, therefore convictions of coin clipping bore severe consequences. The law permitted the punishment of torture and death as well as confiscation of property, which went to the Crown, and the disinheritance of heirs for the offence of counterfeiting. Those accused were held in prison until a special dispensation was issued by the king. A 1232 edict in England prevented the exchange of old and new money, a restriction that was commonplace throughout Europe. All coins had to be bought and sold only in the king's official exchanges to avoid the "false money" that was in circulation. Further changes were made in 1247 to the coins in an effort to make counterfeiting more difficult but these would turn out to be unsuccessful.[46]

In October, 1278, a council meeting was held at Windsor to discuss the coin clipping problem. The decision was taken to arrest all of the Jews in England, along with all goldsmiths and officials at the mints and exchanges regardless of religion. Over a period of two days in November, those detained were dispersed to fortresses around the country. An estimated 600 Jewish males were taken from all parts of the realm and transported to the Tower of London and commissions were established to hear the charges against the accused. Officers of the king ransacked the homes of the accused looking for evidence of coin clipping and counterfeiting. The king let it be known that Jews might gain their release by paying a fine and some Jews bought their freedom. But the burden of heavy and increased taxation over the thirteenth century meant that the Jewish moneylenders no longer had the wealth or influence they possessed in the previous century.[47]

An unknown number of those arrested were found guilty and executed, including Benedict of Winchester who, along with a fellow Jew from Winchester, Deudone, was imprisoned before he could take up the position of queen's gold keeper. He was taken to the Tower of London on charges of "certain trespasses concerning the king's money." Four of his properties were seized and then forfeited before he was found guilty of the charges. On a cold day in January 1280, he and Deudone were "hanged for felony" and their chattels sold. Where large sums of money were at stake, there was always the risk that the eradication of debt and the appropriation of property were motivating factors in the imprisonment and punishment of moneylenders or that such concerns ran roughshod over judicial procedures. It may also have been the case that he was guilty of the common crime of coin clipping.[48]

Around 200 Jews were executed and 29 Christians, including the king's Master of the Exchange at the London mint, Philip de Cambio, and the assayer, William Harlewyn, who were hanged, drawn, and quartered for making and distributing inferior coinage. The prosecutions were an attempt to end a serious problem but in trying to stop coin clipping, money flowed into the king's coffers. Primarily, Edward's motivations, had more to do with solving the issue of debased coinage and filling his treasury, than it had to do with pursuing a policy based on prejudice toward Jews.[49]

After the appropriations and fines resulting from the arrests and executions, the king began the process of recoinage which netted him around £36,000 in profit. An increase in the money supply does not necessarily enrich society but it does enrich the person or government that monopolizes it; in this case, the king. In May 1279, it was announced that,

> all of the Jews lately "charged, indicted, and convicted of clipping the king's money have now been punished with death, and certain of them have forfeited all their goods and chattels ... and are imprisoned during the king's pleasure ... many Christians ... by ... divers grievances heretofore inflicted upon Christians by Jews endeavour from day to day to accuse and indict certain Jews not yet charged or indicted with trespasses of money by light and groundless ... accusations, charging them to their terror with being guilty of such trespasses, in order that they may by threats of such accusations strike terror into the Jews and that they may extort money from them."

After a lull, in 1283, however, there was an upswing once more in coin offences and other crimes concerning metals.[50]

A costly expedition to Gascony and a large payment given to free Charles of Salerno, the son of Charles of Anjou, on top of the debt owed to the Riccardi (which was nearly £110,000), put Edward in the familiar situation of financial trouble. A clampdown on corruption by England's justices—which brought in large fines and ended in the Chief Justice being exiled—brought in not nearly enough money. In addition, the problem over Jewish debt that grieved magnates and smallholders alike, had not vanished with the Statute. Instead, moneylending was now practiced covertly with false contracts. Deciding to rid himself of the issue once and for all, Edward decided on expulsion, a common punishment and one that Jews had experienced under rulers in France.[51]

In July 1290, Edward commanded that all Jews were to quit England before 1 November. His edict charged that in spite of a previous order that Jews should refrain from usury and earn a living from trade and labor instead, they had continued to lend at interest. The edict went on to scold the Jews for "maliciously deliberating amongst themselves," and merely disguising their usury by calling it "courtesy" (*curialitatum*). Whatever they called it, the king stated, it was still a form of usury and one that he judged even more oppressive than before. He therefore concluded that edicts against usury were ineffective in restraining usurers. The only answer was to expel all Jews from England. In return, Edward was rewarded with the biggest tax of his reign. Even the Church agreed to a tax.[52]

Banishment had been used as a form of punishment since ancient times and the subject of the first biblical story which told of Adam and Eve being expelled from the Garden of Eden. It was regularly used in ancient empires and in medieval times for political transgressions, criminal behavior, vengeance, or to maintain social order. It is difficult to class the expulsions as antisemitic as we commonly understand that word. Brutal, certainly, callous, undoubtedly, but it has to be placed in the context of thirteenth-century England. England was densely occupied with a rising population and many lived on the edges of subsistence, barely scraping enough together to survive. A bad harvest could bring famine and plague in its wake, carrying off the young, old, and weak. It was a world where lives were short and often worth little, where people jostled to see rebels and others rightly or wrongly convicted of crimes against the Crown hanged alive, disemboweled, beheaded or their bodies quartered, where heads were displayed on spikes at city walls or castles and left to rot as a warning to others not to defy the monarch, and where war was an almost constant part of life. Exile and confiscation of property were familiar punishments for those who were condemned for some act against the Crown and was suffered by people of all standing, including clergymen, nobles, and even members of the royal family who had fallen out of favor.

By the time Edward ordered the expulsion in 1290, the Jewish moneylenders had declined financially. Four years after the Jews left England's shores, Edward had the Riccardi arrested as "men who had deceived him." The arrest and confiscation of assets, including the deprivation of the custom seals, came shortly after they were financially crippled by the war between England and France and after the company had refused to extend him further credit. Further arrests and confiscations of the Riccardi in France led to a run on their bank, their demise, and bankruptcy. The king, meanwhile, found new bankers in the form of the Frescobaldi of Florence. In the case of the Jews, debtors and especially those at risk of losing their lands, rejoiced at the expulsion order, but the celebration would not last long. Edward continued to press his people for money, by frequent and onerous taxation, threatening the clergy with outlaw status unless they paid up, and seizing food to feed his armies and goods (such as horses, carts, and boats) in return for future recompense. The battle between the earls, lesser knights, and the king continued but the issue of Jewish debt was no longer part of the discussion.[53]

* * *

On Philip III's death in 1285, his son with Isabella of Aragon was crowned king of France. Philip IV may have been handsome enough to deserve his nickname "the Fair," but he was not universally admired. Bernard Saisset, the bishop of Pamiers, remarked that he was not a man, "but a statue," or an owl because all he can do is stare, which may have been due to his extremely shy nature. He was, like Edward I, big on spending but permanently short of funds, obsessed with money and getting his hands on it however he could. If Edward was a petulant and difficult man for moneylenders, Philip was a creditor's enemy, as the Riccardi found out to their ruin.[54]

Because Philip had expensive wars to wage against England and Flanders, impressive buildings to erect, officials to pay, and, not least, a grand lifestyle to fund, he tolerated usury so long as it benefited him. At the same time, he passed measures that appeared to protect his subjects from its "excesses." He allowed debtors to escape imprisonment if the loans they left unpaid were owed to Jews, while instructing his administrators to collect debts owed to Jews of the king (*Juifs du Roi*). If the goods involved in the transactions were "tainted by usury" then the money was forfeited to the royal treasury.

In need of more money for his war against Flanders, Philip IV debased the currency and then raised it to meet his monetary demands, prompting people to furtively describe him as a *faux-monnayeur* or counterfeiter. The practice of rulers manipulating currency would grow over the centuries and prompted the eminent medieval economist, Nicholas Oresme (c. 1320–1382) in the following century to protest. If usury was "bad, detestable, and unjust," in his opinion, alteration of the coinage was far worse. Coinage belonged neither to kings nor princes but to the people, although the kings and princes would beg to differ as they brought the mints, and therefore the money supply, under their control. The rulers, Oresme wrote, had no right to alter or affect the value of that coinage as this was nothing more than a tyrannical act. By debasing the currency in order to lay their hands on more money they committed "robbery with violence or fraudulent extortion." At least usury was a voluntary transaction between a willing usurer who lent money to a person who borrowed of his own free will. The borrower received some benefit from the loan and, generally, interest was not excessive or harmful to the public. This was especially true if there was competition in the moneylending profession. The alteration of coinage by royal authorities, by way of comparison, was "less voluntary and more against the will of [their] subjects, [who were] incapable of profiting" from such action at all, deeming them "utterly unnecessary."[55]

Philip had no ethical qualms about usury, but, as with most monarchs, he was willing to manipulate and exploit ill will towards moneylenders for his own financial gain. Like the Riccardi, Jewish moneylenders had their goods confiscated, including gold and silver accessories and household goods, sacred objects, clothing, linens, and anything else considered valuable. This action on the part of the king's men indicated to others that Jewish moneylenders were fair game and so encouraged physical attacks. Jews' homes were looted as riots broke out in Paris and other towns but there was little more to take as the Jews were no longer a profitable source of plunder. It was more to Philip's advantage to denounce usury and take on the role of protector of the people against "usurious transactions." Philip had already rid himself of the Riccardi but he was still deeply in debt to Jewish moneylenders and the Order of the Knights Templar. With advice from his councilors, such as Guillaume de Nogeret, an ambitious and unscrupulous former law professor from Languedoc, Philippe decided it was time to rid himself of all of them.[56]

In 1306, Philip decreed the expulsion of the Jews, as had Edward I in England some sixteen years earlier. Over the summer and autumn, an unknown number of Jews left the kingdom of France for other, more welcoming, territories where usury was tolerated. Under Nogeret's guidance, the king gladly took ownership of the exiled Jews' property; as he had of the Riccardi's. Not everyone greeted the exile of Jewish moneylenders with enthusiasm. The chronicler of Philippe's reign, Geoffroi de Paris, wrote:

All the poor people complain
For the Jews were more generous

> In the handling of their deals
> Than the Christians do at present.
> These ask for collaterals and deeds,
> Pledges also, and grab everything
> Until they have stripped them bare . . .
> But if the Jews had remained
> In the kingdom of France,
> Christian souls would have had great relief
> they have no longer.

A Norman chronicler of the fourteenth century was of like mind:

> After the expulsion of the Jews [from France] they could not find any money except by borrowing it through agents from certain Christians, both clerics and laymen, who lent at such an enormous rate of interest that it was double what was charged by the Jews, and who did it in such a way that the debtors did not know the lenders who were in possession of their pledges. This was a dangerous situation, for if the agents died or gave up the business, they did not know where to recover them.

The Knights Templar fared the worst of all. One of the most powerful and wealthy military orders in Europe, the Templars, renounced personal wealth and pledged their permanent defence of Palestine and the holy places. In 1307, an order secretly prepared a month prior, directed the arrest of every French member of the Templars without warning and their property seized. Philippe's attack on the Templars was helped by a schism in the Church. At the beginning of the fourteenth century, Philip's showdown with the papacy resulted in the abduction of Pope Boniface VIII. In 1304, the archbishop of Bordeaux was selected by the conclave as the new pope, Clement V. His decision to remain in France rather than Rome—settling in Avignon in 1309—resulted in a move away from Italian dominance of the papacy, especially as the next six popes were also French.

Beholden to the French king, Clement V called for a council to discuss the Knights Templar arrest and usury in general. In 1311, the Council of Vienne dissolved the Templars. With the Pope's approval, fifty-four Templars accused of apostasy, sodomy, idolatry, and obscenity were burned to death at the Saint-Antoine gate outside of Paris. In 1314, the master of the order, Jacques de Molay, along with Geoffrey de Charnay faced the same fate on a scaffold erected opposite the cathedral of Notre Dame.[57]

The Council also instructed the Inquisition to investigate monarchs who allowed usury. Because so many moneylenders hid interest payments, the Church decreed that lenders be forced to produce their record-keeping books for inspection. The Council further ruled that clergy be allowed to take their anti-usury preaching out onto the streets. This was a step too far for some rulers determined to exert their authority over an overweening pope. When the Inquisition attempted to go into various French towns to combat usury (including the southern towns of Carcassone, Limoux, and Pamiers), it was denied entrance. Philip made it clear that usury and its profits on French soil were solely the king's affair, not the Church's.[58]

In the same year that the Jews were exiled, Philip returned to currency manipulation to fill his coffers. He devalued the currency around 39 percent which led to a dramatic rise in prices. Creditors called in their debts at the higher rate, which had tripled as had rents. One satirist scorned the king as turning "twenty into sixty, then twenty into four; and ten into thirty ... Gold and silver, all is lost/And none will be restored." A riot ensued that was put down by force, with a number of craftsmen hanged as an example to other would-be rioters. Taxation and fluctuation of the currency continued with Philip's reign and it was not long after their expulsion that Lombards and Jews began filtering back to France. They resettled in various towns between 1307 and 1311, even though the expulsion had not been formerly lifted. In November 1314, at the age of forty-six, Philip IV suffered a stroke while out on a hunt and died just over three weeks later at Fontainebleu. It was the new king, Louis X, who officially allowed Jews to return to France.[59]

* * *

The expulsion of Jews in England and France has long been a prime example of medieval antisemitism. Yet it is difficult to assess the actions of kings like Edward I and Philip IV as antisemitic. Their prime motivation did not stem from a personal animus towards Jews or their religion but from the demands for finance brought about by decades of costly wars, the expenditure for crusades, the building of defensive castles, upkeep of the royal household, maintenance of the kingdom, ransoms, bribes, and hospitality. No source of funding was sacred, as was clear from Edward's raid on the clergy's money and both kings attack on the Templars. Punishments for transgressions were harsh, and in some cases, obscenely brutal, with exile a convenient way to rid a monarch of a problem. Regardless of whether a few Jews were moneylenders, whether most had taken up other jobs, whether they were impoverished from years of taxation, or whether they were still active usurers, the perception and understanding in both England and France was that they were only settled in those countries for their capital. When usury became a political problem, and other sources of credit were found, it was expedient to expel them from their lands. Usury was an issue that had stoked violence and civil unrest in the past and would be a source of rebellion in the fourteenth century.

Notes

1. Paul Rapin de Thoyras, *An Abridgement of the History of England* (London 1747), 217; Davis, "The Ethics of Arbitrage," chap. 1; Vincent J. Cornell, "In the Shadow of Deuteronomy: Approaches to Interest in Judaism and Christianity," in *Interest in Islamic Economics: Understanding Riba*, ed. Abdulkader Thomas (London and New York: Routledge, 2006).
2. John W. Baldwin, *Masters, Princes, and Merchants: The Social Views of Peter the Chanter and His Circle* (Princeton 1970); O'Carroll, *A Thirteenth-Century Preacher's Handbook*, 5.
3. Britnell, *The Commercialisation of English Society*, 126; Ferguson, *Ascent of Money*, introduction.
4. Britnell, *The Commercialisation of English Society*, 102, 103, 121; Duby, *The Early Growth of the European Economy*, 231.
5. Cave and Coulson, *A Source Book for Medieval Economic History*, 73; Jones, *The Plantagenets*, "L'Espace Plantagenet."
6. David Nirenberg, *Communities of Violence: Persecution of Minorities in the Middle Ages* (Princeton: Princeton University Press, 1996), 222–23; Robert Chazan, *The Jews of Medieval Western Christendom 1000–1500* (Cambridge: CUP, 2006), 159; Mundill, "Christian and Jewish Lending Patterns," 45; Theodore Evergates, ed., *Feudal Society in Medieval France: Documents from the County of Champagne* (Philadelphia: University of Pennsylvania Press, 1993), 28–30; Mollat and Wolff, *The Popular Revolutions of the Late Middle Ages*, 26; Borer, *The City of London*, 55, 84; Robert C. Stacey, "Jewish Lending," 89, 93–95 and "The English Jews under Henry III," in *The Jews in Medieval Britain: Historical, Literary, and Archeological Perspectives,* ed. Patricia Skinner (Rochester, NY: Boydell & Brewer, 2003), 41; *Materials for the History of Thomas Becket* (Rolls Series, 67, 1875–85), vol. III, 19, quoted in Dobson, *The Jewish Communities*, 4. Following J. Jacobs in *The Jews of Angevin England*, Dobson believes the word *creditores* is an error and that *debitores* was intended. Graeme Donald Snooks, "The Dynamic Role of the Market in the Anglo-Norman Economy and Beyond 1086–1300," in *Commercialising Economy,* 27; Kocka, *Capitalism*; C. Hollister, Robert Stacey, and Robin Chapman Stacey, *The Making of England to 1399* (Belmont, CA: Wadsworth Publishing, 2001), 225–26.

7. John D. Hosler, "Henry II, William of Newburgh, and the Development of English Anti-Judaism" in *Christian Attitudes Toward the Jews in the Middle Ages: A Casebook*, ed. Michael Frassetto (New York and London: Routledge, 2007), 170; Christopher Tyerman, *England and the Crusades, 1095–1588* (Chicago: University of Chicago Press, 1988), 79.
8. Raphael Holinshed's *Chronicles of England, Scotland and Ireland* (1577) quoted in Bernard Grébanier, *The Truth About Shylock* (New York: Random House, 1962), 21–22.
9. Holinshed, *Chronicles of England, Scotland, and Ireland*, vol. 2 (London: J. Johnson, 1807), 204–06.
10. William Chester Jordan, *Louis IX and the Challenge of the Crusade: A Study in Rulership* (Princeton: Princeton University Press, 1979), 98.
11. William of Newburgh, *Historia Rerum Anglicarum*, Book 4, chapters 9 and 10 in *Chronicles of the Reigns of Stephen, Henry II, and Richard I*, ed. Richard Howlett (London: Longman, 1885); Holinshed, *Chronicles*, vol. 2, 210–11; Dobson, *The Jewish Communities*, 12; Shatzmiller, *Cultural Exchange*, 41; Robert R. Mundill, *The King's Jews: Money, Massacre, and Exodus in Medieval England* (London and New York: Continuum, 2010), 80; William of Newburgh, *History*, chap. 9.
12. Mundill, *The King's Jews*, 81; Nirenberg, *Communities of Violence*, 222–23; Chazan, *The Jews of Medieval Western Christendom*, 159; Borer, *The City of London*, 84; Mundill, "Christian and Jewish Lending Patterns," 45.
13. Mundill, *The King's Jews*, 80–81.
14. The quote is by The Anonymous of Béthune; Robert C. Stacey, "Jews and Christians in 12th Century England: Some Dynamics of a Changing Relationship," in *Jews and Christians in Twelfth-Century Europe*, eds. Michael A. Signer and John Van Engen (Notre Dame, IN: University of Notre Dame Press, 2001); Mundill, *The King's Jews*, 81; Jones, *The Plantagenets*, "Hunt for an Heir"; Seabourne, *Royal Regulation of Loans and Sales*, 31.
15. Jones, The Plantagenets, "Salvaging the wreck" and "A Cruel Master"; R.B. Dobson, "The Decline and Expulsion of the Medieval Jews of York," *Transactions and Miscellanies (Jewish Historical Society of England)* 26 (1974–78): 25, 35, and *The Jewish Communities of Medieval England*, 24; Robin R. Mundill, "Lumbard and Son: The Businesses and Debtors of Two Jewish Moneylenders in Late Thirteenth-Century England," *Jewish Quarterly Review* 82.1/2 (July-Oct. 1991): 141; *The Chronicles of Melrose*.
16. Jones, *The Plantagenets*, "Kingship At Last."
17. Joe and Caroline Hillaby, eds., *The Palgrave Dictionary of Medieval Anglo-Jewish History* (Basingstoke: Palgrave Macmillan, 2013), 239–40, 408; John Paul Davis, *The Gothic King: A Biography of Henry III* (London and Chicago: Peter Owen, 2013), Kindle ed.; John Stow, *A Survey of London, Written in the Year 1598*, Project

Gutenberg Ebook (2013), http://www.gutenberg.org/files/42959/42959-h/42959-h.htm; Postan, *Cambridge Economic History of Europe*, 552.

18. Hillaby, *The Palgrave Dictionary*, 240; *Calendar of Close Roles: Edward I*, April 25, 1275, 162; R.H. Britnell, "England and Northern Italy in the Early Fourteenth Century: The Economic Contrasts," *Transactions of the Royal Historical Society* 39 (1989):169; Emilie Amt, *The Succession of Henry II in England: Royal Government Restored 1149–1159* (Woodbridge, UK: Boydell Press, 1993), 92; Borer, *The City of London*, 84, 97–98; Jones, *The Plantagenets*, "Edward At Sea."
19. For the life of Licoricia, see, Suzanne Bartlet, *Licoricia of Winchester: Marriage, Motherhood, and Murder in the Medieval Anglo-Jewish Community* (Portland, OR and Edgware, UK: Vallentine Mitchell, 2009).
20. Evergates, *Feudal Society in Medieval France*, 26, 84–85.
21. Jordan, *Louis IX*, 101
22. Shatzmiller, *Cultural Exchange*, 80–81, 91; Gilbert S. Rosenthal introduction to Yehiel Nissam da Pisa, *Banking and Finance Among Jews in Renaissance Italy: A Critical Edition of The Eternal Life (Haye Olam)* (New York: Bloch Pub., 1962), 13; Robert Chazan, ed., *Church, State, and Jew in the Middle Ages* (West Orange NJ: Behrman House, 1980); John H. Munro, "The Medieval Origins of the 'Financial Revolution': Usury, *Rentes*, and Negotiability," *The International History Review* 3.25 (2003): 507, 518, 521; Steven Runciman, *A History of the Crusades: Vol. 1: The First Crusade and the Foundations of the Kingdom of Jerusalem* (Cambridge: CUP, 1951), 134–35; Geisst, *Beggar Thy Neighbor*, chap. 1; Matthew Paris, *English History from the Year 1235 to 1273*, v.1, 2; Sibon, "Peut-on croire en la parole du juif?," 242; Weiner J. Cahnman, "Socio-Economic Causes of Antisemitism," *Social Problems* 5.1 (1957): 24; Fourth Lateran Council (1215), Canon 67, http://history.hanover.edu/courses/excerpts/344latj.html; Hunt and Murray, *A History of Business in Medieval Europe*, 72; Hawkes, *The Culture of Usury*, 65.
23. Golb, *The Jews of Medieval Normandy*, 421, 422–23, 426, 429; *Layettes du Trésor des Chartes* v. III, 3782 and 3783, Archives Nationales (Paris: Henri Plon, 1902); Thomas N. Bisson, *Medieval France and Her Pyrenean Neighbours: Studies in Early Institutional History* (London: Hambledon Press, 1989), 51; Jeffrey Richards, *Sex, Dissidence and Damnation: Minority Groups in the Middle Ages* (London and New York: Routledge, 1991), 113; John H. Mundy, *Europe in the High Middle Ages, 1150–1300* (New York: Longman, 2000), 100; L. Auvray, *Les registres de Grégoire XI*, v.1 (Paris: E. De Boccard, 1955), col. 691.
24. Reinert and Fredona, "Merchants," 5; John H. Pryor, *Business Contracts of Medieval Provence: Selected Notulae from the Cartulary of Giraud Amalric of Marseilles, 1248* (Toronto: Pontifical Institute of Mediaeval Studies, 1981), 60, 63, 75, 77; Roover, *Money, Banking, and Credit in Mediaeval Bruges*, 12.

25. Pryor, *Business Contracts of Medieval Provence*, 83, 86, 89; Julie L. Mell, "Religion and Economy in Pre-Modern Europe: The Medieval Commercial Revolution and the Jews" (PhD diss., University of North Caroline, Chapel Hill, 2007), 191–92.
26. Mell, "Religion and Economy," 228–29; Pryor, *Business Contracts of Medieval Provence*, 83, 86, 89.
27. Ibid, 115–16; Mell, "Religion and Economy," 192, 212.
28. Mell, "Religion and Economy," 220.
29. Ibid., 200, 206–08 and Mell, *The Myth of the Medieval Jewish Moneylender,* vol. 2, 230–32; Reinert and Fredona, "Merchants," 11–13.
30. Mell, "Religion and Economy," 225–26.
31. Golb, *The Jews of Medieval Normandy*, 423, 429.
32. Jones, *The Plantagenets*, preface, "Kingship At Last"; Dobson, "The Decline and Expulsion of the Medieval Jews of York," 36; Hillaby, *The Palgrave Dictionary*, 240; Zefira Entin Rokéaḥ, "An Anglo-Jewish Assembly, or 'Mini-Parliament' in 1287," in *Thirteenth-Century England VIII: Proceedings of the Durham Conference 1999,* eds. Michael Prestwich, Richard Britnell, and Robin Frame, (Woodbridge, UK: Boydell Press, 2001), 71, 73; A.C. Chibnall, *Sherington: Fiefs and Fields of a Buckinghamshire Village* (Cambridge: CUP, 1965), 51–52; Britnall, *The Commercialisation of English Society*, 128.
33. Dobson, "The Decline and Expulsion of the Medieval Jews of York," 36, 39–40.
34. Robert C. Stacey, "Royal Taxation and the Social Structure of Medieval Anglo-Jewry: The Tallages of 1239–1242," *Hebrew Union College Annual* 56 (1985): 205; Morris, *A Great and Terrible King*, chap. 3.
35. Samuel K. Cohn, Jr., *Popular Protest in Late Medieval English Towns* (Cambridge: CUP, 2013), 277; Davis, *The Gothic King.*
36. Seabourne, *Royal Regulation of Loans and Sales*, 42; Jones, *The Plantagenets*, "The Provisions of Oxford"; Cohn, *Popular Protest in Late Medieval English Towns*, 277; Davis, *The Gothic King.*
37. Morris, *A Great and Terrible King,* chap. 3.
38. Jones, *The Plantagenets*, "The Expulsion of the Jews"; Hillaby, *Palgrave Dictionary*, 296, 392; *Calendar of Close Rolls: Edward I*, 128, 391–92.
39. Morris, *A Great and Terrible King*, chap. 3.
40. Mundill, "Lumbard and Son," 151 and "Christian and Jewish Lending Patterns," 61; R.W. Kaeuper, *Bankers to the Crown: The Riccardi of Luca and Edward 1* (Princeton: Princeton University Press, 2015); Léon Gauthier, *Les Lombards dans les Deux-Bourgogne* (Paris: H. Champion, 1907); Morris, *A Great and Terrible King,* chap. 4; Prestwich, *Edward I*, chap. 9; Britnell, "England and Northern Italy," 178.
41. Morris, *A Great and Terrible King*, chaps. 1 and 4; Seabourne, *Royal Regulation of Loans and Sales*, 32, 41, 61; *Palgrave Dictionary*, 296, 392; *Calendar of Close Rolls: Edward I*, 392–93.

42. Jones, *The Plantagenets*, "The Leopard"; *Calendar of Close Rolls: Edward I*, Nov. 9, 1274, 108; Koyama, "Evading," 3; Mundill, "Lumbard and Son," 147–48, 163 and "Christian and Jewish Lending Patterns," 56; "Archa," in *Jewish Encyclopedia*, http://www.jewishencyclopedia.com/articles/1727-archa; Morris, *A Great and Terrible King*, chap. 4; Mell, "Religion and Economy," 202.
43. Hillaby, *Palgrave Dictionary*, 297; Sara Cockerill, *Eleanor of Castile: The Shadow Queen* (Stroud, UK: Amberley Publishing, 2014); *Calendar of Close Rolls: Edward I*, Feb. 10, Nov. 13, and Dec. 15, 1275, 150, 221, 260; Morris, *A Great and Terrible King*, chap. 7.
44. Robert R. Mundill, "Edward I and the Final Phase of Anglo-Jewry," *The Jews in Medieval Britain*, 63; idem, "Christian and Jewish Lending Patterns," 57; Seabourne, *Royal Regulation of Loans and Sales*, 57; Mell, "Religion and Economy,"170.
45. Zefira Entin Rokéaḥ, "Money and the Hangman in Late-Thirteenth-Century England: Jews, Christians, and Coinage Offences Alleged and Real (Part 1)," *Jewish Historical Studies* 31 (1988–90): 93–96; Cave and Coulson, *Sourcebook for Medieval Economic History*, 128; Paris, *English History*, vol. II, 262–264; Seabourne, *Royal Regulation of Loans and Sales*, 58; Rokéaḥ, "Money and the Hangman," 83–84.
46. Prestwich, *Edward I*, 244; *Capitulary given at Diedenhofen*, Migne, *PCC*, vol. XCVII (Paris 1862), 287 quoted in Cave and Coulson, *Sourcebook for Medieval Economic History*, 132; Rokéaḥ, "Money and the Hangman," 84, 86, 93; Martin Allen, *Mints and Money in Medieval England* (Cambridge: CUP, 2012), 68; John Craig, *The Mint: A History of the London Mint A.D. 287 to 1948* (Cambridge: University Press, 1953), 38; *Palgrave Dictionary*, 296, 392; *Calendar of Close Rolls: Edward I*, 107.
47. Rokéaḥ, "Money and the Hangman," 96; Prestwich, *Edward I*, 245.
48. Zefira Entin Rokéaḥ estimated that 269 Jews and 29 Christians went to the gallows and a small number burned whereas Michael Prestwich suggests a lower number, stating that in the south-east nineteen Jews were hanged. Rokéah, *Medieval English Jews and Royal Officials* (Jerusalem: The Hebrew University Magnes Press, 1999) and Prestwich, *Edward I*, 245; Hillaby, *Palgrave Dictionary*, 297.
49. Rokéaḥ, "Money and the Hangman," 88, 90, 91, 92, 99.
50. Prestwich, *Edward I*, 245; The statement was made in Canterbury, May 7, 1279, *The Calendar of the Close Rolls: Edward I*, 529, Morris, *A Great and Terrible King*, chap. 6; Ferguson, *The Ascent of Money*, introduction.
51. Jones, *The Plantagenets*, "The Expulsion of the Jews"; Rokéah, "An Anglo-Jewish Assembly," 71; Benjamin Z. Kedar, "Expulsion as an Issue of World History," *Journal of World History* 7.2 (Fall 1996): 169; Morris, *A Great and Terrible King*, chap. 7.
52. *Calendar of the Close Rolls: Edward I*, November 5, 1290, 109.
53. Gustave Saige, *Les Juifs de Languedoc Antérieurement au XIV Siècle* (Paris: A. Picard, 1881), 228–29; Golb, *The Jews of Medieval Normandy*, 509, 534; Robert R. Mundill, *England's Jewish Solution: Experiment and Expulsion 1262–1290* (Cambridge: CUP, 1998), Appendix IV, 299–302; Stacey, "The English Jews under Henry III," 41.

There is evidence that some Jews continued to live in Britain after the expulsion. Joe Hillaby, "Jewish Colonisation in the Twelfth Century," *The Jews in Medieval Britain*, 38–39; Seabourne, *Royal Regulation of Loans and Sales*, 65; Morris, *A Great and Terrible King*, chap. 9.

54. Régine Pernoud, *The Templars: Knights of Christ* (San Francisco: Ignatius Press, 2009), 112; Geisst, *Beggar Thy Neighbor*, chap. 2; Stephen O'Shea, *The Friar of Carcassonne: Revolt Against the Inquisition in the Last Days of the Cathars* (New York: Walker Books, 2011), Kindle ed.; Morris, *A Great and Terrible King*, chap. 6; Kaeuper, *Bankers to the Crown*, 227–29.
55. Fra Jacopo Passavanti (1302–1357), *Mirror of True Penitance*, quoted in Koyama, "Evading," 15 and Iris Origo, *The Merchant of Prato, Francesco di Marco Datini 1335–1410* (London: Penguin, 2002), 154. William of Auxerre was a scholastic theologian at the university in Paris. *Summa aurea in quattuor libros Sententiarum* III 48 1, 2 (Paris 1500), 13–14, quoted in Koyama, *"Evading," 14*; Nicholas Oresme, *De Moneta of Nicholas Oresma and English Mint Documents*, trans. and intro. Charles Johnson (London: OUP, 1956), 24, 27–29.
56. Jordan, *The Great Famine*, 8, 19, 114; John Kelly, *The Great Mortality: An Intimate History of the Black Death, the Most Devastating Plague of all Times* (New York: HarperCollins, 2005), 89; David Herlihy, ed., *Medieval Culture and Society* (Prospect Heights, IL: Waveland Press, 1993), 344; Pernoud, *The Templars*, 112; O'Shea, *The Friar of Carcassonne*.
57. Pernoud, *The Templars*, 112.
58. Cave and Coulson, *Sourcebook for Medieval Economic History*, 157; Council of Vienne, decree 29, quoted in Koyama, "Evading," 13.
59. Munro, "The Medieval Origins of the 'Financial Revolution,'" 521; Julien Thèry, "The Expulsion of the Jews in 1306 and the Construction of a French Royal Theocracy," *Religious and Ethnic Identities in the Process of Expulsion and Diaspora*, Central European University Conference, June 5–8, 2013. "Toute pauvre gent se plaint/Car Juifs furent debonaires/Beaucoup plus en faisant leurs affaires/Que ne sont maintenant les chretiens./Garanties ils demandent et liens,/Gages demandent et tout extorquent,/Que les gens plument et ecorchent.../Mais si les Juifs demeures/Fussent au royame de France,/Chretiens moult grande abidance/Eussent eu, qu'ils sont plus." Geoffroi de Paris, "Chronique rimée," quoted by Léon Poliakov, *The History of Anti-Semitism, vol. 1: From the Time of Christ to the Court Jews*, trans. R. Howard (Philadelphia: University of Pennsylvania Press, 2003), 80; Mollat and Wolff, *The Popular Revolutoins of the Late Middle Ages*, 93–94; Golb, *The Jews of Medieval Normandy*, 543.

3

"The Filthy Rich"

In the fourteenth century, maritime insurance emerged in Genoa and other parts of Italy and greater security along roads was ordered and assured by rulers. New business administration and techniques of control and management were devised, as well as innovations in accounting, such as double-entry bookkeeping (also in Genoa, in 1340). These added to the bills of exchange, which allowed merchants to transfer purchasing power without shipping coins, to revolutionize and expand the Western European market economy. Such important steps in the market economy came in a century that was struck by forces beyond the control of kings and clergy and led to serious discontent among the population.

After the economic boom of the previous centuries, catastrophic weather, plague, and a decline in population since the end of the thirteenth century, caused havoc in the fourteenth century. The Black Death of the mid-fourteenth century that sharply added to the decrease in population was not the only catastrophe that struck in that century. Famines in 1316–18, 1328–29, and again in 1346–47, and an epidemic in 1339–40, led to unrest, riots, and rebellion. Religious protest movements denounced the wealth of the Church and its clergy as contrary to charity as well as an insult to the humility of Christ and the true message of Christianity. Dissidents who demanded reform were labeled heretics by the Church and those thought dangerous to the unity of the Christendom were persecuted. Apart from disturbances due to a lack of food, the chief sources of complaint were taxation and bad government, along with high interest rates on the loans they transacted, often to pay the taxes. In the fourteenth century, the flames of rebellion would be well and truly ignited all over Europe.[1]

Giustizia, "justice," was a word that rallied protest groups in much the same way as it does today. The terms "public good" or "common good" were also widely invoked, sometimes as a way for the monarch to intervene in the economy and usurp the rights of the guilds to his own advantage. People rebelled against secular rulers, in protest against taxes, regulations, and other burdens. It was said about William Rufus of England (r. 1087–1100) that he "vexed the people with ... excessive taxes" while his influential minister, the bishop of Durham, Ranulph Flambard, "fleeced the rich, destroyed the poor and stole other men's inheritances" and Gerard the archbishop of York emptied "the purses of those beneath him, even by improper means." Although protesters differed in aim and doctrine over the decades and centuries, they all sought "justice," whether that meant a rediscovery of what they believed to be the ascetic roots of Christianity, more liberties, less taxation, or more privileges. If kings chose war, one lyric poet sang, it was the "miserable citizen" who had to pay for the greed of those who only valued gold, gems, and heaps of wealth. The solution to the corruption that tarnished the world was one that could have come from the fifth-century ascetic monks of Syria and Egypt: strip yourself of riches and die naked (*Exue divitias, nudus cede fatis*).[2]

Since the eleventh century, lay groups had vigorously protested against usury and the Church's moneymaking activities, challenging the Church's orthodoxy. Officially, the Church denounced usury and the lust for riches in the strongest terms. Theologians cursed usury as causing the impoverishment of Christians who took out loans with high interest rates they could ill afford and then falling into destitution when they could not make the repayments. At the same time, the Church told their followers that they were better off without material goods, that poverty was sacred and the highest form of morality and virtue, and that wealth and its pursuit was the mark of the godless sinner. In theory, poverty was the pinnacle of Christian virtue. In reality, the Church had moved far away from the mindset of early Christian ascetics such as Symeon the Stylite, who stood in contemplation on one leg atop a fifty-foot column outside Antioch to prove his faith or the wearing ragged clothes to emulate the poverty of Christ.[3]

The Church had to juggle the demands incumbent upon it to prepare for the World to Come and the exigencies of the here-and-now. It preached the ideal of poverty but reaped the profits of their landed estates. The protest movements spoke of egalitarianism (whatever that meant to them at the time) and castigated the wealthy, whether they were popes, clergymen, kings, barons, merchants, or usurers. In the eleventh century, the protesters included the "blind, the unkempt, the miserable, [and] the hopeful" who were opposed the wealthy—described by detractors as being "filthy" or "stinking" rich—the greedy, conspicuous consumption, the lust for wealth, and self-indulgence. The term "rich" was, from the tenth century, defined as wealthy and not, as it meant earlier, powerful. Convinced that they were the true Christians, they set themselves against what they saw as a Church that was more concerned with storing up treasure than relief for the poor. In ridiculing and challenging its authority, they provided a new acronym for Rome: *radix omnium malorum avaritia* (the root of all evils is avarice). The itinerant preacher, Robert of Arbrissel (1045–1115) roamed the French countryside in rags, followed by people ranging from noble to peasant. The disheveled Peter the Hermit (1050–1115) also journeyed around France (in his case, on a mule), while a disgruntled monk from Antwerp by the name of Tanchelm (d. 1115) wandered the Low Countries. He gathered support throughout Flanders, Zealand, and Brabant to his cause and urged his growing bands of disciples—townsmen, fishermen, and farmers—to reject the sacraments and refuse to pay their tithes owed to the Church. Worshipped as a god, Tanchelm's disciples were said to have drank his bath water and watched with reverence as he married a statue of the Virgin Mary.[4]

These ragbag groups headed by leaders given divine or semi-divine status, drew on the book of Revelation and other apocalyptic literature that focused on the End of Days. Selfishness and greed were omens that the world was nearing destruction, while corruption and a decay in ethical values were interpreted within the boundaries of apocalyptic theology. The eleventh-century poet and deacon Egbert of Liège grumbled that money had become a goddess more sought after than honor while the French theologian and poet Walter of Châtillon (1135–1180) claimed that a man's purse had to vomit money for him to achieve success in an Episcopal court.[5]

In the twelfth century, as the Church grew richer—with monks afforded a comfortable and, at the highest level, a lavish lifestyle—and the role of the moneylender grew in importance, asceticism began to flourish again. The Cathars (or Albigensians) were the most numerous and influential dissident group. Their movement gained the support of men such as the Count of Toulouse and the first Cathar synod met in the late twelfth century near Toulouse. This signalled a serious threat to the Church, which formally denounced the movement in 1178, excommunicating several of its leaders. Another dissident group, the Waldensians (known as the poor Men of Lyons), were led by Peter Waldo, the name coming from either the word Valdenses from *vallis densa* (thick or shaded valley) or from a derogatory word meaning sorceror. Born in the French city of Lyon around 1140, Waldo was a prosperous, illiterate merchant who, after a religious vision, gave away his wealth to the poor. He proclaimed:

> No man can serve two masters, God and mammon . . . . My friends and fellow townsmen! Indeed, I am not, as you think, insane, but I have taken vengeance on my enemies who held me in bondage to them, so that I was always more anxious about money than about God and served the creature more than the Creator. I know that a great many find fault with me for having done this publicly. But I did it for myself and also for you: for myself, so that they who may henceforth see me in possession of money may think I am mad; in part also for you, so that you may learn to fix your hope in God and to trust not in riches.[6]

In Waldo's world, riches were antithetical to virtue and he challenged the Church's commercial activities, such as the sale of water for baptisms, or earth for burials, and a variety of other sacraments he regarded as futile for salvation. To the French theologian Alain de Lille the mass of Waldo's followers were "ratchatchers," and their leader was a man guided by his emotions who was "an irrational philosopher, a prophet without vision, an apostle without a mission, a teacher without an instructor, and his foolish disciples have led the simple folk astray . . ." Yet, despite these groups' condemnation of riches, it was these heretical movements that were tainted with accusations of usury. Heresy flourished in regions that experienced rapid economic growth, such as Toulouse, and debt due to interest loans was common in such expanding towns. One man was condemned in Toulouse in 1178 of both heresy and usury while Waldensians were accused of usury by the Cistercian prior Caesarius of Heisterbach who claimed that the rich usurers in Metz belonged to this sect. It may be that there were usurers committed to dissident movements but it was irrelevent. The charge merely gave the Church an additional and effective weapon in its ruthless persecution and eradication of these groups.[7]

With such grave dissent, the Church decided it was time to address accusations that it was corrupt and avaricious and it did so by bringing some of the ideas of the protestors within the boundaries of Rome. Poverty as a central theological concept was now disseminated by two new mendicant orders sanctioned by the pope, the Franciscans (the Grey Friars) and the Dominicans (the Black Friars), whose members would evangelize in the streets and market squares.[8]

In the small Italian town of Assisi, Giovanni Bernadone (1181/2–1226), called Francesco by his father, had a life-changing epiphany. He was the son of a wealthy silk merchant, and it was as he was selling velvet and silk for his father in the marketplace that he had an encounter that radically changed his life. He met a beggar. Acting on impulse, Francesco emptied his pockets and gave all he had with him to the alms seeker. His life from that moment on was dedicated to the poor. He embarked on "the courtship of Lady Poverty," connecting the love of God to an ascetic life. While this did not mean the complete renunciation of the world—to Francesco nature was a gift from God with all its beauty—it did mean a repudiation of material possessions, including money. *Caritas* had to defeat *avaritia.*[9]

Francesco became better known in history as St. Francis of Assisi or *Il Poverello* ("the poor one"), and it was rumored that he came from a heretical Cathar family. His order became known as the Franciscans and they followed Jesus' command to "acquire no gold, no silver, nor copper," as they set out into the "midst of wolves" like the first apostles. The Franciscans stressed actual poverty over symbolic poverty, voluntarily renouncing their fortunes (if they had one), selling their belongings and distributing the income to the poor, clothing themselves in worn, patched garments, and becoming "servants of God and the followers of most holy poverty." Reviving asceticism as a crucial tenet of Christianity once more, they held similar values to populist movements, such as the Cathars and Waldensians, labeled heretical by the Church. Yet, unlike the Cathars and Waldensians, the Franciscans operated within the Church and their religious intensity, austerity, and poverty were approved by the papacy. In this way, the pope sought to combat animosity against the clergymen who had grown exceedingly fond of material and sensual comforts. By supporting these reform movements, the Church also brought the ascetic impulses that had caused widespread dissension and popular protest under the Church's control.[10]

From the outset, the Franciscan movement set themselves the lofty goal of individual religious perfection so as to teach by example, while rebuking others in the Church for worldliness. Franciscan Anthony of Padua (1196–1231), the patron saint of the poor, preached against the sins of usury and avarice. The sanctity of poverty was also circulated by another Franciscan, Giovanni Parenti, who praised the character of Lady Poverty in his book *Sacrum Commercium* (1227). Lady Poverty's bitter foe was Avarice, who was the "unmeasured lust to gain and hold riches." Greed was idolatry and the symptom of a corrupted conscience. To avoid the ownership of land, which was forbidden by the order, the properties in which the Franciscans' dwelt were purchased and held by patrons. Nevertheless, this opened them up to the same criticism that had been directed at monks that they were not leading the life they preached.[11]

The friars view on Jews and moneylending was mainly negative but, like the rest of society, it was never homogeneous. Unlike the black-robed Dominicans, the Franciscans saw a place in society for pawnbroking, which helped the poor to survive day to day, as long as the rates of interest were kept low. Usury in the form of loan transactions was condemned and the friars spread their anti-usury message in the urban centers, often to the irritation of the local clergy who resented the intrusion of these brash newcomers into their parishes. To make their message more relevant to their audience they based their sermons on popular oral culture, folklore, and animal stories. With tales of abuse and corruption, they castigated the rich, the greedy, and the profit-seekers. The mendicant orders became so influential that, by the end of the thirteenth century, for a town to have any true importance it required a mendicant monastery. At the University of Paris and in Tuscany, the Franciscans reflected on theological and canonical writings about absolute poverty and believed that, through their spiritual guidance and inspired by their simple lifestyle, the Church would be revitalized and freed from the corrosive poison of riches.[12]

In the aftermath of Francis of Assisi's death, lay preachers launched bitter attacks on Franciscans that led a life contrary to the founder's vision. The Grey Friars were accused of indulging in simony and wallowing in excess, whether it be drinking, whoring, eating, wearing luxurious clothing, or purchasing sumptuous furnishings. This internal dispute led to a schism that set those loyal to the spirit of poverty as the "inspiration, the strength, the very soul of his Order" against other Franciscans who their critics accused of being "devoured by avarice and the love of wealth." Giovanni Parenti followed the first path, seeing poverty as the redemption of humanity. At a time when Western Europe was saturated with mysticism, a sect of Franciscans was formed known as the Spiritual Franciscans (*Fratelli*). Driven to despair over the state of the church, the Spiritual Franciscans were strongly influenced by the apocalyptic mystic Joachim de Fiore and End of Days scenarios that they hoped would usher in a new world of pure spirituality free from the taint of greed. And that also meant, in their opinion, free from moneylenders. In their insistence on total poverty as a mark of goodness, they became consigned to the edges of Christian society and, seen as dangerous to the Church, they were declared heretics by Pope Boniface VIII in 1296 and subjected to the Inquisition.[13]

The exultation of poverty as the spiritual ideal was marked in many poets, artists, and troubadours. In Italy, Jacopone dei Bendetti's reputation as a greedy and materialistic lawyer prompted his devout wife to secretly atone for his sins by self-mortification and wearing a hairshirt. When she was killed in an accident and he discovered her attempts to expiate his transgressions, his shame was so great that he dispensed with all of his worldly goods and entered into holy orders. He became the poet Jacopone da Todi who described poverty as the mark of virtue. Jacopone's poem "*De la Santa Povertá e Suo Triplice Cielo*" (On Holy Poverty and Her Threefold Heaven) elevated poverty to the highest form of spirituality while disparaging the love of money:

> Poverty, high wisdom deep and sure,
> Unsubdued by earth and earthly lure,
> Scorns created things, detached and pure,
> Scorning, yet possessing utterly.
> . . . He whose wants are master, is a slave,
> Sells himself for what his longings crave,
> Him his purchased riches cannot save,
> He hath bargained very foolishly.
> . . . Riches will steal thy time away;
> Learning vanish like the winds at play;
> Fame will nurse and nourish, day by day,
> Every form of vile hypocrisy.

Popular resentment against the rich also came from pilgrims as they made their way, many barefooted, to the popular pilgrimage sites. As they travelled to holy places such as Santiago de Compostela in northwestern Spain to visit the shrine of St. James or to the Abbey Church of St. Foy in Conques, France, they passed the time singing verses, ridiculing those at the top of society. One Anglo-Norman song objects to the oppressive taxation that the king imposed to fund his wars:

> Since the king is determined to take so much,
> He may find enough among the rich;
> And he would get more and do better,
> As it appears to me,
> To have taken a part from the great and to have spared the little.
> He sins who takes the money of the needy without cause . . ..
> It is no trouble to the great thus to grant to the king a tax;
> The simple must pay it all, which is contrary to God's will . . ..
> The property of the poor taken without their will, is as if it were stolen . . ..

The idea of the rich robbing the poor, picking him "full clean," was common, as was the idea of the rich lording over them "without any right." This theme was favored by the lyric poets known as troubadours who traversed the lands of Western Europe singing their *sirventes*, moral or religious songs of Provençal that satirized social vices such as greed and corruption. Their lyrics mocked the wealthy as being "*Paupres de coret d'aver poderos*" (poor in heart and heavy in riches) as they played the lute, the tambourine, the hurdy-gurdy, or the fiddle-like rebec. The German troubadour Walther von der Vogelweide (1170–1230) wandered from court to court, attacking Innocent III for demanding further taxes to fund yet another crusade. As Vogelweide had participated in a crusade, it seems likely that his ire was directed more at the taxes than the crusade itself. Addressing his poem to the offertory box, Walther accused the pope of sending the box to the German people merely to enrich himself and impoverish the population ("*daz ir in rîchet und uns Tiutschen ermet unde pftendet?*"). The people pined and withered while the pope "filled his chests again."[14]

Matfre Ermengaud of Béziers, a thirteenth-century troubadour and Franciscan friar, targeted "lazy" merchants who sat all day in the town square or spent their time hunting. He charged them with lying about payments in the hope to be paid twice, of swindling their customers by showing them perfect goods but selling them rotten ones, of deceiving foreign traders about local prices and buying up seigneurial rights and then raising taxes. He accused them with fixing weights and measures to their advantage, which was enough of a problem for kings to hand over the responsibility of weighing and measuring to religious houses. Not short on complaints, Ermengaud was further enraged by the stockpiling of commodities which he referred to as hoarding, which was, according to many, such as the Dominican friar Johannes Teutonicus, a sin.

Theologians also condemned the avarice they believed to be rampant in the Church. Robert Grossteste, the bishop of Lincoln, had founded Oxford university in 1240 so that scholars would not have to take on loans from Jewish moneylenders or pawn books with them by providing loan chests for the students. But it was all usurers that bore his wrath. He accused the Vatican of being riddled with "cupidy and avarice," chasing "greedily after gain." The Church robbed the poorest of the poor, pillaged their community, and tore "the flesh from their bones." And Christian moneylenders, shielded by Rome, impoverished a substantial part of the population. On his deathbed in 1253 Grosseteste spoke out against both usurers and Pope Innocent IV:

> Yet now the Lord Pope's merchants or money-changers practise their usury publicly in London, to the disgust of the Jews . . . . [the Christian moneylender, lending a sum of 100 marks (about £67), asks to be repaid £100, even if the loan is repaid in a shorter term] . . . . This is worse than a Jew's condition, for the Jew will receive the principal courteously whensoever thou shalt return it, with only so much interest as is proportionate to the time for which thou hast it in hand.[15]

It was not only amongst Christians that ascetic sectarianism emerged. In Germany, radical pietist Jews emerged who were harsh critics of usury and profligate living. In the twelfth-century, this small, elite sect known as the Hasidim (*Haside Ashkenaz*) laid claim to the correct interpretation of God's Will. Only these Godfearers were righteous. All other Jews—and of course, all non-Jews—were branded "wicked," "evil," "violent," and "immoral." In the case of profit, the Hasidim held views close to many of the ascetic Christians. Wealth was God's property and it was not for men, who were merely custodians of it, to make a gain at the expense of others. The censure of profit by the Hasidim, however, applied only to the Jews. It was acceptable, indeed, honorable, for Pietists to be creditors to Christians as this put them in a position of strength against their enemy.[16]

In censoring the usurer, Judah the Pietist wrote about a sage who ordered his children and students not to buy grain for profit. A profiteer is happy when his grain appreciates in value and sold for a higher price. "But it is written, 'He that is glad at calamity will not go unpunished' (Proverbs 17:5). Out of concern for his own gain, he is not concerned for the welfare of the majority." The common good here is a form of egalitarianism. It was inconceivable to ascetics, Jewish or Christian, that the common good could be produced from the same source that made the merchant profitable.[17]

A popular thirteenth-century tale told of a man begging in the streets of a town for bread. Mindful of the Church's teaching to be charitable to the poor, many passers-by were moved to give him food and money. When his hands and pockets were full, the beggar hid his alms and walked the streets once again to plead for more. Before the beggar could reap the benefits of his accumulated hoard, the devil suffocated him. After his death, the townspeople were outraged to discover that the beggar they bestowed with charity was far from destitute. On the contrary, he was the proprietor of three houses, which were promptly seized by town's angry populace. In a public show of revenge and punishment, children dragged the false beggar's naked corpse through the town and then unceremoniously hurled it in the river. The moral of this popular story, warned the Franciscan friar Salimbene de Adam, was to "Beware, lest by your miserliness you provoke the madness of children." Hoarding was seen as an evil practice that only brought tragedy and efforts were made throughout Europe to prevent merchants from stockpiling goods, or stop people from hindering goods' coming to market, or any other measure which would drive the price up through collusion and conspiracy. In canon law, monopolies were "filthy gain" (*turpe lucrum*) like usury.[18]

The idea that a merchant might buy grain when it was plentiful and then sell at a higher price when it was scarce was not good business as it had been under Roman law; it was uncharitable and abhorrent. In the same way that critics believed a just person lent money to his neighbor out of charity and not out of the desire for profit, a just person shared his goods in times of crisis. "He who buys cheap in order to sell dear, seeks shameful profit," was the mainstream view amongst medieval clergy. The call for the regulation of grain and other essentials was more commonly voiced as a preventative against hoarding. Part of this regulation was the implementation of a just price that would be "fair" to the buyer and seller.[19]

The doctrine of a just price had been around for centuries and was a favorite topic of a number of popes. Under Charlemagne's rule in the ninth century, the just price was the market price and, if a person was charged more, the local priest could settle the price with "humanity." The majority view of the Scholastics—the Christian philosophers who used dialectical reasoning as their intellectual method—maintained this definition; the just price was the market price free of any deceit or collusion, unless a public emergency compelled the authorities to step in and control the prices. Many of those arguing for a just price advocated price controls that took into allowance scarcity and abundance as well as other factors that might affect grain. For them, a just price was not simply a case of a willing buyer and a willing seller agreeing upon a particular price. A truly just price, they argued, must be determined by the government or government-approved guilds. It was a form of charity and advocates of government control, such as the friars, believed that it represented the common good.[20]

The most important thirteenth-century scholar to raise and revise the issue of the just price was the Italian Dominican friar, Thomas Aquinas, who sought to harmonize Greek philosophy with Christian doctrine. He had no doubt that "wealth shines in giving rather than in hoarding: for the miser is hateful, whereas the generous man is applauded." It was impossible for happiness to be found in wealth although, unlike the mendicants, he did not find poverty to be exalting. Poverty deprived the individual of performing acts of charity that were the essence of the common good. Wealth, then, had its benefits but what mattered was how that wealth was obtained, how much wealth was retained by an individual, and to what use it was put.[21]

Born in Lombardy around 1225, the son of Landulph, count of Aquinas, and Theodora, countess of Tiano. before he was even born, it was rumored that Thomas' future as a great theologian was foretold by a hermit. Whether a fable or not, Aquinas became one of the foremost proponents of scholasticism, the quest of which was to reconcile theology and philosophy in the form of rational thought. When it came to the Jews, Aquinas had no patience for forced conversions or mob violence, nor did he consider Jews to be heretics or the devil's minions. It was for their role in usury that Aquinas condemned Jews. Usury, he wrote, is "unjust in itself, because this is to sell what does not exist, and this inevitably leads to inequality which is contrary to justice."[22]

In a series of letters he wrote to Margaret of Constantinople, countess of Flanders, Aquinas contemplated the rights and wrongs of usury. He made a distinction between natural wealth (necessities for everyday life such as clothing, food, and housing) and what he called artificial wealth (money that was "invented by the art of man, for the convenience of exchange, and as a measure of things salable"). He also drew upon Aristotle's volumes *The Nichomachean Ethics* and *Politics*, which were translated into Latin in the mid-thirteenth century. Following Aristotle, he agreed that making money off money was unnatural because it went against money's nature to use it as a method of exchange. As money was unchanged when it was loaned out, the lender could not, in good conscience, claim a profit, as they could with goods.[23]

What Margaret wanted to know from Aquinas was two-fold: was it legal to take goods from Jews if they resulted from the "depravity of usury?" And should a Jew be financially punished if he or she committed a sin? To the first query, Aquinas replied that usury was nothing more than extortion and concluded that Jews could not legally retain these goods. But neither could Margaret, unless the items in question had been extorted from her or her ancestors. Barring that exception, the goods were to be returned to those who relinquished the monies due to a pawn or to an unpaid loan. If this was not possible, the property should be put to charitable use or for the "common utility" of Margaret's land. To the second question, Aquinas replied that Jews were naturally prone to avarice, so should not benefit from the "iniquity" of usury. As punishment, they should be accorded an even greater fine because of their extortion, although, the Dominican added, any financial penalty received was not Margaret's to keep but to be allocated to pious purposes.[24]

Aquinas laid the blame for usury not only on Jews but also on those rulers who did not compel Jews "to work for their own living." The lack of physical labor involved in moneylending had long been a weapon in the arsenal against usury. By living "without occupation," Aquinas accused Jews of growing "rich by usury, and thus their rulers [were]. . .defrauded of revenue." That the issue was usury and not the Jews *per se* Aquinas made clear; his rules were equally applicable to Christian moneylenders, such as the Lombards and Cahors, who were also dependent on "the depravity of usury."[25]

It was one of Aquinas' students, Giles de Lessines, who wrote the first complete medieval treatise on usury. While he retained his mentor's concept of a just price, he rejected the idea that it was iniquitous. In Lessines' view, moneylending was a useful service in society and if the moneylender made a profit it was as justified by the factors of risk, labor, and expense in much the same way as a seller made a profit on oranges, silk, or salt. Thomists were also countered from another angle by the followers of the Franciscan scholastic Duns Scotus who calculated the just price to be cost, plus normal profit and recompense for risk.[26]

For Thomists, charity should compel a seller not to pursue gain as an end in itself and a buyer to recognize the seller's need to sustain himself and his family according to their social status. To pursue further riches, was the definition of greed and usury, a practice that was malicious, unjust, and destroyed the sense of community. Because there was no limit to people's greed, there was need of regulation to ensure that interest rates were not "excessive." How that was defined and who was to make that determination were highly debatable questions. Yet, such ideas were found in the fourteenth century by the mathematician and theologian Henry of Langenstein the Elder (1325–1397) who defined the just price to be nothing over and above that needed for his labor and expenses in order to maintain his status. If it went beyond this, it was avarice. It went against the common good.[27]

* * *

There were ominous warnings at the end of the thirteenth century of the economic discontent to come. In 1285, one chronicler reported that rebels in Barcelona led by Berenguer Oller planned to attack the "clergy, the Jews and all the rich men of the city who were not willing to recognize him, that they should all be killed and that their houses with all they contained should be confiscated for the benefit of his followers." Oller's revolution did not materialize. King Pedro III of Aragon had him dragged at the tail of a mule and then hanged with his co-conspirators.

Oller's followers were not the destitute or of the lowest strata in society but those small merchants, shopkeepers, and artisans who had taken out loans to expand their business as Barcelona's economy grew. This was one of the many signs of unrest and dissatisfaction with the status quo. It was in the next century that these rumblings would explode into a series of open rebellions that sought to upend society in search of a more egalitarian world or, perhaps, invert the hierarchy. In a brutal world where the average lifespan was thirty-five, a reversal of the social order was worth risking the gallows. The new money-free utopia would reward the good—that is, the poor and their advocates—and the rich and the usurers would be condemned.[28]

* * *

From 1310 to 1320, the winters were bitterly cold, the summers wet, and when it came the snow was so deep it would not melt. This mini ice-age made the growing season shorter, bringing heavy rain, and leading to high food prices and famine. In 1315, rain washed away villages, destroying farmland and transforming peasants into beggars. The great famine affected millions people and resulted in hunger and disease (especially typhus) as food was scarce and prices skyrocketed. The increase in the price of bread and salt, staples in people's diet, put them out of reach for peasants. It was said that those driven mad by the lack of food ate corpses, digging up those recently buried. Harvest yields were already dropping before the wet weather inflicted mold, rust, and mildew on the crops. As prices soared, bands of people roamed the lands stealing animals and goods, murdering those who got in their way, and robbing houses of their possessions.[29]

The famine ended in 1317, although its effects were felt for several years after. In these difficult years, protests and rebellions spread quickly throughout Western Europe. Despite the term "peasant wars" that is often used to describe these movements, these revolts involved not only peasants but artisans, wage laborers, urban workers, small tradesmen, and minor nobility as well. With scarcity of food stuffs and commodities there was also hostility towards anyone suspected of hoarding. Higher food costs due to a decrease in supply stirred anger towards anyone making a profit from the increase in prices, whether through monopolizing grain or speculating. Demands for a new social order included the end of villeinage, the removal of corrupt, worldly priests, and the redistribution of Church land.[30]

Money "makes the poor man lose his house, vineyards, furniture and all his roots, casting everything into disarray. The whole world is plagued by its curse and where money prevails many things are overlooked . . . although the monks curse [money] in public, they hoard it in cups and glasses in the monastery . . . It turns the servant into the master, the master into the servant and all things everywhere obey its call." That damnation of money appeared in the fourteenth-century book, *Libro del buen amor* (The Book of Good Love), by Juan Ruíz. It did not matter whether the people were kings, clergy, nobles, or peasants, money lured everyone from all walks of life to commit sin, worship the golden calf, and neglect their spiritual duty. In another century, Walter of Châtillon had expressed the same opinion. "Money is the victor," he wrote, "money reigns supreme over all."[31]

It was a common refrain amongst preachers. "What is meritorious is not that a man should be poor, but that, being poor, he should love poverty." It was said that the words of the Valencian Dominican preacher Vincent Ferrer (c. 1350–1419) moved those who heard him to give all their worldly belongings to the poor. He traveled across Spain, a land "rich with olives, overflowing with grapes, fertile with harvests . . . . girded by a temperate band of sky," preaching against usury and riches. When he approached the city gates of Spanish towns, he was rapturously met by people of all occupations and status. Crowds jostled to see him and wandering penitents accompanied him like a guard of honor. His public sermons, delivered with thunderous energy, left his audience with frightening visions of cosmic dimensions; darkness falling on the earth until Christ returns and saves the good with life everlasting. Despair, fear, and then hope. People should care for their souls, he warned, and not lust after material possessions; otherwise, Christians were no better than Jews.[32]

It was one of the Avignon-based popes who, in 1322, overturned the Church's doctrine of Christ's poverty that had emphasized his humble birth and lack of material wealth. Determined to weaken the Spiritual Franciscans, who he considered to be excessive in their asceticism, Pope John XXII (Jacques d'Euse) ruled that to deny that Christ had possessions was now a heresy and against official Church teachings. Despite this change of policy, the exaltation of poverty was widespread and rooted in popular criticisms of usury. Around 1330, the Florentine artist Giotto painted a fresco entitled *Allegory of Poverty.* The beautiful Lady Poverty, standing in front of red roses and white lilies, barefooted with thorns encircling her white, patched robe, is married by Christ to that other icon of virtuous poverty, St. Francis, with Hope and Charity as her bridesmaids. Giotto's depiction of Lady Poverty, commissioned by the Franciscan order, was not particularly reflective of his own lifestyle. For extra income, he rented out looms to impoverished weavers at a startling interest rate of 120 percent.[33]

In literature, an English rendition of a popular French treatise on Christian morality, *Ayenbite of Inwyt* (Remorse of Conscience, c. 1340) named usury as the first root of Avarice. The "courteous lender" was described as someone who does not make "bargains for profit, either in pence . . . or in cups of gold, or in silver, or in robes, or in tuns of wine, or in fat swine, or in services of horses and carts, or providings for himself or his children, or in any other things that he takes by reason of the loan." To do so is "evil and foul" and the domaine of the wicked:

> The third manner of usury is in them that have shame to lend with their own hand, but they lend their pence through their servants or other men. These are the master money-lenders. Of such sin great men are not quit, who hold and sustain Jews and usurers that lend and destroy the country; and the great men take the rewards and the great gifts, and oftentimes the ransome money of the goods of the poor.[34]

In his late fourteenth-century moral poem, *Apparicion Maistre Jehan de Meun*, Honorat Bovet tried to encourage Christian rulers to demonstrate godly behavior and not their own self-interest by rejecting usury. In his imaginary interfaith dialogue between a Christian, Jew, and Muslim, Master Jean reproached the Jew:

> Vile Jew, most wicked:
> Why, against the edict of the king,
> Do you come into this country?
> Don't you know that, some time ago,
> Because of our great iniquities,
> Because of usury, through your sins,
> You were thrown out of this kingdom?

The English poet John Gower (1330–1408) painted his literary Jews as liars, cheats, and thieves in his poem *Confessio Amantis* (The Lover's Confession), a line of which read that a "true" Jew was allowed to "Bereve [deprive] him [the Christian] bothe lif and good." One of the most famous literary rebukes of usury was in Geoffrey Chaucer's *The Prioress Tale* which depicts it as a Jewish activity contrary to Christian life:

> There was in Asie, in a great citee,
> Amonges Cristen folk, a Jewerye,
> Sustened by a lord of that contree,
> For foule usure, and lucre of vilanye,
> Hateful to Crist and to his companye.[35]

By this time, there were plenty of Christian moneylenders and it was not always the Jews who were the target of literary anti-usury attacks. Chaucer's merchant-usurer in his *Merchant's Tale* was not Jewish but was an outwardly respectable Christian who conducts illegal business transactions as well as usury. The Italian satirical writer Giovanni Boccaccio (1313–1375) had trained as a banker in Naples and was well connected to traders and financiers. Yet, the world appeared to Boccaccio as one infected with the sin of usury that was motivated by human greed. It was not the Jews who epitomized greed, however, in his masterpiece *The Decameron*. It was the lecherous, worldly friars who "cry down luxury, whilst they wallow in all kinds of debauchery. They condemned usury and unjust gains, in order to gain some great benefice or bishopric, by what is given them by way of restitution. . . ." One of Boccaccio's characters, Abraham the Jew, is prompted by his friend's desire that he convert to Christianity, Abraham travels to Rome to see the workings of the papacy first-hand. What he found was a Church filled with gluttonous clergy, "greedy and avaricious," who "bought and sold for money," and "employed more brokers than the drapery trade and all other trades of Paris put together."[36]

In this climate of dissent, unrest, economic downturn, and famine, with usury blamed for causing debt that led to the loss of land, possessions, and sometimes life, protest was ignited once more. In 1320, a popular crusade by the *Pastoureaux* (the shepherds) spread across Spain and France. The rebellion was denounced by the papacy, as well as King James II of Aragon and his son Prince Alfonso, who threatened to hang those who committed acts of robbery or violence and ordered officials to shield their Jewish subjects. Inspired by leaders who claimed to have visions of the Virgin Mary and the Holy Spirit, the rebels combined ideas spread by theologians that the poor were the spiritually elect and furious resentment toward those they believed to be their oppressors and responsible for their deteriorating circumstances in the wake of famine. They burst into castles, abbeys, town halls, and farms, plundering and burning as they went. Their anger was directed both at the rich and the Jews who they accused of bleeding the poor dry with high-interest loans. According to the Carmelite friar Jean de Venette, the rebels massacred Jews at Aquitaine and then marched on towards Carcassone in the Languedoc region which had been a stronghold of the heretical Cathars. Here the *sénéchal* (the royal officer in charge of justice) put the Jews under his protection as *servi camerae regis* (subjects of the king), for "all they have are the king's."[37]

Even with these attempts to protect the Jews, attacks continued. In the small French village of Montclus, known for its credit business involving large and small loans to all sectors of society, Jews were murdered, their homes looted, and documents pertaining to debts and property deeds were burned or stolen. Land belonging to Jews was taken over illegally. The Crown, which benefited from the outstanding loans owed to Jews who died without heirs, commanded that the spoiled and missing documents be recreated. This led to further objections that borrowers were being compelled to pay debts they had already settled, increasing the bad blood between lender and creditor and inflaming the already fraught situation.[38]

Protest movements spread to other parts of Western Europe and included townsmen (*bourgeois* or *burghers*) who chaffed against the financial burdens placed on them by authorities. In 1323, a serious revolt in Flanders was triggered by heavy taxation and lasted for five years. Debt was also a source of resentment amongst the protesters, who included anyone with a grievance against the government. In some places, particularly the Rhineland and southern Germany, modification to debts were made between 1315 and 1322 because usury was "horrible and dishonest." It was claimed that usury drove up prices, reduced the cost of exports, and, therefore, was a national disaster by destroying the home economy. Some Christian usurers demanded laws which restricted competition by Jews while ensuring that those same laws did not hinder their own profit-making. A French fable tells of a Christian usurer who changes the words of the Lord's Prayer, inserting his own meanings into the traditional verse. After the sentence "and we forgive those who trespass against us" (*pardonnez-nous comme nous pardonnons*), the usurer added, "these accursed Jews have plotted to ruin us by lending to our customers at a lower rate than we do . . ." (*Ces maudits juifs ont fait le complot de nous enlever nos pratiques et de nous ruiner, en prêtant à un intérèt plus bas que le notre*).[39]

The situation was not helped by the outbreak of what would become known as the Hundred Years' War between France and England (1337–1453). It was an enormously expensive venture costing hundreds of thousands of pounds. The soldiers' wages in the year 1359 alone amounted to £133,000. In England, Edward III (1312–1377) took out a loan of 340,000 florins to equip his troops and fund their campaigns. One of his creditors was Vivelin le Rous (Vivelin the Red), a Jewish financier from Strasbourg whose consortium lent the English king 140,000 florins. Edward also took out loans from two of the largest Christian Italian banking and trading companies; 900,000 gold florins from the Bardi and 600,000 from the Peruzzi. In the 1340s, these two firms, in addition to the Buonaccorsi bankers, failed. The fall of these giants that had extensive operations in the Mediterranean region and Western Europe was similar to the demise of

Edward's grandfather's bankers, the Riccardi. A domino effect was set off by the collapse, and smaller companies to which the Bardis and Peruzzis owed money also crashed.

The reason for this banking failure, according to the politician Giovanni Villani (1275–1348) was usury:

> O cursed and greed usury, full of the vice of avarice reigning in our blind and mad citizens of Florence, who from covetousness to gain from great lords put their wealth and that of others in their power and lordship to lose, and ruin our republic; for there remained no substance of money in our citizens, except in a few craftsmen and lenders who with their usury consumed and gained for themselves the scattered poverty of our citizens and subjects.

Villani's anger was intensified by his own involvement in the banking crisis. He lost both his reputation and fortune, ending up in a debtor's prison because of his involvement with the Buonaccorsi firm. He attributed the crash to the funding Florence received in their war against the city of Lucca, and the bank's huge loans to Edward III, without having the necessary capital to cover such large transactions. Yet, Villani's assessment may not be accurate. Both the Bardi and the Peruzzi merchant banks were cautious about furnishing loans if repayment was not guaranteed either in wool (Bardi's main commodity) or cash. Rather than due to mismanagement of high-risk loans, the failure of the Peruzzi bank has been attributed by some historians to the grain market's decrease in profit margins, which was their staple commodity. In addition, it has been argued that Edward repaid more of the debt than previously believed, although the dangers of lending to profligate monarchs and magnates remained a real source of bankruptcy and worse.[40]

In May 1347, a plague that came to be known as the Black Death spread from Constantinople to the commercial cities of Europe. It preyed upon the largely agricultural populations weakened by famine with catastrophic effects. The deadly disease moved rapidly to other regions—to Spain in the south-west and north to Normany in France and the Low Countries. In 1348, the plague was found in England and then outbreaks were reported in Scandinavia and the Germanic lands. The final death toll is unknown but certainly many millions and prompted hysteria, rumors of conspiracies, and widespread desolation.[41]

Giovanni Boccaccio watched the plague spread in Florence. Swellings the size of an egg or as large as an apple appeared on the groin or the armpit and spread throughout the body. Soon after, black or livid spots appeared, the sign that death was not far off. Doctors were ignorant of the causes or treatments and as the plague spread just like "fire catches anything dry," laws fell into decay as those in authority fell sick, died, or fled. People carried scented bouquets to ward off the sickness, others drank, some shut themselves away, and many left for areas yet untouched by the contagion. Brother abandoned brother, parents left their children, and death covered the earth. *Momento Mori* (Remember you must die) became a familiar phrase of a macabre culture that grew used to groteque deaths. Skeletons danced across paintings and poems lingered on the decay of the body: ashes to ashes, dust to dust. The figure of Death was the constant reminder that fleeting life was for living. For the short time that a human being was on this earth—and in the medieval world, it was usually a very short time—life was to be enjoyed. It was also a grim reminder to reflect on human mortality, live a moral life, and mend erroneous ways before the grave beckoned. With war decimating much of Europe and earthquakes shaking the ground with a "column of fire" reported over Avignon, riches were no help against nature's cruelties.[42]

Restrictions on moneylending made it more difficult in such bad economic periods to raise the necessary capital for the next agricultural production and to weather the crop failures. With shortages came higher costs of goods, which encouraged a black market and speculation. The hoarding of goods by speculators, considered by many as nothing more than thievery and fraud, was condemned by the French king, Louis X. Calling speculation "avaricious cupidity," he ordered his officials to hunt down those hoarding salt and those conspiring to hoard.[43]

Corruption was rampant with people taking advantage of vulnerable people in perilous circumstances and interest rates were often extraordinarily high due to the greater risk of nonpayment in times of widespread mortality. With a rise in the cost of labor due to the shortage of workers came efforts by rulers to freeze wages. As the plague made its deadly way through Europe, protest intensified. In its aftermath, one chronicler complained that people were reaping riches through disaster and had become greedy. Food, furniture, merchandise, and labor were expensive and donations to charity dropped. People, he lamented, seemed more interested in wealth than their soul.[44]

The attempts at wage control encouraged more rebellion. In Strasbourg, a massacre of Jews in 1349 was condemned by the city's council. Those opposed to the local government included nobles, artisans, workers, and peasants, who accused the council of being corrupted with Jewish gold and forced the dissolution of the council. One of the magistrates, Peter Schwarber, was sent into exile and had his property appropriated. In France, a rebellion led by an affluent merchant protested demands by the Crown for money to pay for ransoms during the

Hundred Years' War. The Jacquerie peasant revolt of 1358 in France was triggered by onerous taxes to fund the war with England, as well as a law which ordered peasants to protect the nobles' castles. Out of all the revolts during the fourteenth century, this rural uprising was one of the most brutal. Rebels targeted the rich nobles and knights. Savage attacks were launched on men, women, and children with no mercy. In one account, a knight was said to have been roasted alive in front of his wife and children, his wife violated by ten to twelve rebels, and the flesh of the knight forcibly served to his wife and children. Whether or not this was a factual occurrence, a fearmongering rumor, or a mix of the two, it was certainly true that lawlessness was rife and marauding gangs made up of all ranks of society roamed the countryside. They took hostages, plundered, and murdered. Theft was common, especially of corn, with even clergymen stealing from abbeys. Conflicts between local lords, Church landowners, and the townspeople and peasants resulted in pillaging and demands for more rights.[45]

In Italy, serious riots broke out in Siena in 1355 involving both nobles and plebeians opposed to the government. The most dangerous revolt in the country took place in Florence 1378 and was known as the Ciompi rebellion. Like the disorder in France, the riots were violent and unplanned, provoked by a hatred of the rich and those to whom they were indebted. In Rouen in 1382, insurgents attacked the king's officials, former members of local government, monks, Jews, and anyone thought to have money. Paris was the site of multiple attacks with a mob ransacking Jews' houses in 1380. Further protests spread over France and into the south. In the face of weakness by King Charles VI (known as "the Beloved" as well as "the Mad"), anti-Jewish attacks continued intermittently until the king signed an edict to expel the Jews in 1394. The fever of popular revolution crossed the English Channel where the Peasants' Revolt of 1381 was sparked by the imposition of a poll-tax and also by the ideas of John Wycliffe (1320–1384) that were spread by poor parish priests. Wycliffe attacked the papacy, rejecting its authority as there was no scriptural justification for that office, and castigated the monasteries for their accumulation of wealth. For the rebels, it was not only the clergy that was the target. It was anyone with wealth. The revolt began on Corpus Christi (June 13), a day that had become associated with protest against high taxes and perceived corruption. Rebels from rural areas and towns such as St. Albans, Norwich, Yarmouth, Bury St. Edmonds, Ipswich, Winchester, Scarborough, Beverly, and York banded together to assert what they regarded as their rights and liberties. As part of the attack on government, they assaulted the weavers from Flanders and other parts of the Low Countries who had been invited to England

Edward III to assist in the important wool trade. There were, of course, no Jews to plunder.[46]

Most of the rebellions were not aimed at Jews specifically. When they were, it had much to do with their association with moneylending. The most dangerous series of revolts against Jews occurred in fourteenth-century Spain. Nearly thirty years after the Shepherd's Crusade of 1320, Christians attacked the Jewish quarter of Barcelona and in Valencia Jews were assaulted during the summer. These attacks were, if not stirred up, then certainly aided to some degree by the public sermons of the Dominican Vincent Ferrer who denounced wealth and praised poverty in a country devastated by natural and manmade disasters. Assured that God despised moneylenders, rioters had one objective in common and that was to reduce the written contracts between Jewish creditors and their clients to ashes. Jewish moneylenders in Tárrega decided it was unsafe to collect the debts due to them but, if they were not paid, then they would have trouble remitting their taxes and other payments due to the king. In Aragón, Pedro IV decided it was time to intervene. He ordered notaries and scribes to help the Jews in restoring their missing and damaged loan records so they could renew the process of repayment.[47]

In 1378, another Valencian Dominican friar named Ferrand Martínez, the archdeacon of Écjia and canon of the church of Santa Maria in Seville, sent letters to local authorities demanding that they expel the Jews. In response, the large *aljama* (community) of Seville, the richest Jewish community in Spain, sent word to the Castillian king, Enrique II. Social order was paramount to any monarch eager to keep his treasury healthy and so, determined to squash any hint of rebellion or disturbances to his finances, Enrique ordered the preacher to cease his verbal attacks on Jews.

As was the case in the rest of Western Europe, despite the association of Jews and moneylenders that these preachers made, most Jews in Spain were not moneylenders. Among other professions, the majority of Jews were employed in viticulture, artisan work, medicine, farming, sail making, dice making, tailoring, shoe making, silversmithing, and brokering. They worked in the leather, fur, and tanning industries, and often shared workshops with Christians and Muslims. Moreover, Christians were involved in moneylending in great numbers in Spain, largely because of new forms of credit called annuities, or the census, which were accepted as legitimate transactions. A census was sold by nobles, the state, or other landowners and secured by their property, monopolies they may hold, or tax receipts. An annual return was paid from the productivity of the land for a person's life in exchange for a lump sum payment. Such transactions were not generally thought of as usurious by the Church, which participated in them. As the buyer of the annuity was hoping to make more on the deal than he had paid originally, there were strict opponents of usury who believed that made the transaction immoral. But to most, including Aquinas' student, Gilles de Lessines, annuities were morally acceptable. Lessine's only concern was that the annuities were sold for a just price. He responded to critics by pointing out that the sum the seller received for the annuity was more advantageous to him than the buyer and therefore outweighed the fact that he may pay more to the buyer in the long run. What was valuable to the seller was that he got the capital he needed at that specific time. Annuities, which either could be inherited or ceased on the death of the purchaser, had appeared at the beginning of the thirteenth century in the north of France (Douai and Calais) and the Low Countries, in towns such as Hainault, Picardy, southern Flanders, and Artois. In 1202, for example, a knight named Erlebaud of Vaubercey transformed his fief into an annuity by giving land and woodland to the Cistercian monks of Notre Dame of Larrivour. In return, he, his wife, and heirs annually received grain. By the sixteenth century, 7 percent of Holland's revenues came from the sale of such annuities.[48]

During the fourteenth century, annuities appeared in Spain and were known as the *censal* and *violari*. A *censal* was a permanent money annuity that an investor obtained in return for a cash amount and could be passed on to an heir if the owner died. The interest rate was usually low for the times (around 7–8 percent) and the period of repayment was long-term. A *violari* was a similar kind of annuity but it was not perpetual and the interest rate was higher. These types of loans were relatively safe and although the returns were small, they were regular and both Christians and Jews used both *censals* and *violaris* to pay their taxes and other expenses. Through this new form of credit, investors bought the public debts of municipalities and Jewish *aljamas* (communities) and in so doing, the successful ones obtained control of the credit market. Over the course of the fourteenth and fifteenth centuries, it was Christian moneylenders who held the power financially, and many Jews took out loans, either individually or as an entire community, as the need arose and became indebted to these Christian moneylenders. And it was not only Christian individuals with whom Jews entered into transactions, but also monasteries, churches, and convents. Although there were some wealthy Jewish moneylenders, such as Ibrahim Pacagón, there was no easily identifiable cohort of rich Jewish moneylenders, as in twelfth-century England. Some Jews lent small sums to their Jewish and Christian neighbors or offered short-term loans to people living outside the towns whose lords were demanding their feudal levies in coinage rather than service. In Girona, by the middle of the century about 90 percent of the transactions by Jewish creditors took place in rural areas rather than urban centers.[49]

All over Spain, Jews and Christians borrowed money for taxes, as well as personal needs such as dowries and household or professional expenses. They also pawned their belongings when necessary, such as in 1370, when the Jews of Huesca pawned religious objects to pay the royal treasury. Like most astute monarchs, Spanish rulers were aware that exorbitant taxation carried serious risks that might disrupt social order. They also knew that if their tax-paying subjects were squeezed too hard financially, they had the ability to simply move away to find better opportunities elsewhere. Or, if they were bankrupted they would be unable to contribute anything at all.

By the time King Juan I of Castile was crowned in 1379, the burden of taxation on the Jews under Castillian control and the intermittent political meddling in debt repayment to the Jewish moneylenders meant a more impoverished Jewish community. Five years later, while trying to grab the Portuguese crown during a period of civil war, Juan taxed the *aljama* of Madrid 3,000 *maravedíes* which then went to the convent of Santo Domingo el Real. Another 3,000 paid by the Avila Jewish community funded the town's cathedral. Tax collection within the community often led to disputes, as those collecting the funds showed favor to their friends and penalized others. In Morvedre, the less well-off members of the *aljama* complained to the king that the community's leaders were not paying their fair share and demanded reforms that would give them more power within the community.[50]

From time to time, individuals and communities who were in debt appealed directly to the king (as they did the papacy) to be relieved of their usurious loans. If the monarch decided not to release the petitioner from his debt completely there were other aid measures he might introduce to assist those in financial difficulties, such as tax breaks or exemptions from taxes and contributions. Yet, plans to aid those indebted had damaging effects on others. Price controls satisfied those who could not afford the cost of staple foods as they rose in price but they hindered the merchants whose profits were cut when their product was forcibly reduced in price by royal decree. If the price was cut below cost, the seller could be bankrupted. And while moratoria on the collection of debts was another popular course of action for those in debt, suspending repayments was onerous, even devastating, for moneylenders who relied on those funds being delivered promptly. In 1389, King Juan I of Aragón attempted to gain control over the lending practices of Jews to ensure that the rate of interest did not exceed the amount he commanded. He ordered the appointment of a notary who registered all loan transactions between

Jews and Christians and recorded the pawns left with the Jewish moneylender as collateral. The notary also kept track of the assets of the Jews, a task that had nothing to do with curtailing usury but enabled the monarch to know how much the Jews owned and thereby how much he might increase the revenues due him from the *aljamas*. The king's official declaration that he was protecting Christians from Jewish greed encouraged some protesters who took to the streets to link their economic problems with Jewish "usurious voracity."[51]

Friar Ferrand Martinez continued his incendiary public sermons against the greed, usury, and Jews—despite the fact that Jews were not primarily moneylenders—prompting Jewish leaders to complain to authorities that Martinez was spreading evil rumors about them. Called before a tribunal of theologians and doctors, Martinez refused to respond to their questions, claiming that he answered to the people alone. Archbishop Barroso read the sentence that barred him from preaching on August 2, 1389, a ban to which the preacher paid scant attention. Martinez' zealotry may have earned him a reputation for rebellion and heresy, but it enhanced his popularity with the masses. In 1391, demonstrations and riots targeting Jews struck the *aljamas* in Castile-Léon's bigger cities and towns such as Seville, Burgos, Segovia, and Madrid. Seville was the first town to experience an outbreak of violence on 6 June. When Martinez delivered his sermons in the city, the excited crowds that he gathered around him were encouraged to ransack the Jewish quarter to take what they had been led to believe was justly theirs. Added to the longstanding resentment of burdensome taxes, high-interest rate loans, and irresponsible fiscal policies, the preacher's fierce words imbued the rioters with the idea that their protest were a form of social justice. As rioters murdered and stole the money and belongings of Jews, they were fed the idea that the Jews had robbed them through usury and the looting was righting a wrong.[52]

The courtier, chronicler, and chancellor Pedro Lopez de Ayala noted that, despite the overture of religiosity, the mob was driven by greed rather than piety. Juan Alonso Guzman, the count of Niebla and *alcade mayor* (chief administrator) of the city, and Alvar Perez de Guzman, the *alguazil mayores* (chief justice), captured some of the chief troublemakers in the crowd and publicly punished two of them. But rather than dampening the fervor of the rioters, this act exacerbated the sedition and the Guzmans narrowly avoided being lynched by the angry mob.[53]

Murder and pillaging spread throughout the *aljamas*—Cordova, Ubeda, Jaén, Muradal, Huete, Cuenca, Ciudad Real, and Baeza. By June 18, Toledo was engulfed in rioting as well as Orihuela, Alicante, and Valencia. According to one chronicler, on August 5, a small group set the gates of the Jewish quarter on fire, purportedly killing a hundred Jews. Some of the remaining Jews fled to the royal

Castillo Nuevo for protection. As the authorities struggled to bring the city under control, arrests were made and gallows were prepared to hang the worst of the rioters. This was the trigger for a even more serious rebellion which threatened to overturn the local government. The bailiff's archives were burned and by August 8 the Jews, desperate for food and water, surrendered. Some converted and those who refused were killed despite Church policy that a forced conversion is unlawful. The rioters threatened to murder the clerics and forced them to pay the city's taxes, as well as terrorizing merchants, silversmiths, and anyone with wealth. On August 10, uprisings erupted in Gerona with around forty Jewish victims and calls for the eradication of indirect taxation.[54]

As the violence spread around Spain, some Jews temporarily fled these towns, leaving for North Africa, Crete, or Palestine. The large number of Jews forcibly converted entered into the country's society as New Christians or *conversos*. It had been the law for a convert's property to be confiscated, but this was later changed under King Jaume I of Aragón who allowed Jewish converts to Christianity to keep their property and to still inherit from their Jewish relatives. Some of those who converted under duress secretly retained their Jewish laws and tradition, passing them on to the next generation. They became known as crypto-Jews or, more derisively, *marranos*.[55]

There is nothing to indicate that the violence in 1391 is indicative of a passion by everyone in Spain to rid the world of Jews nor that "Renaissance Western Europe" accomplished what the Middle Ages had at most dreamed of—a world free of Jews—as one historian has claimed. The attacks on Jews were part of the popular revolts that spread throughout a Europe used to wars and brutality, devastated by disaster, angered by taxes, and motivated by hatred towards usury that led many into a downward spiral of debt. Given that moneylending was not exclusively a Jewish profession at this time, the idea that Jews were inherently immoral and so linked to an immoral occupation seemed deeply enough entrenched to lead preachers and rioters to regard any usury as Jewish. But not every town in Spain was affected. There are no reliable numbers as to how many Jews were killed, how many fled, or how many converted but places such as Córdoba and Murcia recorded little in the way of rioting and normal business continued in the small towns outside of Burgos. In the towns that did experience unrest, the riots, whether spontaneous or organized, were stirred by intemperate anger, resentment, and a sense of injustice that had been the dominant narrative of itinerant popular preachers such as Ferrer and Martínez and which had seeped into popular culture through plays, music, art, and literature. But to those who lost their lives, saw their homes plundered and destroyed, and had to make the choice between death or conversion, it was of little consequence whether the attacks were planned or the result of spontaneous rage, a sense of inequality or simply greed.[56]

Despite attempts by the king's officials and other authorities to protect the Jews and restore social order in other towns, they were unable to prevent the looting of the Jewish quarters. Efforts were made, however, to recover their stolen property and mete out punishment to those found guilty of the violent disorder. In the winter of 1392, a number of the "unbridled and incorrigible" rioters were executed and when King Enrique came of age in 1395, he had Ferrand Martinez arrested, some nine years before death finally silenced his fanaticism. In the king's words, it was the "vile people of low estate" who plundered the Jewish communities, although it was not only the peasants who formed the mobs.[57]

* * *

Notwithstanding the difficult periods of war, famine, plague, and weather-related crop failures during the fourteenth century, it would be a mistake to think that all Jews during this period suffered only misery, plunder, and despair. Not only were some Jews actively engaged in commerce in ever greater distances and scope, they were also involved in procuring property, land, as well as continuing in the moneylending business where it was tolerated. This is apparent in the life of one man in the middle of the fourteenth century, a Jewish merchant/moneylender/investor in Marseille named Bondavin de Draguignan. In general, the Jews of Marseille appear more often as debtors rather than creditors. Bondavin was, therefore, an exception but an important one. His life gives us a glimpse at a world contrary to the traditional version of isolated oppressed Jews and unrelentingly antisemitic Christians. He was not an outsider, he was not restricted in his professions, and he comfortably interacted with Christians. Between 1305 and 1361, a period that covers the disasters mentioned above, he conducted 455 acts of credit. He was, like so many other moneylenders, a man of multiple trades. Marseille was a city with high land value, and Bondavin had extensive holdings. His property transactions included fifteen vineyards—viticulture was the city's most important enterprise—a garden, and a walnut grove. Outside of Marseille, in Saint Marcel, he purchased several additional properties and orchards in the villages of Sainte-Claire, Mourriers, Sion, and Saint-Augustin, some of which he bought from the clergy and nobility. With these property deals, Bondavin became part of the viticulture and agrarian production in the region. His personal affairs and business partnerships involved both Jews and Christians where risk could be shared. Affiliating with Christians allowed Jews to get around restrictions imposed upon them by allocating those aspects of business to their Christian partners. When Jews were forbidden to trade via Alexandria, the hub for commerce between Marseille and the East, Bondavin transferred this part of the trade into the hands of Christians. He issued loans to Christian businessmen and funded the Angevin expansion in France, as well as helping to finance nine expeditions between 1330 and 1340 throughout the Mediterranean and investing in various enterprises. He imported brazil wood, sugar, powdered sugar, and cakes to Marseilles, and shipped textiles and coral from Sardinia and Bougie, which was in demand for its supposed magical properties. Jews in Marseille crafted the coral that was pulled from the coastal waters and these were sold not only domestically but exported to Egypt and Syria.[58]

In 1317, Bondavin brought a law case in the city against one of his debtors in an attempt to regain his unpaid loan. More than fourteen people gave testimony in his favor, including two Christians, the notary Paul Giraud and the merchant Faydit Ébrard (who represented him in front of both the secular and ecclesiastical court and who was the legal administrator of his small children). As a creditor of stature, Bondavin was allowed to avoid a public hearing, which potentially could destroy his all-important *fama* or reputation. He opted instead for a public venue and used the occasion to prove his honesty. Twenty-four testimonies were given. One of Marseille's most distinguished aristocrats declared under oath that he considered Bondavin trustworthy in business, virtuous, peaceful, of good name, and sound opinion. As the trial progressed, all of his witnesses vouched for his good nature and honesty.[59]

The vast majority of Jews never achieved the material success nor experienced the level of interaction with Christians Bondavin enjoyed. Yet, the wealth and status of people like Bondavin affected and benefited many other Jews who were allowed to settle alongside Jewish financiers in those cities that were in need of bankers and had invited them to take up residence. Moneylending may not have been the profession of most Jews, but it was one that offered privileges not only to those Jews that practiced it but to many others, including those that despised it. Bonvadin may have been the exception, or perhaps there were many more like him that remain nameless, but the experience of Jews in Marseille—where commerce played a vital part in the economy—was not one of isolation and persecution.[60]

By the end of the fourteenth century, the economy bounced back in Western Europe and grew in the following century. Western Europe was moving in the direction of a more capitalist economy and more of the population were becoming dependent on cash earnings from employers. Production was increasingly subcontracted to specialists who attended to various stages of a product's development, albeit mainly on a small scale with journeymen and their apprentices rather than large scale industries. More partnerships were formed to discover better trade routes and supplies. The traveling merchant buying and selling at the commercial fairs gave way to the sedentary merchant who set up agents in other cities to facilitate long-distance trade, especially in major commercial centers. Business methods were adjusted to allow for economic and technical innovation which led to extensive growth once more. Along with the economic rebound, demand for credit surged as the new century saw the papacy engaged in a war against the Turkish Ottoman Empire, which had conquered Constantinople in 1453, ending the Byzantine Empire. Debt was now such an integral part of daily life that by the end of the fifteenth century, in 1494, the first book on that double-entry bookkeeping was published by an Italian Franciscan mathematician, Luca Pacioli, entitled the *Summa de Aritmetica, Geometria, Proportioni, et Proportionalita*. As permanent armies began to replace the old system of obliged knights and new weapons were developed, the cost of waging war was ever greater. Victory often depended upon credit-rich, well-consolidated states that could obtain and use its resources with the utmost efficacy and, if necessary, wait out long sieges. Supplying these armies with food, horses, weapons, and armor, was vital and involved many creditors.[61]

Italy was the center of banking, and with moneylending an essential component of the economy, Jews were actively sought to provide low-interest rates to the poorer population. In response to pressure by the friars, the Church decided it was time to take moneylending out of the hands of the Jews completely and devised a way to get into the loan business without the sin of usury. As one historian noted, the Christian loan bank—the monte di pietà—was the "death knell of public or licensed usury." The medieval usurer was taking his last breath as the Church professed that God and profit were not incompatible.[62]

Notes

1. Britnell, "England and Northern Italy in the Early Fourteenth Century," 182.
2. Postan, *Cambridge Economic History of Europe*, 429–30; Martha Howell, "Whose 'Common Good'? Parisian Market Regulation, c. 1300–1800," in Middleton and Shaw, *Market Ethics and Practices*, chap. 2; Borer, *The City of London*, 84; "Song on the Corruption of the Time," MS Harl. No. 978, fol. 105, reign of Henry III,

"Contra avaros," 29, 33–35, "A Song of the Times," MS Harl. No. 978, fol. 123, 13th century, 47, all reprinted in Thomas Wright, ed. and trans. *Political Songs in England, from the Reign of John to that of Edward II* (London: The Camden Society, 1839); Britnell, *The Commercialisation of English Society*, 36.

3. Jairus Banaji, *Agrarian Change in Late Antiquity: Gold, Labour, and Aristocratic Dominance* (Oxford: OUP, 2001), 47; Fried, *The Middle Ages*, chapters 2 and 4; C. H. Lawrence, *Medieval Monasticism: Forms of Religious Life in Western Europe in the Middle Ages* (London and New York: Routledge, 2015), 21, 27; John McNamara, "Monks," in *Medieval Folklore: A Guide to Myths, Legends, Tales, Beliefs, and Customs*, eds. Carl Lindahl, John McNamara, and John Lindow (Oxford and New York: OUP, 2002), 275.
4. Peter Brown, "Rise and Function of the Holy Man in Late Antiquity," *Journal of Roman Studies* 61 (1971): 80, 82–84; Colin Wells, *Sailing from Byzantium: How a Lost Empire Shaped the World* (New York: Delacorte Press, 2006), 150; "Song Against the King's Taxes," MS. Harl. No. 2253, fol. 137, reign of Edward II, 184–86 and "Song of the Husbandman," MS. Harl. No. 2253, fol. 64, reign of Edward II, both in Wright, *The Political Songs of England*, 150; David Burr, *The Spiritual Franciscans: From Protest to Prosecution in the Century after Saint Francis* (University Park, PA: Pennsylvania State University Press, 2001), 77, 97; Larissa Taylor, *Soldiers of Christ: Preaching in Late Medieval and Reformation France* (New York: OUP, 1992), 35; John B. Freed, *The Friars and German Society in the Thirteenth Century* (Cambridge, MA: Mediaeval Academy of America, 1977), 5; Fried, *The Middle Ages*, chap. 6; Malcolm D. Lambert, *Medieval Heresy: Popular Movements from the Gregorian Reform to the Reformation* (Oxford: OUP, 1977), 57; Norman Cohn, *The Pursuit of the Millennium: Revolutionary Millenarism and Mystical Anarchists of the Middle Ages* (London: OUP, 1970), 34, 65–66; Dominique Iogna-Prat, *Order and Exclusion: Cluny and Christendom Face Heresy, Judaism, and Islam 1000–1150*, trans. by Graham Robert Edwards (Ithaca, NY: Cornell University Press, 2003), 278; Michael Haag, *The Templar: History and Myth* (Exmouth, UK: Profile Books, 2009), 83; Britnell, *The Commercialisation of English Society*, 36.
5. Richard Newhauser, "Avarice and the Apocalypse," in *The Apocalyptic Year 1000: Religious Expectation and Social Change, 950–1050*, eds. Richard Landes, Andrew Gow, David C. Van Meter (Oxford: OUP, 2003), 112; Little, *Religious Poverty*, 34.
6. Antoine Monastier, *A History of the Vaudois Church from Its Origin, and of the Vaudois of Piedmont* (New York: AMS Press, 1980), 61; Freed, *The Friars and German Society*, 9; O'Carroll, *A Thirteenth-Century Preacher's Handbook*, 6.
7. Alexander Patschovsky, "The Literacy of Waldensianism," in *Heresy and Literacy, 1000–1530*, ed. Peter Biller and Anne Hudson (Cambridge: CUP, 1994), 127; John H. Mundy, *Society and Government at Toulouse in the Age of the Cathars* (Ontario: Pontifical Institute of Mediaeval Studies, 1997), 206–08.

8. Mollat and Wolff, *The Popular Revolutions of the Late Middle Ages*, 28; Rubin, *Charity and Community*, 75.
9. Rubin, *Charity and Community*, 82.
10. Geisst, *Beggar Thy Neighbor*, chap. 1; Fried, *The Middle Ages*, chap. 6; Jeremy Cohen, *The Friars and the Jews: The Evolution of Medieval Anti-Judaism* (Ithaca: Cornell University Press, 1982), 38; Whittock, *Brief History*, 89.
11. Rubin, *Charity and Community*, 122; "Haec est Avaritia quae dicitur immoderate cupiditas acquirendi vel retinendi divinias"; "Cavete ab omni avaritia quae est idolorum servitus, quoniam avarus non implebitur pecunia."; "Haec et his similia illa dicente, aliqui eorum quorum conscientia corrupta erat, statim praebuerunt assensum." Giovanni (da Parma) Parenti, *Incipit Sacrum Commercium Beati Francisci cum Domina Paupertate* (*Here Begins the Holy Converse of the Blessed Francis with the Lady Poverty*), intro. Paul Sabatier (London: J.M. Dent, 1904), 18, 22; Cohen, *The Friars and the Jews*, 36–39; Burr, *The Spiritual Franciscans*, 263; Perry, *The Life and Times of Robert Grosseteste*, 133; Herlihy, *Medieval Culture and Society*, 171; Fried, *The Middle Ages*, chap. 8; Herrin, *Byzantium*, 40, 70–71; Whittock, *Brief History*, 89; St. Francis of Assisi, "Second Rule of the Friars Minor" and "Last Wish Which St. Francis Wrote to St. Clare," *The Writings of St. Francis of Assisi*, E-Book, https://play.google.com/books/reader?id=yRXBDgDFGEYC&printsec=frontcover&output=reader&hl=en&pg=GBS.PA3.
12. Cohen, *The Friars and the Jews*, 36, 41; Freed, *The Friars and German Society*, 11, 12, 25, 35, 52; McNamara, "Exemplum," in *Medieval Folktales*, 123; Dyer, *Making a Living in the Middle Ages*, 226, 231–34; Giovanni Ceccarelli, "Risky Business: Theological and Canonical Thought on Insurance from the Thirteenth to the Seventeenth Century," *The Journal of Medieval and Early Modern Studies* 31.3 (Fall 2001): 614; Perry, *The Life and Times of Robert Grosseteste*, 92; Burr, *The Spiritual Franciscans*, 19, 24.
13. O. C. Edwards, *A History of Preaching* (Nashville: Abingdon Press, 2004), 212; Perry, *The Life and Times of Robert Grosseteste*, 12, 16; Paul Sabatier, intro. to Parenti's *Sacrum Commercium*, xix–xxiv; Burr, *The Spiritual Franciscans*, 34–35, 37; Fried, *The Middle Ages*, chap. 8; Rubin, *Charity and Community*, 72.
14. "The Order of Fair-Ease," MS. Harl. No. 2253, fol. 121v. Edward II reign, in Wright, *Political Songs in England*, 141, 145; Walther von der Vogelweide, "The Collecting-Box," in *Selected Poems of Walther von der Vogelweide, The Minnesinger*, trans. Walter Alison Phillips (London: Smith, Elder & Co., 1896), 111; Fried, *The Middle Ages*, chap. 8.
15. William of Newburgh, *History*, Book 1, Chapter 6:3; Perry, *The Life and Times of Robert Grosseteste*, 212; Paris, *Chronica majora*, quoted by G. G. Coulton, *Social Life in Britain from the Conquest to the Reformation* (Cambridge: University Press, 1918), 342; Mundill, "Christian and Jewish Lending Patterns," 49.

16. Ivan G. Marcus, "The Politics and Ethics of Pietism in Judaism: The Hasidim of Medieval Germany," *The Journal of Religious Ethics* 8.2 (Fall 1980): 235, 238, 240.
17. Judah the Pietist, *Sefer Hasidim*: 1708, quoted in Marcus, "The Politics and Ethics of Pietism in Judaism," 234–35.
18. Jordan, *The Great Famine*, Prologue.
19. Jordan, *The Great Famine*, Prologue; Kelly, *The Great Mortality*, 69.
20. John W. Baldwin, *The Medieval Theories of the Just Price: Romanists, Canonists, and Theologians in the Twelfth and Thirteenth Centuries* (Philadelphia: Philadelphia American Philosophical Society, 1959), 47; Roover, "The Concept of the Just Price," 419, 421.
21. Murray N. Rothbard, *Economic Thought Before Adam Smith: An Austrian Perspective on the History of Economic Thought*, vol. 1 (Aldershot, UK: E. Elgar, 1995), 41; Migne, *Patrologiae Cursus Completus*, vol. LXXVII (Paris 1849), 498, quoted in Cave and Coulson, *Sourcebook for Medieval Economic History*, 127; Thomas Aquinas, *Summa Theologica*, I–II, Q.2, Art. 1, http://www.basilica.org/pages/ebooks/St.%20Thomas%20Aquinas-Summa%20Theologica.pdf; Diana Wood, *Medieval Economic Thought* (Cambridge: CUP, 2002), 46.
22. John Y. B. Hood, *Aquinas and the Jews* (Philadelphia: University of Pennsylvania Press, 1995), 108.
23. There is also the suggestion that the addressee was Marguerite, duchess of Brabant. Leonard Boyle considers Margaret of Constantinople to be the true recipient. See Boyle, "Thomas Aquinas and the Duchess of Brabant," *Proceedings of the Patristic, Medieval and Renaissance Conference 8* (1983): 25–35, quoted in Steven C. Boguslawski, *Thomas Aquinas on the Jews: Insight into his Commentary on Romans 9–11* (Mahwah, NJ: Paulist Press, 2008), 13 n.12; Munro, "The Medieval Origins of the 'Financial Revolution,'" 508; Hood, *Aquinas and the Jews*, 108; Thomas Aquinas, "Of the Sin of Usury, Which is Committed in Loans," *Summa* II–II Q.78.
24. Ibid; Thomas Aquinas, "Letter on the Treatment of Jews," (1271), http://www.ccjr.us/dialogika-resources/primary-texts-from-the-history-of-the-relationship/268-aquinas.
25. Aquinas, "Letter on the Treatment of Jews."
26. Shatzmiller, *Cultural Exchange*, 8; S. Todd Lowry and Barry Gordon, eds., *Ancient and Medieval Economic Ideas and Concepts of Social Justice* (Leiden: Brill, 1998), 494; Wood, *Medieval Economy Thought*, 213; Roover, "The Concept of the Just Price," 424.
27. Aquinas, *Summa*, II–II, Q. 78, Art. 1; Roover, "The Concept of the Just Price," 418; Daryl Koehn and Barry Wilbratte, "A Defense of a Thomastic Concept of the Just Price," *Business Ethics Quarterly* 22.3 (2012): 501–26.
28. Mollat and Wolff, *The Popular Revolutions of the Late Middle Ages*, 43–45, 50–51, 53; Fried, *The Middle Ages*, chap. 7.
29. Kelly, *The Great Mortality*, 59, 104; Jordan, *The Great Famine*, 17–19, 31; Jones, *The Plantagenets*, "Civil War."
30. Mollat and Wolff, *The Popular Revolutions of the Late Middle Ages*, 92.

31. Juan Ruíz, *Libro de buen amor*, reprinted in Olivia Remie Constable, ed., *Medieval Iberia: Readings from Christian, Muslim, and Jewish Sources*, 2nd ed. (Philadelphia: University of Pennsylvania Press, 2012), 421–23; Walter of Châtillon, *Nummus vincit, nummus regnat, nummus cunctis imperat*, quoted in Fried, *The Middle Ages*, chap. 7.
32. Constable, *Medieval Iberia*, 3; Taylor, *Soldiers of Christ*, 28, 47, 97; Alexandra Guerson, "Coping with Crises: Christian-Jewish Relations in Catalonia and Aragon, 1380–1391" (PhD diss., University of Toronto, 2012), 61, https://www.academia.edu/4128456/Coping_with_Crises_Christian-Jewish_Relations_in_Catalonia_and_Aragon_1380-1391.
33. Fried, *The Middle Ages*, chap. 10; Giotto di Bondone, *Allegory of Poverty* (fresco, c. 1330), Lower Church, San Francesco, Assisi; Paul Sabatier, intro. to *Sacrum Commercium*, xviii, 85–86; Origo, *The Merchant of Prato,* 156.
34. *Ayenbite of Inwyt*, quoted in Allen Rogers Benham, *English Literature from Widsith to the Death of Chaucer: A Source Book* (New Haven: Yale University Press, 1916), 257–59; Richard Morris' transcription of *Dan Michel's Ayenbite of Inwyt: or, Remorse of conscience* systematized from the British Museum's manuscript MS. Arundel 57, volume 1, http://quod.lib.umich.edu/c/cme/Ayenbite/1:34?rgn=div1;view=fulltext. The French original work was entitled *Somme de Vices et des Virtus*. It was compiled at the command of Philip the Bold, in 1279 by frère Lorens, a Dominican friar; Jordan, *The Great Famine*, 137, 168, 175;
35. John Gower, *Confessio Amantis*, quoted in Hÿman Michelson, *The Jew in Early English Literature* (Amsterdam: H.J. Paris, 1926), 48; Chaucer, "Prioress's Tale," quoted in Edgar Rosenberg, *From Shylock to Svengali: Jewish Stereotypes in English Fiction* (Stanford, CA: Stanford University Press), 24.
36. Giuseppe C. Di Scipio, "The Decameron," in *Medieval Folklore*, 98; Boccaccio, *The Decameron*, Part 3, novel 7, http://www.gutenberg.org/files/23700/23700-h/23700-h.htm#THE_SEVENTH_STORY3 and part 1, second story; http://www.gutenberg.org/catalog/world/readfile?fk_files=1453287&pageno=29.
37. Jean de Venette continued the chronicle of the monk Guillaume de Nangis who died around 1300. *Chronique Latine de Guillaume de Nangis de 113 a 1300* (Paris: J. Renouard 1843), v; Jordan, *The Great Famine*, 169; Hillaby, "Jewish Colonisation," 18.
38. Nirenberg, *Communities of Violence*, 69, 71–73, 87–88.
39. "La Patenotre de l'usurier," in *Fabliaux ou Contes, Fables et Romans du XIIe et du XIIIe Siècle*, vol. 4, ed. Pierre-Jean-Baptiste Legrand d'Aussy (Paris: J. Renouard, 1829), 12; Whittock, *Brief History*, 61–62; Jordan, *The Great Famine*, 20, 142, 148–49; Koyama, "Evading," 11.
40. Kocka, *Capitalism*; Fried, *The Middle Ages*, chap. 10; Geisst, *Beggar Thy Neighbor*, chap. 2; Mollat and Wolff, *The Popular Revolutions of the Late Middle Ages*, 106–07; Edwin S. Hunt, "A New Look at the Dealings of the Bardi and Peruzzi with Edward

III," *The Journal of Economic History* 50.1 (1990): 149 and idem, *The Medieval Super-Companies: A Study of the Peruzzi Company of Florence* (Cambridge: CUP, 1994), 216; Benham, *English Literature*, 262; Ephraim Russell, "The Societies of the Bardi and Peruzzi and Their Dealings with Edward III 1327–1345," in *Finance and Trade Under Edward III*, ed. George Unwin (New York: A. M. Kelley, 1965), 131; Hunt and Murray, *A History of Business in Medieval Europe*; Kelly, *Great Mortality*, 103; Gerd Mentgen, "Die Strassburger Juden Vivelin der Rote und Simon von Deneuvre. Bankiers europaïscher Fürsten im 14 Jahrhundert," in *Porträt einer europaïscher Kernregion*, eds. Franz Irsigler and Gisela Minn (Trier: Kliomedia, 2005); Reinert and Fredona, "Merchants," 23.

41. Ole J. Benedictow, "The Black Death: The Greatest Catastrophe Ever," *History Today* 55.3 (2005), http://www.historytoday.com/ole-j-benedictow/black-death-greatest-catastrophe-ever.
42. Jones, *The Plantagenets*, "The King's Tyranny"; Robert Mills, "Momento Mori," in *Medieval Folklore*, 267; Cave and Coulson, *A Source Book for Medieval Economic History*, 15, 56; Giovanni Boccaccio, "Day the First," *Decameron*, v. 1, https://www.gutenberg.org/files/23700/23700-h/23700-h.htm#Proem.
43. Jordan, *The Great Famine*, 137, 168, 175; Poston, *Cambridge Economic History of Europe*, 569.
44. Mollat and Wolff, *The Popular Revolutions of the Late Middle Ages*, 113; "Devenus plus riches, les hommes sont aussi devenus plus avides . . . . Grand cherté des vivre, des meubles, des marchandises et de la main-d'oeuvre." Jean de Venette, *Chronique Latine de Guillaume de Nangis* and the translated edition *The Chronicle of Jean de Venette*, Jean Birdsall, trans. and Richard A. Newhall, introd. and notes (New York: Columbia University Press, 1953).
45. Mollat and Wolff, *The Popular Revolutions of the Late Middle Ages*, 68–69, 123; Jehan le Bel, *Chronique de Jean de Bel* (c. 1370), 257, https://archive.org/stream/chroniquedejeand02lebeuoft#page/256/mode/2up.
46. Juliet Barker, *1381: The Year of the Peasants' Revolt* (Cambridge, MA: Harvard University Press, 2014), 10–15; Roger Wood, "Peasant Revolt," in *Medieval Folklore*, 317; Whittock, *Brief History*, 209, 257; Kelly, *Great Mortality*, 89; Fried, *The Middle Ages*, chap. 11; Erik Spindler, "Flemings in the Peasants' Revolt, 1381," in *Contact and Exchange in Later Medieval Europe: Essays in Honour of Malcolm Vale,* eds. Hannah Skoda, Patrick Lantschner, and R. L. J. Shaw (Woodbridge, UK: Boydell Press, 2012), 62; Jordan, *The Great Famine*, 165; Mollat and Wolff, *The Popular Revolutions of the Late Middle Ages*, 135, 167, 170–71; Postan, "England," in *Cambridge Economic History of Europe*, 608.
47. Guerson, "Coping with Crises," 18 28, 32, 33, 34, 35, 68, 94.
48. Alfonso X, *Siete partidas* (early fourteenth century), reprinted in Constable, *Medieval Iberia*, 399–400; Mark D. Meyerson, *A Jewish Renaissance in Fifteenth-Century Spain* (Princeton, NJ: Princeton University Press, 2004), 15; Miguel Angel Motis

Dolader, "The Socio-Economic Structure of the Jewish Aljamas in the Kingdom of Aragon, 1391–1492," in *The Jews of Spain and the Expulsion of 1492*, eds. Moshe Lazar and Stephen Haliczer (Lancaster, CA: Labyrinthos, 2008), 68, 72, 75, 82; Bas Van Bavel, *Manors and Markets: Economy and Society in the Low Countries 500–1600* (Oxford: OUP, 2010), 185–86; Evergates, *Feudal Society in Medieval France*, 86–87; Ferguson, *The Ascent of Money*, chap. 2; Sidney Homer and Richard Sylla, *A History of Interest Rates* (Hoboken NJ: John Wiley & Sons, 2007), chap. 6.

49. Norman Roth, "Coexistence and Confrontation: Jews and Christians in Medieval Spain," in *The Jews of Spain*, eds. Lazar and Haliczer, 12–13, 17; Guerson, "Coping with Crises," 13, 34, 47, 49, 50, 55–56, 60, 61, 63, 66; Dolader, "The Socio-Economic Structure of the Jewish *Aljamas*," 85–86, 88–90; Meyerson, *Jews in an Iberian Frontier Kingdom*, 9, and idem, *A Jewish Renaissance*, 18, 244; Lawrin Armstrong, Ivana Elbl, and Martin M. Elbl, eds. *Money, Markets, and Trade in Late Medieval Europe: Essays in Honour of John H. A. Munro* (Leiden: Brill, 2007), 133; Benjamin R. Gampel, *Anti-Jewish Riots in the Crown of Aragon and the Royal Response, 1391–1392* (New York: CUP, 2016), 93.
50. H. C. Lea, "Ferrand Martinez and the Massacres of 1391," *The American Historical Review* 1.2 (1896): 212–13; Norman Roth, "1391 In the Kingdom of Castile, Attacks on the Jews," 20–22, https://www.academia.edu/6733467/1391_IN_THE_KINGDOM_OF_CASTILE_ATTACKS_ON_THE_JEWS; Guerson, "Coping with Crises," 63, 78; Roth, "1391 In the Kingdom of Castile," 24; Meyerson, *A Jewish Renaissance*, 15.
51. Guerson, "Coping with Crises," 38, 104; Munro, "Rentes and the European 'Financial Revolution,'" 239; Mark D. Meyerson, *Jews in an Iberian Frontier Kingdom: Society, Economy, and Politics in Morvedre, 1248–1391* (Leiden: Brill, 2004), 208; idem, "Victims and Players: The Attack of the Union of Valencia on the Jews of Morvedre," in *Religion, Text, and Society in Medieval Spain and Northern Europe: Essays in Honor of J.N. Hillgarth*, eds. Thomas E. Burman, Mark D. Meyerson, and Leah Shopkow (Toronto: Pontifical Institute of Mediaeval Studies, 2002), 76; idem, *A Jewish Renaissance*, 25; Dolader, "The Socio-Economic Structure of the Jewish *Aljamas*," 67, 86, 88.
52. Lea, "Ferrand Martinez and the Massacres of 1391," 215–16; Roth, "Coexistence and Confrontation," 18 and "1391 In the Kingdom of Castile," 27, 33; Mollat and Wolff, *The Popular Revolutions of the Late Middle Ages*, 215.
53. Lea, "Ferrand Martinez and the Massacres of 1391," 216.
54. Mollat and Wolff, *The Popular Revolutions of the Late Middle Ages*, 219–20, 222.
55. Guerson, "Coping with Crises," 182, 197.
56. Roth, "1391 In the Kingdom of Castile," 25, 27, 29, 35–36; Nirenberg, *Anti-Judaism: The Western Tradition*, chap. 6; Dolader, "The Socio-Economic Structure of the Jewish *Aljamas*," 85.

57. Lea, "Ferrand Martinez and the Massacres of 1391," 217; Meyerson, *A Jewish Renaissance*, 23; S. W. Baron, *A Social and Religious History of the Jews: Late Middle Ages and Era of European Expansion, 1200–1650*, vol. 15 (New York: Columbia University Press, 1965), 105, 255–56.
58. Pryor, *Business Contracts of Medieval Provence*, 63, 67; Blancard, *Documents Inédits*, vol. II, 123, quoted in Cave and Coulson, *Sourcebook for Medieval Economic History*, 108; Juliette Sibon, "Bondavin revisité. Le prêteur juif de Marseille Bondavin de Draguignan (ca. 1285–1361), suite et fin," *Le Moyen Age* 3–4: CXVIII (2012): 648–52; Shatzmiller, *Cultural Exchange*, 141; Mell, "Religion and Economy," 198, 210.
59. Thelma S. Fenster and Daniel Lord Smail, eds. *Fama: The Politics of Talk and Reputation in Medieval Europe* (Ithaca: Cornell University Press, 2003); introduction; Sibon, "Bondavin," 644, 652–623. . ."bon dans sa loi (in sui lege bonum), vertureux, pacifique et tranquille, de bonne renommé et de bonne opinion."
60. "Ainsi la documentation économique revèle le clivage entre la norme qui vise à maintenir les juifs dans l'infériorité, et la pratique qui autorise des exceptions et des contournements. Ce clivage est le fruit de techniques de contact solides et efficacies avec le patriciat chrétien, parmi lesquelles le prêt intérêt est la moins attendée." Sibon, "Bondavin," 652.
61. Reinert and Fredona, "Merchants," 1–3; Wiesner-Hanks, *Early Modern Europe*, chaps. 1, 2, and 3.
62. Roover, *Money, Banking, and Credit in Mediaeval Bruges*, 151.

4 "In the Name of God and Profit"

Italy was at the heart of the new innovations and developments in pre-industrial capitalism. New accounting techniques were developed by Italians, and merchants often inscribed their account books with the words: "In the name of God and profit." The ideas of profiting off money and interest payments were changing the economy, just as law was replacing some forms of custom. The monied class in the rapidly growing towns bought land not for the "preservation of ancient customs" but for investment. It was hoped that the land would yield enough in an efficient manner to allow for a substantial profit. The ever-larger numbers of wage-earners kept coins circulating in ever-greater amounts. This was not a linear progression, however. As we saw in the previous chapter, plague, epidemics, famine, crop failure, extreme weather, and war devastated lives, land, and investment. Plunder on a large scale was commonplace when the opportunity arose. But the expansion of sea trade, with better, more regular, faster, and safer voyages, linked the lucrative Mediterranean trade to north-western Europe, avoiding the dangers of overland travel.[1]

According to Raymond de Roover, foreign trade in Western Europe was basically a monopoly of the Italians from the thirteenth until the sixteenth century, whether Venetians, Genoese, Lucchese, Florentines, or Milanese. Before their collapse, Italian bankers such as the Bardi, Peruzzi, and the Acciaiuoli had set up banking houses in European cities outside of Italy, such as Bruges, to deal with high-level international trade. The city of Bruges was conveniently located for commerce and trade between the Mediterrean and the Baltic. The cloth trade paid for investment in metals (copper, tin, and iron) as well as salt mines. Mines were dug deeper with new machinery and the metal was processed with smelting techniques that increased the quality and quantity. Much of the finished metal was used for weaponry and armour. To create and maintain these innovations, credit was essential. Increasingly, merchants stopped visiting fairs to conduct business and instead made their transactions from their banks, with the aid of partners, factors able to travel to other countries, and correspondents in other lands.[2]

Despite widespead association of Jews and moneylending of all types, it was not always the case. In the Rhineland, the pawnbroking trade was considered *lombardarien*, or lombardian, a word synonymous with the trade, and *un lombard* was a pawnshop. As moneylenders, the Italians lent at high rates of interest, using their own money, and forming business partnerships with family relations. From time to time, they took deposits to increase their working capital, despite a canon law prohibiting deposits with a usurious moneylender. As with every merchant moneylender, privileges were given in exchange for their commercial activities. For example, the Italians might ask for protection against arrest or appropriation of property, or demand a fixed rate of taxes and dues, freedom of movement without molestation, and a favorable regulation of weights and measures. In this, there was little difference between charters made with Jews and with Italian merchant bankers. Likewise, not all Lombard moneylenders were wealthy. Most earned a modest living, some were poor, and some extremely rich, although even the very wealthy could have it all taken away by a capricious ruler or by an economic disaster.[3]

As elsewhere in Western Europe, the Italian moneylenders disguised their usurious loans, dealing with bills of exchange into which the profit could be written but concealed. It was still considered usury to take anything above the principal on a mutuum, or straight loan. Cambium contracts were not considered usurious as they were exchange transactions. Cardinal Cajetan (1469–1534), an Italian Dominican, wrote a treatise defending the use of cambium contracts in 1506, which helped to "lift the barriers that still opposed the march of capitalism." Attempting to defend some aspect of the profit side of the moneylending business, that in previous times would have been condemned as usury, Cajetan placed the emphasis on intention. In a convoluted manner, he explained that someone hoping to gain something above and beyond his capital is a "mental usurer" and therefore has committed the sinful "depravity of usury." If, however, someone makes a loan with a "feeling of benevolence" he is hoping for nothing illicitly and cannot be considered a usurer. The cracks in the theological arguments against usury had been appearing since the eleventh century but, with commerce and capital so important, theologians such as Cajetan were taking another step towards acceptance of interest payments, even if he still spoke in terms of absolute values and just prices. In truth, there was no such thing as absolute value and just prices. Money and objects were only worth what someone was willing to give someone else for them.[4]

What Cajetan did condemn outrightly as usury were dry and fictitious exchanges. Many straight loans or mutuum transactions had their interest payment hidden in fictitious exchange contracts where no goods actually changed hands. It was not difficult to disguise an interest loan with a cambium contract, what was called a dry exchange as there was not real payments. With the assistance of agents abroad, a fake contract was drawn up but no bills of exchange were sent. Or the rate of return could be fixed beforehand and not dependent on market rates that entailed a speculative risk. It was not only theologians who denounced these dry exchanges; they were not acccepted by those merchants who argued that they went against the market forces of supply and demand and were, in nature, unethical.[5]

By the fifteenth century, concealing usury was no longer as big an issue as in previous centuries and the pretence was dropped that interest did not exist. Phrases such as "without cost, without usuries or without any evil covenants" that had been commonplace in contracts in the thirteenth century were now absent, even if usury was still not candidly discussed or wholehearedly accepted. In the early part of the century, municipal licenses in Bruges allowed the Lombards to lend money for a profit of 2d a pound per week maximum without incurring a fine by the authorities. Restrictions only served to make borrowing expensive and to prevent the free flow of capital but it was another move towards accepting interest rates, which incentivized the lending of capital. Also dispensed with was community punishment. It had been commonplace in the medieval period to punish the family or community of a moneylender was convicted of a crime. It was now legislated that if a Lombard was convicted then only the individual perpetrator would be punished.[6]

As was the case for most moneylenders, Lombards in Bruges were socially ostracized because of their profession, which still carried the taint of immorality. Even other Italians did not associate with them. Interest loans may have become an entrenched part of economic life, but not many borrowers, especially those with the most to lose, admired or liked the moneylender. The idea that they were involved in a profession that was based on greed, however erroneous a description, was hard to erase. Like Jewish moneylenders, the Lombards were accused of extorting the poor and needy, or hounding people to their deaths or forcing them into crime in ordert to pay back their loans. In the Italian cities, this conflict between economic reality and the official and popular distaste for usury put friars and civic authorities at odds.

* * *

The merchants and moneylenders—Christian and Jew—who conducted business at such places as the Rialto in Venice that the fictional moneylender Shylock frequented, were vital for the nation's economic health. On the Rialto, merchants, investors, speculators, bankers, agents, brokers, and moneychangers rubbed shoulders amid tourists, criminals, and the idle. Risks were high. Ships ferrying goods and bullion across the vast European seas were at the mercy of pirates and turbulent waters and the sinking of a ship carrying precious cargo could mean the financial ruin of many an investor. Velvet and silks, satins and damasks, as well as spices (ginger and pepper) and sugar, filled the ships that crowded the Italian ports and then set sail with their precious cargo, their crews praying for safe passage. This danger was lessened by the development of marine insurance and the growth in popularity of partnerships that shared the both the risks and rewards.[7]

The Mediterranean was the site for local and long-distance trade since the fourteenth century, with the greatest flow of capital, and largest source of wealth creation. Venice was renowned for its commerce in Asian spices, and shipbuilding, Milan for its shoemakers, weavers, and other tradesmen, while Genoa dominated the Aegean and Black Sea trade. Professionals of a middling status—including merchants, clerks, lawyers, teachers, moneychangers, magistrates, notaries, and moneylenders—made up a greater percentage of the population than in other countries. By the fifteenth century, Italy was the most innovative region for finance, especially in the realm of public debt and the early beginnings of corporations. Genoa was the site of the oldest chartered European bank, the Casa di San Giorgio (founded in 1407), which consolidated the public debt and issued shares (*luoghi*) which could be freely traded. Centuries later, the French philosopher Montesquieu wrote admiringly that the bank gave the people "a certain influence in the government" which bestowed upon them greater prosperity. In other cities, too, public loans made the interests of the people accord with those of the state to their mutual economic wellbeing.[8]

By the early fifteenth century, borrowed money made up almost 70 percent of Florence's income. Commerce and trade were of vital importance not only in Florence but throughout northern Italy. Venice was the first place in Italy to fund its wars by public debt. Many loans in Italy were obligatory, and interest on forced loans were not considered usury but compensation. The *prestiti* in Venice was a forced loan introduced in the twelfth century to fund the Republic's war against the Byzantine Empire. It was meant to be temporary but, in the following century, it was incorporated into a permanent fund called the *monte vecchio*. Wealthy citizens were obliged to buy these long-term loans, which yielded 5 percent annually, although the investor had the ability to sell off these bonds to other investors.[9]

By the fourteenth century, Italian states had a relatively advanced money market and its lower interest rates vis-à vis the other parts of Western Europe had more to do with this developed capital market than diminished risk. In the Tuscan city of Florence, the Duomo's towering 150-foot dome constructed by Filippo Brunelleschi dominated the skyline. The city's medieval dark alleyways that led to piazzas and courtyards were demolished to construct broader, sun-soaked streets built around large public squares edged with colonnades. Market places were packed with traders selling their vast array of goods, from meat, fish, and vegetables to the exotic wares brought to Italy on ships from North Africa, Asia, and other parts of Europe. One citizen bragged of the city's prosperity and its "well-clothed and large population" although Florence, like other cities, had its fair share of crooks, drunks, prostitutes, and gamblers. It was also plagued with political intrigue, famines, epidemics, wars, civil unrest, and religious division.[10]

By the late fifteenth century, Florence was well established as the European center of banking and commerce. with seventy international banks based there, a figure lower than in 1338, before the Black Death, when the number of banks was estimated to be ten more. Private banks were founded by the most prestigious of Florentine families, including the Medici, who made their fortune from foreign exchange and were members of the moneychangers' guild before becoming bankers sitting at benches near the Calvalcanti palace near the Florentine wool market. They also spent much time, when not involved in political intrigues, trying to avoid the charge of usury by handsomely donating to the Church. By 1452, the Medici, had ventured further than Florence and had bank branches in Rome, Venice, Pisa, Milan, and Ancona in Italy as well as Bruges, Geneva, London, and Avignon. These banks provided money changing, deposit services, and foreign transactions, proffering capital for wars, exploration, and business deals at every level.[11]

Early in the fifteenth century, Pope Innocent VII pledged his jeweled mitre to Giovanni di Bicci de' Medici against a massive loan. It was eventually reclaimed by Pope Gregory XII for 12,000 florins which Gregory had to borrow from elsewhere. Pope Paul II borrowed to buy jewels and art while Queen Isabella pawned a ruby and pearl necklace for cash. Paintings of the Madonna and Child, a favorite subject of court artists, were framed in gold and hung in the homes of the patrons not only out of devotion but as a sign that holiness will bring material prosperity. It was a far cry from standing on one leg atop a pillar in the desert to achieve godliness.[12]

* * *

It has been claimed that banking and commerce "formed the backbone" of Jewish economic life in Italy and there certainly were wealthy Jewish bankers and Jewish merchants, who were responsible for, among other things, collecting and paying taxes to the city governments. But most Jews were not professional moneylenders and often lent money in conjunction with another occupation. The series of wars with the Ottoman Empire throughout the fifteenth and sixteenth centuries demanded large amounts of credit but there were many Italian bankers who could provide these large loans. Prosperous Italian states, though, attracted significant numbers of Sephardic Jews from Spain and Portugal, as well as *conversos*. This flow of migrants multiplied after the order of expulsion issued by Spain's King Ferdinand and Queen Isabella to the country's Jewish communities in 1492. Once on Italian soil, some reverted to Judaism, some continued life as a Christian, and others chose to live as both Jew and Christian, choosing whichever identity suited or benefited them in any given situation.[13]

In the Italian countryside, rural debt was high. Capital from moneylenders kept many peasants in their homes and on their land but debt also left others with nothing. It was to lend money to the poorer people in society that civil authorities all over Italy invited Jewish moneylenders into their towns in return for the type of privileges all moneylenders required. Jewish moneylenders opened small-scale private loan banks once they had obtained a charter (*condotta*) from the town authorities. The details of the charter were first decided by the town's authorities, then agreed to or negotiated by the Jewish bankers, and, finally, endorsed by the papal legate or the governor of the region. The likelihood of a moneylender's request to settle in a town depended upon how urgently credit was needed. When in 1456 a famine devastated the Umbrian town of Terni, home of St. Valentine, the local authorities were in desperate need of more moneylenders and eagerly accepted offers from Jewish bankers. After all the agreements were settled, the amount of capital required to open the bank was set by the authorities and then the Jewish moneylender went about his business of lending money at the approved rate of interest, often receiving pawns for security.[14]

Competition for charters in prosperous cities such as Florence and Venice was stiff and some Jews agreed to lower their rates to 5 percent in exchange for the right to reside or remain in these cities. Throughout the fifteenth and sixteenth centuries, fixed-term charters were issued and renewed to allow Jews to lend money in Venice. Terms varied but, in exchange for the ability to provide loans, an annual payment was assessed, and the annual interest rate was set, depending on whether it was a loan with pledges or without. The renewals were not without debate. In 1548, one proposal denounced usury by Jews as something that "consumed and devoured the populace and the poor of this city." As in the rural regions, most cities like Venice and smaller towns invited Jewish bankers solely to provide their services to the poorer members of the community, at these lower rates of interest. This prompted one of Venice's most prominent rabbis, Simone Luzzatto (1583–1663), to claim that it was these low interest rates that encouraged the "peaceful and docile" attitude of the Christian population toward the Jews. If usury made Jews unpopular elsewhere, he wrote, that was not the case in the city of gondolas. Luzzatto concluded that this type of usury helped the poor and was not for the "profit of the bankers." It was not always as genial as Luzzatto imagined as the above quote suggests. In contracts between the town's moneylender and peasants, where the still-concealed interest rate was relatively high for buying crops in advance, the peasant's risk was greater. The most common reason for a peasant selling his land was debt.[15]

As was usual with charters, the privileges that came with them extended not only to individual moneylenders but to all the Jews who were allowed to settle with them. Charters were jealously guarded by Jewish communities and rabbis threatened excommunication for any Jew who tried to infringe on the loan franchise of another Jew. Privileges differed from town to town and charter to charter but usually they included citizenship, equal legal rights under civil and criminal law, the right to slaughter their animals according to Jewish law, the ability to buy land for burial use, exemption from military duties, taxes and tithes (such as the family tax, *gabella de capo et fumo,* or the military service and equipment tax, *gabella della guardia et del fare hoste e cavalcata*), the right to sell pledges that were not redeemed after a year, and the ability to bear arms. Often included in a charter were the prohibition of trading in sacred Christian objects, exporting pawns from the city, and the requirement that Jews stay in their homes from Good Friday through Easter Sunday. Similarly, Jews requested that Christians be forbidden to harass or injure any Jew, especially during the period of Holy Week. This appeal was generally granted as it was in the town's interest to prevent any public disorder or rioting. In addition, Jewish lenders were usually not required to make loans on their Sabbath or holidays and there was no limit on loans to "foreigners" (those from outside the town), so long as capital intended for the local citizens was not used. Finally, Jews often asked for exemption from wearing an identifying badge, which had been stipulated by the Lateran Council of 1215 for all Jewish males over the age of seven on pain of a fine. Again, the exemption was often granted, much to the annoyance of the more zealous friars who pressed local rulers to implement the badge regulation so that it was easy to tell Christians and Jews apart.[16]

Like the merchants in guilds or Christian moneylenders who tried to squash competition, it was commonplace for Jewish bankers to ask for the privilege of a monopoly to keep other moneylenders at bay. In Todi, Consiglio signed a charter with a clause that no other Jewish banker was allowed to conduct business in the town without his consent, although eventually he did permit another Jewish moneylender to open a bank in Todi. But the decision was his to make. It was clearly in the moneylender's interest to restrict the number of bankers in a town as creditors vying for business generally resulted in lower interest rates for borrowers. For the moneylender, a monopoly meant that his interest rate was curbed only by the town's authorities and not by free competition.[17]

Not only did Jewish bankers negotiate for better conditions and rights, they had recourse to a variety of actions to get their demands met or object to unpopular restrictions. Most effective was the same threat used by the large-scale merchant bankers; that is, for Jewish moneylenders to withdraw their banking services and move to another town. This was particularly successful if a town was finding it hard to attract other bankers. In the hilly Umbrian town of Spoleto, Elia's family was granted a charter that expired in 1436. He requested that it be renewed basing his appeal on the hardships his family had experienced following the recent pillaging of the town. He pleaded that due to poverty, the entire family was forced to move to nearby Trevi. Now, Elia begged to return to Spoleto, his family's native land, and to resume moneylending there. Whether his words were flattery to gain a beneficial charter or a heartfelt plea of homesickness, they were effective, and his request was approved by the general council.[18]

The banker Consiglio, who lived and worked in the commune of Gubbio, was denied a renewal of his charter due to his apparent refusal to make loans to the poor. As most Jews were initially invited to settle for precisely the purpose of small-scale lending to those with little money, it is not surprising that his failure to do so resulted in his dismissal. Fortunately for Consiglio, the town had no success in finding a replacement and the Duke of Urbino, Federico of Montefeltro, had little choice but to extend the charter to him for another year.[19]

In return for the charter with all its privileges, Jews had to pay business taxes to the city proportional to the capital invested in the banks. In 1449, the Jews in Città di Castello, in northern Umbria, agreed to invest 2000 florin in the bank to meet the needs of the town's populace. The annual tax was set at sixty florin which was to be paid on the feast day of Florido, the town's saint. Leading members of the Jewish community gathered in the synagogue to discuss the allocation of taxes, electing one of them to collect the monies from every Jew. It was a duty that was a potential source of antagonism. In 1461, Pius II ordered a *vigesima* tax for the war against the Turks and levied 2000 gold ducats on the Jewish community of Umbria. When a banker by the name of Manuele was told of the amount the leaders of the Universitas Judeorum of Perugia had apportioned to him, he strenuously objected. He carried on a prolonged but, in the end, futile protest.[20]

Jews requested to be exempted from the military, but like all citizens, they had to contribute to the city's defense as well as some religious feasts. In the mid-fifteenth century, the Jews of Norcia paid 100 florins for military purposes and in Terni it was decided that Jewish bankers would fund the mid-summer feast of the Assumption in exchange for granting them a monopoly on moneylending in the town. Military taxation also brought in business. As it extended to all of the population, this meant more loans were needed from Jewish moneylenders. In Foligno, the Apostolic Chamber levied a tax on its citizens for the fleet Pope Calixtus III intended to construct to assist in the ongoing war against the Turks. With much of the populace lacking the funds to pay this tax, many were forced to turn to Jewish moneylenders in order to pay their share. Such onerous taxation not only led to resentment against the pope or the local ruler for high taxation but also against the Jews who profited off the loans they had to assume.[21]

The active financial scene in fifteenth-century Italy brought together Jews and Christians in a multitude of ways. In 1436, the prior of Assisi decided to purchase a gift to placate Francesco Sforza, whose mercenaries were devastating the region. He turned to the local Jewish banker Manuele and borrowed 100 florins in papal currency, guaranteed by fifteen of Assisi's wealthiest citizens. And when the Convent of S. Chiara of Spello had insufficient funds to redeem pawns at the bank of Magister Gaio, the abbess and nuns sold a parcel of land to the prior of the church of S. Lorenzo to raise the necessary payment. A bronze mortar and iron pestle from the town's church of San Andrea was pawned to the same

Jewish moneylender and redeemed by the friars after payment. In need of cash, the citizens of Todi pawned the town bell to a Jewish banker while the priors of Perugia used Jewish bankers for their loans of gold florins when required. In Spoleto, the priors bought silver from Isacco and Ventura. The silver was intended as a gift to Pope Nicholas V, the scholary Humanist pope who collected Classic and Christian texts for the Vatican library.[22]

Despite negotiated contracts, inevitably there were times when moneylending transactions and pawnbroking ended up in court. Usually, borrowers insisted they had paid back a loan while creditors vehemently swore it was unpaid. Jews had the same access to the courts when they were in dispute with a Christian. Pope Callixtus III ordered the treasurer of Perugia to return the property of a Jew that was taken illegally. Also in Perugia, two residents who pretended to redeem an expensive embroidered garment and, instead, beat Mosè the pawnbroker and stole his goods, were given the death penalty by default. Some cases spilled over to affect the entire community. In Spello, Constanzo neglected to repay a loan to Ventura (both were Jewish), prompting Ventura to claim that, without repayment, he was unable to pay his real estate taxes to the commune. With their financial interests at stake, the authorities arrested Constanzo and forced him to pay the taxes Ventura owed to the city. In another case, a Jewish moneylender named Abramo showed a fellow Jewish banker Giacobbe a case filled with sparkling jewels. After obtaining a 100-florin loan from Giacobbe, Abramo left the case as security. When Giacobbe went to check the case later, he found it filled with nothing but scrap iron. Found guilty of switching the cases, Abramo was fined 240 florins, the penalty of which if unpaid was the amputation of his right hand.[23]

Jewish bankers were eager to renew their contracts as moneylending, which goes against the often cited comment that Jews were forced into moneylending. In the winter of 1441, the Jewish banker Ventura asked for permission to lend money in Spoleto with the usual conditions. The priors of the town gave their consent and offered Ventura a charter for twenty years with an interest rate at three and a half soldi per month per florin, which worked out to be the hefty, but not unusual, sum of 42 percent per year. The interest rate allowed in some towns was even higher which meant sizeable profits so long as repayment was not only made but prompt. In 1453, a charter was signed between the General Council of Amelia and Manuele, Salomone, his son, and Benedetto, who were allowed to charge the extremely high interest rate of 60 percent. From his moneylending profits, Salomone in Perugia was able to buy a turreted palazzo, which his heir sold for the substantial sum of 800 gold florins. The buyers were two other Jewish bankers from the town, Consiglio and Guglielmo.[24]

Naturally, most complaints about moneylenders concerned these high rates of interest. The rate was set at the time the charter was issued but, as in other countries, if hard times befell a city or town due to famine, crop failure, disease, or political mismanagement, the rate was altered in an effort to alleviate suffering and ease repayment. In 1447, the commune of Perugia reduced the interest rate to two soldi per florin per month—about 24 percent—and banned the export of pawns. In Assisi, the priors instructed Jewish moneylenders to air clothes left as pledges to avoid their deterioration and therefore their financial depreciation by the time the debtor returned to redeem them.[25]

Italy was coming to terms with usury. Yet, there was always those who adhered to what they believed to be a more "moral economy."

Friars denounced usury not only as robbery but as a moral outrage and pressured the papacy to excommunicate towns that allowed it. In the mid-fifteenth century, Friar Cherubino of Spoleto, the author of *Fior di Virtu* (Flower of Virtue), traveled to Assisi to preach against usury and Friar Nicola, also of Spoleto, condemned the town of Terni for charters the authorities signed with Jewish moneylenders. In April, 1462, Friar Michele Carcano of Milan threatened the entire town of Perugia with excommunication if they did not rid themselves of Jewish bankers practicing their accursed usury. Fearful of such a punishment being carried out, the Council of the Priors of Perugia agreed to revoke the loan charter awarded to the Jews. It was only temporary, however, as six years later, Friar Fortunato Coppoli assailed the Jewish banks in the town, which he blamed for the poverty of the population and the recurrent economic crises that struck them. By welcoming moneylenders, Coppoli declared, Perugia's rulers had become the accomplices of the bankers and therefore guilty of a mortal sin.[26]

The medieval economist and Observant Franciscan Bernardino of Siena proposed that prices should be set by the community rather than the individual—either by the authorities for the common good (the legal price) or by the market price which was accepted by the producer (the natural price). Bernardino condemned deceptive business practices—misrepresentation and monopolies—as well as clerical involvement in trade but he also believed "the rich" to be "necessary to the State" and "the poor [to be necessary] to the rich." Usury, which he defined as making an "excessive" profit off banking, was one of the worst and most sinful practices. In his *Tractatus de contractibus et usuris* Bernardino argued that moneylenders did not produce anything useful nor did they do any good to anyone else. He warned that usury concentrated all the wealth into the hands of a small number of people and this was especially dangerous if those few were Jews. To allow this to occur, "the natural warmth of the city . . . is not flowing back to the heart to give it assistance but instead rushes to an abscess in a deadly hemorrhage, since all Jews, especially those who are moneylenders, are the chief enemies of all Christians." His public audience was, according to his contemporary Humanist critic Poggio Bracciolini, unresponsive to the message. Poggio denounced Bernardino for hypocrisy as he did not condemn the root of usury, which was avarice. There was nothing wrong, in Poggio's mind, with money or the desire for gain, but avarice was the source of evil and had not place in the Church. As for the Franciscan's fiery public speeches, people were more inclined "to laugh at than to detest such a great crime [as usury]." After listening to a sermon by Bernardino, the crowd listened intently to his words but, as soon as he departed, they went back to "cards, dice, false hair, rouge pots and . . . even to chess boards." In the face of such indifference, the friars persisted; they remained convinced that for the common good, the banishment of Jewish moneylenders was vital.[27]

If anti-usury friars were successful in their quest, and charters were annulled, the papacy or local governor retained the power to intervene and reverse the action, reinstating Jewish bankers and their charters. In 1449, charters with Jewish moneylenders in Assisi were no longer approved. Within a short period, a series of catastrophes befell the town, natural disasters as well as the sacking of the city, which added to the town's financial woes. In the face of economic ruin, the priors of the town lamented the absence of a bank. Poorer citizens and peasants were forced to take expensive trips to other communes, some far from Assisi, in order to pawn their pledges. To ease the crisis, the priors decided to risk excommunication and reinstated a Jewish loan bank. In addition, Pope Paul II declared the annulment of charters in Assisi illegal and demanded that the rulers abide by the terms made with Jewish moneylenders until their negotiated expiration.[28]

In 1463, the priors of Trevi also reviewed their loan charter with Jews after the preaching of the Franciscan Agostino of Perugia had either persuaded them of the wrongs of usury or put the fear of God into them. They decided to annul the charter signed with the banker Isacco. A year later, they changed their minds, restoring the charter rights to Isacco and other Jewish moneylenders but with additional conditions. Citizens were restricted in the amount they could borrow—no more than four or five florins at one time—and Jews were obliged to wear the yellow O on their clothes that identified them at all times.[29]

In Terni, the threat of excommunication led not to the annulment of charters but to the granting of them. Economic trouble left the town's government owing money to the bishop and to some Roman merchants. With the pope threatening to excommunicate Terni's entire population if it did not bring its financial affairs into order, one councilor proposed that Jews be allowed to lend at interest once more. After numerous negotiations, a charter was eventually approved by the town's authorities and accepted by the Jewish bankers Dattilo and Mosè. Interest rates were set at 30 percent for citizens and 40 percent for foreigners while the moneylenders agreed to pay a yearly commune tax of forty ducats. It was also in Terni that the physician-turned-banker Manuele had his contract terminated by the commune thanks to the incitement of friars. It was only with the intervention of Pope Sixtus IV that he was allowed to retain his banking services.[30]

In some case, not even papal intervention was effective against the agitation by friars. In response to the cessation of Jewish moneylending in Perugia, the bankers Salomone, Elia, and David received a letter from Pope Pius II affirming their banking privileges. But, while ratifying their privileges, the town priors yielded to the demands of the friars and denied them the right to add interest to the loans. Without the possibility of profit, Elia gave up on banking and, instead, formed a partnership with a Christian in a tailoring business. In nearby Cascia, the commune was so worried about the threat of excommunication, they sent an envoy to Perugia to ask the famous jurist Benedetto dei Benedetti (Il Capra) if they could legally sign a charter with a Jewish banker without risking the eternal damnation of their souls.[31]

The Observant Franciscan Bernardino da Feltre appeared in Italian towns and cities railing against "Jewish usurers [who] bleed the poor to death and grow fat on their substance" and scolded Christians for being involved with them. In March 1488, Bernardino delivered the Lenten sermons at the local basilica in Florence. His inflammable words stirred up a gang of Florentine street boys, the *fanciulli*, who sought revenge against the "bloodsucking" moneylenders, although it did not take much to rouse these boys into causing trouble. They spent much of their time producing disorder, rioting, assaulting women, and stone-throwing during the Carnival (*Carnevale*). The "stupid and brutal game" of stone-throwing around Eastertime was denounced by the writer Jacopo Nardi. Stoning was so common an abuse that it was not only carried out by Christians against Jews over Easter (with Jews sometimes paying the local authorities for protection). It was an activity that was widespread and found within the Jewish community as well. In one case, fines were imposed on Manuele of Assisi and one of his brothers for throwing stones at his neighbor Dattilo's house and injuring him.[32]

The *fanciulli* started by looting a Jewish pawnshop. Then, perhaps galvanized by Bernardino's words and energized by the thought of bloodlust or joining in the riot for their perverse amusement, they made their way to the house of Manullino, a Jewish moneylender. His house stood on the Vacca, a street that ran between the archbishop's residence and the Jewish ghetto. Before the boys could do their worst, the town's authorities sent out guards to prevent any bloodshed or looting. Proclamations followed, warning those who participated in public disorder and violence that they faced the gallows. For his part in inciting the mob, Bernardino was arrested and sent to a monastery in San Miniato, and then banished completely from Florence.

It was, ironically, in Florence, the banking center of Europe, that an Italian city briefly turned the utopian dream of these anti-usury friars into reality. At the end of the fifteenth century, a self-proclaimed prophet began his ascent to power in Florence, basing his political platform on the common good and the establishment of the New Jerusalem. Girolamo Savonarola, the son of a merchant and moneychanger from Ferraro, turned his back on the material world and set out to make the Tuscan city a moral beacon. After a series of bad harvests, a famine left the poor starving in the streets and ensuing plagues decimated even more lives. The time was opportune for reform and renewal. But for this New Jerusalem to appear, usury and conspicuous wealth had to be erased from society.[33]

In 1491, this Dominican friar at San Marco gave a series of Lenten sermons which focused on usury, corrupt financial dealing, the greed of the wealthy, and the admiration of the rich for their money. He publicly denounced those who filled their houses with luxuries, ornaments, pictures, and "evil books" and rallied his followers to throw such vanities onto bonfires. With apocalyptic imagery, perhaps colored by the mystical literature of Joachim of Fiore, he brought his audience to tears as he chastised those who burdened the poor with heavy taxation and interest. Echoing Jesus' condemnation of moneylenders in the Temple, the friar reviled priests and laymen for turning God's house into "a den of thieves." Virtue came from working for the common good, not from pursuing self-interest.

Five years after Fra Bernardino's banishment for his part in the anti-usury riot, Piero di Medici (Piero the Unfortunate, son of Lorenzo) reversed the expulsion. Bernardino was allowed back to Florence as part of his own intricate political maneuverings. It was not long, however, before the fall of the House of Medici to a man who despised everything they represented.[34]

By 1494, Savonarola's followers had wrested power from the Medicis who were expelled from Florence. The fall of the Medicis, which included the confiscation of their property, brought with it the long-held desire of the anti-usury faction: the expulsion of the Jews from Florence. The republic that Savonarola envisioned was one built on what one of Italy's most famous political theorists characterized as detrimental to a powerful state. Niccolò Machiavelli, was twenty-five-years-old when Savonarola took power, and, in his assessment, that destructive characteristic was charity. But one thing that he could agree with Savonarola on, and also with his contemporary, Polydore Vergil, was that wealth was destructive for princes and kings. He described avarice as "he who desires to possess by robbery." A master of propaganda, Savonarola utilized a new invention—the printing press—and disseminated his sermons and treatises. Using the words of Revelation, he rebuked Rome as a harlot and as a corrupt seat of power, the evils of which had infiltrated Italian cities. He struck out at the "great masters" (the rich and powerful) who drank "the blood of the poor" and infected society with their extravagance. To exist in his world, they would have to repent.[35]

Savonarola's utopian republic was soon a tyranny. His critics joked that he wanted to turn Florence into a monastery. They were not far wrong, but it was an austere and draconian monastery driven by fear and social division. Savonarola's religious passion, or mania, split the clergy with one monk offering to strangle him with his own hands. His emotional rhetoric and harsh policies also put him at odds with many in the ruling classes, the wealthy merchants who saw him as a threat, a number of influential clerics (especially the Jesuits), eventually the papacy, and, of course, the moneylenders that he cursed.

To both Jewish and Christian critics, the denunciation of wealth and the pursuit of profit were contrary to the republic's interests as well as to those of the individual. In the end, Savonarola's enemies were victorious and the "moral" republic failed. Pope Alexander VI excommunicated Savonarola in 1497 and, in May the following year, alongside two of his fellow Dominicans, the friar was charged with heresy and "stirring up discord in Florence." On the morning of May 23, 1498, the three friars, clad in thin white garments having been stripped of their Dominican robes, were hanged on the gallows and their bodies burned to ashes to deter devout or macabre relic hunters. The ashes were then thrown from the Ponte Vecchio into the River Arno. The New Jerusalem had lasted a mere four years.[36]

Savonarola's execution did not extinguish his message, including his rebuke of the Jews as being "distinguished for avarice." It was the poverty of Christ that transformed the world and freed people from the "solicitude about earthly gains and from the least taint of avarice." In his radical idealistic philosophy, Savonarola was an implacable enemy of the market economy world which was by his definition antithetical to the common good of society.[37]

Usury was an evil in the minds of many friars, but a growing number of them had accepted that it was a necessary evil. For some time, the Church had redefined usury to mean "excessive" interest rather than all interest. With that shift, the solution to Jewish usury was simply to establish a public Christian loan bank. The monte di pietà, as the bank was known, solved two critical issues. It rendered Jewish bankers obsolete by handing the control and profit over financial transactions to Christians and it answered the needs of the poor by offering them low-interest loans.[38]

Friars and others who had spent years preaching against Jewish moneylending and usury now put all their effort into the opening of Christian loan banks. To aid their success, fines were suggested for any prior or officer of the monte who, at the instigation of any Jew or other citizen, endangered its existence. At the Santo Spirito church in Ferrara, Fra Giacomo Ongarelli of Padua, a disciple of Bernardino, promised a dreadful death for any person who rejected the monte di pietà for Jewish moneylenders "thanks to the justice of God." In Perugia, under threat of excommunication, the town's authorities decided to replace the Jewish loan bank charters with a monte di pietà. In Savonarola's Florentine republic, a monte di pieta opened during the summer of 1496 offering loans at rates far lower than private banks, curtailing the need for Jewish usurers. With an alternative to the Jewish moneylenders in place, preachers demanded that Jewish moneylenders be driven out of all Italian towns. Children, Bernardino commanded, should pray three Paternosters and three Ave Marias for the Jews to be expelled.[39]

These sentiments were echoed in the demand made by Fra Marco di Matteo Strozzi, the rector of the small Florentine town of San Miniato, who called the Jews the "enemies of the cross of Christ . . . with their old synagogue, their rites, and their usury." Strozzi supported the monti over what he labeled immoral and extortionate Jewish usury and recommended that all small loans to the poor be transferred into the hands of the monti and the Jews pushed out. In Pisa, it was suggested that the removal of Jews from the city would rid it of the "evil effects" of usury.[40]

A monte di pietà in every major town and city was considered the best solution to the problem of usury and what Cosimo de' Medici the younger, Grand Duke of Tuscany (1519–1574), claimed was the consumption of the poor "by the inordinate usury of the Jews . . ." Since ancient times, the idea of moneylenders as devouring, consuming, and feasting upon the poor were striking images that continued to be effectively evoked by their opponents. Yet, Cosimo had once been eager to entice capital-rich Portuguese *converso* bankers to Florence, such as Dona Gracia from the House of Mendes, and to take full advantage of their services.[41]

Despite the urgent demand of the friars to create these public banks, it was neither an easy nor an inexpensive task. Perugia found it difficult to raise the 3000 florins needed to set up a monte. In the end, the Jews lent the town 1,200 florins and with this money the governor and the papal legate returned to the Jews all their previous privileges, except for one. They still could not practice usury. Their loan, in effect, robbed them of their occupation. Despite the costs involved, over the fifteenth and sixteenth centuries these low-interest Christian loan banks sprung up all across Italy.[42]

For Jewish moneylenders, the monti meant the destruction of loan charters and privileges in Italy and some began to shift into other areas of commerce, as in the case of Elia who gave up banking for tailoring. Some received a charter to trade rags and old clothing, joining the old clothing guild. In Spoleto, Guiseppe monopolized the rag trade in 1477 while Abramo had exclusive rights to collect and buy rags in Trevi which he then sold at the market of Santa Maria delle Lacrime on the first Sunday of every month.

The disruption caused to Jewish moneylenders in Italy by the monti led to other, equally fruitful careers. The Soncino family began their life in Italy as moneylenders protected by the powerful Duke of Milan and Francesco Sforza. When a monte di pietà was established in Soncino, Israel Nathan Soncino abandoned moneylending and turned to the up-and-coming business of printing. He established a Hebrew press which continued in family hands for several hundreds of years. It was Gerson Soncino who published an edition of Pindar's *Trojan War* that contained a poem by the Renaissance poet and dramatist, Battista Guarini (1538–1612). The verse took as its topic the age-long idea of the sterility of money and the Jews' association with usury:

> Why does the Hebrew wear the fourth vowel on his breast?
> Caecilianus was wont to be asked by many.
> He thought, that, condemned to eternal torment,
> The Hebrew bears it as a sign of his grief;
> Or perhaps this vowel is used as a Zero
> Indicating his nonentity among men.
> Or since Jews get rich through usury
> It indicates how they get much out of nothing.

There have been claims that the printing of this poem was a forced decision, although there is scant evidence for this. Gerson had a history of publishing non-Hebrew works, including Catholic material. It may be the case that this poem was not as offensive to Gerson Soncino and other Jews as it appears to historians many centuries later.[43]

It was still possible for a Jewish moneylender to offer an even lower interest rate than the monti or to deal solely with other Jews. But these charitable banks cut off a large portion of the market for many Jewish moneylenders and they did so with state subsidies. Jewish bankers did have one advantage: they were not interested in whether the loan was for rent payment, food, whores, or gambling, whereas the monti, on the other hand, made lending an extension of the preacher's sermon against avarice and sin. They forbade loans to be used for what they considered to be immoral purposes, although this was a difficult, if not impossible, policy to implement. Even so, with the establishment of the monti, there was less need for Jewish capital and, if Jews wanted to stay in the loan business, they would have to compete not only with individual private bankers but also with the new, subsidized, public Christian lending institutions.[44]

Not everyone viewed the monti di pietà as the solution to the issue of usury. Many Dominicans continued to recognize all interest, whatever the amount, to be usurious and sinful and considered the monti to be akin to the Jewish usurer. The Dominicans complained about the superstitious tales of miracles that surrounded the establishment of these loan banks. It was not surprising in a time when miracles were an accepted and even relished part of life that they would be attached to the monti and that such stories might encourage people to donate money to the institution. There was no difference in the eyes of the Dominicans, however, between the usurer connected to the monti and the heretic or Jew, regardless of papal sanction. In stark contrast to the Franciscan preachers who protested against Jewish banking, Sisto Medici, a Dominican friar, thought it beneficial for usury to be limited to Jews. As Jews were already in a state of godlessness, Medici reasoned, it was of no consequence if they undertook such a sinful practice. This not only prevented Christian usury, it aided the poor. But forbidding usury to be carried out by Christians had not stopped them from entering into the business. Christian usurers had been active for centuries and, in some regions, monopolized the trade. The creation of the monti di pietà was acknowledgment of that fact.[45]

In 1588, the Italian writer Bernardo Davanzati spoke at the Academy of Florence where he extolled the virtues of money. It was not only an "excellent invention" but had the power of "doing infinite good." Financial catastrophes or frauds were not the fault of money or the system by which it financed commerce, trade, and entrepreneurship, but the result of its "ill use" by the person or persons concerned. When money was kept only by the rich its circulation was cut off to those on the lower economic strata of society. The world was changing and attitudes towards usury were changing with it. God was still a dominant force in people's lives, astrology was still consulted in decision making, big and small, and superstition was still rife with charms, potions, and amulets in abundance. But the technological and scientific discoveries of the Italian Renaissance and the economy that fueled them, placed man and his own ability to make rational decisions at the center of the world. Taking inspiration from ancient Greek and Roman texts, the focus was more and more on the world that existed, and not just the world that was to come.[46]

Notes

1. Roover, *Money, Banking, and Credit in Mediaeval Bruges,* 155, 162; Britnell, "England and Northern Italy," 175; Léopold Genicot, "Crisis: From the Middle Ages to Modern Times," and Robert S. Smith, "Spain," in *Cambridge Economic History of Europe*, 438; Reinert and Fredona, "Merchants," 8.
2. Roover, *Money, Banking, and Credit in Mediaeval Bruges,* 13, 15, 29, 31; Wiesner-Hanks, *Early Modern Europe*, chap. 1.
3. Roover, *Money, Banking, and Credit in Mediaeval Bruges,* 14, 117–18, 124.
4. Thomas Cajetan, *On Exchange and Usury*, trans. Patrick T. Brannan (Grand Rapids, MI: Acton Institute for the Study of Religion and Liberty, 2014), 37, 71–72. The quote about capitalism is in the introduction by Raymond de Roover, ibidem, xxxii.
5. Roover, *Money, Banking, and Credit in Mediaeval Bruges,* 17, 54, 81.
6. Ibid., 104, 107–08, 113, 116–17, 126, 149, 153.
7. Goetzmann, *Money Changes Everything*, chap. 11.
8. Britnell, "England and Northern Italy," 168, 171; Wiesner-Hanks, *Early Modern Europe, 1450–1789,* chap. 1; Rubin, *Charity and Community*, 283; Postan, *Cambridge Economic History of Europe*, 428; Ferguson, *The Ascent of Money*, chap. 2; Goetzmann, *Money Changes Everything,* chap. 17.
9. Britnell, "England and Northern Italy," 168, 171; Homer and Sylla, *A History of Interest Rates*, chap. 8.
10. Reinert and Fredona, "Merchants," 5; Germain Sicard, *The Origin of Corporations: The Mills of Toulouse in the Middle Ages* (New Haven: Yale University Press, 2015), 223; Baron de Montesquieu, *The Spirit of Laws*, Book 2 (Glasgow: David Biven, 1793), chap. 3, 18; Wells, *Sailing to Byzantium*, 67. Tom Mueller, "Brunelleschi's Dome," *National Geographic*, Feb. 2014, ngm.nationalgeographic.com; The quote is by Leon Battista Alberti, quoted in Fried, *The Middle Ages*, chap. 11; Kelly, *Great Mortality*, 103.
11. Britnell, "England and Northern Italy," 171; Herlihy, *Medieval Culture and Society*, 172; Wells, *Sailing to Byzantium*, 71. The Medici bank was founded in Florence in

1397 by Giovanni di Bicci de Medici, a Roman banker, and was no longer in business by 1494. Geisst, *Beggar Thy Neighbor*, chap. 2; Carol Bresnahan Menning, *Charity and State in Late Renaissance Italy: The Monte Di Pietà of Florence* (Ithaca: Cornell University Press, 1993), 11; Lauro Martines, *Fire in the City: Savonarola and the Struggle for Renaissance Florence* (Oxford: OUP, 2006), 21; Raymond de Roover, *The Rise and Decline of the Medici Bank 1397–1494* (Washington, DC: Beard Books, 1999), 16; Koyama, "Evading," 11; Ferguson, *Ascent of Money*, introduction.

12. Roover, "The Concept of the Just Price," 428; Lisa Jardine, *Worldly Goods: A New History of the Renaissance* (London: Macmillan, 1996), 128.
13. Robert Chazan, *Reassessing Jewish Life in Medieval Europe* (New York: CUP, 2010), 128–29; David B. Ruderman, *Early Modern Jewry: A New Cultural History* (Princeton: Princeton University Press, 2010), 61; Benjamin Arbel, "Jews in International Trade: The Emergence of the Levantines and Ponentines," in *The Jews of Early Modern Venice*, eds. Robert C. Davis and Benjamin Ravid (Baltimore: Johns Hopkins University Press, 2001); Postan, *Cambridge Economic History of Europe*, 428.
14. Ariel Toaff, *The Jews in Umbria*, vol. 2: 1435–1484 (Leiden: Brill, 1993), 649, 685, 693.
15. Dana E. Katz, *The Jew in the Art of the Italian Renaissance* (Philadelphia: University of Pennsylvania Press, 2008), 82; Brian Pullan, "Jewish Banks and the Monti di Pietà," *The Jews of Early Modern Venice*, 64; Luzzatto quoted in Benjamin Ravid, "The Venetian Government and the Jews," in *The Jews of Early Modern Venice*, 12, 29, and also in Brian Pullan, *The Jews of Europe and the Inquisition of Venice, 1550–1670* (London: I.B. Tauris, 1997), 159; Postan, *Cambridge Economic History of Europe*, 428.
16. Toaff, *The Jews of Umbria*, 492, 581, 482, 694–95, 790; Rosenthal intro. to Yehiel Nissim da Pisa, *Banking and Finance*, 16, 21–22.
17. Toaff, *The Jews in Umbria*, 565, 575.
18. Ibid., 512.
19. Ibid., 605–06.
20. Ibid., 569, 673–74, 704, 705, 706.
21. Ibid., 481, 505, 634.
22. Ibid., 469, 480–81, 503, 557, 564, 566, 572–73, 574, 593, 625; Wells, *Sailing to Byzantium*, 106, 107.
23. Toaff, *The Jews in Umbria*, 486, 535, 659, 723, 729.
24. Ibid., 529, 542, 666, 507, 601, 604, 617, 479.
25. Ibid., 567, 616.
26. Ibid., 754.
27. Menning, *Charity and State*, 15, 21–22; Bernardino da Sienna, "How much usury is in opposition to God and renders the usurer an idolater. And how grave a blasphemy of God and his faith is it to allow moneylending," quoted in Franco Mormando, *The Preacher's Demons: Bernardino of Siena and the Social Underworld of Early Renaissance Italy* (Chicago: University of Chicago Press, 1999), 187–88; McNamara,

"Franciscans and Dominicans," in *Medieval Folklore*, 124; John W. Oppel, "Poggio, San Bernardino of Siena, and the Dialogue *On Avarice*," *Renaissance Quarterly* 30.4 (1977), 572, 573, 575; Middleton and Shaw, eds., *Market Ethics and Practices,* intro.

28. Toaff, *The Jews in Umbria*, 588.
29. Ibid., 751, 755.
30. Ibid., 960, 736, 751, 818, 860, 864.
31. Ibid., 607–09, 801, 878, 883, 884, 890.
32. R. Po-Chia Hsia, *Trent 1475: Stories of a Ritual Murder Trial* (New Haven: Yale University Press, 1992), 25; Toaff, *The Jews in Umbria*, 625, 629, 631, 633; Menning, *Charity and State*, 48; Karen Bezella-Bond, "Games and Play," in Lindahl, *Medieval Folklore*, 168.
33. Donald Weinstein, *Savonarola: The Rise and Fall of a Renaissance Prophet* (New Haven: Yale University Press, 2011), 88; Ross King, *Machiavelli: Philosopher of Power* (New York: Atlas Books/HarperCollins, 2007), 37; Menning, *Charity and State*, 41.
34. Weinstein, *Savonarola*, 38.; Martines, *Fire in the City*, 10, 16–17, 23, 23, 25, 88; Luca Landucci, *A Florentine Diary: From 1450–1516* (New York: Books for Libraries Press, 1969), 24–27, 47, 116–17.
35. Landucci, *A Florentine Diary*, 110; Diane Owen Hughes, "Bodies, Disease, and Society," in *Italy in the Age of the Renaissance*, ed. John M. Najemy (Oxford: OUP, 2004), 19; Martines, *Fire in the City*, 75, 87, 93, 102–04, 136.
36. Martines, *Fire in the City*, 161, 276–77; Weinstein, *Savonarola*, 1; King, *Machiavelli*, 12.
37. Girolamo Savonarola, *Triumph of the Cross* (1497), chapters 3, 5, 7, and 8, http://oll.libertyfund.org/index.php?option=com_staticxt&staticfile=show.php%3Ftitle=2248&layout=html#chapter_212774; Weinstein, *Savonarola*, 310.
38. Toaff, *The Jews in Umbria*, 718–19, 736; Koyama, "Evading," 18.
39. Toaff, *The Jews in Umbria*, 792, 807, 850; Menning, *Charity and State*, 48.
40. The poor meant not the destitute, who would not be able to offer a suitable pledge, but those who were unable to live at the appropriate level demanded by their place in the social hierarchy. See Pullan, "Jewish Banks," 54; Weinstein, *Savonarola,* 72–73; Katz, *Jews in the Art of the Italian Renaissance*, 106.
41. Landucci, *A Florentine Diary*, 45, 101 n.1; Tribaldo de' Rossi's *Ricordanze* also related the events surrounding Bernardino's preaching in Florence and is quoted in Katz, *The Jew in the Art of the Italian Renaissance*, 106. On the *fancuilli* see, Michel Plaisance, *Florence at the Time of the Medici: Public Celebrations, Politics, and Literature in the Fifteenth and Sixteenth Centuries* (Toronto: Centre for Reformation and Renaissance Studies, 2008), 99 n.58; Richard C. Trexler, *Public Life in Renaissance Florence* (Ithaca: Cornell University Press, 1991), 478; Weinstein, *Savonarola*, 73, 173; Mormando, *The Preacher's Demons*, 191; Letter from Cosimo de' Medici to Federigo de' Conti da Montauto, June 10, 1568, cited in Menning, *Charity and State*, 235,

238, see also, 44–45; Toaff, *The Jews in Umbria*, 1175; Andrée Aelion Brooks, *The Woman Who Defied Kings: The Life and Times of Doña Gracia Nasi* (St. Paul, MN: Paragon House, 2002), 194.

42. Toaff, *The Jews of Umbria*, 1175, 723, 732; Katz, *The Jew in the Art of the Italian Renaissance*, 81.
43. Battista Guerini, "ad Caecilianum Cur Judaei ferant literam O," was included in an edition of Pindar's *Trojan War* printed by Gerson Soncino in 1505.
44. Pullan, "Jewish Banks," 57. Monti were opened up all over Italy, including Umbria, the Marches, Veneto, Lombardy, Emilia, and Tuscany. Menning, *Charity and State*, 29.
45. Menning, *Charity and State*, 30, 104; Pullan, "Jewish Banks," 53.
46. Geisst, *Beggar Thy Neighbor*, chap. 2.

5

A Dangerous Game of Monopoly

Critics of the capital-based economy had long sought the eradication of monopoly, which was generally characterized as a deceptive and immoral practice and one that went hand in hand with hoarding. It was a subject that came to the fore in the sixteenth and seventeenth centuries as a terrible and bloody war spread across Europe. Known as the Thirty Years' War, this religious conflict erupted as new dissenters appeared to challenge the power in Rome. Unlike previous heretics, these Protestants succeeded in creating a new church that challenged the Holy See and that was stripped of icons, sacraments, and the money-making methods of the papacy, such as indulgences. In this battle for souls, the debate over usury was resurrected.

The seminal figure in the Protestant Reformation was a German theologian, Martin Luther, who wrote bitterly on the subject. In his *Long Sermon on Usury* (1520) and *On Trade and Usury* (1524), Luther's hatred of moneylenders flowed from his pen without restraint. He defined usury as all interest-loans and not, as was becoming more commonplace, "excessive" or "abusive" interest rates. How was it just, he asked, that a laborer toiled all day in the field and made a fraction of what the usurer earned without exertion of any kind? In Luther's mind, profit was not earned and no risk was taken. Usury protected the rich and the greedy and burdened the poor and the needy. And it was Jews who he considered to be the main purveyors of usury in Europe, and therefore instruments of a social evil.

Through their usury, Luther argued that Jews held Christians "captives" in their own country: "they have us work in our noses' sweat . . . while they sit behind their stoves, in laziness" eating and drinking. Their breath "stinks for the gold and silver of the heathen, since no people under the sun always have been, still are, and always will remain more avaricious than they [the Jews] as can be noticed in their cursed usury." Everything the Jews possess, Luther wrote, "they have stolen from us . . . and robbed through their usury, since they have no other income." It was the moral duty of Christian rulers not to allow their money or possessions, or those of their subjects, to "serve Jews through their usury."[1]

For Lutherans, both lender and borrower were sinful, a view shared by another Protestant sect, the Anabaptists, but not by the man who would influence England's religious path, John Calvin. Whereas Luther's argument rested on prohibitions in the Hebrew Bible, Calvin completely rejected Jewish law for Christians. If Christians followed Jewish law as prescribed in the Bible, he reasoned, then they would be Jews and not Christians. He regarded the biblical ban on usury to be a specific Jewish policy from centuries ago which was neither universal nor binding on any other peoples or generations. The onus was on Christians to follow the example of Christ and his protection of the poor, the weak, and the oppressed. He thought it "a very rare thing for a man to be honest and at the same time a usurer." But, while it was a Christian duty to help the poor and not to charge them interest, usury should not be forbidden to the rich who entered into an agreement honestly and fairly.[2]

In his work, *On Usury* (1545), Calvin accepted a variable rate of interest and in a letter to a friend he wrote that there was no "witness of scripture by which all usury is totally forbidden." To those who pointed to the passage in Luke that instructed Christians to lend without expecting anything in return, Calvin noted the context of that command. One should not expect something back from those who cannot give but, if Matthew 7:12 was followed, it was permissible to "do unto others what you would have them do unto you."[3]

Calvin's ideas about usury cannot be separated from his theological doctrine. Unlawful usury was when it plundered and devoured the poor. If it did not, then there was no compulsion to forbid a practice that had widespread utility. Unlike Luther, he had little patience with early theologians who shaped the "frivolous" anti-usury argument. It was childish to assume that money could not produce money, any less than a farmer benefits from the sale of land. The farmer who rents out a field is doing nothing different from the usurer who rents out money.

It was not only Protestants who challenged the supremacy of Rome but also the secular rulers who were distancing themselves from papal jurisdiction. Since 1356, the emperor of the Holy Roman Empire had not been crowned by the pope but chosen by electors comprised of three archbishops and four princes, all German. The Holy Roman Empire spread out over 680,000 kilometers. Tall, thick medieval walls dotted with towers and gatehouses surrounded the towns. Outer fortifications were a seventeenth century addition to strengthen defenses and gates were closed and guarded as dusk fell. Within its boundaries, the empire included modern Germany, Austria, Luxemburg, Czech Republic, much of western Poland and Alsace and Lorraine. It also incorporated most of modern Netherlands and Flanders and some of northern Italy into its realm. There were over two thousand towns, 150,000 villages, and other communities. Wealth came from the agrarian economy—the farming of rye, oats, wheat, and barley—mining in the Tyrol and the Austrian interior, and textiles in upper Austria, Bohemia, and western Moravia, while the Rhine was one of the most important rivers for commerce. The imperial diet, the Reichstag, was an early form of representation in Germany. It met at the emperor's command settling laws, voting for taxes both for internal order and to raise money for the costly war against the Turks and, now, the Protestants.[4]

* * *

In Flanders, professional moneylenders had been making credit transactions since the eleventh century. Even though it was under the rule of the Catholic Emperor Charles V, it had become a significant center of Protestant ideology and Antwerp was a city where the influential merchant bankers tended to put business above the dogmas of religion. By 1531, it boasted the first stock exchange, although there were as yet no stocks. Rather, the exchange was a place where bills of exchange were cashed from cities all over Europe, loans were floated, commodities and currency were bought and sold, and capital was accumulated. It was a Flemish mathematician from Antwerp, Simon Stevin, who published *Tables of Interest* in 1585, which detailed how to calculate interest rates, including compound interest, using decimals for more accurate results. Cloth, silk, damask, iron, fish, copper, amber, and goods from the Portuguese and Spanish Indies arrived in Antwerp, luring merchants from all over Europe, including many New Christians and crypto-Jews, to its market place. It was to this city that Doña Gracia Mendes, a New Christian on the road to reverting back to her family's Judaism, relocated her banking business after the death of her husband.[5]

The House of Mendes was one of the most important private bankers in Western Europe. It had been started by a converso family, headed by Francisco Mendes and his brother Diogo, who had moved to Portugal after the expulsion of Jews from Spain. In Portugal, they continued to amass silver and provide short term credit to merchants with high interest rates to cover the possible loss of goods due to a ship sinking or piracy. The Mendes family set up agents in other commercial centers to ensure interest payments were collected and formed partnerships with other bankers to combine capital large enough to secure monopolies. Around 1512, Diogo settled in Antwerp, a city that had all the "complex machinery of modern capitalism," but lacked regulations. In the mercantalist world, it was common to try and corner the market or rig it to the traders' advantage. Diogo and the House of Mendes created a consortium with the Affaitati family, who were Italian-Flemish merchants, and some Sephardic Jews to buy up all the spices bound for Antwerp and everything for sale in Lisbon. This way they secured a monopoly over the import and export of spices coming into Lisbon. With this monopoly anyone who wanted pepper in Europe had to buy off the Mendes-Affaitati syndicate, including the biggest German banking family, the Fuggers. By negotiating this contract with the syndicate in exchange for a loan to finance the India fleet, King João III put himself in enormous debt. In 1543, the king owed the syndicate a total of 2,169,252 cruzados, an amount several times greater than his revenues.[6]

In 1532, Diogo was arrested in Antwerp and charged with secretly practicing Judaism and illegally monopolizing the spice trade, which resulted in the appropriation of his entire estate, including his merchandise. As King João III was in desperate need of the money due to him from the peppers and spice contract, he personally intervened. He wrote to Charles V on Diogo's behalf, stressing the large amount of money that was at stake and that the confiscation of the spices and peppers and other merchandise was delaying his repayment as the seized goods could not be sold. His wife Catarina of Austria, who was Charles' sister, added her pleas in a separate letter, also noting the financial ramifications of the arrest for the Portuguese economy, which had held up the payments to the Portuguese Crown. Charles relented and Diogo was released within two months. His reputation, however, was sullied.[7]

There was always the risk of lending large amounts of money to monarchs and also with monopolizing markets. If a king could not pay the interest payments then he had options that were not advantageous to the lender. The friction between the Crown and the syndicate continued until 1549 when João announced that any buyer could come to Lisbon and purchase pepper and he was reducing his debt payments. If one of the keys to a successful banking enterprise was a amicable connection with the monarch who granted those monopolies and took out large, long-term loans, then the syndicate had failed. In their relationship with the Portuguese king, the Mendes-Affaitati group had pushed too hard. But it was not only with the Portuguese monarchy that the Mendes bank negotiated. They struck up a relationship with the English Crown, creating an ally in Thomas Cromwell (the chancellor of Henry VIII), as well as Emperor Charles V.[8]

After the death of Francisco Mendes, his young wife (who was also his niece) Beatriz de Luna decided it was prudent to leave Lisbon and involve herself more in the business in Antwerp. It was here that Beatriz learned the merchant banking business and extended the House of Mendes into Italy and, later, the Ottoman Empire. Clad in the sumptuous gowns of the time and adorned with jewels, she now took the name Doña Gracia and began her journey back to life as a professing Jew, although never an orthodox one. When her brother-in-law Diogo died, she was one of the wealthiest women in Europe at the age of thirty-three. As was the law following Diogo's death, his ledgers and other documents were confiscated for auditing on the orders of Charles V and his sister Queen Marie, who governed the Low Countries in his name. With war looming against German Protestants, Charles and Marie were eager for loans and other financing to pay for weapons, infrastructure, defense, and armies.[9]

Moneylenders were not powerless, especially when they had the kind of wealth that the House of Mendes possessed. They had an effective weapon with which to retaliate. Bills of exchange and a network of agents throughout Europe made it relatively easy to transfer money and move their business to another place. Merchant bankers like Doña Gracia were able to devise ways to remove themselves, their household, and her firm to more agreeable or business-friendly regions, although this had to be done with some stealth in order to avoid imprisonment or the seizure of goods by the Crown. She paid off Charles V with interest-free loans and, leaving the confiscated chests full of accounts behind her, Doña Gracia and her entourage quietly decamped to Italy. She set up residence in a *palazzo* along the Grand Canal and it was here that agents on her behalf reached an agreement with authorities in Florence that allowed the Portuguese Jews to officially live and trade there.[10]

* * *

The Holy Roman Empire was left in bad economic shape by the melancholic, and intermittently insane, Emperor Rudolf who, at his death in 1612, owed two-and-a-half million florin in back pay to officials and servants. This was a more acute problem due to the outbreak of an expansive, deadly, and costly war that divided Catholics and Protestants into two warring camps. The Thirty Years' War (1618–1648) forced Catholics to leave Sweden within three months on pain of death and in Protestant Württemberg, the duke founded Freudenstaat as a sanctuary for Protestant exiles from Graz. Less than forty years after the end of the conflict in 1685, Louis XIV of France revoked the Edict of Nantes (1598) that had granted rights to the country's Huguenot Protestant minority. Protestant ministers were given two weeks to leave France while all other Protestants were forbidden to leave for fear they would take their wealth out of the country. An unknown number of Huguenots defied the order and fled to Protestant lands.[11]

A long and hard-fought war needed a lot of capital. With the cost of the war amounting to around 250 million gulden for the Holy Roman Empire (its allies Spain and the papacy contributed very little to that amount), Emperor Ferdinand II (r.1619–1637) required large loans to pay for mercenaries, horses, maps and field glasses, arquebuses, gunpowder, wheel-lock pistols, muskets, and cannons. So tight were the purse strings, soldiers often were unpaid, which led, as in the past, to mutinies and looting of urban centers. Town officials often needed protection money to shield them from rampaging soldiers who had additional financial problems. Until the 1640s, when prisoners were exchanged, those who were captured during the war had to pay for their own release. These kinds of war-related expenses led one British secretary of state for war to later declare that, "All modern Wars are a Contention of Purse."[12]

Many people, Jews and Christians, saw a downturn in their economic status as war led to plundering, the burning of villages and towns, political instability, and the devastation of land. Yet enormous losses by merchants during the Thirty Years' War opened the door for moneylenders who operated through an international credit system. The largest and most powerful creditors in the Holy Roman Empire since the fifteenth century were the Christian Fugger bankers who had financed the election of Emperor Charles V in 1519. Jakob Fugger (1459–1525) had that characteristic essential to a successful banker—the ability to tolerate risk—but by the end of the war, the firm had been dissolved.[13]

Jews were also active moneylenders in the empire, supplying credit and matérial for wars and court costs. The most elite of these were the agents known as court Jews (*Hoffjuden*) or court factors (*Hoffaktoren*). Military supplies and army contracting were the staples of the court Jews' economic life. They were small in number and exceptional in the history of Jewish financiers, just as Aaron of Lincoln was in the past or James Rothschild would be in the future. Their wealth, which helped to create Jewish settlements in urban centers, created a false image that *all* Jews were rich and influential. But, as in other countries, most Jews were not involved in finance and those who were usually carried out deals on a small-scale. They were far removed from the high finance that occupied court Jews, who, with their profits, bought mansions and filled them with gold-framed paintings, exquisite carved wood furnishings, and beautiful tapestries. Dressed in silk and the latest fashions, they attended and threw lavish parties where the silver candelabra gleamed in the reflection of the lit tallows while the guests were waited on by servants and clerks. They were exempt from a number of restrictions, and enjoyed land, honors, and riches. They were not, as has been written, "a symbol of the sufferings and martyrdom of the Jewish people over the centuries." Nor were they "indispensable," as there were always other moneylenders ready to advance cash and supplies. They were certainly vulnerable, as were all bankers to monarchs and emperors in these times. They were moneylenders whose skills and capital were exchanged for protection, privilege, and settlement, much like moneylenders in Renaissance Italy but on a grander scale. Jews were no longer serfs of the chamber (*Kammerknechte*) or servants of the king (*servi camerae regis*) as in medieval times, but they still had to be invited into towns and cities, with privileges granted by the local authorities in return for their banking services. They still lived and worked at the pleasure and whim of the ruler.[14]

Although some court Jews had tragic fates, this was not the case for all of them. Like all people, their lives were varied and complex. Some died rich men, others were executed for treason. Most court Jews enjoyed great wealth, political influence, and the benefits of a powerful patron who was generally a ruler who was keen to streamline his bureaucracy, modernize his civil service, make taxes more regulated and tax collecting more efficient, unify and codify laws, and invest in trade, commerce, and industry. Frederick William I, the Great Elector, of Brandenburg, took power during the last years of the Thirty Years' War and was committed to strengthening the state through trade, commerce and an efficiently run bureaucracy. Canals and locks were constructed to ease shipping, make it cheaper to move goods and connect cities, while foreigners were invited in to form colonies and assist in the financial expansion of the state. To increase a country's wealth, the monetary system was restructured, factories were founded to boost the crown's revenues, and higher taxes were implemented. Control of the economy introduced regulations, laws, and protectionist measures such as those placed on the export of raw materials and the importation of finished goods. In this world, financiers, merchants, and tradesmen had a key part to play because the modernization of the state and the waging of war all required staggering amounts of capital.[15]

A court Jew was not only a banker and merchant, but someone deeply immersed in political and diplomatic life. While the position often brought great wealth and status, a close alliance with a particular ruler who granted monopolies, capriciously tied the court Jew's fortunes to that individual. Monopolies cut out all competition, causing costs to rise although the banker's fate usually rose and fell not with market fluctuations but with the success or failure, or the life and death, of his benefactor. They encountered the same difficulties that every moneylender faced—nonpayment, imprisonment, bankruptcy, and possibly death (for both real and imagined offences). They also made political enemies, either personally or through their patron, who were keen to exact their revenge when their security was no longer assured. On the other hand, some managed to live their lives in great comfort and, relatively speaking, free from torment.

Samson Wertheimer (1658–1724) was called the "wealthiest Jew in Germany," earning him the nickname the *Judenkaiser* (the Jewish emperor). He bought multiple properties that were located in Worms, Frankfurt, Vienna, Prague, Eisenstadt, and Nikolsburg. Lemle Moses of Mannheim was the *Obermilizfaktor* of the Palatinate in the last two decades of the seventeenth century. Elias Cleve (Elijah Gomperz, d. 1675) hailed from a prominent Jewish family and established a bank in Emmerich, subsequently opening another in Berlin. Elias was the financial advisor to Frederick William, the Elector of Brandenburg, who was eager to build his cost-effective, efficient, bureaucratic, modern state, as well as a banker for the Dutch government and a purveyor for the Dutch military. A relative, Reuben Elias Gomperz, was a purveyor to the Elector of Cologne. Dutch Sephardic Jews, meanwhile, supplied matériel to William of Orange, the Stadholder of the United Provinces. Probably the most successful court Jews was Samuel Oppenheimer of Heidelberg (1630–1703), Wertheimer's uncle and the financial agent and army controller for Elector Karl Ludwig of the Palatinate. He settled in Vienna, the first Jew to do so after the expulsion of Jews in 1670, and became the Imperial War Purveyor. He worked with a large network, including family members and other court Jews but he also allied with Christian firms. He formed a consortium with several Christian groups to provide millions of gulden to the emperor and provisions and matériel for the military, especially the Austrian army in the Rhine during Franco-Dutch War (1672–1677) and the Austrian war against the Ottoman Empire (1667–1683). During the Nine-Years'

War (1689–1698), Oppenheimer supplied the Austrian military fighting the French in Germany and the court of Vienna with wine, jewels, spices, sweets, and livery.[16]

A combination of protection and privilege made for an unstable framework in life especially when it was linked to monopolies and in between wars, Oppenheimer's services were not as essential. In 1700, when a chimney sweep ridiculed a friend of Oppenheimer, a riot ensued during which a mob ransacked the impressive house of Oppenheimer on the Bauernmarkt in Vienna. Windows and doors were smashed, furniture overturned and broken. Rioters made straight for commercial papers, ledgers, contracts, and correspondence which they ripped to pieces or took away with them. Oppenheimer and his family escaped while the main instigators of the riot—the chimney sweep and a sword cutler—were swiftly arrested. They were summarily hanged from the railing at the entryway to Oppenheimer's house as a warning to others who might be tempted to violate social order. The stolen property was ordered to be returned to its rightful owner. When Oppenheimer died in 1703, his son Simon Wolf Oppenheimer, carried on the banking firm and was the court Jew of the Electorate of Brunswick-Lüneburg in Hanover. His son Jacob carried on the business, employing a thirteen-year-old boy as an apprentice by the name of Mayer Amschel Rothschild.[17]

Everything hinged on the desires, longevity, and power of the benefactor, as well as the honesty of both the moneylender and his protector. This was true in the case of Lippold ben Chluchim (1530–1573) who was court factor and master of the mint in Brandenburg. While this garnered him wealth and status, Lippold was charged with implementing a policy of currency debasement, a common occurrence in medieval Europe and one that continued into the early modern era. This less valuable money was then forced on merchants who had to accept the degraded coins at the higher face value. Fraud of this kind was especially common in northern Germany, and it was how Lippold's patron, the Elector Joachim II Hector, helped to finance his court (in addition to taxation). With Joachim's sudden death in 1571 at his hunting lodge, resentment against his fiscal policy flared into an anti-Jewish riot. The new Elector, Johann Georg, did nothing to stop the burning of synagogues or plundering of the Jewish quarter. Indeed, he may have found the disorder to be a convenient way to avert attention away from his father's currency corruption and tax policies.

Lippold was accused of poisoning his patron by sorcery. With a confession extracted by torture, his fate was secured. The grisly execution took place on the Neuer Markt near the Lutheran Marienkirch in Berlin where his body was broken on the wheel and then cut into quarters. Any connection to financial wrongdoing or unpopular fiscal policies could clearly have serious and violent consequences, as in Lippold's case. With no police force yet and no disinterested forms of jurisprudence, it was difficult to know whether the allegations were legitimate or false or whether the punishment was driven by politics, personal vengeance, or merely the laws of the land. But actions taken against court Jews in Germany arose mainly due to such complaints about unfair business practices. The charges of monopolization, "hoarding" (speculation), were not exclusively directed at court Jews but at bankers in general—an indication that the resentment felt by the accusers was primarily against the profession.[18]

Jacob Bassevi (1570–1634), a Bohemian court Jew who was the head of Prague's Jewish community, provided loans for Emperors Rudolph II, Matthias, and Ferdinand II. His star rose higher when he was ennobled. Bassevi took the more distinguished name von Treuenberg and was granted his own coat of arms, was free to reside where he wanted without restriction, and permitted to travel freely. With his wealth, he purchased properties with beautiful gardens in the best parts of Prague. It was said that he was the "most important Jewish leader during the Thirty Years' War." In the course of the war, trade and manufacturing was interrupted when the silver mines were stripped bare. With silver production closed down, the dearth of precious metals led to governments prohibiting silver's exportation, causing its price to skyrocket. As silver was both a commodity and a means of exchange, this increase in value led to more frequent coin debasement. The manipulation of the currency value by financiers produced inflation and a further rise in prices. Complaints came thick and fast from farmers, nobles, and townsmen, some of whom lost their life's savings. Soldiers were frequently left unpaid, adding to the discontent.[19]

Like Joachim II, Emperor Ferdinand II, in his need for ready cash, decided to debase the currency to raise funds. He created a money consortium and gave it the power to mint coins. At the head of the mint he placed Bassevi and a Christian, Hans de Witte, who were charged with purchasing as much silver as their agents could gather and paying for it with less valuable coins alloyed with copper. Once the silver was purchased, it was likewise smelted with copper, flooding the market with devalued silver. With the coins debased, money no longer had the same buying power and people saw any savings they had accumulated greatly diminished in value. It was the same idea as today's habit of printing reams of money to pay for what cannot be afforded otherwise. Soldiers, when they were paid, were given this less valuable currency, while merchants refused debased coins and insisted on payment with the purer silver money. The rise in inflation and the increased cost of staple foods, such as bread, resulted in impoverishment, famine, unrest, and looting. As in Brandenburg, anger was directed at those people who made profits off this scheme. Not Ferdinand, who initiated the scheme, but Bassevi and Witte. The fury toward them may have been exacerbated by the fact that Bassevi was a Jew and Witte a Calvinist but it was not their religion that sparked the hostility. The accusations of coin debasement leveled against them were sound. Expelled from Prague, Bassevi sought and received refuge at the castle of one of his benefactors, Albrecht von Wallenstein, in northern Bohemia.[20]

Moses Jacobson de Jonge, a Dutch Jew, built up a thriving international business with Poland, Lithuania, and Livonia. In return for his financial services to the Great Elector, Frederick William of Brandenburg, Jonge paid no taxes and had the right to purchase houses in Memel even though Jews were excluded from the duchy of Prussia. He also enjoyed other privileges that included permission to visit the annual fairs and to hold religious services in his home. He nearly monopolized the important salt trade by restricting the amount imported to Germany from Holland to keep the price high. The ships that transported De Jonge's imports were laden with so many goods, local merchants grumbled that they were being driven out of business. Their complaints fell on deaf ears as de Jonge paid 80 percent more in custom taxes than any of the other merchants, giving the Elector a substantial amount of revenue. When De Jonge was physically attacked by four Christian merchants, Frederick I of Prussia was quick to severely punish them and renew the business privileges. Not surprisingly, this aggravated the already aggrieved merchants and their many supporters.[21]

The most infamous court Jew to be caught up in a financial and political scandal was Josef Süss Oppenheimer (1698–1738), known as Jud Süss. His notoriety was ensured by the nature of his death and his reincarnation in the twentieth century as the subject of a sympathetic literary portrayal by the German-Jewish novelist Lion Feuchtwanger. Conversely, he was the epitome of corruption and greed in a Nazi propaganda film. In reality, Oppenheimer was a religious skeptic who ridiculed tradition, had contempt for Judaism, and enjoyed affairs with Christian noblewomen and ladies of the court. In spite of this, he obtained permission for a Jewish community to settle in Württemberg. As the financier to Karl Alexander, the Duke of Württemberg, Oppenheimer is a prime example of the pitfalls of political alliances and how quickly a person can fall from grace. The complex details of his life and career, reveal the hazards of a court factor's life tied to the fortunes of a particular ruler and involved in activities unpopular with a vast segment of the populace.

Oppenheimer's power rested in the hands of Karl Alexander, who became the Duke of Württemberg in 1733. In keeping with the trend of the times, he was intent on reforming the state by centralizing it and revitalizing the economy. In March 1734, Oppenheimer was appointed Resident in Frankfurt am Main and given an annual income of 500 florins. His main job was to raise funds to fill his patron's war chest. Karl Alexander had converted to Catholicism in 1712 to fortify his connection to the powerful Austrian Habsburgs, marrying the princess of Thurn and Taxis in the process. Oppenheimer's responsibilities included the administration of domains, taxes, and control over the mint. He took as his model Prussia where, thanks to the reforms made by Frederick William I's, which included streamlining government bureaucracy and instituting protectionist measures, the economy recovered from near bankruptcy. He advised Karl Alexander to order every subject with an income to pay tax, which became known as the "Jewish *groschen*" as it went straight to him. He set up an office that bestowed titles on the untitled in return for payment (*Gratialamt*) as well as a fiscal office (*Fiscalatamt*) that investigated allegations of economic wrongdoings. For a price, these investigations would be quietly dropped. Such practices to raise and maintain credit were part of an economic system that was based on monopolies and dominated by cartels, whether they were Jewish, Christian, or a combination of the two.[22]

Like many a functionary, power had a heady and intoxicating effect on Oppenheimer. He made a fatal mistake when he overstepped his reach with widely unpopular measures and possible financial misappropriation. Operating on the premise that every subject's possessions belonged to the ruler, Karl Alexander requested Oppenheimer to introduce a monopoly on salt, an essential preserving agent. This had been done in other parts of Germany—as mentioned, Moses de Jonge had a near monopoly on the salt imported to Prussia. The problem was that the duke's measure went against the Württemberg constitution which prohibited monopolies. Oppenheimer counseled Karl Alexander to follow that most autocratic of monarchs, Louis XIV, and behead members of the Landschaft (the representatives of the Estates) who protested his anti-constitutional action. By now, suspicion had fallen on the court Jew. Oppenheimer's attempt to establish a public bank in Stuttgart came to nothing due to the common belief that he wanted the bank purely for his own financial benefit.

While Karl Alexander was alive and in power, Oppenheimer was safe. But on March 12, 1737, at the age of fifty-two, the duke suddenly died, leaving the duchy in the hands of his nine-year-old son. As with Lippold, Oppenheimer was put on trial. In his case, there were no charges of sorcery disguising the economic reasons for the arrest. Instead, he was charged with high treason, for which the penalty was death. He also stood accused of an array of financial crimes: fraud, embezzlement, and bribery, as well as other offences such as lechery and plotting with Catholics to overthrow the constitution and Lutheranism. Found guilty, on February 4, 1738, just under a year after his benefactor's death, he was led to the gallows and hanged. As was the macabre practice of the times, his body was left to rot on display in a large bird cage just outside Stuttgart until Duke Karl Eugen's inauguration, when the new ruler ordered its burial.[23]

Complaints against financial agents were not uncommon but most court Jews did not end up like Oppenheimer. De Jonge, who angered merchants with his bulk buying, monopolization, and trading with other Jews to the detriment of the Christian majority in Memel, also faced a trial. But unlike the unfortunate Lippold and Oppenheimer, he was found not guilty. What is clear from these examples is that in times of financial corruption, monopolies, privilege, and political instability, being a court Jew was a profession that brought wealth and influence but also great risks and temptations. The higher the rewards, the greater that risk. This was no different to others in the same position who were not Jewish. Wealth and power linked to kings and princes was unstable and not only due to their possible downfall or death. Losing the ruler's favor was always a danger.

The Court Jew lived a life that was far from the experience of most German Jews who were generally poor to middling with some more comfortably off. In Frankfurt, the long, dirty street of the Jewish ghetto was flanked on either side by oppressive five story houses, the roofs crammed with chimneys, with chamber pots and dirty bedding visible at the windows. Like the rest of society, there was a hierarchy in the Jewish communities with the *Betteljuden* ("begging-Jews") at the bottom. In some German towns, Jews lived side by side with Christian neighbors, shared houses with them, or rented from them. Some Jews were involved in finance, although not at the level of the court Jews. In Worms during the 1650s, currency exchange was a popular occupation and transactions occurred mainly between Jews, whereas in Emden, a seaport in Lower Saxony, 60 percent of loans were made by Jews to Christians. For a long-term loan, Jews were allowed to charge 12 percent interest, double the usual rate allowed to Christian creditors. For short-term loans, the rate was higher, anywhere from 12 to 24 percent. Jewish merchants petitioned to live in better areas closer to their places of business and prestigious neighborhoods were sought after by the wealthy, such as Abraham Jacob, the head of the Jewish community of Steinbiedersdorf, who bought an impressive estate consisting of a substantial house, court, garden, and stable.[24]

With much of the business of pawnbroking and loans conducted in the home it was easier for women to involve themselves in jobs such as bookkeeping or taking charge of business affairs while their husbands traveled. In the case of their husband's death, they often continued at the helm of the business, as had Licoricia in England and Dona Gracia in Portugal. The widowed Jewish moneylender Glückel of Hameln was not in the same financial league as Licoricia or Gracia but she managed her business well enough to provide a decent life. Her adage was to be "honest in money matters, with both Jews and Gentiles, lest the name of Heaven be profaned." To illustrate her point, she told the story—apparently well known in Hamburg—of two Jewish conmen. Hearing of a burgher in Norway who had "a goodly share" of some uncut diamonds, they sought him out and quickly befriended him. He cordially invited them to spend the night, an offer that they gladly accepted. When dawn broke, the two Jews "fled . . . and hiring a small boat fancied they had brought the matter to a happy conclusion." The burgher was not to be so easily robbed of his property, however, and, after tracking down the thieves, they were condemned to the gallows. One converted to avoid death. "We should learn from this," Glückel wrote, "not to be misled by the love of worldly goods." To accrue wealth by deceit was to lose one's "share in the world to come." Wealth was not sinful unless it was gained through dishonest means, and this no longer necessarily meant moneylending.[25]

Glückel's father was a precious gems dealer, although the fashion at the time was more for gold chains than jewels. The family, along with other Jews, were forced out of Hamburg before she was three years old. They settled in Altona, which was then part of Denmark, before resettling in Hamburg at the "mercy and favour of the Town Council." Her marriage at fourteen took her to her husband's home in Hameln where they continued the business of trading precious stones. They also conducted small loans, like so many other Jewish financiers, and partnered with Glückel's relatives, transacting business in Amsterdam as well as at the fairs in Leipzig and Frankfurt. With her husband's death, Glückel sold off what she could and within the year had cleared her debts, using the remaining money to continue her moneylending business.

At the Mariners' Tavern in Hamburg, which was close to the stock exchange (Börse), Glückel stayed with her children as she conducted her business. It was an inn "packed with drivers and travelers," where she revived herself with "good fare" and "good beer." Jewish and Christian moneylenders drank with one another while working out deals and, because the inns and taverns were relatively secure, counted out their earnings. Glückel's life was comfortable but it was a far cry from that of the court Jew. Court Jews represented their communities as *shtadlans* (from the word meaning "to intercede on behalf of"). They were the go-betweens for the Jewish communities and court authorities, and, in that capacity, they were instrumental in bargaining for favorable conditions and for collecting taxes due to the state. They were, in effect, the absolutist leaders of their communities in an absolutist Europe.[26]

It has been said of the court Jew that he was the essence of modern capitalism with their manipulation of money; that they were "bearers of a new and revolutionary political and economic conception which was bitterly attacked by the old legitimatist powers." Oppenheimer has been labeled the "first Jewish representation of the new spirit of Enlightenment." But this is inaccurate. The economic system which gave rise to the court Jew and sustained his wealth and power (however transient) was monopoly and privilege rather than the competitive market championed in the next century by Enlightenment economists. Monopolies restricted the market and hindered prosperity and freedom by hampering competition. They impinged not only on the economy, but also on civic liberty. The German Jewish philosopher Moses Mendelssohn (1729–1786) despised monopolies, the contracts for which were often won through bribery rather than merit, with dishonest state officials gladly lining their pockets in exchange for a contract. A proponent of the eighteenth-century Enlightenment philosophical ideals—such as liberty of the individual, freedom of thought and expression, and natural rights—Mendelssohn valued free trade as a component of personal liberty. As with the individual, the economy had to be unshackled of manipulation and over-regulation and allowed to be dictated only by supply and demand. Indeed, it was commercial services provided by Mendelssohn to the state and monarchy (his family's wealth came from the textile industry), which included a proposal to relax government interference in the private sector, that allowed him to reside in Berlin.[27]

The power of the state and its wellbeing were the guiding principles of Europe's absolutist monarchs who were eager to enrich, modernize, and bureaucratize their kingdoms and empires. Louis XIV's famous aphorism "*l'etat c'est moi*" (I am the state) epitomized his kingship, during which he continued the centralization of France, a process that would not be complete until the late nineteenth century.

* * *

For those who saw the credit market as inherently dishonest and immoral, there was no shortage of financial scandals that assured them that their view was correct. The so-called *Kipper- und-Wipperzeit* (1619–1623) involved moneylenders who, like the medieval coin-clippers, debased coins by changing the weight, metal, value, or quality, and who tampered with the scales used to weigh them. They then exchanged this lesser coin with the unsuspecting tradesmen, peasant, and artisan, devaluing the price of money. Eventually, the coins were worthless. Some saw this kind of coin debasement as intrinsic to the market economy in general and usurers in particular, and not simply the action of dishonest moneylenders who shortchanged their customers in the same way that dishonest merchants cheated the customer on the length of cloth, the number of apples, or the amount of ale. In short, it was a matter of individual probity or lack thereof.[28]

By the seventeenth century, the dominant economies were no longer in the Mediterranean south but had shifted northward to the chillier climes of the Dutch Republic and England. Protestantism had replaced Catholicism in both countries as the dominant religion and the two nations now embarked on an age of empire. New trade routes to America, Africa, and Asia made both countries formidable powers. With the need for capital, interest payments were gaining legitimacy as prohibitions were eased and commerce increased. Usury was to be redefined once more. There was a momentous transformation in the air. As God was pushed more and more to the wings of the stage, economic policies were evaluated for their ability to be efficient and produce steady revenue rather than their morality. In order to handle the government debt, national banks were founded, as well as a variety of other credit institutions. Centralized banking gave the government control over people's money and national banks ushered in the bank note system, establishing the foundation for the modern banking system in Europe. The Bank of England, modeled on the Bank of Amsterdam, was founded in 1695 in the wake of the Glorious Revolution which brought the Dutch-born William of Orange and Mary, daughter of King James II, to the British throne. And it was in these lands that the spirit of commerce and industry took a giant step forward as bankers immersed themselves in a new cosmopolitan world.[29]

Notes

1. Jerry Z. Muller, *The Mind and the Market: Capitalism in Western Thought* (New York: Alfred A. Knopf, 2002), Kindle, chap. 1; Michael Wykes, "Devaluing the Scholastics: Calvin's Ethics of Usury," 39, http://web.mit.edu/aorlando/www/SaintJohnCHII/CalvinUsury.pdf; Geisst, *Beggar Thy Neighbor*, chap. 2; *The English Usurer or Usury Condemned*, collected by John Blaxton [1634] (Norwood, NJ: W.J. Johnson, 1974), 43, 49. On Luther, see, Walther Bienert, *Martin Luther und die Juden: Ein Quellenbuch mit zeitgenössischen Illustrationen, mit Einführungen und Erläuterungen* (Frankfurt am Main: Evangelisches Verlagswerk, 1982) and Christopher J. Probst, *Demonizing the Jews: Luther and the Protestant Church in Nazi*

Germany (Bloomington, IN: Indiana University Press, 2012); Martin Luther, *The Jews and Their Lies* (Los Angeles: Christian Nationalist Crusade, 1948), 27, 42, 48.

2. Norman L. Jones, *God and the Moneylenders: Usury and the Law in Early Modern England* (Oxford: B. Blackwell, 1989), 14–15.
3. There are many reasons advanced by historians why such a difference existed in the assessment of usury by these two reformist theologicans. Some suggest it was their environment that was a key issue to their varying positions on interest loans and trade. Calvin was from a prosperous family from Noyon in France, the city in which Charlemagne was crowned emperor. As a young man, he lived in a number of cities including Orléans and Strasbourg as well as Geneva, a place dependent on commerce, industry, and banking. Some have argued that, in addition to his urban upbringing, and maybe because of that upbringing, Calvin had a better grasp of economics than did Luther. Munro, "Rentes and the European 'Financial Revolution,'" 243; Jones, *God and the Moneylenders*, 17–18; Hawkes, *Culture of Usury*, 83; Geisst, *Beggar Thy Neighbor*, chap. 2; Wykes, "Devaluing the Scholastics," 41–43.
4. Peter H. Wilson, *The Thirty Years' War* (New York: Palgrave Macmillan, 2010), 13, 14, 15, 56, 61; Roover, "The Concept of the Just Price," 428.
5. Bailey W. Diffie and George D. Winius, *Foundations of the Portuguese Empire, 1415–1580* (Minneapolis: University of Minnesota Press, 1977), 413.
6. Selma Stern, *The Court Jew* (New Brunswick: Transaction Books, 1985), 3; H. P. Salomon and Aron di Leone Leoni, "Mendes, Beneviste, de Luna, Micas, Nasci: The State of the Art (1532–1558)," *Jewish Quarterly Review* 88.3–4 (1998): 137; Brooks, *The Woman Who Defied Kings*, 20–21, 47, 50, 60–61; James C. Boyajian, *Portuguese Trade in Asia Under the Habsburgs, 1580–1640* (Baltimore: Johns Hopkins University Press, 1993), 9; Diffie and Winius, *Foundations of the Portuguese Empire*, 413–15.
7. Salomon and Leoni, "Mendes," 138, 142; Brooks, *The Woman Who Defied Kings*, 58–59, 71–72–73, 86, 127.
8. Diffie and Winius, *Foundations of the Portuguese Empire*, 415.
9. Brooks, *The Woman Who Defied Kings*, 102, 16–107, 110, 151, 169, 203; Salomon and Leoni, "Mendes," 139.
10. Brooks, *The Woman Who Defied Kings*, 219, 237.
11. Ceasefire between religious factions was obtained for a while with the Religious Peace of Augsburg in 1555 which prompted a split in Lutheranism. Moderates followed the humanism of Philipp Melanchthon, an intellectual leader of Lutherism who hoped for reconciliation with Catholicism, while their opponents—the Gnesio Lutherans—saw their fight as that of the true Christianity against evil. This branch was particularly strong in Saxony, the birthplace of Lutheranism. In addition, Calvinism in Germany was particularly notable in the Palatinate, Brandenburg, and Hessen. Wilson, *The Thirty Years War*, 27, 35–36, 38–39, 359.

12. Wilson, *The Thirty Years' War*, 21, 76, 81–2, 404; Henry Dundas, Viscount Melville, quoted in Niall Ferguson, *The House of Rothschild: Money's Prophets 1798–1848* (New York: Viking, 1999), 83.
13. Greg Steinmetz, *The Richest Man Who Ever Lived: The Life and Times of Jakob Fugger* (New York: Simon & Schuster, 2015).
14. The first statement on court Jews is from Stern, *The Court Jew*, 153–54, 246. See also 1–2, 5, 8–9, 11, 35, 43, 137, 143, 228, 231; The second quote is from Wiesner-Hanks, *Early Modern Europe*, chap. 11.
15. Wilson, *The Thirty Years War*, 39; Kenneth Dyson, *States, Debt, and Power: "Saints" and "Sinners" in European History and Integration* (Oxford: OUP, 2014), 174.
16. Stern, *The Court Jew*, 19, 86, 88, 91, 140–41; Jonathan I. Israel, *European Jewry in the Age of Mercantilism, 1550–1750* (Oxford: Clarendon Press, 1985), 102, 103, 104, 109, 116.
17. Craig Koslofsky, *Evening's Empire: A History of the Night in Early Modern Europe* (Cambridge: CUP, 2011), 166; Stern, *The Court Jew*, 36.
18. Albrecht Beutel, *Spurensicherung: Studien zur Identitätsgeschichte des Protestantismus* (Tübingen: Mohr Siebeck, 2013), 81–82; Stern, *The Court Jew*, 145.
19. "Jakob Bassevi von Treuenberg 1570–1634," Jacob Bassevi von Treuenberg Collection, Leo Baeck digital collection, Leo Baeck Institute, New York, PID 1642215, Call no. AR 3480, http://access.cjh.org/home.php?type=extid&term=1642215#1; Stern, *The Court Jew*, 163.
20. Steffen Leins, *Das Prager Münzkonsortium 1622/23. Ein Kapitalgeschäft im Driezigjährigen Krieg am Rand der Katastrophe* (Münster: Aschendorff Verlag, 2012); Wilson, *Thirty Years' War*, 796.
21. F. L. Carsten, *Essays in German History* (London: Hambledon Press, 1985), 132–33.
22. Stern, *The Court Jew*, 76,. 116, 117–18, 122, 125, 147.
23. Ibid., 131, 132, 133, 158, 159.
24. Ibid., 179; Claudia Ulbrich, "Eheschließung und Netzwerkbildung am Beispiel des jüdischen Gesellschaft im deutsch-französischen Grenzgebiet (18. Jahrhundert)," in *Eheschliessungen Im Europa Des 18. und 19. Jahrhunderts: Muster und Strategien*, eds. Christophe Duhamelle and Jürgen Schlumbohm (Göttingen: Vandenhoeck & Ruprecht, 2003), 315; Joachim Whaley, *Religious Toleration and Social Change in Hamburg 1529–1819* (Cambridge: CUP, 1985), 85.
25. Robert Liberles, "On the Threshold of Modernity, 1618–1780," in *Jewish Daily Life in Germany, 1618–1945*, ed. Marion A. Kaplan (Oxford: OUP, 2005), Kindle; *Glückel of Hameln*, trans. Marvin Lowenthal (New York: Schocken Books, 1977), 3–4, 92.
26. *Glückel of Hameln*, 9, 23, 3–34, 48, 67, 76, 81; Liberles, "On the Threshold of Modernity."
27. Stern, *The Court Jew*, 1, 13, 19, 35, 86, 88, 91, 115, 139, 140–41, 151, 159, 163, 168, 171, 238–40; David Sorkin, *Moses Mendelssohn and the Religious Enlightenment*

(Berkeley, CA: University of California Press, 1996), 112–13; Carsten, *Essays in German History*, 132–33; Werner Sombart, *The Jews and Modern Capitalism* (New Brunswick: Transaction Books, 1982); Wilson, *The Thirty Years' War*, 117.

28. Charles P. Kindleberger and Robert Z. Aliber, *Manias, Panics and Crashes: A History of Financial Crises* (London: Palgrave Macmillan, 2011), Kindle, chap. 3.
29. Peter Temin and Hans-Joachim Voth, *Prometheus Shackled* (Oxford: OUP, 2013), chaps. 1 and 2.

6 The Virtue of Vice

"Gold in your God," West African tribesmen told the Dutch traders, a sentiment they shared with King Charles X of Sweden (1622–1660). When a Dutch diplomat spoke to the king about religious freedom, he produced a gold coin saying, "There is your religion!" In the eighteenth century, the French encyclopedist Denis Diderot wrote of the Dutch Republic as the country where "money makes up for all vices," and where "the corruption of morals is making headway along with the growth of luxury and wealth."[1]

As was true of the human body, so it was that for the body politic, circulation must be vigorous, and consumption, if excessive, devoured the individual. For the first time, the word competition was used to describe the market. The Spanish Jesuit and scholastic Luis de Molina wrote that it was competition amongst buyers that caused market prices to rise and that few buyers cause them to decline. Man was not yet the measure of all things but the influence of religion on moneylending was on the decline and the opprobrium against credit, while still lively, was ultimately on the wane. Privileges handed out by kings were a form of monopoly and monopolies were increasingly condemned as conspiratorial collusions that went against liberty. Leonardus Lessius, a Belgian Jesuit, did not dismiss the prince's right to grant exclusive privileges but these, he wrote, must be based on cost, risk, and market conditions.[2]

The seventeenth century was the age of exploration with improved navigation, better maps (although not always accurate) and faster, bigger ships. It has been argued that it was the economic system of mercantilism that first dispensed with the idea that market behavior was a moral issue and developed the figure of economic man. Sixteenth-century mercantilism was a method that advocated maximizing net exports and high tariffs as the most effective way to national prosperity. While we can find ideas present in mercantilism in medieval times, as a system that was attached to the self-conscious idea of the nation, it was in the seventeenth century that it dominated as "a deliberate pursuit of the economic interest of the state, irrespective of existing law, privilege, and tradition." It was also irrespective of religion. Mercantilism was a zero-sum system that rested not on morality but on the gold theory of wealth, which meant that wealth meant bullion rather than land, as in feudal times. According to the economist Antoine de Montchrétien (1575–1621), a nation's economic health depended upon four things: a favorable situation, abundant national resources, a large and industrious population, and careful regulation of the first three by a vigorous sovereign. "Order," he wrote in 1615, "is the entelechy of states." And, as it was generally believed that only a certain amount of gold and other valuable substances existed in the world, efforts were directed by nations' leaders to secure as much of it for themselves as possible. Regulation of economic policy was aided by centralized political power. Merchants lobbied to secure lucrative monopolies from monarchs, which protected them from the effects of competition and unstable markets. Mercantilism meant, therefore, the shoring up of the nation's treasury in the form of gold and silver, increasingly from colonies abroad, as well as opening and maintaining overseas markets.[3]

In an age of burgeoning empire, wealth was a vital matter of state. It was no longer feasible to erratically tax the population or sporadically borrow to wage a present or imminent war. The drive to enrich the state promoted trade at home and overseas. National banks were established, stock exchanges appeared as the commodity market began to expand, and factor markets started to emerge (i.e., labor markets, capital markets, and markets for raw materials, management, and entrepreneurial resources). No absolutist king controlled the royal expenditure in the seventeenth-century United Provinces, as the Dutch Republic was also known, or in England after the civil war (1642–1651). It was parliament that ultimately held the purse strings, and, with that, it was hoped would come an end to the debasement of currency that had been so common, or the regular defaulting on debt. Compared to France, where the kings retained their absolutist status and the Estates General, comprised of the clergy, nobles, and burghers) only met occasionally (if at all), defaults continued and privileged public offices were sold to raise money. By the eighteenth century, England and Holland, unlike France, were no longer predominantly agricultural economies. At the beginning of the century, fewer than 25 percent of laborers worked on the land while the middle classes increased in wealth and stature. Goldsmiths began issuing paper bills (banknotes) in exchange for the gold and silver their customers deposited with them. These receipts grew in popularity for the ease of use and transport they offered. In other cases, depositors opened book accounts which could be transferred to others by means of a cheque, which became known as bank deposits. Loans now were not only in the hands of the moneylender but the province of national banks, subsidized by the state and run for the interest of the state.[4]

* * *

In 1556, the Habsburg Netherlands, the region that encompassed the Low Countries (including present-day Belgium, Luxembourg, the Netherlands, and Nord-Pas-de-Calais), passed into the hands of Spain's king, Philip II. As the son of the Holy Roman Emperor Charles V, Philip represented the Spanish branch of the Habsburg dynasty. With the Seventeen Provinces now under Catholic Spanish control, many Protestants and Jews fled to Germany and England, or retreated into Holland and Zeeland. The seven northern provinces were brought together under the Union of Utrecht in 1579 and the autonomous Dutch Republic was created in 1581. The founders who rebelled against Spanish rule, saw the republic as a New Jerusalem. Protestant reformers hoped that this new state would combine the civic prowess and philosophy of Athens and the religiosity of Jerusalem. And it was in this here that two ideas long considered antithetical were fused: Virtue and wealth.

Dutch self-defense transformed into imperial conquest and an empire of trade and commerce. By 1590, the Dutch Empire was one of the most important powers in world trade, especially in shipping and colonial commerce but also in the arms trade, even selling weapons to Spain after the cessation of hostilities between the two countries. In turn, the region attracted more investment and credit, making Amsterdam the world financial center and the hub for talent—the Silicon Valley of its time. Debt was becoming not only acceptable but coveted, and annuities (fixed income securities that had been popular since the thirteenth century) were abundant. These included life annuities and tontines, whereby multiple investors paid into a common pool of money and received a regular dividend in accordance with their share. This helped lessen the risk for the issuer of the annuity. Age-contingent annuities appeared in the late seventeenth century and in 1671 the Dutch republican politician Jan de Witt wrote *Value of Life Annuities in Proportion to Redeemable Annuities*. The study of statistics became ever more important in analyzing the risk and the value of invested capital as people sought to minimize the former and maximize the latter in their hope of financial security or quick riches.[5]

On the subject of usury, the Dutch legal scholar Hugo Grotius (1583–1645) declared that interest was compensation for the use of money and was "neither repugnant to natural law nor revealed law." An interest loan only became usurious if the rate was greater than the risk. That was a significant shift from medieval times where usury was a sin on a par with murder and considered an unnatural vice. Where once usury was condemned because it involved no risk to the lender, now the notion of risk in credit was clearly acknowledged and rewarded. Capital was in great supply and investor confidence was high. Between 1632 and 1752, Dutch debt increased from 50 million guilders to 250 million and there was no sign that there would be any default on that debt.[6]

In Leiden, the French scholar and Calvinist Claude Saumaise (Claudius Salmasius) published *De usuris liber* in 1638. In his work, Saumaise argued that there was nothing immoral about moneylending. The individual moneylender could be immoral but that was not due to the profession. It was a business like any other business. High interest rates were due to restricting moneylenders and if there were more moneylenders then competition would naturally drive down the rate. There was, Saumaise noted, no words uttered by Jesus against usury and Jews only prohibited it amongst themselves due to political and tribal reasons. There was no reason to ban or restrict usury other than the pope's laws and, as a Calvinist, there was no need to pay attention to those. With the average interest rate on loans to the poor in Amsterdam being 16 percent, by the time the moneylender's expenses were taken into consideration, that amount was cut by half, which was hardly a scandalously high amount of profit.[7]

The Dutch United East India Company (*Vereenigde Oostindische Compagnie* or VOC) was chartered in 1602 out of six smaller East India companies. Along with the East India Company in England, the VOC was one of the early joint stock companies that appeared in the seventeenth century to facilitate and attempt to monopolize colonial trade. Its early days, however, were focused more on capturing hostile ships than trade. It was afforded the right to implement laws, negotiate treaties, and enter into conflict overseas. When it did turn towards trading, it claimed a monopoly on Dutch trade east of the Cape of Good Hope and west of the Straits of Magellan, especially in cloves, mace, and nutmeg—

spices all in high demand in Europe. Stock in the company was sold in the covered Beurs (*bursa*) near the Town Hall and the stock price had a steady rise over the seventeenth century. "If one were to lead a stranger through the streets of Amsterdam and ask him where he was," Josef de la Vega wrote in the first book known to describe a stock exchange, "he would answer 'Among the speculators,' for there is no corner where one does not talk shares." Vega was a Spanish Jew whose family had been crypto-Jews until they fled first to Antwerp and then Amsterdam, while one brother went on to London. In his description of the stock market, he repeatedly refers to it as a game, "the fairest and most deceitful [business] in Europe" as well as the "finest and most vulgar." Whether it was fair and fine, or deceitful and vulgar depended on the participant, who he divided into three classes: the big financial capitalists who lived off the interest of their large fortune, never visited the exchange but conducted their business through a broker, and had the dignity of princes in their business dealings. The second was the merchant, who took risk into account as much as profit, who was content to make a small amount with relatively little risk, and who may or may not frequent the exchange or use a broker. The third category was the speculator or gambler, whose thrill was the pursuit of massive gain, excelled in tricks such as collusion, cheating, concealment of facts, and other deceits, and who sometimes swindled the brokers.[8]

People in Amsterdam had begun speculating in the mid-sixteenth century on grain, herring, spices, whale oil, and, most famously, tulips. The bourse had humble beginnings in an open-air market before moving twice and ending up in the stock exchange built by merchants in 1611. By the end of the seventeenth century, most of the terms utilized today in trading were in use, including the word "share" ("*actie*," 1606), puts, calls, options, and pools. On weekday mornings, business was conducted on The Dam, a square that faced the Town Hall, from 10 a.m. to 12 p.m. At noon, trading switched to the Exchange until it closed at two o'clock. Just before midday, the "crowds gathered in great haste in order not to be fined for coming late" to the exchange, which shut its gates promptly at noon. It was, by Vega's account, a raucous atmosphere with much handshaking, shouting, hand-slapping, pushing, insults, and rudeness. One contemporary English traveler claimed that most of the speculators were Jews, trading in the main business, which was the buying and selling of shares in the VOC. But Vega makes no mention of the religion or ethnicity of the traders. They either behaved decently or lost their reputations. Some made a good living, others gambled for amusement, some out of vanity, others were spendthrifts. Profit were used for family life and the upkeep or homes, or squandered on card games, women, wine, lavish clothing, and many more luxuries.[9]

To combat the abuses that were possible in the stock market, edicts were published forbidding certain practices, such as short selling, trading shares not actually in the seller's possession, trying to manipulate the market or falsely depress the price of shares by spreading rumors, and using insider information that was not available to other investors. No regulations could end all corruption and rigging the market continued to be a problem for shareholders and traders. Despite the potential for cheating, the stock exchange was an essential step in the evolution of capitalism, as it allowed the free flow of capital that aided economic expansion. The temptation some felt to gamble and get rich quick was certainly one of its pitfalls, but, for the more sober, it allowed people to raise the capital they needed to grow their business by giving investors a share in their company.

The most important development on the road to a fully-fledged capitalism and the acceptance of interest and the financial professions, went hand-in-hand with the stock exchange. The Bank of Amsterdam, founded in 1609, was most important national bank on continental Europe. Originally, it was simply an exchange bank (*Wisselbank*) that did not extend credit but, over time, the public bank offered its clients a range of services such as the ability to deposit, transfer, invest, and lend money. It became a resource for both private and municipal investment, funding cheaper, long-term loans. The bank solved the problem of the multiple currencies in the United Provinces, including many foreign coins, as merchants set up accounts in standardized currency. This enabled more commercial transactions so long as the bank's reserve was greater than the deposits. More than at any other time, large sums of money were made off financial dealings and speculation rather than trade and, with mercantilism still the dominant (if ailing) economic theory, creditors still vied for privileges, exclusive rights, and titles. The principal borrowers remained the monarchs, who negotiated loans to fund their political and social designs at home as well as the numerous wars that erupted in the seventeenth century.[10]

It is not surprising, that people from other nations with money and ability flocked to Amsterdam—as well as other Dutch cities—attracted by its economic power and, in turn, stimulating its economic growth by investment and trade. The Dutch Republic became not only a place for Jews and *conversos* who left Spain and Portugal to live freely, whatever religion they chose, but also a place of dynamic economic opportunities for them. In Amsterdam, Jews were involved in many businesses; they were diamond cutters, butchers, poulterers, bakers, wholesalers, in shipping, as well as present in the financial trades, brokers, moneylenders, and moneychangers. By far, however, the wealthier financiers and largest fortunes belong to native Dutch patricians and regents, not Jews. That notwithstanding, fortunes and comfortable livings could be made by anyone in the Dutch Republic in comparison to other cities. When Hamburg's burgesses assigned a wealth tax to the Jewish community, it brought the annual tax in 1690 to 4000 mark, an amount which was raised again in 1697 to 4,500. That was only part of new financial tariffs designed to ease the city's fiscal problems. The Portuguese Jews were to pay a special tax of 20,000 while the German Ashkenazic Jews were responsible for a 30,000 levy. To avoid paying these onerous taxes, there was the age-old solution. Rather than handing over such a high sum of money, the richest Portuguese Jews departed Hamburg for other places, some did not go far afield and chose Altona, just outside of Hamburg, while others chose to settle in Amsterdam and other parts of the Netherlands, and enjoy better economic opportunities and more liberty.[11]

The Dutch Republic was a religious madhouse according to Jean-Baptiste Stouppe, who, although a Huguenot, joined the French army and took part in the French invasion of the Dutch Republic in 1672. As well as the Sephardic Jews from Spain and Portugal, Anabaptists such as the Mennonites, Lutherans, Calvinists, Quakers, Socinians, and all kinds of *chriétiens sans église* settled in this new republic that put trade and commerce before religion. With such diversity of religion, a compromise was reached between the Calvinist House of Orange and the political forces of the various Dutch provinces to resist anything that interfered with trade. The Dutch, Stouppe observed, "are addicted to *Commerce*." So long as they can "heap up Money" the merchants of Holland would trade with "Infidels" in their colonies and, unlike the Spanish and French, were not even bothered to convert them. Andrew Marvell, the English poet, agreed, referring to the Dutch Republic as a "Mint of Schism" and a "Staple of Sects."[12]

Even though were no formal ghettos, the natural tendency was for people to live in close proximity with others who shared their religious and cultural traditions. Religious Jews had another reason to segregate themselves in their own communities apart from Christians. Many Jews arriving in Amsterdam were returning to Judaism from Catholicism and knew very little about Judaism. As a result, they were inconsistent in their devotion or straddled the two religions. The focus of the community, though, was not theological. Leaders of the Jewish community were both commercial laymen (*parnassim*) and rabbis but it was the *parnassim* that were the real power in Jewish lives. They appointed the rabbis, fired them, and made all major decisions concerning the community. They have been called unimpressive due to the fact that they were chosen as community leaders because of their wealth and economic power and because of what they might be able to do for the Jews in Amsterdam rather than their religious knowledge. But that was a strength not a weakness.[13]

Most Sephardic Jews made their money from trading merchandise, importing from the South such commodities as woods, sugar, dyes, spices, jewels, precious metals, and exporting raw materials from the North and finished goods. It was the breadth of economic possibilities rather than religious piety that drove Antonio Lopes Suasso (1614–1685), a merchant banker from Belgium, to leave Antwerp and go to live in Amsterdam. Suasso had been born into a New Christian family in Bordeaux where his brother was a professor of Catholic theology. Once in Amsterdam, Suasso transformed into a Jew, taking the name Isaac Israel Lopes Suasso. He promptly married Violenta, the daughter of Abraham de Pinto, the richest Jewish merchant in Amsterdam. This connection enabled him to be appointed the secretary-treasurer of the Jewish community despite not having completed the requisite residential period. As a banker, he not only helped to finance the Stadtholders—the nobles who represented the Dutch Republic—he also maintained strong ties with Spain, in spite of the expulsion. It was from the Spanish king, Charles II, that Suasso received the title Baron d'Avernas le Gras for his diplomatic ventures.[14]

Suasso's tenure as treasurer also coincided with the arrival of a number of Jews fleeing the colony of Recife in Brazil following the Portuguese recapture of the territory from the Dutch in 1654. Most of these refugees were wealthy Sephardic Jewish financiers, brokers, sugar and slave merchants. Some resettled in the Dutch Antilles, helping to establish the sugar trade there, a few went to the Dutch colony of New Amsterdam (New York), while others, along with Dutch exiles, arrived in Amsterdam. Their arrival came at the right moment. Around the same time, thousands of Jews fled from cities such as Vilna when Sweden invaded Poland but, unlike the Sephardim, these Ashkenazic Jews reached Amsterdam penniless. It was up to the wealthier Spanish and Portuguese Jews to make sure that they were fed, clothed, and housed, and did not become a burden on the state, for the sake of the entire community. In this respect, these secular leaders of the community, again, were anything but unimpressive. Their wealth and influence were vital for these refugees.[15]

The 1650s were a time of economic prosperity and that continued into the next century. It was in the Netherlands that the first diversified investment fund was created called *Eendragt Maakt Magt* ("unity makes strength"). The focus of the fund was not on shares but bonds, which were issued against the fund's pooled assets. Its success was short-lived, as Holland's role as a great power was in the drawn-out process of decline. Much of this was due to their own success. Their productivity led to deflation and their competitive economy prompted other powers such as France and England to put protectionist tariffs into place that stifled freedom in economic movement and closed off major markets. Costly wars eroded financial stability, such as the invasion of the Dutch Republic by an alliance consisting in 1672 of Sweden, England, France, Cologne, and Munster. Multiple wars against England ended in eventual victory for the latter. After the fourth Anglo-Dutch war (1780–1784), the English parliament passed the Navigation Acts, which barred foreign ships from trading in English ports. By this time, the Dutch Republic had been economically surpassed by other powers, in particular, England, which was embarking on its first phase as a global empire and was eager for capital.[16]

* * *

Just before his death in 1553 and Elizabeth's coronation, Edward VI prohibited usury as "a vice most odious and detestable." It had been banned by Henry VII in 1487 and again in 1495 but as its enforcement relied on informants, it was difficult for the anti-usury law to be effective. In reality, interest rates of 10 percent were widely acceptable. Lower than that, the principal was forfeited; higher, and a fine was imposed of three times the value of the loan. The growing acceptance of some sort of interest payment as a normal part of the economic system was an indication that, in a period of colonial expansion, economic considerations were outstripping moral qualms about interest rates.

On New Year's Eve, 1600, 218 merchants were granted a royal charter by Queen Elizabeth to trade with the East Indies, giving them a monopoly of trade east of the Cape of Good Hope and west of the Straits of Magellan. It was a company backed by the state in a world in which protectionism was the basis of mercantilist policies. The company's interests were married to the nation's global aspirations. To placate British merchants at home, Elizabeth expelled the German traders who, as competition, were bitterly resented, along with the Lombards who were physically attacked. Trade increased in volume and the number of bankers rose.[17]

Once lagging behind financial centers in Flanders and Italy, London became the place for new forms of capital ventures in both agriculture and industry. The expanding international economy made life ever more prosperous and comfortable for a larger number of people. Poverty remained a serious social problem in Elizabethan England, but the poor were richer than in previous times. New houses were fortified by timber frames and plaster. Carpets were laid down on stone floors instead of straw, beds had sheets, blankets, pillows, and soft mattresses instead of bare wood, and upholstered furniture replaced hard seating. Tapestries decorated the walls. If you had the money, exotic luxuries could be purchased such as expensive textiles for clothing, jewels to adorn the body and dress, and spices to make food taste more palatable.

"I do not knowe," the diplomat and privy councillor Thomas Wilson (1524–1581) wrote, "anye place in christendome so muche subject to thys foule synne of usurie as the whole realme of Englande ys at thys present, and hathe bene of late yeares." Usury was fraud and theft and the usurer was "a deceitful false man, an errant thief, and an extreme extortioner." Even though Jews were no longer in England and moneylending had long been practiced by Christians, Wilson still attached usury to Jews. They were hated, he wrote, because they robbed "all men that deal with them and undo them in the end." Bishop John Jewel (1522–1571) was another strident enemy of usury. Profits via interest were "filthy gains, and a work of darkness .... a monster in nature .... the plagues of the world, and the misery of the people. It is theft, it is the murdering of our brethren, it is the curse of God and the curse of the people." The pamphleteer Philip Stubbes (1555–1610) adduced that the "number of those whom the pestilence of avarice hath swallowed up, is greatter than the number of those whom the sword hath destroid." It was, indeed, as impossible to borrow money in England without recourse to usurious practices as it was a dead man to speak. While acknowledging that the civil laws allowed for earning interest, Stubbes wrote that the usurer butchered his "patient," drawing out his suffering and "sucking out his hart blood" for "lucre and gaine," killing not only the husband but his family, destroying both the body and soul.[18]

In the two decades before Shylock was brought to life by Shakespeare, Parliament passed the Act of Usury in 1571, which made the charging of interest "open and legal." The wording of the 1571 legislation still revolved around God's law and moral rectitude, limited the interest on a loan to 10 percent, and defined usury as interest charged at an excessive rate. How excessive "excessive" was depended on the government that regulated it. The Usury Act of 1624, which replaced the 1571 statute, contained no reference to God. The passing of the new act marked the transformation of loans at interest from being sinful and an act against God to having a legitimate role in economic life and in the national interest. It was now a question of what percentage was to be regarded as "immoral" and "exploitative" and what interest was acceptable—by no means an easily answered problem. In his 1640 history of Canterbury, William Somner denounced Jewish usurers not for their profession but for exacting "unreasonable interest upon the loan of Money" while Gerald de Malynes, himself a merchant, cautioned people not to avoid loans but not to trade with hearts "overfrozen with the Ice of uncharitablenesse."[19]

After a civil war that opposed the royalists against the parliamentarians, Charles the I was beheaded, his son exiled, and Oliver Cromwell's Commonwealth replaced the monarchy. It was envisioned as a Puritan version of the ancient Jewish mission with Cromwell as the Protestant Moses leading Britain out of the dark wilderness of the Catholic world. In this heady atmosphere of king slayers and messiahs, Cromwell desired to make England a prosperous and a great commercial nation. That meant that it was open to moneylenders and it was not long before a great influx of financiers and merchants from the continent streamed into England looking for more economic opportunities. French Huguenots and Dutch Jews of Spanish and Portuguese birth or descent brought their continental business practices and capital to London. As there had never been any legal stipulation that Jews could never return to England after the expulsion, it was decided that no official edict or readmission was necessary. Wealthy Jewish merchants and bankers who settled during the Interregnum were officially given access to the Royal Exchange, where people traded stocks as a side business, and where other merchants dealt in clothes, groceries, and medicine. Cromwell also employed Jews as army contractors for his New Model Army. Moneylenders such as Antonio Fernandez Carvajal imported large sums of Spanish money and silver into England. Diego Rodrigez Marques, a London-based Portuguese Jewish merchant who was particularly active in the gem trade, was also in the process of bringing gold and silver into the country when he died. His will lists not only the amounts of money that he owed to other Jewish merchants and moneylenders but also the debts due to him by English companies and individual bankers. One debt was for the enormous sum of five thousand pounds.[20]

Jewish financiers and traders continued to arrive in England during the Restoration of Charles II, which began in 1660. Sephardic Jews and *conversos* from the Dutch Republic made the journey, including Henrique Mendes da Costa, from the House of Mendes, who had once aided Cromwell and now offered loans to Charles II. When in 1688, the pro-Catholic James II was deposed, and the Dutch William of Orange was installed as King William III along with his co-regent Queen Mary II, Dutch financial innovations also crossed the channel. William's campaign was partially aided by some of the Sephardic financiers in Amsterdam and Antwerp. For this "Glorious Revolution," insofar as it was bloodless, Solomon de Medina, the first Jew to be knighted in England, supplied funds to William and was also the commissariat contractor to John Churchill, the first duke of Marlborough. William was also assisted by Antonio Lopes Suasso, who had previously seized the opportunities offered by the business-friendly environment of Amsterdam. It was rumored that he gave 2,000,000 guilders in an interest-free loan to the future king of England to fund his invasion.[21]

Sephardic Jews who moved from Antwerp and Amsterdam to London settled in what is still today the financial district. Antonio (Abraham) de Porto lived at St. Mary's Axe (where the building nicknamed the Gherkin stands today), Domingo (Israel Roiz) Francia resided in Leadenhall Street, Diego Rodriguez Aries on Fenchurch Street, and Augustin Coronel Chacon, Duarte Henrique Alvares, and Antonio Robles all lived on Duke's Place. They met regularly to worship at the house of Rabbi Moses Israel Athias on Creechurch Lane, just off Leadenhall Street, the site of the first synagogue in London. Towards the end of the seventeenth century, more Jews from Lithuania and Germany arrived in London and this flow of Jewish migrants from the continent continued into next century, necessitating a more spacious house of worship. The Great Synagogue, founded in 1690 by Benjamin Levy and renovated in 1722 by Moses Hart was built for this new Ashkenazic community and was separate from the new Sephardic synagogue, Bevis Marks, established in 1701 and located nearby off Heneage Lane. It was during the eighteenth century that the city gates were removed in order to widen the streets as commerce boomed. Amongst the new Jewish immigrants was a man whose son would significantly contribute to the history of economics. Abraham Ricardo left Amsterdam where his father had been a successful stockbroker and, in 1759, settled in London, where his son David was born in 1772.[22]

The changing economic landscape shaped the towns and cities as merchant-bankers rose in importance. Business had long been conducted in taverns and inns, such as the ones in which Glückel of Hameln stayed during her travels. As tastes changed, deals were conducted in coffee-houses. In preparing for his role as Shylock on the stage, the actor Charles Macklin visited these new venues to observe the merchants and bankers at work. The new thinking was that the stimulant coffee was more conducive to closing business deals than sleep-inducing ale. *Coffy-huysen* had opened in Amsterdam and other parts of the Dutch Republic, where merchants and investors drank coffee, chocolate, milk, or tea in warm rooms, filled with books and board games. Here they conversed, smoked, learned the latest news, negotiated, and closed deals. In the same year as the Glorious Revolution, Edward Lloyd opened a coffee shop on Tower Street in the City of London where merchants, sailors, and shipowners gathered for trustworthy shipping information. In the Parish of St. Peter's in Oxford, a Jew named Jacob opened a coffee-house before trying his luck in London. A year or two later, in 1651, the better-known Pasqua Rosée (a Ragusan) established his coffee house in Oxford and, a year later, in Cornhill within London's financial district. By 1700, four to five hundred coffee-houses were located around London.[23]

* * *

In his eighteenth-century travel memoirs, *A Foreign View of England in the Reigns of George I and George II*, César-Francois de Saussure observed that the English:

> are very fond of wealth . . . their first inquiry [on making an acquaintance] will be "Is he rich?" In this country one is esteemed for one's wealth more than anything else . . . . Merchants come after the clergy, and in England commerce was not looked down upon as being derogatory, as it is in France and Germany. Here men of good family and even of rank may become merchants without losing caste . . . . London is assuredly the greatest commercial city in the world.

In England, unlike France, it was thought that commerce fostered manners and civility and economic activity had the ability to stimulate patriotism. Commerce, trade, and the investment capital that allowed their expansion were no longer at odds with societal values. What was of concern, as always, was the possibilities of corruption and immoral actions rather than an economy based on capital. The East India Company that Elizabeth I had chartered was a state-controlled company and ultimately beholden to the Crown. However, many MPs held stock in the company and it was in their financial interest to protect and aid this monopoly. As a result, the EIC had largely free rein in its policies and action in India, foreign competition was hindered, and the company's directors saw themselves more and more as legally distinct from the Crown. Its power was further enhanced by a standing army that grew to around 20,000. Such monopolies and the purchasing of stock raised concerns over corruption and a decay in morals.[24]

Forms of limited-liability affiliations dated back to the thirteenth century, with the Bazacle Milling Company in Toulouse, but it was from the sixteenth and especially during the seventeenth century that they flourished. Joint stock companies allowed multiple investors to pool their money for riskier and more expensive endeavors and allow that risk to be shared. Apart from the East India Company, the Virginia Company was another joint stock company with a royal charter—this time by King James I in 1606—to colonize the north-eastern coast of North America. Before 1689, there were fifteen major joint stock companies with their business predominantly overseas. At the end of the seventeenth century, when banking was liberalized, giving companies the greater ability to borrow funds, there were 140 such businesses with capital totaling £4.5 million and with wider interests and a keener focus on domestic affairs. These new joint stock companies raised money by selling shares to investors who then had a vested interest in the strength or weakness of the company. The proliferation of shareholders provided more money than ever before to fund vast and unprecedented ventures around the globe.[25]

With this transformation, a new profession sprang up: the stockbroker or stock jobber. Specialized jobbers, predecessors of the modern brokers, appeared around 1700, acting as the intermediary between lender and borrower. The London securities market had a humble beginning at the Royal Exchange, which had been opened by Elizabeth I in 1571. It was the hub of commerce for the city of London, along with various coffee houses in Change Alley such as Jonathan's Coffee House and Garroway's, which often hosted the brokers who were thrown out of the Royal Exchange for indecent and raucous behavior. Brokers ran from the coffee house where financial news was posted, then over to their clients with the latest stock and commodity prices, and back to the coffee house with their instructions on what to buy and sell.

By the end of the seventeenth century, about a fifth of all the recognized brokers in the vicinity of Lombard Street were described as "Jews or foreigners," with their own areas or "walks" in the Royal Exchange. One author complained in a 1719 essay that the alley thronged with "Jews, jobbers, and brokers." Many of the private bankers, however, were neither Jewish nor foreign, including Francis Child, John Campbell (Coutts Bank), and Richard Hoare, who opened up the credit market to more of the general public. Most loans were collateral-based, although banks moved towards unsecured loans. Collateralized loans were mainly due to low interest rates as these were restricted to 6 percent and reduced to 5 percent after 1714. It was argued that lower interest rates encouraged international trade, although low, fixed rates handcuffed private bankers, making it difficult for these lenders to compete during a credit crunch. For those who covertly contracted a loan at a higher interest rate than legally allowed, the punishment was a fine of three times the original loan plus interest. Unlike in medieval times, usury laws that protected these rates were upheld not for religious and moral reasons but by the English law courts as a matter of economic policy.[26]

A national bank was called for based on the one already established in Amsterdam "whereby the profits in usury will supply his Majesty more plentifully than ever to carry on the war, exempt the nation from land tax, great customs, exceedingly promote trade and navigation, and give England many other advantages." It was hoped that the bank would carry the national debt and free the country from extortioners and usurers, which by now meant someone who lent at what was considered to be an exorbitant rate of interest. To its critics, the opposite was more likely; a national bank would produce innumerable brokers and jobbers relishing the chance to prey on their fellow man as well as corrupting morals. With the founding of the Bank of England in 1694, London boasted an institution that could manage the ever-larger sums of capital and it also presented significant competition to private bankers. Merchants and goldsmiths now had a place to deposit their surplus funds, rather than their previous option of keeping them at the mint in the Tower of London.[27]

It was unabashed self-interest—the desire for profit and betterment—that epitomized the banking and stock market professions. It created prosperity not only for the individual, however, but for the rest of society, even if there was always a wide gap between the very rich and the very poor. The financial professions were also a way for those who were not born into nobility to climb the social ladder, although this new middling sort were disinclined to imitate what they saw as the moral decadence and economic profligacy of the aristocracy.

Critics of the capital economy did not vanish, but the focus shifted toward the machinations of speculation, which tended to increase as the rate of interest declined. Keen to keep up the same standard of living or dramatically improve their circumstances, some financiers turned to riskier and potentially more profitable speculative enterprises when they could no longer count on a high interest rate return. Speculation attracted the honest risk-takers, as well as the unscrupulous, fraudulent, and the foolish. The craze for "get rich quick" schemes exploded with overexcited speculation on all manner of companies and weird inventions as people scrambled to invest before the door of opportunity was shut on them. The author Daniel Defoe warned of the menace of this new financial era which, he believed, brought to the fore the dishonest, the manipulative, and the gullible who were easily tricked out of their money. It was not that Defoe was against this new world of finance. His hopes, like many before him, were that if such dishonesty could be stifled, then finance could transform society for the better and avoid the corrupting of morals.[28]

If money had been regarded as sterile in ancient and medieval times, there was little doubt in the modern world that money was very fertile indeed. Money made money and then even more money. And along with the sound investments there were a multitude of unsavory and shady business deals. As one economic historian put it, "rational exuberance" morphed into "irrational exuberance," resulting in "economic euphoria." With so much money invested in dubious or unprofitable businesses, it was only a matter of time until the bubble burst.[29]

It did so spectacularly in the eighteenth century, rather more so with the Mississippi Bubble in France but to a lesser extent with the South Sea Bubble in England. In 1715, France was in bad financial shape. Despite high taxes, war and mismanagement had left the country in on the verge of bankruptcy and defaulting on its debt. Into this scenario came a Scotsman by the name of John Law, a financier and gambler, who had broken out of Newgate prison in London, after being sentenced to hang for the dueling death of another man. He put his two talents together to devise a scheme to help debt-ridden Louis XIV out of financial trouble. Entranced by the Scotsman's professed abilities, Louis gave him a charter to the royal bank. The bank took in coin deposits but issued loans and withdrawals in paper. Law then created the Mississippi Company, which held a twenty-five-year monopoly, granted by Louis, over the commerce in French-controlled Louisiana. Shares in the company were sold publicly and both the French and foreign investors were encouraged to buy. The national debt was to be paid from the revenue elicited from the sale of stock. With Law misrepresenting the profitability of Louisiana and the money that could be made through investment in the company, people flocked to buy shares. The bank then issued credit for people without the ready cash to buy shares. Anxious not to use up the bank's reserve of gold and silver, Law capped the amount of profit that could be taken in coinage. This meant that more paper money was printed—far more than the bank had reserves of gold and silver—to fund this bubble which was financed by selling new shares rather than its profits. The bubble burst in 1719 when a large number of people attempted to convert their shares into coin, which the bank was unable to cover. France's financial development was critically damaged, as the reaction of the government in the aftermath of the financial collapse was to refrain from any further use of paper money or stock markets. This only augmented the state's financial woes.[30]

In England, The South Sea Company had been set up 1711 to consolidate and reduce that country's national debt, along with the Bank of England and the East India Company. In financing the government's debt, the South Sea Company was given a monopoly in South America to trade slaves. The company exchanged its own shares for treasury bonds (government debt) and the government paid interest to the company. Drunk and delirious with expectations of vast wealth, aristocrats, gentry, politicians, bankers, merchants, and many others rushed to buy shares, boosting the price of shares, unaware of the mismanagement of the company, the extent of fraud and bribery conducted by insider traders and politicians, or the unlikelihood of the South American monopoly ever producing a profit. When this Ponzi scheme crashed, many people were financially ruined. To the economist Adam Smith, the scandal was a result of "knavery and extravagance" on the part of the company's personnel. It was one of many such fiscal scandals, a boom-and-bust story of people ready to throw their money at any venture, no matter how insubstantial or ludicrous, in the fear that they would miss out on the one golden investment that would make them unimaginably rich. Isaac Newton was one of those caught up in the mania, making a profit initially but then, with a second investment, incurring a loss of £20,000.[31]

Although the consequences were not as severe in England as they had been in France, in both countries there was a sudden decrease of credit. Critics complained about "unsavory" financial professions and the distasteful nature of making of money from money. In 1716, one critic griped:

> From this corruption of companies in Trade, breeds the vermin called stockjobbers, who prey upon, destroy, and discourage all Industry and honest gain for no sooner is any Trading Company erected, or any villainous project to cheat the public set up, but immediately it is divided into shares, and then traded for in Exchange Alley, before it is known whether the project has any intrinsic value in it, or no . . ...

The buying and selling of stock remained to many outside the profession as just another form of gambling, an immoral activity that did nothing to elevate the nation's economic wellbeing. Rather than seeing these rash activities as individual human error, archetypes of the financier were used to further the idea that he was nothing more than a villain who preyed on the poor, the foolish, and the vulnerable. Far from contributing to the common good, the stock exchange was a sinkhole of degradation. That there were cheats and frauds is, of course, true. But there were strict limits on the financial activities of stock market associates for this very reason. The concern was that if one person suffered a large loss in trade or banking, it would have a domino effect on others. This initial loss would then cause further losses and eventually destabilize the market. There was also the personal disaster of financial ruin, the inability to repay debts, and bankruptcy. In 1810, out of despair, Abraham Goldsmith shot himself when his business failed and he was left owing a massive debt of £466,700, mainly to the government.[32]

To those who pointed the finger at extravagant and reckless investments, misdeeds, and corruptions as examples that the economic system was intrinsically immoral, the Anglo-Dutch mercantilist economist Bernard de Mandeville responded with *The Fable of the Bees* (1714). The common good and individual interest were not adversaries. Vices were "inseparable from great and potent Societies," he wrote, and "Wealth and Grandeur" would not exist without them. But that was not to say that anyone guilty of vice should not be "continually reprov'd, or not be punish'd for them when they grow into Crimes." In poetic form, Mandeville claimed that the self-interest of the individual was synonymous with the good of the state. Rather than vilifying wealth and those who moved in the world of finance, effort should be made to celebrate both. For Mandeville, vice and virtue went agreeably hand-in-hand, to the benefit of all:

> Thus every Part was full of Vices,
> Yet the Whole Mass a Paradise;
> Flatter'd in Peace,
> And fear'd in Wars,
> They were the Esteem of Foreigners,
> And lavish of them Wealth and Lives,
> The Balance of all are Hives.
> Such were the Blessings of that State;
> Their Crimes conspir'd to make the Great:
> And Virtue, who from Politicks
> Had learn'd a Thousand Cunning Tricks,
> Was, by their happy Influence,
> Made Friends with Vice:
> And ever since,
> The worst of all the Multitude
> Did something for the Common Good.

In other words, it is not industry that causes the bees to work; it is their vices which pushes them to be industrious and a benefit to society. Even when money was pursued for individual enrichment, investment, and speculation, the result was the prosperity of nations. What caused economic downturns, in Mandeville's assessment, was not the supposed greed of bankers and stockjobbers but underconsumption.[33]

* * *

Eighteenth-century France was a country gripped by the problem of economic growth and how best to achieve it, mainly because France was in such dire straits economically after wars that depleted the treasury. Louis XVI relied on heavy taxation, especially of the Third Estate burghers. Tax was a "sacred debt" and denunciation of tax avoiders was encouraged as a virtue. But the free spending of extravagant monarchs, who believed they were God's representative on earth and who refused to make the necessary cuts and reforms, meant that taxes were unable to fund the economy. It was time, many believed, for the economy to be free from the grasping fingers of meddling kings and incompetent government officials and replace them with a free trade economic system given the name "*laissez-faire*" (leave to be). The "bumpy and indirect" history of free trade began prior to the eighteenth century, in Parisian suburbs such the *faubourg* St. Antoine as well as St. Seurin and St. André in Bordeaux, which were "free enterprise zones" and outside of guild regulations. But it was with the Enlightenment writers that free trade became a part of a larger philosophy and consciously linked to the political and social life.[34]

Enlightenment ideals were discussed in different countries at different times and marked by discrete characteristics, but they were arguably given their most prominent platform in France. Despite regional differences, a common set of overarching ideas defined the movement: a passion for liberty and the individual. Ideas included men being born with natural rights, that subjects should become citizens with civic duties and rights, and that governments should dispense with absolutism to become representative of the people. It was a turning point for Europe, and it was with a moral sense of disdain and superiority that the Enlightenment philosophers dismissed the medieval world as full of barbarism and superstitions, the miserable "Dark Ages" that would be obliterated by the brilliant glare of Enlightenment.

By the mid-eighteenth century, there was a mania in France about how best to improve the economy. Debates over the morality or immorality of commerce and usury had writers churning out books on political economy quicker than novels, with subjects covering the agrarian economy, commerce, manufacturing, and economic theory. In 1638, the French Protestant Claude Saumaise had argued that if bankers were given free rein and not hampered by usury laws, interest rates would naturally fall due to competition. But over a hundred years later, it was a Scot, not a French man, whose book would become the bible for free-trade capitalism.

In 1764, Adam Smith (1723–1790), at the age of forty, left his post as the chair of moral philosophy at Glasgow University and took up the position of tutor to the duke of Bucchleuch. He had already become well-acquainted with members of the Scottish Enlightenment, such as David Hume, and now, during his time in Europe, Smith, met with their counterparts on the Continent. He was introduced to the French economist Anne-Robert-Jacques Turgot, as well as philosophers well versed in the current debates over the economy, wealth, and virtue. Smith met François-Marie Arouet, better known by his *nom de plume* Voltaire, as well as the Swiss philosopher Jean-Jacques Rousseau, whose dislike of authority and belief that all men were born free, chained only by the tyranny of oppressive governments, formed the basis of his book *The Social Contract,* published in 1762.[35]

Many of the *philosophes* with whom Smith debated were linked to the physiocrats, economists who argued for deregulation in agriculture and intensive farming and promoted *laissez-faire.* The physiocrat Dupont de Nemours wrote that "Freedom of exchange . . . serves the general good, for it engenders competition; each takes pain to economise on the costs of his labor, and this economizing necessarily works to the advantage of all." Free trade was the most effective way to increase prosperity by expanding trade without restriction of government interference. Their economic manifesto of the physiocrats included the right to one's own person, labor, and goods. Every man should have the right to buy and sell freely—whatever he wants, to whomever he wants, for whatever price he chooses. Interest rates should be dictated by the degree of money in circulation rather than by moral qualms. The French government should have a hands-off policy and not encroach upon anybody's liberty. Those who opposed free trade were ignorant of everything but "the surface appearance of things," and therefore capable only of demanding regulations, price controls, and the end of market speculation. But it was land, the traditional source of wealth, that was the source of true wealth for physiocrats. Finance and speculation were forms of "unreal" wealth and they categorized people in these professions as a selfish "sect of egoists." The worker of the land, the peasant, was the symbol of national virtue. Farming was to be encouraged as this would lead to modesty, tranquility, and gentleness, and prevent all manner of vice. Land was solid, tangible. Finance was hazardous, ephemeral.[36]

Smith returned to Scotland, his thoughts trained on what constituted and encouraged economic and therefore civil and social progress. Financially secure thanks to a pension from the duke, in the little village of Kirkcaldy he sat down to write what would become the definitive book supporting the principles of free trade and capitalism, although that term was never used by Smith and coined only in the late nineteenth-century. Essential to his task were the abundant notes he had accumulated from all of his travels, debates, and correspondence over a period of seventeen years. *The Wealth of Nations*, written in the year the American colonies cast off British rule, argued for limited government intervention in the economy and rejected the policies of mercantilism. Denouncing the "wretched spirit of monopoly," he believed that it was only through free trade that the steady increase of wealth Europe now expected and desired could occur.[37]

With the belief that free men were naturally inclined to improve their financial condition, Smith supported the "natural price," based on competition, over the mercantilist idea of monopoly and fixed prices and the physiocrat's focus on land as the best source of wealth. Mercantilism operated under the premise that there was a finite source of wealth, which was bound to lead to conflict with nations battling to obtain the world's riches. Physiocrats mistakenly valued land as the sole producer of wealth but the same deregulation that they argued was beneficial for the agricultural economy was also necessary for commerce. And those who imagined that protectionist measures enacted by the government aided prosperity were mistaken. Only an economy left as much as possible to market forces—the systematic exchange of labor and products based on supply and demand—increased wealth for everyone and enriched society. It was summed up by Smith's term, the "invisible hand." Certainly, not everyone would enjoy equal wealth, but most people would experience an improvement in their own personal economy.[38]

Although Smith and Mandeville both applauded self-interest, Smith was more inclined towards David Hume's philosophy. The desire for gain, in Hume's view, encouraged productivity and entrepreneurship and was a necessary incentive and one that prevented indolence. But this should always be harnessed by self-control and frugality, not excessiveness and greed. Smith disagreed with Mandeville's underconsumption theory and his depiction of self-interest as a beneficial vice. Instead, Smith contended that mercantilism rested upon too many government regulations to keep exports high and imports low and that was opposed to his free market system. He also believed that self-interest—as with Hume, this meant self-control and prudence—was a virtue, not a vice as it was the cause of the increase of capital; one which led to admirable characteristics such as industry, economy, discretion, and attention. Liberty in all walks of life was a matter of restraint that would foster self-regulation in the economic world. Market forces were not, and should not, be based on a subjective morality, nor should they be linked to charity. As free traders such as Smith saw it, wealth was not shameful, and it was not immoral for a person to attain wealth and not give it all away.[39]

By the time Smith wrote his treatise, usury was broadly defined as the charging of "excessive" rates of interest with the malicious intent to fleece the borrower. Smith agreed that interest charges were usurious if they were "biting," if they devoured the poor, if they exploited the vulnerable, if they bled the nation dry. But what was excessive? Did it mean 5 percent interest? 10 percent? Or, perhaps,

100 percent interest? It potentially meant all of these and anything in between or over. In the age that created the idea of free trade, it was clear to its proponents that the rate should not be controlled by the government but by market forces and competition. Government intervention, said its critics, was crucial in difficult economic times. And in late eighteenth-century France, those theories were put to the test.

* * *

In the eighteenth century, Man took center stage. The mercantilist theory of wealth was being pushed aside as new ideas were formulated that were based on liberal Enlightenment ideals. The divine right of kings gave way to the idea of a constitutional monarch or an elected assembly based on a *mutually* agreed contract with the people. *Laissez-faire,* or free trade, was opposed to a highly regulated economy and was based on the theory that wealth was created when free people followed their economic interests without undue hindrance by state authorities. Self-interest, self-regulation, reason, and utility were the watchwords of the free market modern economy.

With the vast sum of £20,000, Nathan Rothschild came to England from Frankfurt. His father, Meyer Amschel, had founded the House of Rothschild in Frankfurt in 1764 dealing in coins and gold. With his family connections throughout Europe—Frankfurt, Naples, Vienna, and Paris—and a network of agents and couriers who ferried information as well as gold, Rothschild was often in receipt of important financial information ahead of others. And the year Nathan landed in England was one that changed the face of Europe. It was 1789.[40]

Notes

1. Amy Chua, *Day of Empire: How Hyperpowers Rise to Global Dominance—and Why They Fall* (New York: Anchor Books, 2007), 155; Charles Lipton, "The Social Thought of Diderot," *Science & Society* 8.2 (1944): 130, 131.
2. Roover, "The Concept of the Just Price," 425–27.
3. Mark Blaug, *Economic Theory in Retrospect*, 5th ed. (Cambridge: CUP, 1997), 29; Israel, *European Jewry*, 2; Antoine de Montchrétien, *Traicté de l'oeconomie Politique* [1615] (Paris: E. Plon, 1889), 24–25, 101; Charles Woolsey Cole, *French Mercantilist Doctrines Before Colbert* (New York: Octagon Books, 1969), xiii, xiv, 6; Whaley, *Religious Toleration and Social Change*, 77–80, 83; Jardine, *Worldly Goods*, 95; Kocka, *Capitalism*, chap. 2; Franco Franceschi, "The Economy: Work and Wealth," in *Italy*

in the Age of the Renaissance, 124–25; Temin and Voth, *Prometheus Shackled*, chaps. 1 and 2; Geisst, *Beggar Thy Neighbor*, chap. 2.

4. Ferguson, *The Ascent of Money*, chap. 2; William Doyle, *Venality: The Sale of Offices in Eighteenth-Century France* (Oxford: Clarendon Press, 1996), 3 *passim*; Kindleberger and Aliber, *Manias*, chap. 3; Sennholz, *Age of Inflation*, 11.
5. Majia Holmer Nadesan, *Governmentality, Biopower, and Everyday Life* (New York: Routledge, 2008), 49; Kocka, *Capitalism*, chap. 1.
6. Ferguson, *The Ascent of Money*, chap. 2; John Lothrop Motley, *The Rise of the Dutch Republic: A History* (New York: Harper & Brothers, 1883), 247; Wilson, *The Thirty Years' War*, 130; Geisst, *Beggar Thy Neighbor*, chap. 2.
7. Rothbard, *Economic Thought Before Adam Smith,*144–45.
8. Goetzmann, *Money Changes Everything*, chapt. 18; Josef de la Vega, *Confusion de Confusiones* [1688] (Mansfield Centre, CT: Martino Publishing, 2013), v, 5, 16, 18, 22, 28.
9. Ibid., v, viii, xii, xiii, xix, 21, 29.
10. R. D. Richards, *The Early History of Banking in England* (Abingdon, UK: Routledge, 2012), 135; Ferguson, *Ascent of Money*, chap. 1.
11. Vega, *Confusion de Confusiones*, viii.
12. Temin and Voth, *Prometheus Shackled*, intro and chaps. 2 and 3; Geisst, *Beggar Thy Neighbor*, chap. 2; Richards, *The Early History of Banking*, 135; Wilson, *The Thirty Years' War*, 134–37; Kocka, *Capitalism*; Kindleberger and Aliber, *Manias*, chap. 3; Jean Baptiste Stouppe [Giovanni Battista Stoppa], *La Religion des Hollandois* (Cologne: P. Marteau, 1673); Richard H. Popkin, "The First Published Discussion of a Central Theme in Spinoza's *Tractatus*," *Philosophia* 17.2 (1987): 104. Martin van Gelderen, "Turning Swiss? Discord in Dutch Debates," in *The Republican Alternative: The Netherlands and Switzerland Compared*, eds. André Holenstein, Thomas Maissen, and Maarten Prak (Amsterdam: Amsterdam University Press, 2008), 151–52; Stouppe, *La Religion des Hollandois*, 101–05; van Gelderen, "Turning Swiss?" 152–53.
13. R. H. Popkin, *Spinoza* (Oxford: Oneworld, 2004), 33–34.
14. Henry Méchoulan, *Être juif à Amsterdam au temps de Spinoza* (Paris: Albin Michel, 1990).
15. Popkin, *Spinoza*, 14–15.
16. Goetzmann, *Money Changes Everything*, chap. 19.
17. Geisst, *Beggar Thy Neighbor*, chap. 2; Jonathan Gil Harris, *Sick Economies: Drama, Mercantilism, and Disease in Shakespeare's England* (Philadelphia: University of Pennsylvania Press, 2004), 3, 5; Borer, *The City of London*, 90, 103, 135–37, 146, 182; "The East India Company," *The Economist*, Dec. 17, 2011, http://www.economist.com/node/21541753.
18. Thomas Wilson, *Discourse Upon Usury, by Way of Dialogue and Orations, for the Better Variety and More Delight of All Those that Will Read This Treaty* (London: F. Cass, 1962), 178, 196–97, 220, 229, 353; Bishop Jewel, "A Paper on Usury," *The*

Works of John Jewel, Bishop of Salisbury (Cambridge: Cambridge University Press, 1848), 1293–98; Richard L. Greaves, *Society and Religion in Elizabethan England* (Minneapolis: University of Minnesota Press, 1981), 547–48, 599, 605; Philip Stubbes quoted in Jones, *God and the Moneylenders*, 27, 83; Stubbes, *The Anatomie of Abuses* (London: R. W[ard] for William Wright, 1583), 119, 123, 126–128, http://www.archive.org/stream/phillipstubbessa00stubuoft/phillipstubbessa00stubuoft_djvu.txt.

19. House of Commons committee quoted in Wilson, *Treatise on Usurie*, preface, 103, 106, 115; William Somner, *Antiquities of Canterbury, Or a Survey of That Ancient Citie, with the Suburbs and Cathedrall* [1640] (London: R. Knaplock, 1703), 125; Gerard de Malynes, *The Maintenance of Free Trade, According to the Three Essentiall Parts of Traffique: Namely Commodities, Money and Exchange of Moneys, By Bills of Exchanges for other Countries* (London: I. L[egatt] for William Sheffard, 1622), http://www.efm.bris.ac.uk/het/malynes/malynes.txt.
20. The Will of Diego Rodrigues Marques dated 1675, *SynagogueScribes.com*, http://synagoguescribes.com/blog/the-will-of-diego-rodrigues-marques-dated-1675; Richards, *The Early History of Banking in England*, 132–34; Edward Stringham, "The Emergence of the London Stock Exchange as a Self-Policing Club," *The Journal of Private Enterprise* 17.2 (2002): 4.
21. Ferguson, *The Ascent of Money*, chap. 2.
22. Albert Hyamson, *A History of the Jews of England* (London: Chatto & Windus, 1908), 174–75.
23. Borer, *The City of London*, 210; Kocka, *Capitalism*; Vega, *Confusion de Confusiones*, 35.
24. César de Saussure, *A Foreign View of England in the Reigns of George I and George II: The Letters of Monsieur César de Saussure to His Family*, trans. Madame van Muyden (London: John Murray, 1902), 207–08, 215, 216; John Shovlin, *The Political Economy of Virtue: Luxury, Patriotism, and the Origins of the French Revolution* (Ithaca: Cornell University Press, 2006), 6, 12; William Dalrymple, "The East India Company: The Original Corporate Raiders," *The Guardian*, March 4, 2015, https://www.theguardian.com/world/2015/mar/04/east-india-company-original-corporate-raiders.
25. On the mills of Toulouse, see, Sicard, *The Origin of Corporations*; Geoffrey Poitras, *Valuation of Equity Securities: History, Theory, and Application* (Singapore: World Scientific Pub., 2011), 108; Temin and Voth, *Prometheus Shackled*, chap. 2; Kindleberger and Aliber, *Manias*, chap. 3; Stringham, "The Emergence of the London Stock Exchange as a Self-Policing Club," 4; Ferguson, *The Ascent of Money*, chap. 2.
26. Richards, *The Early History of Banking in England*, 133, 134; Temin and Voth, *Prometheus Shackled*, chapters 2–4.
27. Larry Neal, *The Rise of Financial Capitalism: International Capital Markets in the Age of Reason* (Cambridge: CUP, 1993), 45; Borer, *The City of London*, 151, 203, 204–05; Temin and Voth, *Prometheus Shackled*, chap. 1.

28. Daniel Defoe, *An Essay Upon Projects* (1697), Project Gutenberg, https://www.gutenberg.org/files/4087/4087-h/4087-h.htm; Goetzmann, *Money Changes Everything*, chap. 18.
29. Kindleberger and Aliber, *Manias*, chap. 1
30. Ferguson, *The Ascent of Money*, chap. 3.
31. Borer, *The City of London*, 207; Temin and Voth, *Prometheus Shackled*, chapters 1 and 5; Muller, *The Mind and the Market*, chap. 2; Kindleberger and Aliber, *Manias*, chap. 3.
32. Goetzmann, *Money Changes Everything*, chapt. 19; Temin and Voth, *Prometheus Shackled*, chap. 7; quote is by Anon., *Thoughts on Trade and Public Spirit* (London 1716), quoted in Ranald Michie, *London Stock Exchange: A History* (Oxford: OUP, 1999), 23, 34, 45; *The Anatomy of Exchange Alley* (1719), 378, reprinted in J. Francis, *Chronicles and Characters of the Stock Exchange* (1849), 359–83, quoted in Richards, *The Early History of Banking in England*, 134.
33. Bernard de Mandeville, *The Fable of the Bees, or Private Vices, Publick Benefits*. 6th ed. (London: J. Tonson, 1729), A6, 5.
34. Florin Aftalion, *The French Revolution: An Economic Interpretation*, trans. Martin Thom (Cambridge: CUP, 1990), 12–14, 18, 67, 87; Howell, "Whose 'Common Good' "; James R. Farr, *Artisans in Europe, 1300–1914* (Cambridge: CUP, 2000), 85.
35. Temin and Voth, *Prometheus Shackled*, chap. 1; Geisst, *Beggar Thy Neighbor*, chap. 2; Shovlin, *The Political Economy of Virtue*, 37.
36. Dupont de Nemours quoted in Aftalion, *The French Revolution*, 46–47; Giesst, *Beggar Thy Neighbor*, chap. 8.; Nicolas Bandeau, "De l'esprit agricole," *Éphéménides du citoyen, ou Chronique de l'esprit national* 1. 4 (1765) and *Journal oeconomique* 1 (1751), both quoted in Shovlin, *Political Economy*, 109, 75 and see also 2, 67.
37. Adam Smith, *An Inquiry into the Nature and Causes of the Wealth of Nations*, Ebook, http://www.econlib.org/library/Smith/smWN.html; Nicholas Phillipson, *Adam Smith: An Enlightened Life* (London: Allen Lane, 2010), Kindle ed., chap. 1.
38. Smith, *Wealth of Nations*, Book 1, chap. 7; Kindleberger and Aliber, *Manias*, chap. 3.
39. Smith, *Wealth of Nations*; Muller, *The Mind and the Market*, chap. 3; Middleton and Shaw, *Market Ethics and Practices*, intro.
40. Geisst, *Beggar Thy Neighbor*, chap. 3.

7

The "Regeneration" of Jewish Usurers

"The more democratic a government is, the more suitable it is for a commercial people whose prosperity depends on maximum freedom in its enterprises. No one understands the intents of the business man better than he does himself. As soon as some authority mixes in lessons or laws, everything is lost." Denis Diderot, whose massive *Encyclopédie* was a canon of Enlightenment thinking, wrote this when he still believed in the regenerative power of technology, commerce, and manufacturing and when his vision of the perfect society was one akin to the early Roman Republic; a nation of small-property holders united in their efforts to create a moral, equal world.[1]

Diderot's despair was mainly directed to what he saw as the imposition of luxury into society, the greed of merchants, and the corruption of society and government by gold. Concern over luxury was longstanding. Mendicants had also rebuked people, including other clergy, for their show of wealth. But what Diderot despised, others saw as the progress of society, produced by trade and commerce, funded by capital. By 1750, Paris boasted around 600 cafés. Items once exorbitantly expensive now graced many tables and pantries. Sugar, tea, coffee, chocolate, and all kinds of spices were affordable for most all but the poorest of society. Chinaware, calico, and lacquerware were commonplace. Those of middling status wore finer clothes and filled their homes with art and more comfortable furniture. Even the poor's standard of living was much more prosperous in comparison with the poor of the previous century, to say nothing of the lives of the impoverished masses in the late medieval period. Sound finance was key to a well-ordered and wealthy state and the loosely connected group of French Enlightenment thinkers known as the *philosophes* spent much time debating the economy within their new universe filled with salons, societies, clubs, lodges, and coffee-houses. They imagined a world that was full of citizens with inherent natural rights and not subjects of a God-sanctioned king, who had unfettered private property rights rather than privileges. But as new ideas and new ways of life share space with old ones, there were still many (including Denis Diderot and his circle) who maintained that wealth should be equally distributed, and that the Jewish usurer was detrimental to this vision of a nation. At a time when the country experienced the most radical disruption in European history, an issue that became labeled the "Jewish Question" peaked.[2]

Corruption had been a concern for the mercantilist economist Antoine de Montchrétien in the sixteenth century, especially if those involved were foreigners. Montchrétien complained that foreign competition, especially the English, was destroying the French economy as inferior foreign goods were given preference over superior French goods. He urged French manufacturers to stop buying from foreigners and called for a ban on foreign imports. "The gold of France," he wrote, is "changed into iron by the fraud of foreigners." Moreover, such an economy leads to degeneration of the French people and, therefore, along with the import ban and regulations, there should be a reduction of luxury. Foreign traders were nothing more than "leeches who attach themselves to this great body [of France], suck out its best blood and gorge themselves. They are ravenous lice who suck its juice and feed to bursting on it but who would leave it if it were dead . . .. They amass all the gold and silver in France, and take it away, some to Seville, some to Lisbon, some to London, some to Amsterdam, some to Middleberg." One historian has taken Montchrétien's comments to refer solely to Jews but it is clear from his text that he was referring to all foreigners, especially the English who he claimed cheated French merchants through deceptive weights and measures, monopolies, regulations, and taxes, and the Spanish who shut the French out of the Indies trade.[3]

The denunciation of bloodsucking leeches and luxury continued into the eighteenth century. Diderot injected morality back into the economy—that is, if it every truly left—albeit in an atheist manner. God was a mere figment of the imagination for Diderot, but the argument of the freethinking *encyclopédiste* would have received a vigorous nodding of the head from many past theologians. Unrestrained luxury and the "affluence of gold" corrupted morals. Gold had become the measure of success and luxury, inequality and opulence were social evils that needed to be corrected by a modern, utilitarian education, and wise laws. And like many of those theologians who denounced usury, Diderot's economic views tended to be romantic idealism that was wrought with "confusion and contradictions." He was a strong advocate of property rights and freedom, especially freedom of trade and private enterprise, representative government, and control of the state by property owners. But he was also a critic of the inequality of wealth, colonial commerce that exploited native populations, large-scale property, and what he considered to be an over-development of production. In the end, these social concerns led to him yearn for a simple, primitive, land labor that was communal, whereby wealth was distributed and "all belongs to all."[4]

In Alsace, which was conquered by France in the seventeenth century, credit was hard to come by for the peasants who needed capital to buy seed, farm animals, equipment, and to pay their taxes to the Crown. Jewish moneylenders travelled to the villages offering loans and, in 1778-1779, when some of those loans were called in, a large number of receipts written in Hebrew were produced by Alsatian peasant debtors as proof that their outstanding loans had been paid. Their Jewish creditors protested that the receipts were forgeries and that the debts were still owed. One moneylender, Benjamin, had agreed to loan a certain amount of money in 1771 to two Alsatian Christians, Henri Mouches and Jean-Georges Oberlin. Eight years later, when Benjamin complained that the loan had still not been settled, Mouches and Oberlin offered a receipt in Hebrew that they insisted proved that part of the loan had been repaid. The receipt, Benjamin contended, was not genuine.

French authorities were loath to turn a blind eye to the non-payment of debts, if indeed the receipts were fake. To solve the issue, a royal commissioner promised the debtors extended periods for repayment, at which point most of them dropped their claim. In addition, a decree was issued in July 1778 requiring that all present and future loans be registered and witnessed by officials. That way, repayment would no longer be hostage to a person's word. It was a law that satisfied no one, however, because it introduced additional registration expenses. Anti-Jewish riots followed, encouraged by pamphlets and books accusing the Jews of fiscal deception. The Crown's investigations found the receipts to be forgeries and led to multiple arrests for fraud. In one case, thirty-two people were arrested, including two Jews, the merchant Joseph Lévy of Leyman and Marx David of Zinswiller. Some of those found guilty were lashed or sentenced to the life of a galley slave, three convicted men were hanged, and all were branded with a hot iron indicating their crime.[5]

One of those arrested in the middle of February 1780 was a bailiff from Alsace named François-Joseph-Antoine Hell. Imprisoned in the Strasbourg citadel, a five-sided fort overlooking the Rhine, Hell was charged not only with forging receipts but as being the mastermind behind the crime. He was also found to be the author of a pamphlet condoning the forgeries. In his pamphlet, honest, hardworking peasants were destroyed by treacherous and greedy Jewish moneylenders who forced excessive interest-rate loans upon naïve and desperate borrowers, exploiting their vulnerability and deepening their misery. Caught in a cycle of debt, the peasant borrowed more money from other Jews to pay the first loan, and so on it went, spiraling out of control, with always "another bloodsucker [wanting] to be sated." In Hell's stories, fathers despaired as debts mounted while anxious mothers had no food to feed their starving children; all were victims of usury by Jews who were blind to their suffering and unmoved by homeless families or individuals sinking into depravity.[6]

Hell was himself in debt to various lenders as a result of speculation and wasteful spending. Although it is not known whether his creditors were Jewish or Christian or both, his experience led him to find common cause with peasants over the issue of Jewish moneylenders. His fate, though, was kinder than that of co-conspirators who were hanged or were sentenced to become galley-slaves. Petitions for his release resulted in his freedom, as the authorities tried to defuse the potentially destabilizing situation at a time when the scent of revolution was already in the air. To avoid further trouble, Hell was exiled to Dauphiné in southeastern France, but his exile was not for long. He returned to Alsace in 1782, where he was celebrated as a hero who had fought for the poor and oppressed against the "bloodsucking" Jews.[7]

A year after Hell's arrest, a Prussian civil servant by the name of Christian Wilhelm von Döhm wrote a treatise on the civil improvement of the Jews. One of the key words in eighteenth-century economics was utility and this now was applied to the Jewish communities in France. As was clear in the Alsace receipt fraud case, the small-scale moneylending practiced by many of the Yiddish-speaking Jews brought them into contact and sometimes conflict with peasants. In his pamphlet *Concerning the Amelioration of the Civil Status of the Jews* (1781), Döhm, an advocate of Jewish political emancipation, held the same point of view as the anti-finance lobby in France. Hatred against Jews, he surmised, rested upon their tendency to "deal crookedly with others [not of their religion] and to disregard their rights." It was due to the oppression and contempt experienced by the Jew that left him "no honest means of earning a living" that it was "natural that he falls into criminal practices and fraud, especially since commerce more than other trades seduces people to such practices." It was not an inherent or religious flaw, but the profession of banking and commerce that had such a deleterious effect on the Jew's "moral and political character." This "defect," as Döhm saw it, could be removed by forcing Jews to give up finance for the morally uplifting and socially beneficial artisan occupations and agriculture.[8]

In 1788, one year before the storming of the Bastille set off a bloody revolution and destroyed the Old Régime, a contest was held by the Royal Academy of Metz, in northeastern France. The topic was how to encourage Jewish moneylenders to abandon the "parasitical" and "unneighborly" trade of moneylending and become useful citizens. Three prizes were awarded. One went to the Protestant lawyer Claude-Antoine Thiéry, who considered usury and the Jewish moneylenders' passion for gold to be an obstacle to the assimilation of the Jewish community. This, he wrote, was not the fault of the Jews, however, but the injustice of a society that forced them into usury. A young curé, Henri Grégoire, was also honored. He showed concern for Jews but loathing for their economic practices. In business, they were not to be trusted. The third essayist, Zalkind Hourwitz, a Polish Jew living in Metz and the curator of the Oriental manuscripts at the royal library, laid out an expansive argument for both autonomy and political, social, cultural, and economic integration. But he, too, advocated restricting financial and commercial deals between Jews and Christians. It was a physiocrat's argument, only land was not just the source of true wealth. It was also the source of moral well-being.[9]

In his work *L'anti-financier* (1762), Edmé-Francois Darigrand insisted on the primacy of agriculture as the key to economic health and reform. Commerce produced vampires who drained the lifeblood of the landowning people. People had to get back to the land in order to regenerate themselves and the nation and to avoid corruption. It was not in the nation's interest to create a sector of society that simply accumulated money and wallowed in luxury. The "crisis" of luxury was a consequence of the new commercial world as constantly improving material conditions was not, it was argued, the way to a better life, but instead, the pathway to decadence. As people gained more, they desired more, leading to a never-ending, insatiable lust for an array of merchandise. Luxury not only resulted in inequality and misery, it also led to "a confusion of ranks and estates" and so disturbed the stable, hierarchical order of society.[10]

In a similar vein, the Abbé Emmanuel-Joseph Sieyès wrote in his *Essai sur les privileges* (1788) that the rebuilding of the common good was a "necessary brake in the passion for riches." If Jews were to be accepted into a rejuvenated and cleansed France, they had to dispense with their moneylending activity and entered into artisanal or agricultural work. Only by renouncing usurious practices—the stock market, speculation, banking—could a person be socially virtuous and useful. Only then could that person be a citizen of the new republic that was just about to send shockwaves throughout Europe.

* * *

In the latter half of the eighteenth century, a "horribly ugly little man" with questionable hygiene left his family home in Prussia to make his way around the continent. He was destined to play an important role in the coming revolution but, in the meantime, Jean-Paul Marat (1743–1793) lived for a time in England, Holland, and Italy before settling in Paris. He survived as a self-taught physician. He became better known, however, for his aggressive and radical politics which, for an ambitious man who thought highly of his ability, was the launching-pad for popular adulation and political power. Marat hated bankers, speculators, and stockbrokers with every fiber of his being. In his ideal world when justice was served, they would be among the first of those enemies of the state to hang from their doors.[11]

Sacrificing the rich was—and still is—a populist idea, favored by many French revolutionaries. "Should not a few perish, so that the greater number be saved?" queried the corpulent Honoré Gabriel Riqueti, the comte de Mirabeau. But, as the Duc de la Rochefoucauld astutely observed a century earlier, virtues are often vices in disguise. "What the world calls virtue," he observed, "is usually a phantasm created by our passions, to which we give the name virtue in order to do what we want with impunity." People dress up selfish pursuits and desires or petty emotions such as envy in magnanimous words such as "Common Good" or "Justice." There were plenty of men like Mirabeau who castigated the rich while accumulating their own wealth.[12]

Financiers, meanwhile, were eagerly reading the new works on mathematical probability as it related to efficient markets, which was sorely lacking in France. The government was paying high rates of interest on its loans and had borrowed "to the limits of its taxation and revenue-generating powers." France was on the verge of collapse. Revolts had erupted in France during the seventeenth century due the poor economic conditions, which was mostly the fault of a spendthrift monarchy and the lack of a sound set of financial institutions—a national bank, a stock exchange, and the free flow of credit. Now, in the spring of 1775, crop failure and unproductive land that had been stripped of its nutrients had led to an insufficient harvest. This meant shortages, a rise in the cost of grain, and a sharp increase in the price of bread. Many blamed the crisis on speculators, as well as the liberal reforms by Turgot, who was the Controller-General of Finances under Louis XVI. An edict by Turgot in September 1774, had established free trade in the grain industry, much to the anger and disapproval of those who benefited from its monopolization and from price controls. A conspiracy theory spread that grain was being deliberately withheld from the population by speculators for the benefit of the elite. It fed into the rumor that financiers were hoarding vital foodstuffs and crushing the poor in their attempt to make a hefty profit. The food shortages in France had a rather more mundane reason. On top of the bad harvests, there were problems with distribution and inefficiencies in government as the switch from guild monopolies to free trade was implemented.[13]

The knowledge that grain was being moved to other markets rather than being distributed to the famine areas led to riots in the northern, eastern, and western regions of France where people now struggled to provide bread for their families. Suspected hoarders were killed during what became commonly known as the "flour war" (*guerre des farines*). Pressure was put on the government to regulate the price of bread, which was fixed to a "fair" price. It was a way to feed the hungry and stave off riots and disorder but it did little to improve the economy. Economic power shifted to the royal authorities who gained control over the production and trade of wheat. Short-term, price control aided consumers who were struggling to provide for their families. In the long-term, regulations that interfered with supply and demand economics encouraged merchants not to sell their grain if it meant selling below market cost. Hiding goods and black markets flourished as some saw an opportunity to sell inferior goods, such as poor-quality grain, undercutting the government price controls.[14]

More revolts raged throughout the countryside during that momentous year of 1789 as revolutionaries set fire to chateaux and abbeys and the deeds held within them. Resistance to the Old Régime meant not only burning the houses of nobles and clergy. It meant refusing to pay taxes or looting government salt stores. For many French revolutionaries, patriotism meant the redistribution of property, labor meant physical labor, and usury meant idleness and the "judaization" of society. Revolutionaries had battled over private property, free trade, and the free movement of labor. But there were wide discrepancies between men such as Maximilien Robespierre, Diderot, Voltaire, Rousseau, and Georges Danton. To varying degrees they supported property rights, the rights of the people, equality under the law, and representative government but there was a wealth of difference about the scale of these aims and how they were to be implemented. The net national wealth, for those like Diderot and Robespierre, had to be divided evenly so that a great divide between rich and poor was avoided. "Cursed be he," Diderot wrote, "who set up gold as the idol of the nation." His solution was ostensibly similar to the physiocrats and those whose essays urged the regeneration of the Jews: agriculture. It was only through agriculture that the nation could avoid the corruption that modern industry and the pursuit of luxury brought, and which led to misery and poverty to the majority.[15]

A republic was ushered in after the fall of the Bastille on July 14, 1789. Resentment and personal feuds, as well as sheer brutality, were unleashed in the cobbled streets of France. In the bloodiest manner, the populace vented their fury on the aristocrats, their loyal servants, the clergy, and any other person labeled an "enemy of the people." Louis XVI and his queen, Marie Antoinette, were imprisoned, awaiting their trial, while the inauguration of the National Assembly swept away all vestiges of the Old Régime's system of royalty and privilege and introduced a new system of citizenship. Citizens were equal before the law, although not in wealth, ability, status, occupations, and countless other ways. The attempt to straight-jacket people into that sort of equality would come in a future revolution.[16]

Like Saturn, the revolution ate its own. Mirabeau's comment about sacrificing the rich was made shortly before power passed into the hands of the new Jacobin dictatorship headed by Robespierre in the first years of the 1790s. This shift led Mirabeau to secretly conspire with the king and the Austrians while the Jacobins decided to take Mirabeau's rhetoric to its logical conclusion. Mass slaughter of the enemies of the French Republic, they decided, was the road to a just, equal, and purified society. In Mirabeau's honor, and before his treachery was discovered, one of the many nicknames given to *la guillotine* that ended the lives of those enemies was Mirabelle, the feminine form of his name. Two of its victims were Louis and Marie Antoinette who were transported by an ignoble cart to the steps of the guillotine. [17]

During the blood-soaked days of 1793–94, many revolutionaries ended up as victims of The Terror, taking "*La Monte-à-regrét*" (the regretful climb) to their deaths. Marat would have delighted in the orgy of execution but he, too, was already gone, a victim of Charlotte Corday who, in 1793, plunged a knife into his chest as he lay in his medicinal bathtub. She had, as she confessed, "killed one man to save a hundred thousand," encapsulating the sentiment Robespierre had uttered as the king was condemned to death—Louis must die so that others may live. As the streets of Paris turned red, another man whose neck met the steel blade of the guillotine for his support of the monarchy was the former Alsatian bailiff and counterfeiter François Hell, who had become a member of the National Assembly.[18]

Hell was one of the thousands who succumbed to the revolution's appetite for revenge but, before his death, he had declared himself in favor of Jewish political emancipation. The assembly defined citizenship as a social contract as meaning not only rights but duties to the state. In return for citizenship, in the land which now promoted "liberty, equality, fraternity," everyone, including Jews, had to renounce their old communal way of life that relied on courtly privilege and alliances with rulers. There would be no more charters. No more invitations or requests for settlement. No more negotiations of services and no more privileges. Every citizen was equal under the law.[19]

For the Sephardic Jews living in southwestern France, the new conditions of political existence were of little consequence for they were well assimilated. But for the more traditional Ashkenazic Jews of eastern France who preferred to live in their own semi-autonomous world, the new concept of citizenship required a monumental transformation on their part that many rejected. On December 21, 1789, Count Stanislas-Marie-Adélaide de Clermont-Tonnerre (1757–1792), in a speech on religious minorities and questionable professions (such as actors and executioners), had outlined the new political arrangement that made everyone an equal citizen and rejected the old hierarchy that was structured around communities. Clermont-Tonnerre's ideal was to implement a constitution based on the one in England. As he stood before the assembly, the count presented the new republic's demand for citizenship as the social contract between man and state. It was applicable to everyone, including the Jews in the east who were determined to hold on to their traditional way of living.

One of the prerequisites for Jewish French citizenship was the abandonment of usury:

> Every mode of worship has but one proof to offer with regard to society . . . which is that of morality. It is here that I am attacked by the adversaries of the Jews. That people, they say, are unsociable. Usury is enjoined them . . . . [But] Usury is not enjoined the Jews by their laws; lending upon interest is forbidden among themselves and permitted with strangers. *Non feneraberis nisi alieno*. This text is a benevolent law among them, that does not enjoin them usury with us. The sense of it has been altered, because the Jews, in fact, are usurers; and their laws have been traduced, because their conduct impeaches them. That usury, so justly blamed, is the offspring of our own laws; men who have no other property but money to improve, must make the best use of it: there is the evil . . . .

Clermont-Tonnerre's solution was the same one that had been previously suggested by Döhm and the Abbé Grégoire, among others: Make Jews more productive by forcing them into agriculture and away from the immoral trade of moneylending. He continued:

> let them possess lands; let them enjoy the blessings of a native country, and they will lend no longer: there is the remedy . . . you should deny the Jews everything as a distinct nation, and grant them everything as individuals . . . they should form in the state neither a political body, nor a separate order; they should be individually citizens . . . if they refuse it, banish them from among you. It is repugnant to sound policy to see in the state a society of men that are not citizens; to see a nation within the nation . . . . In a word, gentlemen, the supposed state of every housekeeper in any country is that of being a citizen.[20]

Jews' involvement in finance was a key issue in the debate over whether to permit or deny them citizenship. The bias held by deputies in the National Assembly against financiers echoed the longstanding stigma that equated moneylenders with dishonesty, greed, and the destruction of the nation. The most extreme revolutionaries ranted that justice demanded the death penalty for speculators, those "assassins of the people" and "vile hoarders," along with "their wretched capitalists." What had been accepted as the economic arm and inspiration of Enlightenment philosophy, free trade, was replaced by government regulations and price controls as the government evolved into a tyrannical dictatorship. The irony that these were the same failed policies that had led to protest, riots, and revolution appeared lost on the advocates of governmental seizure of the economy.[21]

The role of the medieval theologian denouncing the wealthy who devoured the poor, was now taken up by the revolutionary. Anti-speculation and anti-usury laws were cast in moral and patriotic garb. Jacques Roux, an ex-priest and demagogic revolutionary popular with the Paris masses, called for the physical annihilation of speculators and hoarders who were traitors to the new order. A "silent, insidious and invisible war," the political dramatic satirist and revolutionary Fabre d'Eglantine called speculation. In the name of the poor and oppressed, anti-hoarding laws were enacted which, instead of leading to plenty for all, resulted in scarcity. Crisis led to inflation, which led to further price controls, which led to more state control. Famine reappeared, exacerbated by government intervention as well as a new round of warfare launched by the French republic. Stock companies and the stock exchange, the homes of "vile speculators" who conspired against the new republic, were closed down. Rights were not those of the individual. They were of the nation. National interest ruled supreme, supplanting individual freedoms, including economic ones.[22]

The English were among the villains the French denounced. Attitudes in England towards usury certainly diverged from those in France. Two years before the revolution was unleashed in France, the English Utilitarian Jeremy Bentham wrote his *Defence of Usury* (1787). Christians who "judaized" by practising the sinful craft of usury were once considered morally corrupt; now Bentham ridiculed Christians who "were too intent upon plaguing Jews, to listen to the suggestion of doing as Jews did, even though money were to be got by it." The issue in England, unlike France, was no longer over usury. It was how to structure an economic world revolving around capital, interest, and profit without it leading to extortion, unrestrained greed, or to a society that considered money to be the root of all goodness.[23]

In pondering on the right course of action for a prosperous nation that would avoid the fate of France, the British statesman Edmund Burke rejected the idea that it was the opulence of the elite that gauged a nation's wealth. Yet, he was concerned that the "love of lucre" could be taken to a "vicious excess." When the motivation of financiers is greed, he warned, it results in reckless economic activity, corruption, and criminal acts. Nevertheless, Burke, like Bernard de Mandeville and Adam Smith, believed that if this "love of lucre" was honestly accomplished and effectively focused, it was the key to global prosperity. And despite his warnings about the possible abuse of the economic system, Burke staunchly defended the free market and felt that it was up to the government to support those involved in the world of trade and finance from "the ignorance and envy of farmers and consumers" who too readily looked to the government for regulations and protection against competition. The poor, unaware of financial affairs, envy and despise those with wealth, Burke wrote, and, reflecting on events across the English Channel, continued:

> But the throats of the rich ought not to be cut, nor their magazines plundered; because, in their persons they are trustees for those who labour, and their hoards are the banking-houses of these latter . . . . When the poor rise to destroy the rich, they act as wisely for their own purposes as when they burn mills, and throw corn into the river, to make bread cheap.[24]

The Terror encouraged people and their fortunes to flee to England to escape the guillotine. The revolution in France wore itself out after the orgy of killing and economic devastation and ended with the seizure of power by Napoleon Bonaparte.

The republic was transformed into the first Napoleonic empire (1804–1815). Chaos in French political life during this period caused chaos in the French financial system, encouraging bankers and other financiers to escape to safety. This was followed by the flight of German bankers who escaped the turmoil in their lands after the invasion by Napoleon's *Grande Armée* and their victory at the Battle of Austerlitz in 1805. Jewish merchants involved in international trade, stocks, and foreign bills of exchange flocked to London "from every quarter under heaven."[25]

With Napoleon's defeat at Waterloo, the globalization of capital—exported from London and Paris and stimulated by free trade capitalism—helped to increase economic growth in the nineteenth century. The permanent debt created by the British government required a more stable and larger market where it could be traded other than the Royal Exchange. By 1698, most brokers, with the exception of those trading in foreign issues, had left the Royal Exchange and set up business in the various coffeehouses. The pressing need to eliminate the rampant fraud and non-payment that blighted the early exchanges led to a group of brokers forming a new self-regulatory stock exchange in Sweeting's Alley in 1773. Called New Jonathan's, anyone could enter by paying a low daily fee. This was, however, insufficient to deal with unscrupulous traders so, in 1801, a bigger and more exclusive premises near St. Paul's Cathedral became the permanent site of the London Stock Exchange. For a fee of ten guineas per annum, a person could request to become a subscriber and the members had the right to expel any person considered dishonorable. That the rules and regulation of financial trading were privately developed, rather than imposed by government, offered the brokers more flexibility in choosing the rules that worked best for them and their clients and dispensing with those that were ineffective.

Private brokers still practiced outside of the LSE but the LSE became a critical part of the nation's capital market by financing the national debt and providing short term funds in long term loans, keeping interest rates relatively low, and stabilizing the nascent banking system. Brokers carried an investor's instructions to the jobber who specialized in certain markets, each one of which was allocated a space on the floor of the Exchange. The importance of the international money market encouraged some Jewish migrants such as Dutchman Raphael Raphael to switch from trade to stockbroking. Raphael moved his banking business to London and built a considerable fortune during the Napoleonic Wars. From stockbroking, his business diversified into bullion dealing, government loans, and handling transactions in American railway stock.[26]

* * *

With capital more necessary than ever before to fund monumental building schemes such as canals, railways, and factories. Far from being unproductive, the diligent banker was as vital to society as he had been to earlier times. Even more so, given the rapidly changing times and the scale of construction, production, trade, and commerce. Capitalism, the economic and political system that was based on the accumulation of capital, freedom of exchange, wage labor, and profit, was founded on the political ideal of freedom of the individual. And, in the nineteenth century, after centuries of stereotyping Jews as disreputable moneylenders, capitalism was once again erroneously identified as a "Jewish" creation by ideologues who excoriated it. The widespread success of socialism in the nineteenth century adopted the idea that Jews were exploiters, greedy, and would ruin a nation in their pursuit of profit. For socialists, the economic value of a product equaled the amount of labor it took to produce it. Capitalism, driven by profit, was robbery, just as theologians in the twelfth century had argued that usury was theft. The state was the instrument through which social justice would be gained through redistribution of wealth, as opposed to the capitalist ideal of accumulation. With the stereotype of the Jews as moneylenders and the stereotype of moneylenders as extortionists and rapacious profiteers of the worst kind, the idea that Jews collectively were harmful to the nation deepened. In an age of nationalist, revolutionary fervor, stimulated by Napoleon's rampage through Europe, the old idea that all moneylenders made money at the expense of society, culture, traditions, and spiritual virtue spread into divergent political philosophies and actions with new and more vicious results.

Notes

1. Diderot, *Encyclopédie* xiii, 394, quoted in Lipton, "The Social Thought of Diderot," 126, 129.
2. Wiesner-Hanks, *Early Modern Europe*, chapter 12.
3. Montchrétien, *Traicté*, 28, 69–67, 92,–93, 37–138, 200–03, 209.
4. Lipton, "The Social Thought of Diderot," 126–27, 135–36, 138, 140.
5. Zosa Szajkowski, *Jews and the French Revolutions of 1789, 1830, and 1848* (New York: Ktav Pub. House, 1970), 202–09.
6. The pamphlet was entitled *Observations d'un Alsacien dur l'affaire presente des Juifs d'Alsace*. Ronald Schechter, *Obstinate Hebrews: Representations of Jews in France 1715–1815* (Berkeley: University of California Press, 2003), 67, 71.

7. Szajkowski, *Jews and the French Revolutions*, 213; Schechter, *Obstinate Hebrews*, 67.
8. Shovlin, *Political Economy*, 179; Christian Wilhelm von Döhm, *Concerning the Amelioration of the Civil Status of the Jews* (*Ueber die buergerliche Verbesserung der Juden*) (Berlin 1781), GDHI, http://ghdi.ghi-dc.org/sub_document_s.cfm?document_id=3647.
9. Phyllis Cohen Albert and Frances Malino, eds., *Essays in Modern Jewish History: A Tribute to Ben Halpern* (London: Associated University Press, 1982), 101–05; Alyssa Goldstein Sepinwall, "L'Abbé Grégoire and the Metz Contest: The View From New Documents," *Revue des Études Juives* 166.1–2 (2007): 273–88.
10. Anoush Fraser Terjanian, *Commerce and Its Discontents in Eighteenth-Century French Political Thought* (Cambridge: CUP, 2013), 29–30; Edmé-Francois Darigrand, *L'anti-financier* (1763), quoted in Shovlin, *Political Economy*, 96, 100, 78. See also, pp. 51, 59, 65.
11. Sarel Eimerl, *Revolution!: France 1789–1794* (Boston: Little Brown, 1967), 55; Shovlin, *Political Economy*, 119, 127, 137.
12. Aftalion, *The French Revolution*, 58; Duc de la Rochefoucauld, Maxim 179, *Reflexions ou Sentences et Maximes Morales* (Paris 1664) Ebook, Project Gutenberg, http://www.gutenberg.org/cache/epub/14913/pg14913-images.html. He reduced this maxim later on to "Nos vertues ne sont le plus souvent que des vices déguisées"; Muller, *The Mind and the Market*, chap. 1.
13. Goetzmann, *Money Changes Everything*, chap. 15; Alessandro Stanziani, "Hoarding, Speculation, and the Public Order of the Market in France, End of the Eighteenth Century-1914," *Law and Social Inquiry* 36.3 (2011): 728; Aftalion, *The French Revolution*, 38–41, 53, 111.
14. Aftalion, *The French Revolution*, 12–13, 22, 39; Roover, "The Concept of the Just Price," 430.
15. Aftalion, *The French Revolution*, 53; Antoine de Cournand, *De la propriété, ou La cause du pauvre*, quoted in Shovlin, *Political Economy*, 194, 198.
16. Gertrude Himmelfarb, *Poverty and Compassion: The Moral Imagination of the Late Victorians* (New York: Knopf, 1991), Kindle ed., chap. 17.
17. Marquis de Mirabeau, quoted in Aftalion, *The French Revolution*, 58.
18. Schechter, *Obstinate Hebrews*, 67.
19. Smith Stickney, "The Bailiff of Landser: A Biographical Overview of Francois-Joseph-Antoine de Hell and Events Leading to the Emancipation of the Jews of Alsace," *Rhodes Historical Review* 18 (2016): 46.
20. Count Clermont-Tonnerre, *Translation of a Speech Spoken by the Count Clermont Tonnerre Christmas Eve Last on the Subject of Admitting Non-Catholics, Comedians, and Jews to the Privileges of Citizen According to the Declaration of Rights* (London 1790), 12–14, https://babel.hathitrust.org/cgi/pt?id=hvd.hxg1dd;view=1up;seq=5.

21. Aftalion, *The French Revolution*, 111, 113–14.
22. Ibid., 126, 127, 140, 145, 148–49, 168–70, 189, 190, 191, 195.
23. Jeremy Bentham, *Defence of Usury; Shewing the Impolicy of the Present Legal Restraints on the Terms of Pecuniary Bargains* (London: Payne & Foss, 1816), archive.org/stream/ripped #page/n9/mode/2up, 98.
24. Edmund Burke quoted in Muller, *The Mind and the Market*, chap. 5.
25. Borer, *The City of London*, 151, 277; *Knight's Cyclopaedia of London* (London 1851), 647, quoted in Michie, *London Stock Exchange*, 18, 21, 28, 32, 43, 68, 69; Himmelfarb, *Poverty and Compassion*, chap. 1.
26. Stanley Chapman, *The Rise of Merchant Banking* (Abingdon, UK: Routledge, 1984), 60; Stringham, "The Emergence of the London Stock Exchange as a Self-Policing Club," 2, 5, 8, 9.

[illegible]

8 The Globalization of Capital

The nineteenth century was a time of big ideas and breathtaking schemes. Economic growth soared and there was plenty of capital to be invested in new schemes and discoveries. If in 1450, one in twenty people lived in a city or town, by 1800 that number was one in ten. In some places, it was higher, such as in the Netherlands where three in ten people were urban dwellers. By the end of the century, people walked along the streets of Paris lit by electric lamps, which created the outdoor café culture now so synonymous with that city and assured them of a safer passage than the dark alleyways of the past. Outbreaks of epidemic disease were fewer and farther between as the sewage system was modernized and sources of infection were understood to be linked to sanitation. Impressionist artists painted in the open air, trying to capture the changing fluctuating light in bright colors and visible brushstrokes. Telephones, phonographs, the internal combustion engine, moving pictures, photographic film, lightbulbs, escalators, machine guns, and the automobile radically changed the way people lived and died.[1]

There was a substantial improvement in the standard of living for all classes. The middle classes made the biggest strides as they became more abundant. There still existed the destitute, those inhabitants of city slums, whose lives were depicted in the late-nineteenth-century novels of Emile Zola and Charles Dickens. But for the working poor, whose expectations were higher than ever, it was more a matter of "felt wants," rather than demanding fundamental needs to live. Life was incredibly hard but their standard of living was improving. As wages rose and hours of work decreased, food costs were lower and tended to fluctuate less, and items once thought of as luxuries were now found on the workers' tables, including meat, sugar, tea, butter, and cheese. Clothes and shoes were more affordable and would become even more so with the arrival of the department store and off-the-peg outfits. Advanced economies all had a central bank that was regulated like the *Wisselbank* and the Bank of England and on the gold standard, including the Banque de France (1800), the German Reichsbank (1875), and the Swiss National Bank (1907). Taxes were not heavy and international trade meant the consumer could buy certain foreign goods that were cheaper than domestic products. With more income in their pockets, consumers bought the products in the new department stores of Paris, Au Printemps and Le Bon Marché. Or they could just enjoy the spectacle of the eye-catching window displays as they sauntered along the streets. In the opinion of the journalist and publisher Émile de Girardin—a man described by Victor Hugo as the "public watchman"—it was "the age of commercial transactions. Religion and Liberty go up and down in value, and every conscience has a fixed price."[2]

* * *

Loans proffered by bankers had positive macroeconomic benefits. Capital was invested in infrastructure and new industries vital to the national economic interest and the stabilization of the global economy. Shares were sold in mines, canals, insurance companies, joint stock banks, property, and international funds. There was perhaps no greater enthusiasm generated, however, than in the new and exciting railway industry, which made transportation cheaper, more secure, and faster. The funding of the rail networks was a boost to economic growth but, with many shares sold on the stock exchange, there was always the temptation into financial recklessness. People anxiously gobbled up stocks and shares in railway ventures without always understanding the soundness of the venture. But the new train lines changed people's lives. Rail travel dramatically altered the landscape and opened up villages and towns that during harsh winters were previously cut off even from their neighboring hamlets. It expanded cities and increased productivity as workers could now commute from ever expanding city borders and suburbs. Leisure time was transformed as more people, not only the rich, took weekend breaks away from the city by train. Families were better able to keep in touch with sons and daughters who had married and moved away. Freight trains carried goods more cheaply and quicker than by water, bringing such products as fertilizer to the farms which significantly increased their agricultural output. It is not an exaggeration to say that the railways helped to unify countries into nations and shaped national identity.[3]

In the summer of 1837, Queen Marie-Amélie of Bourbon-Sicily, wife of King Louis-Philippe I, inaugurated the first passenger railway from Paris to a little town called Le Pecq, near St. Germain-en-Laye. The railway was financed by a banking conglomerate founded by the Jewish bankers Emile and Isaac Pereire, brothers who were of Sephardic Portuguese ancestry. The Pereires supported the Paris-St. Germaine railway, convinced that industrial growth was beneficial to the poorer sectors of society. Emile won the concession to build the network after promising to invest six million francs of his own money to create the Compagnie du Chemin de Fer de Paris à Saint-Germain. If it failed, the Pereires' money would be lost. On its first day of operation, 18,000 passengers travelled on the route, making the venture a huge success and every investor richer. Concessions for two passenger lines were awarded to James de Rothschild and the Fould brothers for the Paris-Versailles route, the former given the one on the right bank and the brothers the one on the left.[4]

With the railway contract, it was the Rothschilds who became the embodiment of the acquisitive Jew to all those critical of capitalism, the modern world, and the changing landscape. Centuries of associating Jews with money and money with avarice led to the Rothschilds being depicted as the personification of greed, whose aim in life was only to enrich themselves through "swindling operations, speculations, and money grabbing." Radicals portrayed the bankers as a vast black octopus with its tentacles firmly wrapped around the globe. The German poet, Heinrich Heine, likened James Rothschild to Richelieu and Robespierre, "the three terroristic names that spell the gradual annihilation of the old aristocracy." This new aristocracy was, instead of land, founded upon "the most unreliable of elements, on money." At the inauguration of the Northern Railroad, it was said that when "a few fanatics" yelled "*Vive* Rothschild!" they were met with "hisses and hootings."[5]

The Rothschild bank dealt in government securities between London and Paris, rising to dominate international banking in the first half of the nineteenth century. It was a success so meteoric that it was rumored to be due to a Hebrew talisman, a story that resurrected the ancient image of the Jewish sorcerer concocting money by magical, even demonic, tricks. From a modest house in the *Judengasse* (Jews' Alley) in Frankfurt, one of the oldest ghettos in Germany, the bank of Mayer Amschel Rothschild, the one-time apprentice of Jacob Wolf

Oppenheimer, spread to the major European cities. His five sons, Amschel, Salomon, Nathan, Carl, and James, set up branches of their banking business in Frankfurt am Main, Vienna, London, Naples, and Paris respectively. In 1815, the capital for the Rothschild branches of London and Frankfurt was £500,000. Thirty years later, that sum had increased to £7,778,200. Most of their profit came from government finance, with James de Rothschild in Paris enjoying a near monopoly in French government finance. In London, the bank's biggest clients were the British and French governments. But the family's main impact on the development of modern capitalism was in the international bond market. Their innovation in this field of finance was issuing in London, Frankfurt, Berlin, Hamburg, and Amsterdam of the dividend payment of an international loan to Prussia was made in sterling and the interest was to be paid in London. This avoided the uncertainty over the fluctuation of currency, making the investment in foreign bonds a more attractive venture.[6]

In the early nineteenth century, Europe experienced a sharp decline in temperature due to the eruption of the Mount Tambora volcano in Sambawa, Indonesia. This eruption and the volcanic debris that was cast into the air had a devastating effect on the climate in Western Europe. With the sun blotted out by ash and snow colored orange and brown, 1816 was so cold that it became known as the "Year Without a Summer." The cool climate, frost, and heavy rain caused a shorter growing season and crop failures and in Germany this led to much higher food prices at a time of high unemployment. People took to the streets in protest, some resorted to looting and rioting.[7]

The cold weather continued for the following two years, causing a subsistence crisis and social unrest. In 1818, the jurist Ludolf Holst published two works dealing with the role of Jews in the economy of Hamburg. In his estimation, the financial woes that he described and denounced (the high cost of living, moral degeneration, artisanal unemployment, the desire for luxury goods) were caused by the Jews. Their tendency, he claimed was to ignore regulations, to flood the market with imports, and to manipulate weights and measures were detrimental to commercial towns and cities. They had no loyalty to the nation, caring only for the opportunity to make money. "The sources of their wealth," he later wrote, "are usury, mercantilist tribal spirit, and trade maxims."[8]

The long Napoleonic wars stirred up nationalist sentiment in Germany which the German Confederation attempted to stifle. Another pamphlet appeared around the same time, written by the German philosopher Jakob Friedrich Fries, a political agitator for the *Burschenschaft* (the student group based on liberal and nationalist ideals). Fries was a radical democrat who was inspired by the German nationalist movement that wanted a unified Germany. The work, entitled "On the Endangerment of the Prosperity and Character of the Germans by the Jews," included accusations that the Jews made money triumph over culture in Germany and that the trading practices of Jewish merchants was unfair due to their connections in other countries. In response to this and to the detrimental effect of Jews on Christians in Germany, there should be restrictions on Jewish immigration and pressure put on Jews to assimilate.[9]

The following summer, a series of planned attacks, named the Hep Hep riots for the call shouted by those involved, broke out in various German cities. Starting in Würtzburg, they spread to other Bavarian towns before flaring up in the central and southwestern region. Bamberg, Bayreuth, Darmstadt, Karlsruhe, Mannheim, Frankfurt, Cologne, Koblenz, Bremen, Hamburg, and Lübeck were some of the towns and cities affected to varying degrees. In certain places, the police were slow to respond while in others the riots were short-lived as orders were given to shoot the perpetrators. These youth movements ignited the call for German unification based on national identity. Over the following decades, it absorbed racial ideas and became part of the revolutionary spirit that enveloped Western Europe in the middle of the century.[10]

New ideas were fomented in this cauldron of political turmoil. Liberalism, based on Enlightenment ideas, supported individual progress and freedom, the means of which was the state, inspired dreams of a better society, and a more just world. Socialism, which was predicated on the state as a means to another kind of justice; that of redistributing wealth to aid the poor and punish the rich. They were the street preachers in modern dress. Both Liberals and Socialists were moral reformers with ideas of a more equal society based on universal ideas, but socialists were committed to a radical economic equality, obtained via state ownership and a planned economy, rather than the liberal equality of merit and opportunity and the pursuance of free trade within a capitalist economy.

In 1830 and, more dramatically, in 1848, liberals and radicals found common cause in destroying the status quo. Motivated by ideas that included democracy (meaning universal male suffrage), the worker control of the means of production, and representative government, the revolutionaries excoriated those they held responsible for all that was wrong in society. Nationalist ideas also came to fruition in the nineteenth century, based on popular racial science espoused by Arthur de Gobineau, Karl Vogt, Ernst Haeckel, and Johann Gottfried Herder. Advocates of this nationalist ideology argued that human beings were not unified by common natural rights and duties or religion but were divided by the concept of race. It was the beginning of identity politics. De Gobineau separated these races into three categories based on color: Blacks, Whites (which included Aryans, the pinnacle of the White "race," Semites, which came to mean solely Jews in Europe, and Hamites, from Northern Africa), and Yellows, as Asians were classified, with each racial classification having traits attributed to it.

The idea favored by French Enlightenment thinkers that it was environmental circumstances that pushed all Jews into finance—as erroneous as that was—could be "remedied" by them taking up other professions. Now it was argued that the notable presence of Jews in banking and speculation was due to innate "Jewish" traits. Such criticism came from those who held capitalism in low regard as a system to be overcome and replaced, along with those who were involved in its perpetuation. Foremost among those people, such critics argued, were Jews, who had innate characteristics such as avarice and shirked physical labor—characteristics in harmony with capitalism. Furthermore, it was claimed that they had an inherent talent for moneymaking, often at other's expense. Many accepted this gibberish as scientific fact, including some of those radicals who manned the barricades during the 1848 revolution and who dreamed of overturning the present order and creating a socialist utopia.

One of the most influential utopian socialists was the French philosopher Charles Fourier (1772–1837). In his hatred of free trade capitalism, Fourier loathed anything, or anyone, connected to it. Foremost on that list were Jews and the English, both of whom he regarded as oppressors of the entire world. The son of prosperous cloth merchants, Fourier spent most of his life in commerce. He grew frustrated with speculation in the industry as well as with the effects of inflation and stagnation, even though the nineteenth century was, overall, economically stable with little inflation. Fourier dreamt instead of a social utopia, a world free from poverty and the disorder he saw around him. Banking and commerce were, to him, different forms of usury, which he defined as a method of exchange in which "the seller has the right to defraud with impunity and to determine by himself without arbitration the profit which he ought to receive." The buyer was at the mercy of the seller who was, in Fourier's world, always avaricious and deceitful. Most responsible for "mercantile depravities" were the Jews, who were the "parasites, merchants, and usurers" who "pillaged the country like pirates":

> What shall I say of the Usurers who, under the name of bankers, are waging war against property owners? Take for example the hordes of Jews and vagabonds who have practically overrun the four departments on the right bank of the Rhine. They would soon have gobbled up most of the French property there if

> the government had not restrained them by decrees and by means of an economic struggle that involved the Bank of France, which is an agent of resistance against usury.[11]

Fourier's idea of a Jewish merchant was a man arriving in France with a hundred thousand pounds in capital (obtained through his first bankruptcy) to swindle and thieve. He did not pay taxes, he robbed the poor, and he peddled debased coins. In 1835, a book by Renault Becourt entitled *Universal Conspiracy of Judaism* echoed this idea, condemning Jews as usurers intent on destroying the wealth of "unhappy [Christian] merchants" who had now been reduced to poverty.[12]

Using the same language as the French revolutionaries, Fourier admonished Jews for not engaging in any useful employment such as agriculture or manufacturing. These unproductive "bloodsuckers" were despised, he wrote, by "every class worthy of respect," including the nobility, clergy, propertied classes, officials, lawyers, artists, and soldiers. Commerce was a business conducted by liars, rascals, and hucksters. And in the age of industry and stockjobbing, the mask slipped and those involved in trade no longer disguised their desire for political power, preferably executed behind the scenes.[13]

Pierre-Joseph Proudhon (1809–1865), who famously called all property theft, also despised capitalism and Jews, who he believed were its chief exponents. He wrote in his diary that the Jews were "the enemy of mankind," and had to disappear either by expulsion, steel, or fire. The Jew, Proudhon wrote, echoing Charles Fourier, was "an anti-producer, neither a farmer nor an industrialist nor even a true merchant." As a middleman, he was

> always fraudulent and parasitic ... [operating] by means of falsification, counterfeiting, and horse-trading. He knows but the rise and fall of prices, the risks of transportation, the incertitude of crops, the hazards of demand and supply. His policy in economics has always been entirely negative, entirely usurious; it is the evil principle, Satan ... incarnated in the race of Shem.

The intermediary between producer and consumer was the "unproductive" part of the chain. It had long been argued that financiers were sterile non-producers in the eyes of those who understood work to mean physical labor that exhausted the body, not the mind, and thought of capitalism was trickery, deception, and exploitation.[14]

"A Jew, a money-lender, a businessman, these are all synonymous to me," thought one of Fourier's and Proudhon's disciples, the naturalist and writer, Alphonse Toussenel (1803–1885), who further developed the connection between Jewish bankers and the destruction of France. As people marveled at the speed of the steam trains, Toussenel rejected the idea that these rail projects were in the interests of the population. On the contrary, their construction was only in the Jews' interests, particularly those of James de Rothschild, who was labeled "the king of the Jews." He criticized the deal which gave Rothschild fifteen to twenty million francs per year for forty years in return for advancing sixty million francs to the government (which paid an additional 100 million francs for the land). Toussenel could have made his anticapitalist criticism without mentioning the Jewishness of Rothschild—Rothschild's business dealings were no different than those of many Christian bankers of the time—but the image of the avaricious Jewish banker had become ingrained in popular culture. The "immoral banker" was a universal synonym for "Jew," just as the word "usurer" had been for centuries. The Rothschilds were also scorned as *les nouveaux riches*, "scions of the Ghetto" who had a "mania for putting themselves forward" with "ridiculous pretentions." According to one observer, Rothschild stood in vulgar contrast to the other wealthy Jewish family who funded railways, the Pereires, who lived simply and without a box at the opera.[15]

Toussenel's attack on monopoly was an appropriate criticism in an age of free trade. Monopolies forced the closure of small businesses and workshops, as the general stores absorbed the small shops. But Toussenel was no free trader. His answer was not more competition and fewer regulations, but governmental control over railways and canals as a means to eradicate monopolies and the Jews from the state. It was the Jews who possessed and profited from monopolies, he argued, to the detriment of the French people who "work and who suffer." A monopoly was like a medieval privilege bestowed on moneylenders and like the vulture that descends on its dead prey, feasting on the entrails so, too, the usurer destroyed "his victim" by extorting "the last penny from the worker's purse." Toussenel could have preached his views in the markets and town squares of medieval Europe and would have not been much out of place.[16]

In Toussenel's opinion, Jews destroyed religion and values with their capital and divided the nation with their corruption. Toussenel's radical nationalist form of socialism was built upon Fourier's core hatred of Jews and England that linked the two as a sinister and corrosive alliance. He spent some forty pages excoriating British colonial mercantilism while praising the France's charitable colonization. His reference to "*Londres-Juda,*" by which the Protestant and the Jew were the same, evoked the specter of a vampire that parasitically invaded and possessed the national body, drinking the blood of the nation, and reducing it to a lifeless corpse. The Jewish merchant-usurer was a spider, a hideous creature with legs, eyes, and belly but no body and heartless. Like the merchant-usurer behind his "Judas" peephole, the spider lurks in dark spaces, watching, and waiting to strike. It dispenses with the corpse of its victim only after draining it of all its blood. Unlike the patriot, merchant-usurers had no homeland. For them "*ubi aurum, ubi patria*" (where the gold is, there is the fatherland). In an age of stirring nationalism that was based not on the individual but on the nation, the animosity towards bankers and wealth was more striking and more virulent than in previous eras.[17]

Toussenel's book *Les Juifs, rois de l'époque* (1847) described his contemporary world as one of financial and industrial feudalism that had produced an army of monopolies with interests diametrically opposed to those of the "people." The "invasion of industrial feudalism" had been brought into France by the Enlightenment physiocrats who had been influenced by foreign, especially English, ideas. It was an economic system that concentrated wealth "in the hands of parasites" who reaped profits at the expense of the people. These new feudalists—that word being as loosely used as fascist would be in a later period—increased the "wound of pauperism." It was a misery that degraded not only the body but the soul. This financial aristocracy lived on the exploitation and wretchedness of a people, motivated by avarice, their hearts shut to compassion as if they were made of bronze armor.[18]

Jews, Toussenel warned, would "soon be the conquering and ruling nation." Rejecting the Enlightenment ideals of the equal citizen with rights and duties, Toussenel wrote that it was impossible for Jews to be French. The words fatherland, religion, and faith were meaningless for the Jews because they had a silver coin instead of a heart. The remedy to this decadence? Yet another revolution. "Death to parasitism! War against the Jews! There is the motto of the new revolution!" Here Toussenel went further than other anti-Jewish authors. His most secret desire he jotted down in his private diary, which he kept to himself and were never part of his published manifesto. What was needed, he wrote, was the annihilation of the Jews.[19]

* * *

In 1842, twenty-five-year-old Karl Marx took a job as a journalist for the *Rheinische Zeitung*. The newspaper was to become an outlet for his new form of socialism based on his version of economic historical development. Marx was at the threshold of becoming the latest in a long line of preachers protesting that the oppression of the poor was due to the greed of the moneylender and the sins of unrestrained wealth.

Baptized into the Lutheran church at the age of six by his father who had converted earlier, Marx eventually abandoned all religious beliefs. Academically, he was influenced by the German philosopher Georg Friedrich Hegel and his idealistic dialectical method with its cosmic concept of alienation. Marx rejected the cosmic element, preferring to construct a materialist version of Hegel's philosophy, that is, a materialist history of economic forces that throughout history have been engaged in a deterministic dialectical struggle. The end point was Communism whereby the state and the desire for profit withered away and people lived in an altruistic community, each according to his ability to each according to his need.

In creating his economic theory, Marx furthered the secularization of the long-standing theological disdain for usury and the abhorrence of making money without physical labor. In an article written sometime in the early autumn of 1856, the now thirty-eight-year-old attacked the spirit of the age. Economic crises in 1817, 1825, 1836, and 1846–47 were, he believed, the product of the capitalist system, which was based on the "present mania" of "universalized swindling." Marx saw nothing in market economics but alienation and division between the rich capitalists and the oppressed workers. This created exploitation, corruption, and misery which had to be overcome with a reinvention of the theological argument that if everyone divided their money, then no one would go hungry. It was only with the abolition of private property that workers could be emancipated and the burden of exploitation could be eradicated.[20]

If Smith and Mandeville argued that capitalism, that is, deregulated economic competition based on a free market supply and demand system, was the answer to peace and prosperity, Marx's view was that it encouraged war and made each person think as an isolated individual rather than a member of a community. For Marx and his colleague Friedrich Engels, capitalism was an immoral system based on self-interest. Unlike Adam Smith's definition of self-interest, Marx's characterization was simple greed and selfishness. While he recognized capitalism's ability to generate industrial growth and progress, he believed it did so at the expense of the proletariat working-class, benefiting only the capitalist classes. The owners of the means of production did not care about their workers, their working conditions, their poverty, their health. They were only driven by the lust for money and desirous of ever-greater profit which they grasped by immoral means such as speculation, which was nothing more than gambling. The triumph of communism over a decrepit capitalism would end the alienation caused by the modern division of labor. In an image that was common to the nineteenth century, Marx compared capitalists to vampires, their self-interest creating an "atomistic, antagonistic" world of individuals that sucked the lifeblood from their victims, the workers.[21]

In Marx's ideal world, there would be no more need for something as sordid as profit or, indeed, the free market world of Adam Smith for whom competition and self-interest were vital engines for economic progress and a higher standard of living. There was no doubt that the transformation from a preindustrial economy into an industrial one was not immediately beneficial to everyone. But the dire conditions that Marx and Engels reported were a testament to the old economy that was in its death throes. The standard of living for the working classes rose over the course of the nineteenth and into the twentieth centuries. Between 1850 and 1865 in England, the real wages of the British factory worker rose by 17 percent, the standard of living was about 50 percent higher at the end of the century compared to the middle, and while the country's GDP for the years 1770–1815 was 1.5 percent per annum, that figure doubled in the years 1815–1831. The number of hours full-time employees spent at the workplace was on the decline. Fewer hours in the workplace led to the creation of leisure time and people took advantage of the new railways to escape from the city and spend time in the countryside or at the seaside. Factories produced more and cheaper goods, railways sped up not only the transportation of people but of this greater array of products (thereby lowering costs), and steam engines cut the price of energy, as did abundant coal. Entrepreneurs invented new machines and methods of production, invested in stocks and shares, and expanded the economy, bringing to market a greater number of products of wider variety than ever before. All of this depended upon the financiers who provided the necessary capital. Marx's dire predictions of a capitalist European economy in decline were unfounded even though there were serious problems with poverty. The answer was not less capital, however, but more of it.[22]

In Germany, the association between Jews and finance was called *die judische Goldspinne*, the Jewish gold spider that exploited and ruined all those caught in its web. As early as 1843, Marx had raged against the Jews who he believed embodied the economic system he despised. To be a capitalist was to be Jewish; they were Shylocks vying for their pound of flesh, feasting on the misery of the disenfranchised. In a response to another Young Hegelian, Bruno Bauer, on the Jewish Question (*Die Judenfrage*), Marx dusted off an old argument, characterizing modern capitalist society as Jewish:

> What is the profane basis of Judaism? *Practical* need, *self-interest*. What is the worldly cult of the Jew? *Huckstering* [usury]. What is his worldly god? *Money*. Very well: then in emancipating itself from *huckstering* and *money*, and thus from real and practical Judaism, our age would emancipate itself.[23]

For Marx, the modern age was a Jewish age of usurious profiteering and, as he put it, huckstering. Money was the "jealous god of Israel, beside which no other god may exist." Like so many others who viewed the world in terms of economic classes and monetary inequality, Marx was convinced that "the Jews," through their financial strength, "determine[d] the fate of the whole [Habsburg] Empire." Through their money alone, they shaped the destiny of Europe. It was the accomplishment of Jews, with their "Jewish spirit" of practicality, that money became a global power. To the "Jew," the world was nothing more than a giant stock exchange, where everything—and everyone—had a price, and where man's objective was to be "richer than his neighbor."[24]

Marx contended that there surely were, in the past, "gambling manias before corn manias, railway manias, banking manias, cotton-spinning manias . . ." But now every aspect of government and commerce seemed to be "invaded by the spirit of speculation." And, in his view, this was not a good thing. Even the socialists—who he despised as heretics to his brand of orthodoxy—he attacked for their "stock-jobbing and philosophical swindling." It was a common argument that misunderstood the nature of speculation and one that is still in use. As Neil Ferguson noted, it was the scandals that stayed in people's minds not the fact that their lives were infinitely more comfortable than those of their ancestors. There was reckless speculation, of course, prompted by laziness, greed, and ignorance, but there was also speculation that required the investor to be well-informed, have good business acumen, and clear-sightedness. Far removed from such informed speculators who studied and understood the market were the mere gamblers, who only needed to spin the wheel or flip a card. They were the people described by one newspaper in 1895 who lived in "the sphere of speculation," that existed of "regularly recurring cycles of excitement." The desire to make great sums of money quickly was a dream that spanned the generations. From the tulip mania in the seventeenth century when investors tried to lay their hands on every bulb they could, to the eighteenth-century South Sea Bubble which "floated gaily for a time," infatuated financiers and merchants "crippled their resources" chasing after the prospect of easy riches and dividends.[25]

Marx's excoriation of capitalism and the inextricable fusing of a stereotyped Jew with an economic system that, he argued, worshiped at the altar of money and resulted in alienation, echoed in the revolutions of 1848 and beyond.

* * *

In the spring of 1848, an uneasy coalition of protesters demanded freedom of speech, more democracy, better working conditions, and brought an end to the rule of the Orléanist king Louis-Philippe in France. A former mason named Pierre Leroux (1797–1871) became mayor of Boussac in central France and, later, a radical member of the Legislative Assembly. Leroux, who was credited with coining the term "socialism" in his article "*De l'individualisme et du socialism*" in 1834, detested the private enterprise system. It was, he wrote, pioneered in large part by the Jews, who had a "great greed for money and eagerness to make it." Elucidating on what he meant by using the word "Jew," he informed his readers that "*the Jewish spirit*" was "the spirit of profit, of lucre, of gain, the spirit of *commerce*, of speculation, in a word, a *banker's spirit*."[26]

In Germany, when he was not manning the barricades, Richard Wagner was working on a new opera. It turned into a cycle of four operas called *Der Ring des Niberlungen* and would take him around twenty-six years to complete. The plot was taken from Norse myth; the chief of the Niberlungen and keeper of their treasure, Alberich, forges a magic ring from gold stolen from the Rhine maidens. The ring bestows upon its possessor power over the entire world. The dwarf Alberich is "swarthy, swampy, and sulphurous," while his brother, Mime, is "gruesome, grizzled, and gray, cramped and crooked, with hanging ears stretching, bleary eyes staring."[27]

Wagner admired socialism and hosted guests in Dresden such as the Russian anarchist Mikhail Bakunin and the composer and conductor August Röckel. Röckel was the editor of a radical newspaper in Dresden called *Volksblätter* and was involved, along with Wagner and Bakunin, in the May Uprising in Dresden in 1849. With its failure, Röckel and Bakunin were given death sentences (later commuted to life imprisonment) while Wagner fled to Zurich. The composer was also influenced by the work of the Proudhon and shared his attitude toward Jews. Employing the popular racial ideas, the composer believed Jews to have an inherent lack of culture, so obsessed as they were with base materialism and money-making. It is a topic of much debate whether this view was reflected in the Ring cycle with the misshapen, thieving, covetous dwarves representing Jewish capitalists who "stole" the nations' gold in order to control the world.[28]

In his 1850 essay, *Das Judenthum in der Musik* (Jewishness in Music), Wagner portrayed the Jew as someone who converts art into "a mere article of exchange." Jews were not interested in, and had no ability for, creativity and art. Their world was solely that of the stock exchange or bank. As long as money "continues the power before which all our doings and strivings are as naught, [the Jew] will continue [to dominate] . . . . What the Roman and medieval tyrant did to people in the past, Jews were [doing] now—converting torment and suffering . . . day to day into gold." It was not art, beauty, or sentiment that excited the Jew, only "some special and selfish interest. Either . . . his material profit . . . his personal vanity . . ." It was a depiction that was shared by the man who would become known for the creation of the term "antisemitism."[29]

Like Wagner, the radical journalist Wilhelm Marr took to the streets during the 1848 revolutions, aspiring to install a "socialistic policy" in Germany. Marr admired Wagner and his new festival at Bayreuth and, like Marx, linked Jews collectively to ill-gotten wealth and the capitalism he abhorred. Also like Marx, Marr was anti-religious, detested liberalism (which they both regarded as weak), professed to be a guardian of the working classes, and was revolutionary in temperament. He would prefer, he pronounced, to "live under the iron rod of a despot, even that of Nero, than under the power of money and the bourgeoisie." It was a choice many revolutionaries made who made cult heroes out of tyrants. He despised what he called "the aristocracy of money," with Rothschild being one of his prime targets. But as a German nationalist whose head was filled with racial types, Marr rejected Marxist internationalism, and this led him to question to place of Jews in German society.[30]

In the 1860s, Marr's solution to the so-called "Jewish Question" was the complete assimilation of Jews by exogamy. By the late 1870s, he changed his mind. Successful assimilation was unworkable due to the inalienable differences of race. Driven by a desire to separate his secular and racial anti-Jewishness from religiously inspired prejudice, he popularized the term antisemitism. The Jewish Semite was opposed to the Germanic Aryan. Unable to live together, in a cosmic battle, a clash of civilizations, one must inevitably and catastrophically vanquish the other. Jewishness was no longer a term used to describe religious adherence. It was fundamental to a person's being, and as much a part of the person as having straight hair, green eyes, or an even temperament. It was a product of the modern mania for categorization and national identity. It would have been an idea incomprehensible to medieval and early modern society.

Marr's 1879 publication, *Der Weg zum Siege des Germanenthums über das Judenthum* (The Way to Victory of Germanness over Jewishness) marked a turning point in anti-Jewish rhetoric. For the first time, an argument against Jews was based on purely "racial" categories, imbuing all Jews with the age-long mantel of the usurer and his history as shaped by his opponents. The fundamental basis of

Marr's antisemitism was the alleged economic corruption and dishonest livelihood of Jewish usurers. Like Marx, Wagner, and others, Marr spoke about the "Jewish spirit" that was inimical to the common good. This phantasmagorical spirit was created by and fed on the lust for money, moneylending, and commerce—all of which were portrayed as contrary to culture and humanity—and those who involved themselves in these pursuits and professions were judaizers. On the face of it, the foundation of Marr's thinking is not so different to medieval theologians but in attaching usury—by which was meant corruption, exploitation, and deceit—to Jews as an inherent trait, he stepped in a different direction to the critics of usury in past times.

In response to this literary attack, German Jews retaliated. In a variety of arguments, Jews countered that they were not shirkers or parasites, and that more Jews were engaged in artisanal work rather than in finance. Others defended the presence of Jews in commerce. Some Jews, however, who also despised the world of finance, wholeheartedly agreed with Marr's characterization of Jews as usurers, suggesting that Jews refrain from such activities so as not to bring opprobrium upon the whole of Jewry.[31]

Marr experienced another shift in his views towards Jews at the end of his life. He roundly rejected overtures from Protestant Socialist anti-Jewish groups to join with them, dismissing offers by Adolf Stöcker, Kaiser Wilhelm II's court chaplain, to become part of his organization. He made it clear that he would not "consider cooperating with orthodox, church-Christian anti-Semitism." As the antisemitic movement became coopted by men such as Stoecker, Marr put a distance between himself and organizations he disparaged for their "commercialized and businesslike anti-Semitism" and their "*commercialized fraud*" which made them "more Jewish than *the Jews themselves*." Not only did he loathe what he branded a corporate antisemitism, which he saw as authoritarian and capitalist, he also despised the kind of beer-hall firebrands and German mystics who venerated the nation's blood and soil that were attracted to these groups. He did not have, he remarked, "the ability to be a drunken anti-Semitic vandal." Nevertheless, his antisemitism rooted in economics, encapsulated in a capitalist "Jewish spirit" at war with a "German Kultur," would be adopted by these very groups he rejected.

Marr disassociated himself and the ideology he named. For him, the movement had become a crude, popularized movement appealing to the basest instincts of mankind. In his mind, his earlier attempts were not vitriolic tirades against the Jews as people but against their role in commerce. If they were to remove themselves from commerce, then there would be no antisemitism and a *modus vivendi* could be accomplished. Yet, he also claimed that even if all the Jews were beaten to death, the Jewish spirit—the commercial moneymaking proclivity—would still exist in modern life, which cared only for money and profit and power. It cast its long, ominous shadow over the golden hills of the communal past Marr romanticized and idolized. Modern society, in his eyes, would "end its days in social suicide."[32]

Marr's antisemitism was a malleable notion that soon attached itself to political parties and candidates. The theme of extortion, the commonplace image of the Jew sucking the poor dry, became the rallying cry for the electoral candidates running on behalf of the new antisemitic parties that had sprung up in various cities throughout Europe. Otto Böckel (1859–1923), a librarian and folklorist, published a pamphlet in 1886 entitled *Die Juden—Die Könige unserer Zeit* (*The Jews: The Kings of Our Time*) in which he presented his own radical anticapitalist and antisemitic viewpoint. He shared many of the same views as Wilhelm Marr. It was not the religion of the Jews that was the trouble. What Jews believed, whether they were acculturated, highly observant, or baptized (which, outside of racial theories, made them non-Jews), was irrelevant to the antisemite. Conversion was merely the means for ambitious Jews to reach the highest echelons of society and promote the interests of their race. The Jews, Böckel wrote, were powerful because of their money and because people were afraid of them. It was not even unthinkable that it was the Jews themselves who hired *agents provocateurs* to stir up the so-called antisemitic riots that had broken out in various towns and cities. Presumably, they did so in order to pin the blame on antisemites. Central to Böckel's thought was the economic force of "the Jews." They were the ruin of the peasantry. They were to blame for the so-called hunger-typhus (a combination of starvation and epidemic) and poverty in the Spessart region of Bavaria and Hesse; and in West Prussia (where Jews were "extraordinarily widespread") they were the "fundamental evil" that confronted the peasant classes. The Rothschilds and their financial power, which was evident in global affairs, were nothing less than the guardians of Germany. The blame he placed on Jews and capitalism was strikingly different to the medical scientist and reformer who witnessed the poverty and disease Böckel referenced. For Rudolf Carl Virchow, the answer to this crushing poverty was "full and unlimited democracy." That included more capital being placed at the disposal of more people, not the restriction of capital. It was by broadening capitalism so that it was not concentrated in the hands of a few, that liberty and prosperity thrived.[33]

In 1887 at age twenty-seven, the "handsome, energetic, and resourceful" Böckel was elected to the Hesse government, surprising his Conservative opponent who was sure he was on the road to victory. Böckel ran on a pro-peasant platform that urged them to free themselves from Jewish middlemen. The economic downturn that hit the German peasants in the 1870s meant more farmers were plunged into debt and bankruptcy but as Virchow observed this had to do with the stifling bureaucracy, retention of hierarchy and aristocracy, and the lack of economic liberty that fostered apathy rather than an excess of capitalism or a Jewish conspiracy. But Böckel's diatribes against the "robber" Jews who, he said, exploited and manipulated the misery of the peasants were especially effective. In the same year, the German sociologist and admirer of Marx, Ferdinand Tönnies, published *Gemeinschaft und Gesellschaft* (Community and Society). While family and tradition were the building blocks of community, the market and its moneylending merchants belonged to society. With a brief comment that trade can, of course, be carried out honestly, Tönnies went on to write that as capital enterprises became more "purposefully" carried out on a larger scale, deceit was used to cover up losses or gain higher profits. The desire for wealth made the capitalist an "unscrupulous, egoistic, self-willed" speculator who used everyone as a means to his own ends. The capitalist was, as had been long argued by opponents, the antithesis of the common good.[34]

* * *

In France, the first country in Europe to politically emancipate Jews, there were Jewish judges, Jewish deputies in the House of Representatives, and military officers who had attended the elite military school, the École Polytechnique, in Paris. Even so, antisemitism found fertile ground. In a legislative election in September 1889 for the ninth *arondissement* of Paris, Adolphe Willette (1857–1926) stood as the antisemitic candidate. It was not Hitlerian in character—there were no calls for mass incarceration or extermination. Instead, antisemites wanted Jews—who were no longer regarded as "racial" compatriots—to be driven from the economy and, in some cases, from the land as an alien element that was working against the "true" French people.

Willette, an art nouveau painter, illustrator, lithographer, and caricaturist, had studied at the prestigious École des Beaux-Arts in Paris. Some of his Pierrot paintings hung in the famous cabaret *Le Chat Noir* in the bohemian art district of Montmartre, situated on a hill north of Paris' center. Montmartre was a place where cheap accommodation was to be found; it was also the "home of every kind of artist" as well as workers, retirees, and "the starchy ladies of the rue Bréda." Willette's works did not attain the fame of posters by his friend Théophile-Alexandre Steinlen (whose black cat advertisement for the cabaret has remained a staple in poster art), nor did his work achieve the acclaim of that of another friend, Henri Toulouse-Lautrec, whose art captured the bohemian culture and sexual freedom of the cafés, brothels, and cabarets of Montmartre. Politics proved to be a more successful venue for fame and fortune in Willette's case.[35]

As a "man of the people," a champion for the downtrodden and oppressed, Willette objected to Jews not because of their religion but because of their "tyranny." The poster he created for his political campaign proclaimed "Judaism, there is the enemy." The heroes he drew were laborers and soldiers—honest Frenchmen in the candidate's eyes. The Jew in his artwork was not hard to spot. He was the small figure behind a pig's head held up by one of the hardworking, decent Frenchmen. Not only did he sport a hooked nose, but also a top hat and umbrella—symbols typifying the businessman. The message was: Here is the man who does not toil, unlike the soldier, the sailor, the factory worker, and the farmer. In text accompanying the artwork, Willette urged the French to protest against the despotism of the racially alien Jews who enslaved them.[36]

An obsession with the supposed decadence of the French nation followed the country's defeat in the Franco-Prussian war of 1871 and the fall of the Second Empire (1852–1870). After Napoleon III's ignominious defeat by the Germans, a third republic came into government which was immediately put to the test with the establishment of the short-lived Paris Commune by a mixed group of communists, anarchists, and socialists. Some journalists noted a sense of hysteria in contemporary France, although this was not completely unwarranted. The seizing of power in Paris by revolutionaries, the regular occurrence of bomb attacks, successful and failed assassinations, and other anarchic activity augmented the spirit of defeat that marked the nation in the aftermath of the war.

In 1882, the French stock market crashed, sending shockwaves through the nation. One of the triggers to the debacle was the fall of the Société de l'Union Générale, a Catholic bank founded in 1878 by Paul-Eugène Bontoux, a former employee of the Rothschild railway company. In its first years, creditors flocked to put their money in the bank, and Bontoux invested that money in other banks and in a railway system in the Balkans. Shares in the Union Générale rose from 500 francs each in 1879 to just over 3000 at its height. With the prospect of quick riches, speculators rushed to invest and, as in any time of frenzied stock buying, they often spent more than they had in hand, counting on making money before their debts became due. As interest rates rose and margins on the loans increased, a crash loomed. To add to the problems, it turned out that the bank had less capital than it claimed; it was actively trading its own stock and doctoring its records to indicate a profit it did not have. It was, in effect, a fraudulent Ponzi scheme whereby the investors' money was spent on further speculative projects.[37]

With the collapse and bankruptcy of the Union Générale and the ensuing crisis in the Paris stock market, allegations were made that Jews, particularly the Rothschilds, in association with Protestant bankers conspired together to bring down the bank. The bank had not failed due to mismanagement or corruption, it was said, but because of the manipulative machinations of the Rothschilds who resented the competition from the institution started by their former associate.[38]

Antisemitic newspapers reveled in reports of mercenary Jewish bankers supposedly responsible for the economic crises. Underneath the sophisticated exterior of the wealthy Jewish banker they spied the imagined repellent moneylender of medieval times. The suit may have been handmade at the finest tailors, but it could not disguise the Shylock who wore it, the grasping, duplicitous usurer, ready with his bloody dagger to take his pound of flesh. After ridding the nation of its monarchy in a revolution that decapitated enemies of the state in a frenzied bloodlust, the crown and throne had now simply passed to the capitalists, with the industrialists now the new aristocracy single-mindedly pursuing nothing but self-interest. These men, insatiably hungry for larger and larger profits, exploited their workers without conscience, immorally gambled through the stock exchange, and stole from the poor and oppressed.

As the eminent late-nineteenth-century social theorist Max Weber would write in *The Protestant Ethic and the Spirit of Capitalism*, this way of thinking was based on one of the greatest "illusions" in economic history. The pursuit of profit driven by selfish greed was not a definition of capitalism nor was it the "spirit" of an inanimate system. It was how the critic wanted to define a system they blamed for every economic woe. Individual flaws, such as dishonesty, were personal to the individual, not the fault of an inanimate economic method. No matter. To the anticapitalist, self-interest was not advantageous to anyone other than the "self." To those who started with the idea that equality rather than liberty was the more important pursuit in life, and that fairness meant economic and social egalitarianism, then all efforts had to be directed towards the leveling of all peoples' lives. Self-interest, in this perspective, was not viewed as the incentive to work and produce but as morally indefensible greed. For a wide array of people, the Jews personified this system and sometimes a scandal involving Jews, or, as in the following case, people of Jewish descent, would give spurious ammunition to their prejudice.[39]

The crash of the Union Générale was not the only financial scandal that focused attention on Jewish bankers. Early on the autumn morning of November 20,

1892, a Sunday, Baron Jacques de Reinach's valet made his way to his employer's bedroom at his house on the rue Murillo. The baron was a gregarious, easy-going businessman involved in a variety of financial enterprises, and had arrived in Paris as a young man from Frankfort to work with the established bank founded by Baron Samuel Kohn. His impressive mansion stood near the Parc Monceau, the perimeter of which was developed by Emile Pereire. The park, the subject of sunlight-dappled paintings by Claude Monet, had been redeveloped in the mid-nineteenth century by Baron Haussmann. The banker Moise de Camondo also lived nearby, as did Adolphe de Rothschild and Pereire himself.[40]

The valet's intention was to wake the fifty-two-year old baron to ride with his hunt. As he entered the room, he was surprised to see Joseph Reinach, the baron's nephew, was already there and that the baron was dead. The uproar that ensued over Reinach's death was connected to his involvement in the biggest monetary scandal in nineteenth-century France, the corruption surrounding the building of the Panama Canal. For keeping the financial trouble of the Panama scheme quiet, so as not to alarm investors, members of the Third Republic government were given bribes. The baron was due to appear before the House of Deputies to account for the large sum of money given to him by the Panama Canal Company, funds that, supposedly were for publicity, but were strongly suspected to have been used as bribery.

One of the last people to see Reinach was his colleague Cornelius Herz, who was also implicated in the scandal. He had since fled to England and refused to return to Paris, claiming ill health. Herz, the son of a German father and French mother, grew up in the United States. He traveled to Heidelberg to study medicine and it was during his time there that his parents were financially ruined. Forced to sell his *objects d'art* to pay his debts, he left Heidelberg for Paris, where his first job was looking after a pharmacist's dog for a franc a day. On completion of his studies, Herz was married to a Catholic washerwoman by a Protestant minister in front of his atheist friends. For services in the Franco-Prussian war (he set up a field hospital), he was awarded the Legion of Honor. He returned to New York after the death of his wife and became the chief medical officer at Mount Sinai Hospital. Once back in Paris, he married for a second time and, with a growing family, Herz made the acquaintance of the Rothschilds and became involved in a variety of business ventures, which included setting up the Electric Force Transmission Company. As for his involvement in the Panama scandal, it was alleged that Herz was the intermediary between the Panama Canal Company and the ministers accepting bribes. Found guilty *in abstentia* and sentenced to five years, attempts to extradite Herz back to France from England failed.[41]

Such scandals were the fodder for novelists, journalists, and pamphleteers who took up their pens to chronicle their times or put contemporary debates into narrative. It was not a matter of one or two corrupt people but a scandal that was indicative of an entire people. One of the papers that launched an attack on Reinach and Herz was *La Libre Parole*, the journal founded by a French journalist named Edouard Drumont in the wake of the Panama affair. Drumont was convinced that one of the reasons the scandal had not come to light earlier was that the newspapers and publicity media were in the hands of Jews, either through ownership or financial dependency. Disgusted, angered, and motivated by what he regarded as the evils of "Jewish" capitalism, he launched a vicious attack on Jews. In April 1886, he published his mammoth two-volume work, *La France juive* (Jewish France), which lambasted the effect of Jewish bankers and financiers on the nation. The Jews were foreigners, "Semites" who had "vomited from the ghettoes of Europe, [and were] . . . now installed as the masters of the historic houses that evoke the most glorious moments of ancient France." In grabbing wealth through usury, Jews had made themselves the most "powerful agents of disorder the world has ever seen." Whereas Christians placed little emphasis on money, the Jews made it of paramount importance, creating capitalism to manipulate and oppress laborers. For Drumont, it made no difference if the capitalist was an aristocrat or a Christian; their financial business made them all Jews.[42]

In Drumont's hyperbole, hatred of Jews was primarily a question of economics, albeit mixed with racial animus. In his writings, he combined a strong nationalist fervor with socialist ideals that regarded capitalism as unfair, corrupt, a scourge on the poor, and, as Fourier had argued earlier, dominated by Jews and the English. Heavily influenced by Toussenel, Drumont's extravagant claims bolstered the idea that Jews had gained riches from greed and fraud. He also made the untenable contention that they possessed at least eighty billion of the one-hundred-and-fifty billion that made up the wealth of France. The Sephardic Jew's "crooked fingers" were ready to grab gold while the Ashkenazic Jew was like the medieval usurer, a counter and "circumciser" of ducats: the former was a "jumping and joyous flea" while the latter resembled "a mellow and sticky lice, living parasitically off the human body."[43]

In contrast to the spirit of free trade, which was based on competition and minimal regulation, Drumont proposed the expropriation of Jewish wealth by an Office of Confiscated Jewish Wealth, which would act in the same way that the revolutionary Office of National Wealth had during the Revolution. Basing his proposal on revolutionary practices gave it legitimacy, or so he thought. He also considered it a legitimate action because this Jewish wealth had been obtained by "parasitical and usurious" means, through speculation and capitalist ventures. The expropriation of wealth was justified because Jews—all Jews in his eyes—did not make money through physical labor. All profit produced from capitalist business was automatically suspect as it enriched the Jews at the expense of the "real workers."[44]

Drumont claimed that the Semite (the racialist characterization of Jews) were obsessed with crushing the "Aryan" into servitude. While he chose to use the current racial terminology, he looked back to the twelfth century to find support for his socialist economic policy. Quoting Peter the Venerable, Drumont wrote that the wealth of the Jews should benefit Christians, even if it had to be forcibly taken. It was the Jews, "the manipulators of gold against the poor . . . the sons of Judas," who persecuted "the servants of Jesus Christ." Jews were taught from a young age, especially through the reading of *Aesop's Fables*, how to be cunning and swindle Gentiles.[45]

Avaricious and cunning Jewish bankers who were ready to cheat and steal became common villains in late nineteenth-century literature. In V. Roustane's *Le Juif de Sofiefka* (1894), a Jew swindles a man who had once saved him from destitution. Taking over his estate, the Jew then proceeded to drive the village peasantry into ruination, while he and his co-religionists subject them to an array of humiliations. Another Jewish banker, Baron von Horn, appears in Henri Lavedan's satire *Prince d'Aurec* (1894). Motivated by greed, Horn delights as the debts owed to him by a desperate nobleman mount, causing the borrower's impoverishment. In *Décadence* (1901), by Albert Guinon, the Jewish banker Strohmann schemes to defraud people in Paris of their life savings. Strohmann is unremittingly cold, calculating, and covetous, his fingers itching to grab the wealth of Frenchmen.[46]

The villainous Jewish banker was also the subject of a book by the French writer, journalist, musicologist, and agriculturalist Guy de Charnacé (1825–1909). Appearing in 1885 novel, *Le Baron Vampire* was a caricature of the Rothschilds and based on his investigations into the railway business. For eight years, he explored the business transactions of the Railways of the North. De Charnacé regularly visited the literary salon in Dresden of the Polish aristocrat Countess Eveline Hańska and where he became acquainted with Richard Wagner. In marrying Claire d'Agoult, Charnacé became related to Wagner when the composer married Claire's half-sister Cosima. He was also involved in his musical endeavors. Along with his musical ability, Charnacé was an expert on rural economies and a recipient of the Legion of Honor.

Le Baron Vampire was written at Charnacé's Chateau de Bois-Monbourcher, nestled in the Loire Valley in Anjou, and follows the story of a poor German Jewish peddler, Rebb Schmoul, on his journey to becoming one of the richest bankers in Paris. That this was achieved through deception and intrigue both mirrored and solidified the commonplace association of Jews and unscrupulous finance. Gleeful in times of financial crisis, when he profited by buying stocks at a lower price, and immune to the suffering of those destroyed by such economic crises, Schmoul typified what Charnacé believed to be the typological nature of the Jew. The Jews, he wrote, made human sacrifice holy and that sacrifice was accomplished by the impoverishment, destitution, and starvation of the French people by the covetous and duplicitous Jewish financiers.[47]

Guy de Charnacé's attitude may have been colored by his own financial recklessness. A business deal involving livestock from England ended in failure and resulted in a large loss of money, much of it from his wife's dowry, and the destruction of his marriage.[48]

These literary condemnations of modern society were stimulated by a variety of economic disasters, such as the stock market bubble that occurred in the 1870s. It led to bank failures in France and what was known as the *Gründerkrise* in Germany. Some pointed the finger of blame at Jewish financiers who had a notable but far from unique presence in the exchanges. These financial crises had nothing to do with a mythical Jewish conspiracy and more to do with the euphoric and foolhardy expansion of credit which turned to a lack of confidence in the market and the sell-off of shares. All it took was the whiff of scandal, the hint of corruption, bankruptcy, or any other negative event to turn the mood from over-confident to panicked.[49]

In an opinion that would become a leitmotif over the generations, the philosopher and economist Eugen Dühring noted that the press, "in so far as it is an instrument of money" and makes gold into a Moloch or deity, "all higher interests are sacrificed to [the Jew]" He accused the business world and the press of manipulating politics and, as the business world and the media were "Jewish," this meant that Jews guided politics towards their own ends. It was the same argument that had been made by Wagner. Everything was in the market for sale. Those with power and influence got the best deal. For Dühring, corruption was attached to two things: supply and demand, the basis of capitalism. While not solely responsible for economic corruption, the Jews were, by their inherent nature, monopolistically minded, insofar that they worshipped a god that tolerated no other god, and they coveted global power. The portrait of Jews built up by various philosophers, composers, and economists in the nineteenth century, therefore, was one of a corrupt, covetous, and thieving cabal, plotting to rob the world of its wealth, and then grasping for dominion over the earth. No one encapsulated this image more for anticapitalists than the Rothschilds and other barons of industry.[50]

* * *

Reform was a key word in the nineteenth century, as people looked for ways to perfect society. There was a growing sense that the private sector was inadequate in the battle against poverty and that taking care of the poor via charity was insufficient. Dismissive of *laissez-faire* economics, reformers began to advocate for government intervention to redress inequality in society. The answer to poverty and scarcity, was to increase governmental control and public spending on programs that would benefit society as a whole. It was, however, the opposite that was true. Interference in the economy (price controls, wage controls, quotas and taxes on imports, corporate taxes, personal taxes, surcharges and so on) led to a loss of liberty. The more control the government obtained over the economy, the more liberty the individual had taken away and the more likely tyranny of some sort would arise. And it was in the next century that the individual freedoms heralded by the Enlightenment were crushed by ideologues imposing their vision of the perfect society.[51]

Notes

1. Wiesner-Hanks, *Early Modern Europe*, 1450–1789, chap. 6.
2. Kocka, *Capitalism*; Ferguson, *The Ascent of Money*, chap. 1; Dean de la Motte and Jeannene M. Przyblyski, eds., *Making the News: Modernity and Mass Press in Nineteenth-Century France* (Amherst: University of Massachusetts Press, 1999), 354.
3. Niall Ferguson, "The Rise of the Rothschilds: The Family Firm as Multinational," in *The World of Private Banking*, eds. Youssef Cassis and Philip L. Cottrell (Farnham, UK: Ashgate Publishing, 2009), 10; Michie, *London Stock Exchange*, 51, 68; World Trade Organization, "The Economics and Political Economy of International Trade Cooperation," *The GATT/WTO at 60: WTO World Trade Report Examines Six Decades of Multilateralism in Trade* (2007), 35, https://www.wto.org/english/res_e/booksp_e/anrep_e/wtr07-2b_e.pdf; Eugen Weber, *From Peasants Into Frenchmen: The Modernization of Rural France 1870–1914* (Stanford, CA: Stanford University Press, 1976).
4. Michael Graetz, *The Jews in Nineteenth-Century France: From the French Revolution to the Alliance Israelite Universelle* (Stanford, CA: Stanford University Press, 1996), 148;

Jim Harter, *World Railways of the Nineteenth Century: A Pictorial History in Victorian Engravings* (Baltimore: Johns Hopkins University Press, 2005), 137.

5. Telemachus Timothy Timayenis, *The Original Mr. Jacobs* (New York: The Minerva Pub., 1888), https://archive.org/stream/TheOriginalMr.JacobsAstartlingExpose/OMJ_djvu.txt; Ferguson, *The Ascent of Money*, chap. 2.
6. Ferguson, "The Rise of the Rothschilds," 1, 8.
7. "1816, The Year Without a Summer," *In Our Time*, BBC Radio 4, http://www.bbc.co.uk/programmes/b077j4yv
8. Kindleberger and Aliber, *Manias*, chap. 3.
9. Götz Aly, *Why the Germans? Why the Jews? Envy, Race Hatred, and the Pre-History of the Holocaust* (New York: Metropolitan Books, 2011), 55–56.
10. Moshe Zimmerman, "The 'Hep Hep' Riots in Hamburg. Ludolf Holst's Treatise 'On the Relationship of Jews to the Christians in Commercial Towns,'" *Key Documents of German-Jewish History*, http://jewish-history-online.net/article/jgo:article-190#section-1.
11. Nicholas Valentine Riasanovsky, *The Teaching of Charles Fourier* (Berkeley and Los Angeles: University of California Press, 1969), 164–65; Bryan Taylor, "The Century of Inflation," *Economic Thought Journal* 2 (2006): 101; Charles Fourier, "On Free Exchange," and "The Vices of Commerce," in *The Utopian Vision of Charles Fourier: Selected Texts on Work, Love, and Passionate Attraction* (Boston: Beacon Press, 1972); Fourier quoted in Bernard Lewis, *Semites and Anti-Semites* (New York: W. W. Norton, 1986), 111.
12. Edouard Drumont, *La France juive,* v. 2 (Paris: C. Marpon & Flammarion, 1886), 335; Timayenis, *The Original Mr. Jacobs.*
13. Fourier, *Fable of the Jew Iscariot and the Six Christians*, quoted in Dan Cohn-Sherbok, *The Crucified Jew* (London: HarperCollins, 1992), 159; Wistrich, *Antisemitism: The Longest Hatred*, 191; Riasanovsky, *The Teaching of Charles Fourier*, 166; Fourier, "On Trade," *The Utopian Vision.*
14. Pierre Joseph Proudhon, diary entry for December 26, 1847, *Carnets* (Paris: M. Rivière, 1960); Lewis, *Semites and Anti-Semites*, 111.
15. Adolphe Toussenel, *Les Juifs, rois de l'époque: Histoire de la féodalité financière*, vol. 2 (Paris: G. de Gonet, 1847), 44, 47, 75, 75, 86 http://archive.org/stream/lesjuifsroisdel02tous#page/28/mode/2up; Ferguson, *The House of Rothschild*, 429; Timayenis, *The Original Mr. Jacobs*; Richard Wagner, *Judaism in Music* (*Das Judenthum in der Musik*), trans. William Ashton Ellis, http://www.jrbooksonline.com/pdf_books/judaisminmusic.pdf.
16. Tousssenel, *Les Juifs*, 80; Sarah Juliette Sasson, *Longing to Belong: The Parvenu in Nineteenth Century French and German Literature* (New York: Palgrave Macmillan, 2012), 143.

17. Toussenel, *Les Juifs*, 338, 75, 86, 95–96; Drumont, *La France juive* v. 2, 334; Ceri Crossley, "Anglophobia and Anti-semitism: The Case of Alphonse Toussenel (1803–85)," *Modern and Contemporary France* 12.4 (2004): 459–72.
18. Toussenel, *Les Juifs*, 5.
19. Jacob Katz, "A State Within a State: The History of an Anti-Semitic Slogan." *The Israel Academy of Sciences and Humanities Proceedings IV* (1969/70): 25; Pierre Birnbaum, *L'Aigle et la Synagogue: Napoléon, les Juifs et L'État* (Paris: Fayard, 2007), 28–29, 256.
20. Karl Marx, "The Economic Crisis in Europe," *New York Daily Tribune*, Oct. 9, 1856.
21. Ibid and idem, *On the Jewish Question*, reprinted in *The Marx-Engels Reader*, 2nd ed., Robert C. Tucker, ed. (New York: W. W. Norton, 1978), 51.
22. Muller, *The Mind and the Market*, chap. 7; C. H. Feinstein, "National Statistics 1760–1920," in *Studies in Capital Formation in the United Kingdom, 1750–1920,* eds. C. H. Feinstein and S. Pollard (Oxford: Clarendon Press, 1988).
23. Marx, *On the Jewish Question*, 48.
24. Ibid., 49–50.
25. Marx, "The Economic Crisis"; Louis Guenther, "Investments and Speculation," in *Business Administration: Theory, Practice and Application*, ed. Walter D. Moody [1910] (London: Forgotten Books, 2018), 121; *Dundee Evening Telegraph*, Sept. 3, 1895, 2.
26. Pierre Leroux quoted in Edmund Silberner, "Pierre Leroux's Ideas on the Jewish People," *Jewish Social Studies* XII (1950): 368–69. Original emphasis.
27. *Nibelungenlied* (*The Song of the Nibelungs*) was an anonymous Middle High German poem dating from around 1200 CE. It told the tale of the tragic history of the Burgundian royal family and the death of the dragon-slayer Siegfried.
28. Albrecht Classen, "Nieberlungenlied," in *Medieval Folklore*, 290; Leon Stein, *The Racial Thinking of Richard Wagner* (New York: Philosophical Library, 1950), 73.
29. Wagner, *Judaism in Music*, 5–6, 14–15. For different interpretations of Wagner and whether his anti-Jewish beliefs affected his art or not, see, for example, Stein, *The Racial Thinking of Richard Wagner*, chap. 16; Marc A. Weiner, *Richard Wagner and the Anti-Semitic Imagination* (Lincoln, NE: University of Nebraska Press, 1995), chap. 4; Jacob Katz, *The Darker Side of Genius: Richard Wagner's Anti-Semitism* (Hanover, NH: University Press of New England, 1986).
30. Marr was influenced by Ludwig von Feuerbach's Hegelian works such as *Das Wesen des Christentums* (*The Essence of Christianity* [1841]). Moshe Zimmerman, *Wilhelm Marr: The Patriarch of Antisemitism* (New York: OUP, 1986), 15, 16–17, 21, 25, 27, 74–75; Wilhelm Marr, "Zur Charackteristic des deutschen Liberalismus," *Der Mensch und die Ehe* (Leipzig: W. Jurany, 1848), 331, http://archive.org/stream/dermenschunddie01marrgoog#page/n7/mode/2up.
31. Zimmerman, *Wilhelm Marr*, 80.

32. Wilhelm Marr, *Testament eines Antisemiten* (1891) reprinted in Zimmerman, *Wilhelm Marr*, 136, 137, 140, 149, 151, 153–55. Original emphasis.
33. Otto Böckel, *Die Juden—die Könige unserer Zeit* (Berlin: Rusch, 1886), 4–7, 12; Rudolf Carl Virchow, "Report on the Typhus Epidemic in Upper Silesia," *American Journal of Public Health* 96.12 (2006), https://www.ncbi.nlm.nih.gov/pmc/articles/PMC1698167/.
34. Muller, *The Mind and the Market*, 230; Mark Strauss, "Anti-Globalism's Jewish Problem," *Foreign Policy*, November 2, 2009, http://foreignpolicy.com/2009/11/02/anti-globalisms-jewish-problem/; Albert S. Lindemann, *Esau's Tears: Modern Anti-Semitism and the Rise of the Jews* (Cambridge: CUP, 2000), 152–53.
35. "The Lure of Montmartre 1800–1900," *Metropolitan Museum of Art*, http://www.metmuseum.org/toah/hd/mont/hd_mont.htm.
36. Nelly Wilson, *Bernard-Lazare: Antisemitism and the Problem of Jewish Identity in Late Nineteenth-century France* (Cambridge: CUP, 1978), 67.
37. Eugene N. White, "The Krach of 1882 and the Bailout of the Paris Bourse," 14, 19–20, http://econweb.rutgers.edu/ewhite/Krach%20of%201882 %20June2005.pdf.
38. Kindleberger and Aliber, *Manias*, chap. 4.
39. Roger Boesche, "Tocqueville and Le Commerce: A Newspaper Expressing his Unusual Liberalism," *Journal of the History of Ideas* 44.2 (1983): 283; Muller, *The Mind and the Market*, chap. 9.
40. Maron J. Simon, *The Panama Affair* (New York: Scribner, 1971), 26, 105; "The Panama Scandal: Baron de Reinach's Suicide," *The Argus* (Melbourne), January 21, 1893, 9.
41. *The Argus*, 9; This biography is according to Marius Tallon who claimed to be a friend of Herz in his early days in Paris. *The Argus* (Melbourne), February 25, 1893, 4.
42. Barbara W. Tuchman, *The Proud Tower: A Portrait of the World Before the War 1890–1915* (Cambridge: CUP, 1993), 57. Drumont, *La France juive*, xiv–xvii.
43. In 1888, a one-volume edition was published by Victor Palmé. Michel Winock, *Nationalisme, antisémitisme et fascisme en France* (Paris: Seuil, 1990), chap. 4; Gerald Krefetz, *Jews and Money: The Myths and Reality* (New Haven: Ticknor & Fields, 1982), 5; Frederick Busi, *The Pope of Antisemitism: The Career and Legacy of Edouard-Adolphe Drumont* (Lanham, MD: Rowman & Littlefield, 1986), 6; Drumont, *La France juive*, 35–38.
44. Drumont, *La France juive*, 524–26.
45. Drumont quoted in Albert S. Lindemann, *The Jew Accused: Three Anti-Semitic Affairs, Dreyfus, Beilis, Frank, 1894–1915* (Cambridge: CUP, 1993), 86; Drumont, *La France juive*, Book 2, 151, 524.
46. Moses Debré, *The Image of the Jew in French Literature From 1800 to 1908* (New York: Ktav Pub. House, 1970), 34, 35, 41–42.

47. Debré, *The Image of the Jew*, 33; Guy de Charnac, *Le Baron Vampire* (Paris 1885), 161, quoted in Sara Libby Robinson, *Blood Will Tell: Vampires as Political Metaphors Before World War I* (Brighton, MA: Academic Studies Press, 2011), 129–30.
48. Alan Walker, *Franz Liszt: The Weimar Years 1848–1861* (Ithaca: Cornell University Press, 1989), n. 24, 437.
49. Muller, *The Mind and the Market*, chap. 9; Kindleberger and Aliber, *Manias*, chap. 5.
50. Eugen Dühring, *Die Judenfrage: Racen-, Sitten- und Culturfrage* (Karlsruhe and Leipzig: Verlag von H. Reuther, 1881), https://archive.org/stream/Duehring-Die-Judenfrage-2/DuehringEugen-DieJudenfrageAlsRacen-Sitten-UndCulturfrage1881167S.Scan#page/n0/mode/2up, and quoted in Christophe Cobet, *Der Wortschatz des Antisemitismus in der Bismarckzeit* (Munich: W. Fink, 1973), 74, 81; Dühring, *Die Judenfrage*, 14.
51. Himmelfarb, *Poverty and Compassion*, introduction; Sennholz, *Age of Inflation*, 12, 21.

9 Sharing the Wealth

In 1913, the French writer Charles Péguy observed that, given the vast number of innovations introduced into society, the world had changed more in the past thirty years than it had since the time of Jesus Christ. Airplanes soared through the skies, cars raced around country lanes at top speeds of forty miles per hour, and telephones and electric lighting were fitted into a greater number of homes. In 1911, a telegraphic message was relayed from New York to London in just thirty seconds. Free trade ruled the seas, budgets were balanced, money was sound, and empires seemed stable. The three decades before 1914 were, as one historian has put it, "the golden years for international investors." That would change with the war that would set the world ablaze.

The Great War would foment revolution, which was nothing new, but what was new was the combination of a highly technological world and, in the heart of Europe, an inflexible and deadly idealism where the moral authority was a totalitarian dictator. Standing against that were the Western countries that had developed a strong tradition of individual liberty, freedom of thought, freedom of movement, and a free economy. And the bastion of those values, and the greatest exponent of capitalism, was the United States. It was in the US that economic ideas and techniques, mainly abandoned by Europeans immediately following the bubbles in the early eighteenth century, were tested, as Americans experimented with land banks, paper money, and private corporations. But it was in the aftermath of the 1914–1918 war that the "American attitude towards investing" arose that diverged from the idea that money was made through hard physical labor, land, and thrift. The ideal of the postwar era was, Julia Ott writes, that of a "shareholder democracy," and, depending on the advocate of this vision, that could mean unregulated markets or the development of an entirely new bureaucracy to oversee and regulate.[1]

* * *

The United States, after its independence from Britain in 1776, inherited its usury laws. All states, except California, had restrictions on the practice before the Civil War. Due to the commercial basis of the early settlers, however, these laws were generally ignored by the colonizers and this tendency continued after the revolutionary war. The neglect of the usury laws led not to the sort of financial scandals and failures that were seen in eighteenth-century England and nineteenth-century France and Germany, where the financial system was more tightly regulated, but to a more stable economy. Funding generally came from equity rather than bank deposits in the two central banks, the First and Second Bank of the United States which made the banks "more like venture capital firms," as one historian has described the setup. The banks funded businesses directly and therefore came close to the exemplar of what a financial intermediary should achieve. By 1830, the United States enjoyed a higher per capita income than its former colonial master.[2]

In the United States, then, usury laws were no longer pertinent or enforced, although no one wanted to be accused of extortion. Without restrictions imposed by such laws, more of the population profited from manageable loans and the credit market was not rationed as it was in countries where interest rates were kept artificially low. In eighteenth-century England, for example, and into the early nineteenth century, wars prevented consistent and substantial economic growth. That, combined with the hindrance of usury laws and other regulations, impeded the private sector and, therefore, the entire economic health of the country. With the abandonment or neglect of such restrictions as the Corn Laws, a protectionist measure that was repealed in the 1840s, England embarked on free trade which unleashed rapid economic growth.[3]

America, however, became the standard bearer of the idea that trade and commerce could only be carried out and improved if loans were readily available. Payment for the monetary loan was seen as no different than a payment for the hiring of any other item. Objections to interest loans and money were, for a greater and greater number of people, a thing of the past. Neither was the connection automatically made between bankers and Jews. The men of the nineteenth century who were given the disparaging nickname of "robber barons," were not Jewish—men such as Cornelius Vanderbilt, Andrew Carnegie, J.D. Rockerfeller, and J.P. Morgan—but there were certainly Jews involved in banking, especially in investment banks such as Goldman Sachs, Lehman Brothers, Kuhn Loeb, and the Salomon Brothers.[4]

Jacob Schiff (1847–1920) was born in Frankfurt-am-Main to a father who went from selling shawls to stockbroking. He left his home country for New York in 1865 where he was taken under the wing of William Bonn, a banker at the firm of Speyer & Co. Returning to Germany to take up a post at the Warburg bank, Schiff met Abraham Kuhn in Frankfurt and soon after he was back in New York. He accepted a position in the Kuhn, Loeb company, which became one of the most influential investment banks in New York. Schiff, who headed the company by 1885, was key in pushing the bank into taking greater risks supplying funds for new or expanding railroads and other industries and forging international relationships with other bankers in London, Paris, and Hamburg. In the spirit of the times, he helped fund these railroads, as well as reorganizing those in trouble, such as Union Pacific. It was during his time working on this railroad that Schiff developed a close bond with the railroad entrepreneur Edward H. Harriman.[5]

Schiff was a successful banker and philanthropist and gave generously to Jewish organizations and charities. He was the epitome of an era abounding with grand schemes, business empire-building, and the mad whirl of speculation. Speculation was not hoarding, greed, and exploitation, although there were many who still thought of it in those terms. So long as it was practiced by honest men, who observed the market with detachment and rational thinking, speculation was a way of making money no different from any other profession. The fact that speculators could profit handsomely in bad markets that meant losses for many, upheld the view that it was immoral as profit should not come at the expense of others.[6]

Alongside Schiff in the echelons of finance was one of his partners and the husband of his wife's sister. Paul Warburg was one of the main advocates for a central banking system in the United States as a "lender of last resort." The Federal Reserve System (1913) established a central banking system as a response to financial panics, especially the "rich man's panic" in 1907. The federal banks, its supporters believed, would help to stabilize the economy, including the regulation of long-term interest rates. The involvement of some Jews in the setting up of the

Federal Reserve system became part of the antisemite's arsenal that foreign Jews controlled the organization. Some of the sponsors were German immigrants, but they were both Christian and Jewish. Moreover, the seven members of the Board of Governors of the Federal Reserve System were nominated by the president of the United States and confirmed by the Senate. It was not then, and is not now, a tool for Jews, or Zionists as antisemites currently claim, but for the US government to intervene in the economy.

* * *

In June 1914, the Archduke Ferdinand and his wife were assassinated in Sarajevo by a Bosnian Serb nationalist leading the Austro-Hungarian empire to declare war on Serbia in July. Within another month, the whole of Europe was at war. The four years of mass slaughter would radically transform Europe's map and create massive discontent and disorder. Young men marched off to the front—to rat-filled trenches knee deep in mud, to the sight of mangled corpses left to rot in no man's land, and to the terrifying sound of shells exploding or the deadly rattle of machine guns. It was the first part of a long European conflict that by 1945 left millions of people dead and be foolishly labeled the "war to end all wars." President Woodrow Wilson famously told the US Congress in 1917, the war would "make the world safe for democracy." He could not have been more wrong.

World War I encouraged the growth of government intervention and in their aftermath, this continued as planned economies and welfare states expanded. In the broadest sense, the beliefs were not so different from the medieval theologians who pitted charity against usury. A moral economy was one which took care of the poor (the definition of which was wide and changeable) and where "excessive" wealth should be redistributed. The U.S. had a different economic history to Europe, however, even though politically it grew out of colonial Britain. It had been built on the framework of the independent pioneer and, in the twentieth century, the free market economy was not only accepted as the best existing financial system but as part of the "American Dream."

Two years into the fighting, at the annual dinner for the American Newspaper Publishers Association, the American investment banker, Otto H. Kahn (1867–1934) gave a speech on high finance. Kahn, who was Jewish, was born in Mannheim, Germany and began his illustrious career as a junior clerk. After working for the Deutsche Bank in London, he immigrated to New York in 1893, taking up an offer to join the Speyer bank. He relocated to Kuhn, Loeb &

Company where he worked alongside his father-in-law Abraham Wolff, Paul and Felix Warburg, and Jacob Schiff, becoming a senior partner in 1920 after Schiff's death.[7]

In a speech at the Waldorf-Astoria, Kahn addressed the issue of financial institutions and war. He praised American finance for its "immense services to the country." There had been no "gambling frenzy" in the US financial markets as had been seen in South Africa during its "mining craze," which led to a number of "questionable episodes" of wrongdoing. There had been no scandal as great as the Panama affair in France. This showed that when handled properly, finance mobilized and organized the wealth of the country to its benefit. Yet, even so, there was still "widespread attitude of suspicion" toward finance in the United States and, in some cases, "virtual hostility" was directed "toward the financial community," especially Wall Street.[8]

This kind of mistrust of bankers, investors, and speculators affected Kahn as rumors surfaced that his wealth was due to fraudulent activity during and after the war. One of his friends, the successful financier Bernard Baruch, was also the target of such accusations. Baruch became an advisor to President Wilson in 1915 and, shortly thereafter, the suspect of illegal trading. It was claimed that Baruch had vital information about the European war before it was made public and, with this knowledge, he and others on Wall Street, such Kahn, had sold short a substantial number of shares. Laws against insider trading were on the horizon with the Securities Exchange Acts in the 1930s but the 1909 US Supreme Court ruling in *Strong v. Repide*, 213 U.S. 149 stated that a member of the board of directors of a publicly-traded company could not buy and sell shares if they were aware of information unknown to the other buyer or seller. Although there were no true regulations against insider trading before the 1930s, the practice was generally agreed to be illicit and, additionally, that there something unsavory about short selling. After the war, there were rumors that brokers who engaged in this type of trading were bankrolled, with or without their knowledge, by the newly formed Soviet Union in an effort to sabotage the American economy. Baruch vehemently disagreed that there was something irregular with this practice and contended that it prevented people from buying securities at exorbitantly high prices. In January 1917, he sat before the congressional committee investigating the allegations, and when he gave his occupation as "speculator" it was as if he had declared himself immediately culpable. After questioning, he gave the committee a coherent lecture on the stock market, successfully defended his reputation, and emerged from the inquiry unscathed.[9]

The war profiteer existed—there were disreputable people of all kinds who were not averse to using the war to enrich themselves. But the idea of the war profiteer expanded to include anyone making a profit during the fighting and it was to this that Kahn objected. While he had no patience for the "war hog" or those who exploited the war for political purposes, he saw no contradiction between profit and patriotism. There was, he told his audience, "an astonishing lot of hazy thinking on the subject of the uses of capital in the hands of its owners." And he strenuously objected to the idea that business gained financially from the battlefields. On the contrary, it was easier to make money in peacetime rather than in times of conflict when governments imposed price controls, more regulations, and heavier taxation. Yet the idea that a profit was tantamount to treason persisted at a time when the fear of espionage and disloyalty was paramount, and people were inclined toward rumor even more than usual.[10]

Anticapitalists in a multitude of forms had long demonized the free market economy as a soulless, exploitative system that widened the gap between rich and poor and oppressed the workers. For intellectuals such as György Lukás, capitalism was spiritually empty and morally inadequate. It was communism that was more alluring to intellectuals concerned with vague concepts such as the "totality" of life and "alienation." With its promise of an equal society and zero unemployment—even if that infringed on individual liberty—communism appealed to those who retained the age-old hostility towards the rich and those in the financial professions. It was not surprising, then, that as the war dragged on there was talk of it being "a rich man's war and a poor man's fight," and that it had been fomented by "big business" for selfish gain. It was another depiction which Kahn rejected. This idea he regarded as "hateful calumny . . . a malicious perversion or ignorant misconception of the facts." But not every financier was opposed to the Wilson government's crackdown on profit making during wartime, as Bernard Baruch, whose fortune had been made under free market conditions, sided with the administration's policy.[11]

Baruch's objection to war profit may have been an attempt to show the nation that the speculator was not a man of greed and was as patriotic as any other. Whatever his motive, the banker helped an administration that introduced a type of war socialism that restricted free trade, raised taxes, drastically increased the public debt, and gave the government unprecedented involvement in the economy. In 1918, Baruch was appointed chairman of the War Industries Board, which put him in the position of regulating business. Price controls were essential, he maintained, so that companies did not profit off the war, although not everyone in business agreed. Those who did not comply were threatened with the appropriation of their property.[12]

The wartime state intervention in the economy and government management of the economy did not recede postwar. The success of the Bolsheviks, led by Vladimir Lenin, in overthrowing the tsarist government in Russia in 1917 excited many in the West disillusioned with their own world and led them to attach their own utopian dreams onto the Bolshevik coup. The radical change from empire to communist state revitalized ideas of planned economies from the top down. Economic gurus such as J. M. Keynes proposed that after all the bloodshed, misery, and destruction a new world of greater prosperity and more equality could be offered to the masses through government regulation and public spending. Such intervention into the economy was seen as a remedy for fiscal instability, even if that was often caused by government manipulation of the money supply in the first place. Depressions, unemployment, wage fluctuations, and inflation were to be fixed with price and wage control and copious amounts of stimulus spending. Planned economies were not only advanced after the war by Keynes in England, but also by Benito Mussolini in Italy, and Walther Rathenau in Germany who advocated justice and the public good via wealth redistribution. Yet, control over the money supply by governments—which meant printing more when it needed to fund social programs—did not solve the problems long-term. Constantly issuing new money to cover government deficits produced inflation, which encouraged even more government intervention in the vain hope of regulating the economy. It was as effective as the postwar League of Nations' promise to prevent another war.[13]

* * *

By the 1920s, the consumer in America had a lot of new technology to acquire. In the aftermath of a horrifying war, the general desire was to forget the past and revel in the present. Car production grew rapidly, the number of houses with telephones increased, radios brought the outside world into the comfort of home, and movie theaters opened, giving the public a new form of entertainment with the creation of Hollywood and new idols in the shape of the movie star. In the 1920s, consumer debt in the United States was roughly $6.4 million for a population of 60 million. For most, debt was no longer abhorrent and borrowing on credit was not a sinful, immoral act. Credit bought the Ford Model T, a new home, modern appliances, furniture, and clothes from the big department stores such as Sears, which opened its first stores in 1925, and Macys.

The trend towards government intervention in the economy was the topic of a speech given by Otto Kahn at the American Bankers Association. In the wake of the creation of the Federal Reserve Bank, he criticized the menace of paternalism—the encroachment of the bureaucratic state into people's lives. It was the enemy of private enterprise and the kind of individual initiative that encouraged each person to put forth their best effort. France, he noted, had been "atrophied" by paternalism, which had retarded the nation's economic development and driven wealth out of the country. Russia's paternalism had ended in revolution, anarchy, and bloodshed. In Germany, paternalism combined with militarism and had created disaster by making the state a deity. In Kahn's view, individualism had come to an end in Europe. And with the end of the war, another war loomed. On the one side were the Bolsheviks, demagogues, utopianists, iconoclasts, intellectuals assured "of their mental and moral superiority," professors, and other teachers who were "disgruntled and acidified." All were sentimental, emotional, envious or demagogic, hankering for unattainable perfection by any means necessary. On the other side were those people with "accumulated wisdom of centuries," who found individualism—and that meant free market economics—to be "ordered, enlightened, progressive, [and] sympathetic." Communism, with its system of shared property and equal compensation, had been tried and had failed. Government, which was fundamentally the nullification of competition, had to be restricted as bureaucracy was either "wasteful, stagnant, and inefficient" or "ruthless, obnoxious, and morally poisonous." This was a strong and reasoned validation of the free market system, the individual, and the benefits of private enterprise, all of which Kahn feared was being jeopardized in Europe.[14]

In 1919, Kahn branched out from his business in New York and funded some property on the west coast of the US. The land had been bought by another lapsed Jew, Adolph Zukor, on which he was to build a new temple for the masses in the shape of the movie theater. With his collaboration with Zukor, Kahn now added another string to his already well-strung bow: film producer in Hollywood.

In the early days of the Hollywood movie industry, a loose network evolved based on the main entrepreneurs' shared Jewish background and family connections. William Fox, the Warner brothers, Adolph Zukor, Harry Cohn, and Louis B. Mayer were all born Jewish. Jesse L. Lasky was related by marriage to Samuel Goldfish (1879–1974). Goldfish, who changed his name to Goldwyn, became a collaborator with Mayer in creating Metro-Goldwyn-Mayer (MGM) in 1926 which, in the 1930s, became the most powerful movie studio with such popular actors as Clark Gable, Jean Harlow, and Greta Garbo under contract. From 1931 to 1940, the combined profits of Hollywood's Big Eight studios totaled $128.2 million; MGM's profits were $93.2 million—nearly three-quarters of the total. Its motto? *Ars Gratia Artis*: Art for art's sake.

MGM's motto might have drawn derisory laughter from those who were firmly of the opinion that Jews were only interested in money, not art. In his book on capitalism, the German economist Werner Sombart declared that Jews were not creative beings but calculating speculators, weighing up risks and profits, which had been the position of Richard Wagner. Keynes, too, drew a line between culture and money by describing the "rentier" class, those living on income from properties or securities, as preferring compound interest over the arts of enjoyment. Jews, he claimed, were the quintessential usurers who had "done the most for the principle of compound interest." Just to make his distaste for this type of person clearer, he wrote "avarice is a vice . . . the exaction of usury is a misdemeanour, and the love of money is detestable." Keynes, like many people then and still today, saw art and money as adversaries. The image of the starving artist in the garret was not a new phenomenon. It had been cultivated in the previous century by writers and painters, such as Honoré Balzac, as the *sine qua non* of creativity. It was the continuation of the medieval preachers' argument in secular culture; money was a vice and poverty a virtue. If it could be achieved, what was best was to have the wealth but still present the image of the cultured and compassionate soul disdainful of money and scornful of capitalism. This was Balzac's dilemma and one often voiced by his literary characters: to find a way to benefit from the comforts and materialism of the modern world while retaining the sacred virtues of poverty and suffering.[15] [16]

It was widely accepted that money was not meant to be the motivation or purpose of art—whether the visual arts, the performing arts, or literature. Cultural critics such as Sinclair Lewis attacked the wealthy as leading empty lives while the American economist and sociologist, Thorstein Veblen denounced what he called "conspicuous consumption." Financiers, critics grieved, were caught up in the capitalist world of buying and selling and made culture nothing more than a business. The marketplace reduced everything to a product and tarnished the finer sentiments in life. Art was supposed to be removed from the seedy world of money but, in reality, art and artists could not survive or create without it. Throughout history, the rich had occupied the post of patron of the arts and in the modern era it was either wealthy benefactors or the taxpayer.

The perceived, or desired, gulf between art and money was a general critique of capitalism but there were people in America who followed Sombart and Wagner and directed this reproach directly at Jews. According to its detractors, Hollywood, the metonym for the movie industry, was run by Jews who had turned art into a marketplace for lowbrow entertainment. The notion that Jews corrupted high culture by commercializing it was held by one of the most successful entrepreneurs, the car maker Henry Ford (1863–1947). Ford had developed the Model T, the first affordable and mass-produced automobile for the American middle classes. But the "Jewish Question" was a topic he regarded as critical to the United States and a subject on which he wrote extensively. To those who objected to his opinions, he answered that the only prejudice he had was the prejudice that favored American values over others. A "nasty Orientalism" had crept into some capitalist ventures, he wrote, which was "traceable to one racial source," that is, the Jews. The solution to the "Jewish Question" was in the hands of the Jews themselves. Like Wilhelm Marr in his early day, the answer was assimilation. In rhetoric that was similar to Marx and Marr's "Jewish spirit," Ford argued that rather than making America Jewish—by which he meant debasing the culture by making everything about money—Jews should strive to become American.[17]

This "Orientalist" money-chasing he ascribed to a Jewish spirit which he thought was most visible in the new mass popular culture of Hollywood. The aim to "give the people what they want" was contrary to elevating minds to higher forms of art. *The Dearborn Independent*, a weekly newspaper published by Ford, ran articles about the vulgarity of show business—the fact that the word "business" was part of the definition was enough to show the grubby and factory-like nature of Hollywood. Its creator was the Jewish entrepreneur whose interest was not culture or art but dollars. In place of high culture and creativity, Jews produced "frivolity, sensuality, indecency, appalling illiteracy, [and] endless platitude[s]." And they did so, the paper claimed, for ignoble reasons.[18]

Henry Ford was convinced that money lay at the heart of the collective Jewish soul, and that money was the means to power. He was convinced that Jews had a master plan for economic domination, and hence political dictatorial power, and would seek out all duplicitous and disreputable methods to obtain wealth. As examples, Ford offered the involvement and influence of Jews in secret societies, lodges, orders, unions, committees, and federations. As a free trader, Ford was opposed to monopolies, which were made possible by government intervention in the economy. Yet, he felt compelled to associate monopolies only with Jews—not particular Jews, but Jews in general.[19]

To those who might protest that there were many Jews who were opposed to trade unions and even disliked their immigrant Russian coreligionists who streamed into the Lower East Side of New York, the *Dearborn Independent* had an answer. "Jewish power" was made up of two groups: German-Jewish financiers who ran the monopolies and Russian/Polish Jews who ran the trade unions and populated the lower ranks of industry. Together, they sought to control the economy of the United States. Their success, these articles claimed, was built on the harnessing of economic benefits through government manipulation rather than fair and open free trade.[20]

In Ford's opinion, the venture capitalist Bernard Baruch was the epitome of the corrupt Wall Street Jew. Even though Baruch married the daughter of an Episcopalian minister, had no religious convictions, and was associated with no Jewish organizations, in an age of racial categorization, his critics regarded him as a quintessential Jew. To Ford, he was the "pro-consul of Judah in America," and a "Jew of Super-Power." At the Paris Peace Conference in 1919, it was rumored that Baruch, a delegate at the conference, was pro-German because he favored lenient terms for Germany with regard to financial reparations, that he gave political advice based on his own financial interests, and that he was one of the wealthy Jews who had financed the Bolshevik revolution. This was far from the truth.

Baruch believed that Russian despotism had fostered the Bolsheviks, which was not the same thing as declaring support for the Russian revolutionaries or funding them. He also argued that it was undemocratic to isolate the new Russian regime on ideological grounds, even as that government was embarking on a murderous attack on their opponents. In 1920, Baruch made the statement that "The Russian people have a right, it seems to me, to set up any form of government they wish." This was either naïve or willful distortion of the facts. Lenin's regime was not a democratically-elected government in Russia with free and fair elections, but a brutal dictatorship that was in the process of appropriating personal property and killing or neutralizing its opponents. Nevertheless, in spite of its communist nature that was opposed to capitalism and the private ownership of property, businesses all over the US and Europe lined up to welcome Soviet delegations, ready to export Russian's natural resources and sell their goods to the new regime. Trade would moderate the communists, it was contended, as trade and commerce led to profitable and mutually beneficial relationships. Baruch was not the exception in voicing his support for establishing an affiliation with Lenin even though his hands were bloody, nor had it anything to do with the fact that he was born Jewish.[21]

* * *

On October 24, 1929, on a day that would become known as Black Thursday, the Wall Street Crash saw the Dow fall by 13 percent and continue to decline over the following days. Many, including Baruch, thought the worst was over by mid-November but it was the start of an economic depression that would become the Great Depression. Paul Warburg, who had been one of the founders of the Federal Reserve System, had warned in February that stock prices were overheated. But when stocks are going up and up and money is being made hand over fist, no one wants to listen to the voice of Cassandra.

By spring 1930, the stock market had rebounded enough to recoup half of the losses from the crash and President Herbert Hoover was convinced that the worst over. At the end of the year, however, hundreds of bank failures sent the country into an economic downturn again, a crisis sparked by the failure of the Bank of United States (BUS). The BUS, despite its lofty-sounding name, was a provincial bank in New York. It was established in 1913 on Delancy Street, one of the main roads running through New York's lower east side, the area into which most Jews immigrated. The bank's founder, Joseph S. Marcus, was a Jewish immigrant born in Germany of Russian ancestry, and its customers were mainly Yiddish-speaking middle- and working-class Jews employed in the garment trade. At its height, the bank had branches in Manhattan, the Bronx, and Brooklyn. With Joseph's death in 1927, his thirty-seven-year-old son Bernard took over as the president with Russian-born Saul Singer as vice-president. Singer had started as a two-dollar-a-week garment worker, working his way up to own his own clothing business. He then turned to the real estate market and banking. The Democratic Senator Carter Glass of Virginia dismissed the BUS as a "pawnshop" and Marcus and Singer as "corner-grocery" shopkeepers. For Carter Glass, who was one of the men instrumental in bringing the Federal Reserve into being in 1913 and thus creating a centralized banking system in the US, men like this were merely playing at being bankers.[22]

In 1930, rumors swept the area that the BUS was broke. Marcus and Singer had seriously damaged the bank's assets by risky speculation with the bank's stock which they used as collateral for real estate ventures. Attempts to rescue the bank came to nothing. Panicked that their money would be lost to them, people rushed to get their deposits out before the bank was ordered closed. And it did close, on December 11. The bank shut the doors of all its eighty-two branches, making it the largest bank, money-wise, in US history to collapse, and prompted customers of other banks around the country, fearing their money was no longer safe, to withdraw their deposits just in case. The fact that the failed bank had the United States in its name led many people to mistakenly assume it was a federal bank and that contributed to the run on other banks. Marcus and Singer were indicted for the misappropriation of funds. On the stand, one of the bank's directors, Joseph

C. Brownstone, admitted to losing $250,000 in speculaton on the stock market. Marcus and Singer were convicted of fraudulent bookkeeping, claiming the bank had a surplus profit of $10,000,000 when, in reality, it owed $4,000,000. The men served their prison sentences at Sing Sing.[23]

Some believed that Communist activists were behind the bank failures and stock market declines with anonymous officials in the New York Banking Department claiming to have traced a thousand depositors on a bank run to Communist sources, which was stopped by the "energetic intervention" by the office of John A. Broderick, New York's Superintendent of Banks.[24] Radical anticapitalists emerged to point the finger at those who were to blame for the dire economic times. Father Charles Coughlin (1891–1979), a controversial Catholic priest born in Ontario, Canada, moved to the United States in the early 1920s, settling in Detroit. In 1926, he became the priest of the Shrine of the Little Flower in Royal Oak, Michigan and it was from this point that his preaching thrived. Only his venue was not the market square or the steps of a city cathedral. It was radio.

The first commercially licensed radio station—KDKA in Pittsburgh—broadcast for the first time in 1920. Ten years later, around 40 percent of American households regularly gathered around the radio and listened to dramas, comedies, news, music, and educational programs. If movies were a form of escape for many people, radio was a potent force in spreading information and an outlet for those with populist ideas, such as Coughlin. From 1926, the priest hosted an hour-long program on WJR once a week during which he attacked socialism, the Soviet Union, and Wall Street capitalists—a vague term that encompassed anyone he despised. These capitalists were corrupt, he told his audience, and it was their greed that drove the average American into the arms of the Communists. He strongly backed Franklin D. Roosevelt in the 1932 election, coining the phrase "the New Deal is Christ's Deal," and applauded any efforts to rein in and regulate the "money-changers."[25]

By 1933, Roosevelt was in the Oval Office. The 1932 Revenue Act had produced the largest tax hike in US history during the Hoover administration. Under FDR, the plan to help the economy increased the deficit spending and redistributed income on a grand scale. Roosevelt's efforts to intervene in the economy to aid recovery, however, failed to end the financial disaster and even prolonged it. His New Deal extended government economic control, which limited competition in product markets and his sponsorship of stronger bargaining powers for the unions led to higher wages but reduced employment. Individual entrepreneurship, the source of prosperity, was crushed by public works.[26]

Coughlin had high hopes for Roosevelt in his campaign against the rich. His large following tuned in to hear him denounce Wall Street bankers who he accused of colluding with international financiers to destroy western civilization. The men pulling the strings, Coughlin argued, to the detriment of the average man and woman, were the Jews. In a 1933 broadcast entitled "Banks and Gold" he singled out the Kuhn-Loebs, the Rothschilds, the Morgans, and others, as well as the Federal Reserve (which he mistakenly believed to be in private hands), as responsible for shackling "the lives of men and of nations with the ponderous links of their golden chain." The interest on the money they loaned was something they got "for nothing." Using language that stretched all the way back to ancient times, interest-bearing loans—usury—were theft and, therefore, immoral. While neither J.P. Morgan nor the influential Wall Street broker William Read were Jewish (and the Morgan bank was the most powerful in the country), Coughlin's reference to bankers not having Christianity "flowing in their veins," as well as his frequent mention of moneychangers polluting the temple, makes it clear that like so many before him, the financial profession was "Jewish" and deleterious to a spiritual life.[27]

Huey Long (1893–1935), a Democratic governor and then senator of Louisiana, was, like Coughlin, a populist. Born in that southern state, Long grew up in an impoverish region dotted with wooden cabins and small farms that scraped by. His father grew cotton and corn and raised hogs on scrubland but, when the town grew due to the new railway line, he became successful enough to build a substantial home with modern conveniences. Such a life was not for his son. After a time as a travelling salesman, Huey passed the bar and began his law career. But his intention was not to spend his days in litigation—it was to enter into the fray of political life as an advocate of the people, in particular, the poor who were left in destitution as a result of the depression. In May 1928, he realized his ambition to become governor of his state. Like Coughlin, Long disseminated his message about wealth redistribution on the radio and with his newspaper, *The American Progress*. His fiscal and monetary reforms were similar to other American populists of the time: the capping of incomes, personal wealth, and inheritance.[28]

It was the anticapitalist populists like Coughlin and Long, along with anticapitalist socialists, some of whom were admirers of the Soviet Union, who believed they could create a utopia on earth. The latter included the so-called "Silvermaster group" that comprised Treasury and Department of Justice members organized by Nathan Gregory Silvermaster, Harry Dexter White, the assistant secretary of the Treasury, Solomon Adler, also at the Treasury, and Lauchlin Currie, Roosevelt's administrative assistant. Roosevelt's move against a free market was successful due to the ever-popular desire to penalize the rich, especially in an economic downturn, and because the mood of the country was hostile to that amorphous enemy, Wall Street.[29]

In his inaugural address on March 4, 1932, which was dominated by the economic crisis, the new president indicted the "[p]ractices of the unscrupulous money changers" who have in the past induced people to follow their "false leadership" with the "lure of money." They were a generation of "self-seekers" devoid of vision:

> The money changers have fled from their high seats in the temple of our civilization. We may now restore that temple to the ancient truths. The measure of the restoration lies in the extent to which we apply social values more noble than mere monetary profit.

In language that was familiar, Roosevelt condemned material wealth as false and spoke of bankers as indulging in "callous and selfish wrongdoing." Speculation with other people's money must, he told his audience, be eradicated. It was the kind of language that was in need of specifics. Illegal trading and speculating by dishonest people had to be stopped, of course, but that was not the way of most bankers and speculators. It was just that after a calamitous market crash, it was the kind of hostile language that resonated with a large number of people.[30]

With millions of people out of work and people lining up at soup kitchens, the economic slump was used as the justification for the government's nationalization of gold. In 1933, in response to the bank failures, the Banking Act—or the Glass-Steagall Act after its sponsors Carter Glass and Henry B. Steagall—extended the Federal Reserve control over banking by putting into place banking reforms and the Federal Deposit Insurance Corporation. The FDIC guaranteed a depositer's money in an insured bank of up to $250,000. In that same year, under executive order 6102, Roosevelt's administration made it illegal for Americans to privately own or to trade gold anywhere globally. The Vice-President John N. Garner joked with Roosevelt that one of their "greatest friends," Bernard Baruch, possessed "a whole bankful of gold bricks." The Gold Reserve Act of 1934 called for all gold and gold certificates to be placed in the control of the United States Treasury and therefore forced those in possession of gold to sell it to the government in exchange for paper money. The price of gold was then raised from $20.67 per ounce to $35 which devalued the dollar, making the compensation given to those who had unwillingly sold their gold less valuable. It did, however, enrich the government and supported the greatest intrusion by the government into the economy in the history of the United States with a program known as the New Deal, which included the 1937 Social Security Act.[31]

Shortly after his inauguration, Roosevelt issued the Economy Act which cut federal pay. More dictates followed, including the Tennessee Valley Authority Act, the Securities Act, the Home Owners Loan Act, and the Emergency Farm Mortgage Act. The National Industrial Recovery Act of 1933 (NIRA) gave the president the authority to regulate industry and control prices. From the Works Progress Administration (WPA), which employed eight-and-a-half million people to build roads, bridges, and public buildings, to the Federal Emergency Relief Administration (FERA), the United States Housing Authority, Farm Security Administration, and the Civil Conservation Corps, the kind of bureaucracy that Otto Kahn abhorred grew as a steady stream of legislation and executive orders were issued by the administration.[32]

The New Deal policy was applauded by many as a necessary step to stimulate the economy. But it was also widely criticized by a diverse group of people. Critics included the Democratic nominee for president in 1928, Al Smith, who thought that it stirred up class conflict. The prominent newspaper columnist Walter Lippmann also voiced his disapproval. Writing in the *New York Herald-Tribune* in 1933, Lippmann noted that Roosevelt's economic proposals amounted to a constriction of industry, trade, and commerce, insofar as government regulations meddled with free enterprise and the market economy and argued that high taxation hindered the creation of new enterprises and the expansion of existing businesses (and, therefore, jobs). The increasingly centralized governmental control along with "the dictatorial spirit" dispirited and repelled many in the business world who objected, as did Lippmann, to the "bureaucratic control of American economic life." The government, being pushed by radical social planners who saw an opportunity to redress life's inequalities, now invited "discord and jealousy, and hysteria and fear among the people" as it became a "government by propaganda." Some years later, in 1938, the playwright Maxwell Anderson and composer Kurt Weill wrote the musical *Knickerbocker Holiday,* which satirically compared the New Deal to the ideas of the rising fascists Mussolini in Italy and Hitler in Germany.[33]

Back in 1930, before Roosevelt's election, Bernard Baruch explained why he was a Democrat. It was, he said, because he thought "Government should mind its own business . . . the people who are least governed are best governed . . . you cannot make manufacturers prosperous by putting up a tariff wall which because of reciprocal action will drive our manufacturers into other countries . . . [t]he only thing that good government can do is to see that everyone has equally easy access to the door of opportunity." He believed Roosevelt to be a man of fiscal orthodoxy, whereas Herbert Hoover, his Republican opponent for the presidency, was too experimental. After Roosevelt's landslide win, and the implementation of the New Deal contradicted that assessment, Baruch nonetheless backed the government expansion, even though he confided to a friend that there was much legislation with which he disagreed.[34]

Baruch's hope for a high-profile position in the administration went unrealized but he remained loyal to Roosevelt, while harboring private reservations about the intrusion into private business. He spoke about the dangers of bureaucratic statism, just as Otto Kahn had done, lamenting that privacy in the business world was almost depleted. The price of "all this folly," he remarked, was "a four billion dollar government." On the other hand, he suggested a worldwide minimum wage in 1936, which went against his support of giving the private sector as much autonomy as possible.[35]

In 1934, the Republican Representative Gerald P. Nye convened a congressional committee to look into whether the munitions industry had pushed the United States into the First World War. Serving as a legal assistant was a man who would later be unmasked as a Soviet spy, Alger Hiss. Baruch was called as a witness but, as it turned out, Nye and Hiss had other motives for his appearance before the committee. During questioning, the banker was asked to turn over his tax returns for 1916–1919 and the names of securities he owned during that time. Baruch was one step ahead of them, perhaps because of his previous experience before the Senate, and had already furnished that information. More overtly, Huey Long painted Baruch as the power behind Roosevelt's government while Coughlin called him the "Acting President of the United States, the Uncrowned Prince of Wall Street."[36]

Although Coughlin and Long were strong supporters of Roosevelt's New Deal initially, ultimately the president's policies did not go far enough for either man. Believing that Roosevelt had betrayed the promises of the New Deal, they launched a vigorously opposition to the administration. Coughlin founded The National Union for Social Justice (NUSJ) in November 1934 and published a newspaper entitled *Social Justice*. Through these channels, he disseminated his beliefs that reform of the economy was vital to produce an "honest" money supply, as if an inanimate economic system had inherently a moral and therefore human sensibility. It was only its participants who could be honest or dishonest. Coughlin's idealized system would put the money supply in the hands of the government and not private individual bankers who, he claimed, "control our entire economic, social, and governmental system and derive enormous, illicit profits therefrom." Once under government control, Coughlin's solution to economic woes was to increase the money supply through government spending—a recipe for inflation. This is what Roosevelt did, but the president's failure to nationalize the banks created a break between his administration and the NUSJ.[37]

In 1934, Long created the Share Our Wealth Society, which had as its aim the redistribution of Americans' wealth after seizing property and raising taxes. With the effects of the depression devastating families, those most affected were desperate for change. Long's attacks on the rich, the privileged, and the men in charge of the nation's monetary supply were welcomed by the impoverished citizens who struggled to put food on the table. It did not matter whether his reforms made economic sense. His dissatisfaction with the Roosevelt administration's lack of radical reform led him to run for president, with the hope that Coughlin would throw his considerable influence behind him. He knew well that his plan to challenge Roosevelt for the Democratic nomination would fail but believed that the publicity he would gain in the effort would enable him to create a third party. If the third-party strategy failed, he intended to take enough votes from Roosevelt to allow the Republican to win (perhaps Herbert Hoover). As the country disintegrated economically under Hoover, as Long surmised it would, he would be the guaranteed front runner in the next election.[38]

Long crossed the country giving rousing stump speeches in fairgrounds and farming lands. In his shirt sleeves and frequently with a Bible in hand, he drew in not only the poor but the affluent, who liked his energetic charisma and what they regarded as straight talk about fairness and equality. He ran on a platform that advocated home ownership for every American family "equal in value to not less than one third the average family wealth." No family should possess more than 300 times more than the average family's wealth—which meant no more than $5,000,000—and no one was to own less than $5,000. Every wage earner would have an income of no less than a third of the average income and no more than 300 times greater the average income. This meant that incomes would be no less than $2000–$2,500 and no more than $1,000,000. Pensions would be collected by taxing "excess fortunes," "excess incomes and excess inheritances." This would also fund education for all. Long's prescription was thought of as radical but, fundamentally, it was no different than the many voices through the centuries calling for "excess" wealth (that is, whatever the government defines as excess) to be redistributed and given to the poor and needy. What was different in the modern era was the demand that government force the entire population to relinquish their earnings by law on a regular basis without recourse to refuse.[39]

Long's plans were cut short when he was assassinated allegedly by Dr. Carl Weiss on September 8, 1935, over a dispute the Louisiana senator had with a long-time opponent, Judge Benjamin Henry Pavy, Weiss' father-in-law. Long's bodyguards shot Weiss dead. The presidential candidate's murder came just one month after announcing his intention to run.[40]

* * *

In Los Angeles, the fascist Paquita Shishmareff adopted the pen-name L. Fry under which she began to set out her conspiracy theories in print. Basing her hypothesis on the forged *Protocols of the Elders of Zion,* she condemned both communism and capitalism as Jewish inventions in *Waters Flowing Eastward* (1931). In *The Jews and the British Empire* (1935), she sank deeper into conspiracy waters and presented the Freemasons, the Illuminati, Disraeli, the Rothschilds, and the League of Nations as proof that the empire was controlled by Jews to further their own agenda. The economy was the means to power.

These populist agitators in interwar America, while following the same storyline that capitalists were to blame for the economic woes and wars of the world that was found in Europe, did not, in the end, create any serious problems for Jews in the United States. Long had dismissed any comparison between himself and the rising populist leader in Germany, Adolf Hitler. Hitler, Long remarked, was a fool who mixed racial prejudice into his politics. Similarly, the senator clashed with Hiram Evans, the Ku Klux Klan wizard who referred to the senator as "un-American." To Evans, whose organization promoted a white, Protestant America, Coughlin's Catholicism and Long's dedication to all the poor, black and white, made them "aliens." The rhetoric was unpleasant but, despite this, and unlike mainland Europe, there were no government restrictions on Jews, no anti-Jewish legislation, and no physical violence against Jews on a significant scale.

With the Great Depression and ineffective government, populist politics found an inroad. So much so, that, even if Roosevelt felt contempt for Long and Coughlin, he echoed the rhetoric that reviled the rich, despite the fact that he and most of his friends were part of that elite group. In a message on tax revision in 1935, Roosevelt told Congress that "the duty rests upon the Government to restrict [vast personal fortunes] by very high taxes." This "economic royalty" [i.e. the bankers] was to be culled through higher taxes, whether income, inheritance, corporate, or any other tax that could wrest the money from "the privileged princes of . . . new economic dynasties." In words resonant with age old protests against wealth, Roosevelt told Congress in his 1936 speech, "A Rendezvous with Destiny," that his party planned to destroy the "palace of privilege . . . [and in its place] build a temple of out faith, hope, and charity."[41]

Even with talk like this and men like Coughlin and Long, the United States was a secure place for Jews. They could practice their faith, assimilate, and have a hopeful future. There were many Jewish immigrants who emigrated from Europe with little or nothing and went on to build businesses and, in the case of the movies, whole industries. Insofar that, out of every nation, the United States admired the self-made man and put the honest capitalist in a place of honor, not rebuke. It was a place to where European Jews, concerned about the rise of dictators in Europe, wanted to settle. The American demagogues of the 1920s and 30s had their moment on the political stage but it soon vanished and most people would not know their name today. Ultimately, in America, people did not view wealth as intrinsically immoral. On the contrary, if self-made, it was something to admire. It was a situation that could not have been more opposed to the society taking shape in Germany.

Notes

1. Charles Péguy, *L'Argent suite* (Paris: Cahiers de la Quinzaine, 1913), 10; Ferguson, *The Ascent of Money*, chap. 6; Goetzmann, *Money Changes Everything*, chaps. 19, 27; Julia C. Ott, *When Wall Street Met Main Street: The Quest for an Investor's Democracy* (Cambridge MA: Harvard University Press, 2011).
2. Temin and Voth, *Prometheus Shackled*, chap. 8; Geisst, *Beggar Thy Neighbor*, chap. 3.
3. Geisst, *Beggar Thy Neighbor*, chap. 3; Temin and Voth, *Prometheus Shackled*, chap. 8
4. Geisst, *Beggar Thy Neighbor*, chap. 3.
5. Naomi W. Cohen, *Jacob Schiff: A Study in American Jewish Leadership* (Hanover, NH: Brandeis/University Press of New England, 1999), 1, 3–5, 9–11, 13, 14–15.
6. Cyrus Adler, *Jacob Henry Schiff: A Biographical Sketch* (New York: The American Jewish Committee, 1921), 12–16, 22, 37–38.
7. Mary Jane Phillips-Matz, *The Many Lives of Otto Kahn* (New York: Pendragon Press, 1984), 223.
8. Otto H. Kahn, "High Finance," Address delivered at Annual Dinner American Newspaper Publishers Association, Waldorf-Astoria, New York, April 27, 1916, 3–4, 7, 22, 23.
9. "Red Plot to Start Bank Run Revealed by Broderick Aides," *New York Times*, December 26, 1930, 1, 3; James Grant, *Bernard Baruch: The Adventures of a Wall Street Legend* (Edinburg, VA: Axios Press, 2012), Kindle, chap. 8.

10. Otto H. Kahn, "Frenzied Liberty: The Myth of the Rich Man's War," Address given at the University of Wisconsin, January 14, 1918, 36, 37.
11. György Lukás, *Theory of the Novel* (Cambridge, MA: MIT Press, 1971), 64.
12. Grant, *Bernard Baruch*, chap. 9.
13. Niall Ferguson, *The Pity of War* (London: Basic Books, 1998), 395, 397.Avraham Barkai, Nazi Economics: Ideology, Theory, and Policy (New Haven: Yale University Press, 1990); Peter F. Drucker, The End of Economic Man: A Study of the New Totalitarianism (New York: John Day, 1939); Martin Dean, Robbing the Jews: The Confiscation of Jewish Property in the Holocaust, 1933–1945 (New York: CUP, 2008), 51; Sennholz, Age of Inflation, 18–19.
14. Otto Kahn, "The Menace of Paternalism," An Address Before the Convention of the American Bankers Association, Chicago, September 27, 1918, 4–16, 20, 25–26, 30, 38, 51, 55; Kindleberger and Aliber, *Manias*, chap. 3; Geisst, *Beggar Thy Neighbor*, chap. 5.
15. Muller, *The Mind and the Market*, chaps. 9 and 12.
16. See, Honoré de Balzac, "La Peau de Chagrin," *Comedie Humaine*, http://www.gutenberg.org/files/1307/1307-h/1307-h.htm; Graham Robb, *Balzac: A Biography* (New York: Norton, 1995), 185.
17. Henry Ford and Samuel Crowther, *My Life and Work* (Los Angeles: Business and Leadership Publishing, 2003), Kindle ed.
18. *The International Jew* (Boring, OR: Liberty Books, 1995), chap. 10. The four-volume work is a collection of articles from the newspaper *The Dearborn Independent.*
19. *The International Jew*, chap. 7.
20. *The International Jew*, Chapters 7 and 9.
21. Geisst, *Beggar Thy Neighbor*, chap. 5; Grant, *Bernard Baruch*, chapters 6, 10, 11; Richard Pipes, *Russia Under the Bolshevik Regime* (New York: A.A. Knopf, 1995), 215.
22. John Steele Gordon, "A Fiasco That Fed the Great Depression," *Barron's*, http://www.barrons.com/articles/SB122914127585004015; Joseph L. Lucia, "The Failure of the Bank of United States: A Reappraisal," *Explorations in Economic History* 22 (1985): 402–03.
23. Beth S. Wenger, *New York Jews and the Great Depression: Uncertain Promise* (Syracus, NY: Syracuse University Press, 1999), 11; Paul B. Trescott, "The Failure of the Bank of the United States, 1930," *Journal of Money, Credit, and Banking* 24.3 (Aug., 1992): 384–99; *Northern Daily Mail*, January 23, 1931, 10; Grant, *Bernard Baruch*, chap. 13.
24. "Red Plot," *NYT*, 1.
25. Stephen Smith, "Radio: The Internet of the 1930s," *American RadioWorks*, November 10, 2014, http://www.americanradioworks.org/segments/radio-the-internet-of-the-1930s/; Ronald H. Carpenter, *Father Charles E. Coughlin: Surrogate Spokesman for the Disaffected* (Westport, CT: Greenwood Press, 1998), 39, 173.

26. Kindleberger and Aliber, *Manias*, chap. 5; Harold L. Cole and Lee E. Ohanian, "New Deal Policies and the Persistence of the Great Depression: A General Equilibrium Analysis," *Journal of Political Economy* 112.4 (2004): 779–816; Sennholz, *Age of Inflation*, 53, 128.
27. Carpenter, *Father Charles E. Coughlin*, 39; Charles E. Coughlin, *Money! Questions and Answers* (Royal Oak, MI: The National Union for Social Justice, 1936).
28. Richard D. White, *Kingfish: The Reign of Huey P. Long* (New York: Random House, 2006), 5, 12, 36.
29. Kathryn Olmsted, *Red Spy Queen: A Biography of Elizabeth Bentley* (Chapel Hill: University of North Carolina Press, 2002).
30. Franklin D. Roosevelt, "First Inaugural Address," 1933, http://www.c-span.org/video/?5792-1/president-franklin-d-roosevelt-inaugural-address.
31. Grant, *Bernard Baruch*, chap. 13.
32. Ibid.
33. David M. Kennedy, *Freedom From Fear: The American People in Depression 1929–1945* (Oxford and New York: OUP, 1999), 186; Walter Lippmann, "Today and Tomorrow," *New York Herald-Tribune*, July 26, 1933, quoted in Barry D. Riccio, *Walter Lippmann—Odyssey of a Liberal* (New Brunswick, NJ: Transaction, 1996), 107.
34. Grant, *Bernard Baruch*, chap. 13.
35. Ibid., chap. 14.
36. Ibid., chap. 13.
37. White, *Kingfish*, 240; Coughlin, *Money!;* Thomas E. Woods, Jr., *The Church and the Market: A Catholic Defense of the Free Market* (Lanham, MD: Lexington Books, 2015), 108–09.
38. White, *Kingfish*, 242.
39. White, *Kingfish*, 3–4; Huey P. Long, "Share the Wealth," *Radio Address*, NBC, New York, March 7, 1935, http://www.americanrhetoric.com/speeches/hueyplongshare.htm.
40. It is unclear why Weiss came to see Long or why he may have shot him. There were people at the time and still today who dispute the official version of events that Weiss shot Long and, in turn, was shot by Long's bodyguards. Some, including Weiss' family, suggested that Long's bodyguards shot Weiss and Long was killed by a ricocheting bullet.
41. Hiram Evans, "The Klan's Fight for Americanism," *North American Review* 123 (1926): 33–63; Franklin D. Roosevelt, "Message to Congress on Tax Revision," June 19, 1935, Gerhard Peters and John T. Woolley, *The American Presidency Project*, http://www.presidency.ucsb.edu/ws/?pid=15088; Muller, *The Mind and the Market*, chap. 11; Roosevelt, "A Rendezvous With Destiny," Speech Before the 1936 Democratic National Convention, Philadelphia, Pennsylvania, June 27, 1936, http://www.austincc.edu/lpatrick/his2341/fdr36acceptancespeech.htm; Muller, *The Mind and the Market*, chap. 11.

10

The "Tyranny of Usury" Conspiracy

In March 1918, before the war's end, the Bolsheviks signed their own peace treaty with Germany and withdrew from fighting on the side of what he called "reactionary and bourgeoise governments." This freed the Germans from a two-front conflict just as the Americans entered the war on the side of the Allies. Just as it seemed as if the war would continue to drag on, and generals started to prepare for the campaign of 1920, the end of the war came suddenly as the Central Powers collapsed. After the signing of an armistice on November 11, the ceasefire commenced at 11 am on that same day. The Versailles treaty, signed in Paris in 1919, formally ended the war that had caused over thirty-seven million dead and wounded.

In the same year, an emigré Russian newspaper published a document in Berlin which was allegedly found in the pocket of a dead Jew named Zunder, a Bolshevik commander of the 11th Sharp-shooter Battalion. Addressed to all the branches of the "Israelite International League," it claimed "the hour of our ultimate victory is near . . . . We have done everything to bring the Russian people under the yoke of the Jewish power, and ultimately compelled them to fall on their knees before us." This document, the newspaper article continued, boasted of the property and gold taken from the Russians by the Jews in pursuit of their goal of world power: "We buy up Government loans and gold, and thereby we have controlling power over the world's exchanges. The power is in our hands, but be careful—place no faith in traitorous shady powers." This story was disseminated by the publisher Ludwig Müller von Hausen. With the ability to read Russian, Hausen perused the paper founded by monarchist Russian emigrés, *The Call* (*Prizyv*), for antisemitic articles to republish for his German audience. Before the war, Hausen had founded an antisemitic organization called the Association Against the Presumption of Jewry (*Verband gegen Überhebung des Judentums*). Other members of the group included Martin Bormann, Alfred Rosenberg, and Ernst Graf zu Reventlow, who would all go on to become important members of the future Nazi party.[1]

In the same year that the Zunder note was published, the *Protocols of the Elders of Zion* appeared in Germany, England, France, and in the United States the following year. *The Protocols* outlined a plot by a Jewish cabal to dominate the world by monopolizing and manipulating the capitalist economy and the media. Fomenting revolution and global war, Jews would secure global domination in the midst of the destruction. In reality, the work was based on a satire written by Maurice Joly in mid-nineteenth century France against Napoleon III and devised by Matvei Golovinski, a Russian-French author and political activist who knew Maurice Joly's son Charles in Paris. Golvinski's father had belonged to the progressive Petrashevsky Circle, which was comprised of a group of intellectuals including Fyodor Dostoevsky. They were inspired by the utopian socialism of Charles Fourier, who had denounced "parasitic" and "bloodsucking" Jewish bankers.[2]

While taken as a factual account by many, its authenticity was contested by a London *Times* correspondent, Philip Graves, who noted the similarities to Joly's nineteenth-century satire. Yet, this still did not convince everyone that the *Protocols* were fake or that what they alleged was untrue. It was precisely the enthusiasm with which Jews greeted this discovery of plagiarism that most convinced conspiracy theorists such as Paquita Shishmareff that the *Protocols* was authentic. It was not the relief of the innocent that Jews expressed after Graves' revelation, she claimed, it was relief that they had not been found out. The apparent conflict between communism and capitalism was really a smokescreen. Both were a means to power.

The importance of economic power was the first protocol, which declared that "In our day the power which has replaced that of the rulers who were liberal is the power of Gold." Later, under the chapter title, "The Tyranny of Usury," the author discussed how Jews "transfer loans into the external sphere" so that "all the wealth of States flowed into [their] cash-boxes and all the *goyim* began to pay [the Jews] the tribute of subjects." *The Protocols* offered an easy and holistic explanation for global disparity of wealth and power. To oppose the Jews, therefore, was to protect the poor, the workers, the patriots, stand up for the moral and economic good of society, and to prevent the bloody conflicts finagled by those bewitched by profit and power. It was propaganda that in its simplicity had mass appeal.[3]

The credibility given to the *Protocols* was aided by the First World War and the 1917 Russian Revolution which created global turmoil, millions of deaths, and destruction that set economies back decades. In the aftermath of the world's first "total war," borders were redrawn, defeated empires obliterated, new states created, countries reborn, and war continued to rage in Eastern Europe. With most of the trench fighting carried out on French soil, that nation's economy was shattered, its industry in tatters. British debt was equal to 136 per cent of the gross national product. By the early 1920s, the German Reichmark was worthless, with a loaf of bread costing 428 billion marks. The economic devastation of Europe sowed the seeds of future conflict.

Kaiser Wilhelm II abdicated in November 1918, fleeing to the Netherlands, and the following year the Weimar Republic, Germany's first ever representative form of government, was created. The Versailles Treaty signed on June 28, 1919, blamed Germany for the war and responsible for financial reparations. To many Germans, the bill of 132 billion gold Marks that the victors decided was appropriate to repair the destruction incurred during the conflict was too punitive. This was added to the fact that the war had been funded by loans, banking on a victory after which the loans could be repaid. With defeat, the new Weimar government was left with massive debts. Still, at the end of hostilities, the German mark was no worse off than the franc or the pound. By the end of 1923, it had sunk to one-trillionth of its value in 1914. Economic chaos in the shadow of defeat encouraged political strife.

Idealism, Aldous Huxley quipped, is the noble toga that political gentlemen drape over their will to power. And the twentieth century was awash with idealists whose visions of the perfect or just society ended in repression, terror, and mass graves. The modern utopia that was beloved of totalitarians of all stripes began with the annihilation of the individual. When government is a means to an end—no matter how moral or noble that ideal sounds—those who disagree with those aims are marked as enemies of the state. Legitimate opposition, the most vital of safeguards against tyranny and an unjust authority, becomes silenced. The government then may resort to force to push through their vision of freedom, under the mantel of social justice, or equality, or the quest for the perfect society and, soon after, tyranny follows.[4]

The most expedient way of overthrowing capitalism, Lenin claimed according to John Maynard Keynes, was to debase the currency. In the modern era, that meant printing more money. When money is worthless, the economy nosedives into a spiral of inflation, hyper-inflation, unemployment and depression. Through inflation, Keynes wrote, governments can secretly confiscate their citizen's wealth arbitrarily. Most will be impoverished, while the chosen few—those in power—will be enriched. The relationship "between debtors and creditors, which form the ultimate foundation of capitalism, become so utterly disordered as to be almost meaningless; and the process of wealth degenerates into a gamble and a lottery." Those who wanted permanent government intervention in the economy—a means to grab total power—argued that man's freedom came not from economic liberty and fewer regulations in their economic endeavors but from the opposite. What led to true freedom was the individual's absorption by the state which, in the twentieth century, became the idol of a new and modern form of religious faith. True freedom for totalitarians meant one party controlled by one dictator who was the protector of his people and who knew what was best for them. The suppression of dissent was a mute issue for in a utopia there is no dissent. Everyone is forced to hold the only correct view possible to be part of that society. In logic that George Orwell would later ridicule in his novel 1984, as there is only one truth, no other truth is possible, therefore, to think differently to the party view is not possible. Unless, of course, one was mad or an enemy of the people.[5]

Those who yearned for world domination infected their population with truths, half-truths, outright lies, propaganda, spurious ideas, and overblown theories. Their domination was only accomplished by crushing the individual, and their right to free speech and economic freedom, redefining the idea of freedom, and denying each person control over their own lives and destinies. Once the concept of the individual had been eradicated, once the individual felt insignificant or vulnerable without the state, their perfect world could be created. Control of the economy was vital.

* * *

The world had changed a lot over the centuries. But one thing hadn't changed and that was the need for capital to fund such innovation, technology, and war. And even though Jews were far from dominant in the banking business, the stereotype of Jews as money-obsessed financiers and speculators who were out to exploit was reharnessed and used in the pursuit of power, the waging of war, and the brutal attempts to mold the "perfect" society. In the twentieth century, this stereotype encouraged a conspiracy, presented in the *Protocols*, that claimed that Jews were behind all the chaos in the world so that they could bring about the economic downfall of Western civilization and grasp global power. Ironically, this conspiracy theory would be used in aftermath of war by two totalitarian political groups that grasped power, created chaos, and tried to bring down Western civilization: Communism and Nazism.

It was easy to blame people's greed as the cause of the 1914–18 war and the new treasurer Matthias Erzberger promised that "in Germany the rich would be no more." If that was their ambition, the young government was successful. They collected inadequate taxes and embarked on an unrestrained program of spending and capital confiscation. In order to pay for the social benefits to ensure this more egalitarian society envisioned by these politicians, the government printed and borrowed huge sums of money. In 1919–20, Germany had a deficit even before the reparations were imposed. Without overhauling the tax system, the money being spent freely on health, education, and welfare added to the expenses already being allocated to the peace treaty demands, the returning soldiers, the disorder in the streets, the deficits of the industries that had been nationalized, and the general waste that comes with giving people with little experience control over the economy. It was not exactly the cradle to grave security that Marxists demanded but it was closer to it than to the independence of nineteenth-century free trade liberalism. That kind of liberalism was viewed with disgust by up-and-coming radical political groups and by the unemployed, the wounded soldiers who returned from the Front to find a greatly altered nation that seemed to have no place for them, by the housewives who lined up for hours to buy meager foodstuffs, and by the small business owners who struggled to stay afloat as postwar inflation reached dizzying heights.[6]

When spending did not stabilize the economy or create wealth, bitterness and hostility toward the government increased, leading to further spending to placate the radicalism that was fast becoming a serious problem. A general strike in response to the French occupation of the Ruhr in 1923 was funded by printing yet more money and brought hyperinflation and economic catastrophe to a country already mired in debt. Hard hit by the unbridled inflation was the capital market, the source of a healthy economy. Hyperinflation wiped out savings and economic depression left many people struggling to feed themselves and their families as unemployment spiraled out of control. Proudhon had called property theft in the previous century, but it was inflation and burdensome taxation that really stole from the population.[7]

Realizing their opportunity for power in a time of chaos, Fascists and Communists—both anti-democratic, anticapitalist, and anti-parliamentarian forces—battled each other in the streets for political supremacy. Primarily they fought the one thing they despised the most, liberal society and the free economy it rested upon. Added to these radical voices, were those theologians who retained the disdain for capitalism. In Austria, bishops denounced capitalism as an evil force in modern times and the financiers who stole from people "to impoverish them through charging excessive interest rates." The Christian Social Party openly linked hostility towards Jews with the class conflict bred by economic inequities and the capitalism and merchant spirit that had infiltrated and sullied all walks of life, political and cultural.

A new, radical, and violently destructive form of antisemitism took shape as dictators planned their perfect societies in which everyone marched to the same tune. "The Jew," a mythical collective, was blamed by these anticapitalist groups for the capitalist system, even though it was a system that had evolved over many centuries, involved a vast multitude of diverse people, and had greatly enriched Western Europe and its populations—materially and culturally—more than any other economic system. No matter; the extremists fighting in the streets had a will to power that was dependent upon an authoritarian, totalitarian state. The individualistic liberty which was interlaced with the free market capitalism had to be destroyed.

Writers and politicians in Germany blamed its economic troubles not on their own policies but on the greed and malicious intrigues of foreigners, particularly the demand for reparations. The ominous figure of the speculator—an archetype rather than a real person—took center stage once more as the villain on whose back all the economic woes of the country could be heaped. It was not the overspending or the manic printing of money that was the cause of the financial crisis, they argued, but the vicious demands of the victors and the corrupt speculation of international forces that were to blame. That explanation exonerated those who were most responsible for the depression and, in its simplicity, it was eagerly accepted by many Germans. This viewpoint also formed the basis of a political manifesto written by an Austrian ex-corporal which simplified the foreign speculator into the image of "the Jew" that for so long had been linked to finance.

As rival political extremists fought in the streets, that ex-corporal, Adolph Hitler, was asked to surveil the German Workers' Party (*Deutsche Arbeiterpartei*). His mission was to keep the authorities apprised of the party's movements and discussions. That plan did not go as intended. Rather than informing on the parties, Hitler was so impressed by their ideology that he soon became involved with the DA. Within a short time, he had taken over its leadership and transformed a small, radical, rabble-rousing political party into the National Socialist German Workers' Party (*Nationalsozialistische Deutsche Arbeiterpartei* or Nazi party).[8]

From the start of Hitler's leadership, a stereotype of the Jewish financier was used by the Nazis to discredit liberal democracy and the free market. It would become the central theme in Nazi antisemitic propaganda. In the film *Der ewige Jude* (The Eternal Jew), made during the Second World War, the millions of native Germans were unemployed and in misery, Jewish immigrants made fantastic riches in a short time—not through honest labor but through usury, trickery, and fraud. It was propaganda that was formed from the time that Hitler took the reins of the Nazi party. The depression and high prices were the fault of "greedy" bankers, the "unscrupulous" speculators, the "bloodsucking" businessmen. These were "foreigners" who impoverished the honest German workers and those "foreigners" (regardless of their German birth) were Jews. This depiction of Jews by the Nazis was influenced by Werner Sombart's characterization of capitalism as a Jewish creation, which was promoted by two of his students, Otto and Gregor Strasser. The Bavarian brothers were members of the anti-Communist paramilitary Freikorps, but then parted ways. Gregor headed a Freikorps battalion in Bavaria, participating in the Kapp Putsch in March 1920. Otto joined the Bolsheviks. He still labeled himself a national socialist (giving Lenin the title first national socialist) but led a Bolshevik paramilitary group, *Rotfrontkämpferbund* (The Red Front Fighter Association). Gregor's group merged with the Nazis and, joining forces with Otto once more, the brothers laid out a program that advocated an anticapitalist, antisemitic, and anticommunist revolution for the NSDAP.[9]

Nazi propaganda drew upon the longstanding image of the "exploitative" Jewish usurer in molding their Bolshevik-Capitalist-Jewish collective. Most people had little understanding or interest in finance, market cycles, and economic theory and accepted the simple explanation as to why there were so many unemployed, why there were queues for food, and why that food was scarce. This explanation was aided by a number of scandals that were used to promote the image of the exploitative Jewish financier. In 1920, a pamphlet circulated in Germany entitled "The Rat King and His Helpers: The Truth About the Sklarz Case." The subject was Georg Sklarz who had been involved in business with a certain Alexander Parvus during the war and the negotiations with the Germans regarding Lenin's return to Russia. Sklarz was also implicated in the murder of the Marxist revolutionaries Rosa Luxemburg and Karl Liebknetch and accused of financial corruption with members of the German Social Democrats. The anonymous author sketched Sklarz as the king of a society of rats (that is, other Jews) who profited from the German people's misery. He helped to install Bolshevism in Russia by financing Lenin's return and "robbed" people and princes of their cash. This plan worked because, the author claimed, the Jews controlled the international monetary market. It was not simply that Sklarz was an unpleasant and unscrupulous man. To the author of the pamphlet, he was every Jew and every Jew was Georg Sklarz: murderous, rapacious, corrupt, and desperate for power.[10]

One of the earliest Nazi propagandists, Julius Streicher, began his public life as a member of the *Deutschsozialistische Partei* (German Socialist Party, SDP) denouncing "big money," and urging comradeship between nationalists, socialists, and communists. In one of his early articles in the newspaper *Deutsche Sozialist* in the summer of 1920, Streicher wrote:

> Do you really think the Rothschilds, Mendelsohns, Bleichroders, Warburgs and Cohns worry about your poverty? As long as the blood brothers of the Mendelsohns, the Bleichroders and the Cohns are your leaders, and as long as your party leaders are Jewish lackeys, you will be no threat to the big money men. As long as you yourself do not lead the way, and as long as the black shadow of foreign blood is behind you, you will be betrayed and deceived. The black shadow cares for itself, not for you.

Streicher met Hitler some time in 1922 and, according to his own recollection, immediately recognized in the Austrian the strong leader he sought. The following year, Streicher began his propaganda newspaper, the scurrilous *Der Stürmer.* The first copy appeared in May with the words "*Die Juden sind unser Unglück*" (The Jew are our Misfortune) emblazoned across the front. It was a phrase that was to appear on every issue, leaving no doubt who they blamed for Germany's financial calamity. In one illustration, an unpleasant-looking Jew (identifiable by the yellow star) looks through a triangle bearing the words "Washington, London, and Moscow." The accompanying text reads: "The dream of the Jews is to rule the world, therefore he plunges it into murder and horror, to build his throne in chaos." The repetitious propaganda created by Streicher both imposed on readers his vision of Jews as a foreign, corrupting force and manipulated hostility towards capitalism and banking. The imagery was crude, the message was blatant. The illustrated Jews—always ugly, fat, and holding the accoutrements of the businessman (cigar, umbrella, gold)—were at odds with the decent, hardworking German who did "honest" labor.[11]

Throughout the 1920s and 1930s, Nazi propaganda continued to center on the Jews as fat cats who robbed the poor, the peasants, exploited the vulnerable, and made their wealth through unscrupulous means. Using racial theories of the nineteenth century, Germans were transformed into Aryans (meaning "noble"), a constructed categorization of blonde, blue-eyed northern Europeans promoted by Nazi ideologues such as Alfred Rosenberg (1893–1946), and Jews were alien, middle eastern "Semites." This included people of Jewish descent as racialists believed that Jewishness was indelible. So even second- or third-generation Christians were labeled Jews because they had Jewish ancestry. The Jews obtained their wealth through illegal, corrupt, and exploitative methods and channels, Nazi propaganda claimed, so it was for the common good to redress this wrong and any economic disparity through wealth confiscation and redistribution.

* * *

In 1923, the Nazis attempted a *coup d'état* known as the Munich Putsch. For his part in the attempt to overthrow the government, Hitler was given a five-year sentence, of which he served just over a year. While incarcerated, he wrote a manifesto of his political aims, *Mein Kampf*. In the book, Hitler's attack on Jews was strongly economic and he wove together a hatred for Jews, capitalist society, and Bolsheviks. Capitalism was dominated by "physically degenerate" intellectuals and the umbrella-wielding bourgeoisie who were manipulated by Jewish usurers and speculators. The aristocracy, who he despised, was as culpable as the Jews for welcoming such financial exploitation. Their reward, however, was their downfall. With their wealth squeezed out of them by usurious Jews, they were "driven to despair" and left with no money to squander on their idle pleasures. In the United States, he stated, Jewish capitalists controlled the stock exchange, while tightening their grip on the unions and the press. It was against this economic tyranny, that people rebelled and out of which anti-Jewish violence ensued.[12]

While the Jews' financial dealings were facilitated by the parliamentary democracy that they wanted to destroy, Hitler wrote, it was also the "breeding-ground in which the bacilli of the [Jewish] Marxist world pest" grew and spread. In buying up stock in a variety of national undertakings, the capitalist Jew made the country's production "the pawn in a financial game of chess." They encouraged a gulf between employers and employees that led to class consciousness and the class struggle that formed the basis of Marxist ideology, which he referred to as the "Jewish contagion." By dominating the stock exchange, the Jew "secured control of the working power of the nation." The international Jewish cabal, as Hitler described the Bolsheviks, pulled the strings of war in 1914, for it was only in the Jews' interests to annihilate Germany. By 1916–17, Hitler asserted, virtually all production was "under the control of Jewish finance." Trade unions became an "economic weapon which the international Jew uses for the purpose of destroying the economic foundations of free and independent national States, for ruining their national industry and trade and thereby enslaving free nations to serve Jewish world-finance, which transcends all State boundaries." National Socialism, in Hitler's estimation, was the only authentically classless solution to the corrupt capitalist society in a way Marxism was not.[13]

These were the ramblings of a man with little, if any grasp, on economic matters but a mind soaked in racial stereotypes and resentments. Instead of coming to terms with the financial failures of the Kaiser, the lack of economic dynamism and innovation, and the fallout from defeat, Hitler saw the world in terms of a struggle between Aryan and Semite, just as Wilhelm Marr had done in the nineteenth century. The conflict between nazism and bolshevism was not one of ideological differences—there was more similarity between them than differences—but of two powers competing for domination over a liberal democratic and capitalist Western Europe. Hitler was convinced that the *Protocols of the Elders of Zion* were intrinsically truthful for the same reason that persuaded Paquita de Shishmareff: the Jews "so violently repudiated" them as forgeries.

> What many Jews unconsciously wish to do is here clearly set forth. It is not necessary to ask out of what Jewish brain these revelations sprang; but what is of vital interest is that they disclose, with an almost terrifying precision, the mentality and methods of action characteristic of the Jewish people and these writings expound in all their various directions the final aims towards which the Jews are striving.[14]

If a Jew was successful in commerce, it was due to his cunning—his ability to exploit—which trumped the honesty of his "Aryan" competitor. Jews looked at "the commercial domain and all money transactions as a privilege belonging exclusively to himself and he exploited it ruthlessly." It was this type of activity that aroused indignation and hostility, Hitler wrote, especially given the habit that Jews had of flaunting their possessions, including land. They lacked the visceral connection to it that the peasant possessed. To the Jew, land was just another commodity to be bought and sold and exploited. On this Hitler and Marx agreed, the "Jewish spirit" was a corrosive and selfish self-interest, and German culture, influenced by "Jewishness," was reduced to the marketplace.

Hitler had grander ideas than to be leader of a street-fighting gang. To become the leader of a totalitarian state, Hitler could not act without the will of the people and the people had to be convinced of the benefits they stood to gain under the Nazis. And, like any successful propagandist, the Nazis were quick to utilize any scandal. No disaster would be wasted. And post-war Germany's dire economic state of chaos created the perfect storm.[15]

* * *

In 1925, as Hitler transformed the NSDAP, the Barmat affair erupted. It was named after the four Polish-born Russian Jews involved—Julius, Solomon, Herschel (Henry), and Isaac Barmat. They had started a food export-import business, buying goods in the Netherlands and importing them into Germany, including foodstuffs that were in desperate need. That they made a large amount of money from this led to accusations of war profiteering. With much of the German population impoverished and unemployed, suspicion and resentment fell upon people who made money in hard times. Julius Barmat became a member of the Social Democrats, making important connections and, in some cases, rewarding these political friends with gifts. Wilhelm Richter, a Social Democrat and the president of the Berlin police, not only took gifts from Julius but had the Barmat brothers pick up his bills from restaurant meals. That the brothers' firm benefited financially from political patronage was apparent. That kind of cronyism was, unfortunately, not uncommon in politics, then or now.[16]

With loans from the long-established Prussian State Bank, the brothers expanded their business activities into banking, as well as buying up factories, mills, and other works, all the while financially backing Social Democratic politicians and their projects. Over the period of a year, Julius Barmat had borrowed 38 million Marks at a rate below the market price. Hyperinflation drove the value of the currency further and further down, driving up the market price. The Barmats then lent the money they borrowed cheaply at those higher market rates. There was nothing illegal in this, but it fed into the image of the unscrupulous speculator, even though their purchased investments proved unprofitable. The bubble burst for the Barmats when their dabbling in currency speculation failed, resulting in the collapse of the firm and the loss of millions of marks for the bank and their other creditor, the *Reichspost* (the national post office).

An unrelated investigation into the Prussian State Bank revealed that it had lent money without sufficient collateral, which left the bank with liabilities greater than its reserve. The arrest of one man at the center of the scandal named the Barmat brothers as being the recipients of millions of marks from the bank. Prominent socialists, Center party members, and other high-level figures were drawn into the affair, with questions asked about the brothers' status as "quasi-official agents of the government." On New Year's Eve, 1924, Julius Barmat's

Schwanenwerder peninsula villa was surrounded by the police to prevent him fleeing. It took about a hundred policemen to accompany the other brothers into custody while their offices were raided for evidence of wrongdoing. Almost four years later, Julius was sentenced to eleven months in jail while his brother Henry was given six months. In both cases the conviction was for bribery, not fraud as originally charged.[17]

With the run up to the elections in 1925, at the height of the scandal, the Barmat case was used as propaganda by the Nazis (and also the Communists) and forcefully exploited by the propagandist Joseph Goebbels:

> While the front soldier was fighting in the trenches to defend his fatherland, some Eastern Jewish profiteer robbed him of hearth and home. The Jew lives in the palaces and the proletarian, the front soldier, lives in holes that do not deserve to be called "homes." That is neither necessary nor unavoidable, but rather an injustice that cries out to the heavens. A government that stands by and does nothing is useless and must vanish, the sooner the better.[18]

Goebbels' view of the Jews as middlemen, traders, or financiers, and, as such, "unproductive" echoed the long-standing criticism of the financier who eschewed physical labor and made money from money instead. Where it differed was in the tone and degree of vitriol. In other centuries, Jewish moneylenders had been encouraged to move into other professions. In the Nazi ideology, the "unproductivity" of the banker was used merely as an assault.[19]

When another financial scandal erupted in Germany in 1927, the Nazis and the Communists used it to their advantage. Three Eastern European Jewish brothers—Max, Willi, and Leo Sklarek—were charged with fraud and bribery for cheating the Berlin City Bank out of ten million Marks, although the figure may have exceeded that amount. As owners of a Berlin clothing company founded in 1921, the brothers were awarded a monopoly contract to supply clothing and linen to the city. They were charged in 1929 with receiving payment for forged invoices detailing clothing that was, in fact, never delivered. For good measure, they were accused also of bribing the Lord Mayor of Berlin and other high-level officials with large sums of money and luxury goods.[20]

It soon was revealed that the brothers, like the Barmats, were members of the SDP (the Social Democrat party) but some of the crooked officials implicated belonged to the KPD (the Communist party). The brothers went on trial for corruption trial on October 14, 1931, with the antisemitic press denigrating them while the SDP did its best to distance itself from them. Jewish leaders also denounced this "trio of uneducated men, with notoriously gross tastes" who were allowed into the cloisters of the City of Berlin, a privilege not easily granted. That they eschewed an Orthodox Jewish life for one of horseracing and society events was sufficient excuse for the Jewish community to deny they were Jews at all. The hostility toward them by the Jewish establishment was such that it was a Jewish council member who first complained about the Sklareks while their defense was headed by Deputy Bruehn, an affirmed antisemite whose newspaper *Wahrheit* was "a Jew-baiting paper." A close friend of the Sklareks, Bruehn was also a financial beneficiary of the brothers and was a guest at their beach resorts.[21]

Within a world of racial categorization, these scandals propped up the Nazi's theory of a global Capitalist-Marxist-Jewish plot to defraud and impoverish the German worker. The court case and the escalating antipathy between the SDP and the KPD had an effect politically, resulting in greater gains at the municipal polls in November 1929 for both the KPD and the Nazi party. In the election run-up, the antisemitic press promoted class hatred and division between "haves" and "have-nots." Articles spoke of feasts given by the Sklareks and their cronies where "Champagne flowed and pots of caviar were devoured." These articles were contrasted with photographs of abandoned factories and starving, sick children, and the unemployed. Photographs of elegant houses owned by Jews were placed next to images of wounded veterans left to die on the streets. Large department stores owned by Jews were blamed for the ruination of the small business owner who was forced to close their doors. When they later attained power, however, the Nazi attempt to close down these department stores were met with strong resistance from the majority of the population.[22]

The Nazis built their party on these promises using the Jews as the dangerous obstacle to a strong economic German state. A Nazi election poster for the Berlin municipal election in 1929 showed an arm of a party member, replete with swastika armband, whose fist was punching three, fat, Jewish businessmen surrounded by bags of money. The slogan ran: "End the Corruption: Vote National Socialist." A few years later, another election poster screamed "Death to Lies," with a similar arm grasping a poisonous snake with the words "Marxism" and "High Finance" inscribed on its skin. *Der Stürmer* ran cartoons depicting disparities between the rich Jews and the impoverished Germans. In one, well-fed and well-dressed Jews walk in front of a bank while the hungry Germans line up at the unemployment office. In another image, an obese Jew holds in his hand a key inscribed with the word "*Geld*" (money) while a starving German worker is trapped inside a locked wheel that is etched with words such as "wage reduction" and "unemployment." The message was clear and effective. If you are without a job, if you cannot fill your cupboards with food, if you are hungry, if you can't afford medicine for your sick child, there is only one group of people to blame. The Jews.[23]

Photographs and electioneering posters of Hitler presented him as the savior patriarch of the new Germany risen from the ashes of defeat. He was photographed meeting with farmers, stroking the cheek of young children, and paying respects to dead SS members. The message of the Nazi campaign in these early years before the Third Reich was established was simple: what was in place in Weimar Germany was a system that tolerated Jews enriching themselves during the time of economic collapse at the expense of the German worker. Capitalism was a tool of the Jews and their cronies. It was time to "bring down the system."[24]

* * *

Between 1930 and 1932, five emergency decrees increased taxes dramatically in Germany. Existing taxes were raised, new taxes imposed, and exemptions quashed. With no clear principles of, or commitment to, liberal democracy, those in charge of the new Weimar Republic proved ineffectual in combatting the growing radicalism disrupting social and economic order. After political inveigling, in 1933, Hitler succeeded in his aim and was appointed Chancellor of Germany by President Paul von Hindenburg. He now began the process of establishing his one-party, totalitarian Third Reich. Individual freedom was decimated. True freedom, in Hitler's estimation, meant rejecting the free economy and abolishing actual freedom. Adam Smith's Economic Man was dead and buried. The new man was nihilistic, devoid of positive beliefs and ethics, and prepared to sacrifice himself to bring this new world into being by force and bloodshed. Economic status was no longer to be the measure of wellbeing and class distinctions were to be eliminated. Instead, social position was a function of allegiance and usefulness to the state. It was a state in which "a higher form of human civilization" would develop in a "perfect" society.[25]

The Jewish-born scholar Victor Klemperer (1881–1960), who had converted to Protestantism in 1912, wrote in his diary one Monday evening in April 1933 about the red posters that had appeared in the shops. The notices assured shoppers that the premises were a "Recognized German-Christian enterprise." Other posters warned people who bought goods from Jews that they were destroying the German economy. Klemperer saw no difference between Hitler and the Communists, writing that "both are materialistic and lead to slavery," and both were "tyrannical . . . [disregarding and negating] the freedom of the spirit and of the individual." Everything was geared towards crushing the individual under the boots of the Aryan collective. It was an astute observation for the times when both political factions were pitting themselves against each other as if they were worlds apart. Apart from the emphasis on nationalism and internationalism respectively, Nazism and Communism were cut from the same cloth and, like vicious siblings, had an intense rivalry for power as well as a shared hatred of the individual freedom in the economy, thought, action, politics, and movement.[26]

Before the war, a third of Germany's workforce was unemployed. They wandered the streets looking for work, lining up for free meals, returning to crowded rooms inhabited by hungry children and despairing wives. Within four years there appeared to be an economic miracle with full employment. The *volte face* of the economy, however, was "largely an illusion," with wages and pensions at the same level as during the Great Depression. The so-called "miracle" was due to a level of deficit spending never before seen in Germany. The market system was abandoned for a "command order organized for war." The Nazis manipulated the economy and so further gained power over the people, redistributing wealth, robbing Peter to pay Paul. Ideally in Hitler's world, Peter was a Jewish capitalist and Paul was a poor "Aryan" worker. For the Third Reich, state intervention in the economy was a national duty and a means to an end. It was termed a *Volkswirtschaft* (national economy) rather than a *Weltwirtschaft* or *Privatwirtschaft* (global economy or private sector economy). The authoritarian state's needs came first.[27]

After initial misgivings, most industrialists and bankers (apart from Jews) who had resisted Hitler's radicalism until the end of 1932, decided that it was in their best interests to accommodate the party that was on the verge of power and supported the move away from the Liberal economic order. In spite of Hitler's propaganda, his alliance with big commercial and industrial concerns such as I.G. Farben, Deutsche Banke, Telefunken, AEG, and others came at the expense of smaller entities that benefited from a competitive system not dependent on political patronage or crony capitalism. These large-scale industries and businesses might have welcomed the shift to protectionism and monopoly but government intervention on their behalf was, first and foremost, for the financial of the Reich. Businesses were restricted by government decrees on wage control, hiring and firing, product price, and output, with consumption controlled. If businesses did not comply, they could be taken over with the possibility of the owner placed under arrest and charged with treason.[28]

Hitler's economic policy was greatly influenced by Friedrich Zimmerman's book *Das Ende des Kapitalismus* (*The End of Capitalism*). One leading Nazi economist spoke of a "just rate" of interest that would free the nation from the "tyranny of credit capital," just as there was a "fair wage." As a result, the professional classes and small traders saw a decline in their income while wages for the lower economic classes were fixed. Interest on loans, although not abolished, was lowered in the attempt to stifle the "slavery of interest," without regard to risk, overhead, or profit. Private property was allowed, but the Reich had control over its owners and, if need be, the power of appropriation. With a pledge to eradicate unemployment, capitalism was dealt its "death blow," with the sanctioning of the right to work being, as one writer observed, "the turning point from capitalism to socialism." Otto Dietrich, the head of the Nazi press bureau, later wrote, "our socialism is no utopia." It was "natural life . . . the sole egalitarian economy" which would demand and give every German employment. The intent of the Nazi's Four-Year Program was to end both poverty and unemployment through a work creation scheme. To this end, as well as price and wage control, monumental public works were funded, foreign trade heavily regulated; the free market became a fossil from another era. The liberal economic era of maximum output and growth based on individualism and free trade was substituted with slower economic progress, corporatism, regulations such as rent control and price freezes on food staples (including bread, potatoes, and beer), tax increases for corporations and tax breaks for those with low incomes. This new National Socialist economic policy, Goebbels claimed, assured the German population that they would be saved from the economic catastrophes that occurred under both Liberalism and Marxism.[29]

If the Bolsheviks every took power in Germany, Hitler warned, Germany's means of production would fall under the control of "Jewish international finance." For this to occur, outside help would be required, such as an invasion by France, which would bring with it the chaos necessary for the state to be overwhelmed by "Bolshevik storm troops," that served Jews. In their "lusting after blood and money," the whole world was prey to the oppressive Jewish "hydra." The Jew would pursue world domination until confronted by a superior force and, like Wilhelm Marr's vision of a cosmic battle between Germanness and Jewishness, there could be only one victor. While the "Jewish media" beat the drums of war, urging its British and American allies to military action, it was "[i]nternational finance-Jewry" who were behind global conflict.[30]

In 1933, few Jews feared for their lives in Germany. But mounting regulations pushing Jews out of society made life increasingly difficult and insecure. This was especially true from 1935, when the Nuremberg Laws designated Jews as foreign (*Volksfremden*) and as enemies of the state (*Volksfeinden*), stripping them of their German citizenship and any protection or rights that afforded. It is this step that signaled the move from rhetorical antisemitism to an antisemitism that was potentially lethal. Any and all power had been removed completely from the individual Jew, who was now at the mercy of an increasingly hostile state. As non-Aryans, they were excluded from the *Volksstaat*, the "egalitarian" community and a welfare state for those of the "deserving" background. Many Jews decided that it was safer to relocate to other lands and began to liquidate their assets, some falling prey to buyers who benefited from the sellers' urgent desire to emigrate. Victor Klemperer watched as his friends left one by one, for France and Czechoslovakia (until they were conquered), South Africa, Canada, England, America, and Palestine. He sympathized too much with the Arabs to contemplate Palestine and he regarded the Zionists as not so different from and "just as offensive" as the National Socialists, with their "nosing after blood, their ancient 'cultural roots. . . .'" In the end, he stayed, citing his lack of proficiency in French, Italian, Spanish or English as detrimental to securing a suitable job outside of Germany. There was also the conviction on the part of some German Jews reluctant to leave their homeland that the Hitler government would not last and that Germans were too civilized to put up with his bunch of rabble-rousing antisemites for long. But by 1937, the main cities in Germany had lost a third of their Jewish population and, in rural areas, two-thirds of Jews had left their villages and small towns.[31]

The Reich government welcomed the emigration of Jews from Germany but not with their capital. Jewish emigration policies were therefore shaped in such a way as to avoid large amounts of private capital being syphoned out of the Reich. In reality, Jewish enterprises had been adversely affected by the inflation during the Weimar Republic when savings and investments dwindled to a fraction of their pre-1914 worth and by Nazi policies that adversely affected their businesses. A special case was made if Palestine was the destination of emigrating Jews. The Haavara Agreement, through which Jewish émigrés received "capitalist visas" into the British mandated territory, was signed on August 25, 1933 and conducted between the Nazi government and Zionist German Jews eager to get Jews out of Germany and into Palestine. Even though it meant Jews had to give up possessions, they would be allowed to immigrate into Palestine and possibly retrieve these goods as German exports at a later date. In exchange, the German Reich got a compensory export agreement. This achieved the Nazi goal of ridding their country of Jews without economic destabilization. For their part, Zionists helped German Jews escape from economic disaster and obtained more Jewish immigrants to further their hopes for population parity and a Jewish state.[32]

It was in 1938, after the *Anschluss* (Germany's annexation of Austria), that the Reich experienced a serious cash-flow crisis. The departure of Jews had slowed, in part due to the high cost imposed on emigrants. To raise funds and encourage greater Jewish emigration, the Nazis increased and speeded up their confiscation of Jewish assets and investments not previously seized. It was now no longer legal to change the name of a Jewish business, thereby closing off the possibility of disguising it with an Aryan façade. In the case of Jews immigrating to countries other than Palestine, their property was deemed to be the property of the German people and confiscated outright. The Third Reich introduced Aryanization—the process of transferring Jewish businesses into Nazi hands—which was just another name for the expropriation of Jewish property and money. It was robbery on a grand scale accomplished with new laws, intimidation, and physical force.[33]

By the summer, all property was required to be registered and official approval was needed for the sale of Jewish businesses. Under the process of Aryanization—simply, the eradication of the Jews from the German economy—meant that all Jews were forced to reveal all personal assets greater than 5,000 RM to the revenue services so that it could be collected and then redistributed, with Jews forced to accept government bonds in exchange for their assets. Overall, the impact of the Aryanization policy was minimal. By 1938, it was only in the retail industry that Jews held a significant position and most German Jews never did have the kind of wealth others imagined they had. But so strong was the myth that Jews had untold riches it was assumed that substantial revenue would be garnered from these policies.[34]

The flight of Jews from the Third Reich rose considerably after the events of November 9–10, 1938. Known afterwards as *Kristallnacht* (Night of the Broken Glass), Jewish property was vandalized, destroyed, and looted. Ninety-one Jews were killed and thousands arrested, many sent to concentration camps, and a billion RM fine was levied against the Jewish community to repair the damage caused by Nazi vandalization, destruction, and looting. Shortly after the pogrom, the "First Decree for the Removal of Jews from Economic Life" was issued, prohibiting Jews from retail and crafts, trade fairs, and executive company posts. Jews could sell but not own real estate. They could no longer acquire, pawn, or sell certain precious items such as gold, platinum, precious stones or jewels. They were obliged to register any stocks and shares they held and were unable to sell them without official approval. It was, in effect, impossible for Jews to live in Germany. For those propertied Jews who decided that Germany was no longer a safe place to live, a Reich Flight Tax of 25 percent was applied against their assets. These economic policies directed against the Jews had an advantage other than propping up bureaucracies for months at a time. They also meant that the government could avoid raising taxes on German citizens.

Emigration increasingly became the option only for those young or vigorous enough to start their lives over elsewhere on little money, or those who found ways of hiding their assets and syphoning as much of their money and belongings out of the country as they could. Some Jews smuggled valuables out of Germany in the form of rare stamps and hidden diamonds, stashed money under plaster casts, or set up of dummy businesses abroad into which funds were channeled. But most settled their debts—however egregious—and faced the new challenges of beginning their lives anew in a foreign land.[35]

* * *

With war declared in 1939, after the Nazi invasion of Poland, the biggest capitalist entity in the world—the British Empire—was pitted against a revolutionary dictatorial Reich in pursuit of global domination. France fell quickly, and in 1941, the Nazis turned their attention east again, invading their erstwhile ally the Soviet Union, in defiance of the non-aggression Molotov-Ribbentrop Pact signed in August. As the Wehrmacht moved eastwards, Jews were driven into ghettos, such as Lodz, which became an important component in the Nazi economy for the production of all kinds of goods, including furniture and clothing. The Jews that were more likely to survive were the ones that were young, healthy, and with skills that were useful to the German economy. Ghettoization of Jews also solved the problem of homelessness among "Aryans." The apartments and goods once belonging to Jews were given to German citizens, sometimes as rewards, other times to relieve the social tension wrought by Allied bombings that destroyed their homes. A law passed in November 1941 enabled the Reich government to confiscate property and tax deportees who were involuntarily moving from one part of the Reich to another or to a land conquered by it. Technically they were not émigrés, yet in order to seize their possessions the Reich Citizenship Law denaturalized deportees once they crossed the Reich's border, even if they remained in territory occupied by the Germans.[36]

Belongings confiscated from Jews were put up for sale. In the summer of 1943 in Oldenburg, a sale of deported Jews' goods was held. Linens, porcelain, beds, enamelware, and other appropriated items were first offered to the victims of bombings who had not been compensated already. When they had finished picking over the items, families and newlyweds were allowed to purchase the goods. Finally, the sale was opened to the general public who purchased books, ornaments, bedding, and furniture that had previously filled the homes of middle-class Jews. Such requisitioning, they were told, as they tussled over the goods in cash sales and in auctions, was for the common good. Jews were the enemy of the state and therefore an enemy of the people. The longstanding propaganda that Jews accumulated their wealth through theft and greed meant that it was only just for it to be taken from them to aid those in need.[37]

On April 2, 1942, a decree pointedly entitled "The Forfeiture of Jewish Wealth for the Benefit of the Reich" was published giving the regime the green light to seize cash, jewels, stocks, bonds, and bank accounts. Fines were issued on Jewish communities for everything from Allied bombings to the upkeep of Jewish forced laborers. The plunder continued as the Nazis took over Slovakia, Salonika, Rhodes, and Kos. Jewish cemeteries were leveled for the raw materials, such as the stone tombstones and iron gates, or the land was sold off. All in all, the amount of money stolen from Jews was negligible with regard to the German GDP, but with the financial pressures of warfare and the welfare policies for Reich citizens, all revenue was vital. To the individual Jews who lost everything, it was devastating. But far worse was to come.[38]

Once their money and goods had been plundered, once they had been left stateless, and with food scarce, the decision to slaughter the Jews *en masse* was taken. Concentration camps had been in use since the beginning of the Third Reich but now death camps were set up and those Jews not selected to work in the ghettos were sent to them from all parts of German-occupied Europe. On arrival, their usefulness was assessed and those deemed to be "a life unworthy of life" (*Lebensunwertes Leben*) were herded into gas chambers. The Nazis had practiced forced euthanasia on the mentally and physically ill from 1939 under the T4 Program, with the definition of unworthy life given a broad stroke. The cruel and relentless pursuit of the Nazi utopia meant the eradication of those considered a burden, useless, or unproductive. In the eighteenth century, unproductivity was an obsession, but the solution was to "regenerate" and make the "unproductive" "productive," however nonsensical the idea was that all Jews were unproductive. The Nazi answer was to exterminate.

It may be thought that demanding usefulness in society would inevitably lead to ideas that the useless are expendable. But mass murder was not inevitable, and it was not a culmination of centuries of hatred. Hatred in an individual cannot be reified into a substance that travels across time and space, unquestionably handed on from parent to child. There was no sustained transference of hatred from one generation to another, in different countries, at different times. It is not a virus as is often claimed, lying dormant "ready to wake." The hatred that led to the camps came from a specific group of twentieth-century people who lived in a world that looked at everything through group identities rather than individual accomplishments. It was bred in the modern era in a country defeated in a war that was like no war before it, and in which many people despised the individual and loathed the freedoms that emanated from classic liberalism. Most importantly, it came from people who reviled capitalism as the epitome of the mythical "Jewish spirit." That disparagement of capitalism was longstanding but that is not the same as saying it inevitably led to mass murder. Prior criticism of financiers led to debates over a change of occupation, expulsion, imprisonment, or sometimes death. Generally, the attacks were directed at all bankers even if the profession itself was labeled "Jewish." In the twentieth century, there was no debate over the rights and wrongs of usury and how it should be shaped or what would make it more acceptable. The dialogue of Döhm, the abbé Grégoire, or Clermont-Tonnerre had no place in this desolate and terrifying landscape in which the individual had been suffocated by the omnipotent and tyrannical state, whether in the Soviet Union or Nazi Germany. In the world of totalitarian politics, where freedom of thought and speech, economic freedom, and the rights of the individual were denounced and then crushed, those labeled as detrimental to the common good and "unproductive" people were simply unfit to live.[39]

Notes

1. It was claimed in a 1934 edition of the *Protocols* that this information was first published in the short-lived newspaper *Prizyv*, February 5, 1919. It was first published in an Estonian newspaper, *Postimees*, December 31, 919.
2. While at university, Golovinski had joined a secret antisemitic organization called The Holy Brotherhood. Opportunistically, after his studies he worked for Okhrana (the Russian secret police under the tsar) and later, after the revolution in 1917, he changed sides and offered his propagandistic services to the Bolsheviks. Vadim Skuratovsky, *The Question of the Authorship of the "Protocols of the Elders of Zion"* (Kiev: Kiev University Press, 2001); On the Petrashevsky Circle, see N. Troyan, "The Philosophical Opinions of the Petrashevsky Circle," *Philosophy and Phenomenological Research* 6.3 (1946): 363–80.
3. *The Protocols of the Learned Elders of Zion*, trans. Victor E. Marsden (Union, NJ: Christian Educational Assn., 1970), 12, 72; Binjamin W. Segal, *A Lie and A Libel: The History of The Protocols of the Elders of Zion* (Lincoln, NE: University of Nebraska Press, 1995).
4. http://www.huxley.net/ah/huxley-quote.html.

5. John Maynard Keynes, *The Economic Consequences of the Peace* (London: Macmillan, 1919), chapter 6; Ferguson, *The Ascent of Money*, chapter 2.
6. Sennholz, *Age of Inflation*, 70, 82–83; Ferguson, *The Ascent of Money*, chap. 2.
7. Sennholz, *Age of Inflation*, 70, 82–83.
8. Ibid., 79.
9. "Während Millionen des eingesessenen deutschen Volkes in Arbeitslosigkeit und Elend gerieten, gelangten zugewanderte Juden in wenigen Jahren zu phantastischen Reichtümer—nicht durch ehrliche Arbeit, sondern durch Wucher, Gaunerei und Betrug." *Der ewige Jude* (The Eternal Jew) (1940), Deutsche Film Gesellschaft, directed by Fritz Hippler; Sennholz, *Age of Inflation*, 69; Sean McMeekin, *The Red Millionaire* (New Haven: Yale University Press, 2003), 234, 236; As in any movement, there were those who were fervently committed to their cause—even in its nihilism—and those who were dismissed by the more radical as "Sunday Nazis." Drucker, *The End of Economic Man*, 192–93.The diversity of the revolutionary movements, and the fluidity that existed between Communists and Nazis, was apparent in men such as the Strassers. Otto was expelled from the NSDAP for his class-conscious radicalism, creating his own party, Black Front, which had among its aims the expropriation of Germany's industrialists. While disgruntled radicals dabbled with a variety of extreme groups across the political spectrum, Hitler set about ridding himself of his potential rivals. Just as Stalin was rumored to have had his rival Sergei Kirov murdered, Hitler wiped out members of the Strasserite faction, the brownshirt SA (*Sturmabteilung*, the first paramilitary section of the NSDAP), and prominent Conservative anti-Nazis during the infamous "Night of the Long Knives" in 1934. Gregor Strasser was arrested and then assassinated in his prison cell. Drucker, *The End of Economic Man*, 227.
10. Martin H. Geyer, "Contested Narratives of the Weimar Republic: The Case of the Kutisker-Barmat Scandal," in *Weimar Publics/Weimar Subjects: Rethinking the Political Culture of Germany in the 1920s*, eds. Kathleen Canning, Kerstin Barndt, and Kristin McGuire (New York and Oxford: Berghahn Books, 2010), 221–22.
11. It was claimed that as late as 1939 that not many Nazis took this seriously, recognizing as a theme to capture voters. Drucker, *The End of Economic Man*, 17; Julius Streicher, *Ruf zur Tat* (Nuremberg 1937), 11–13, quoted in Randall L. Bytwerk, *Julius Streicher: Nazi Editor of the Notorious Anti-Semitic Newspaper Der Stürmer* (New York: Stein and Day, 1983), 10, 14, 51–52 and illustration no. 18 on p. 91. The text reads: "Der Traum des Juden ist die Welt, Die ihm, als herricher, unterstellt, Drum schlug er sie in Mord und Grauen, Den Thron im Chaos sich zu bauen."
12. Adolf Hitler, *Mein Kampf* [*MK*], 914–22, https://archive.org/stream/meinkampf035176mbp/meinkampf035176mbp_djvu.txt.
13. *MK*, 584, 692–93, 931, 937, 943–44, 946–47, 1750–51, 1860–61, 1863–65.
14. *MK*, 910–11, 945.

15. Drucker, *The End of Economic Man*, 218, 249; Barkai, *Nazi Economics*, 114–15, 169.
16. Bernhard Fulda, *Press and Politics in the Weimar Republic* (Oxford: OUP, 2009), 89.
17. "Barmat Scandal Threatens to Split German Politics," *The Evening Independent*, March 5, 1925, 19; Fulda, *Press and Politics*, 90–91.
18. Joseph Goebbels, "Wir Fordern" (We Demand), *Der Angriff. Aufsätze aus der Kampfzeit* (Munich: Zentralverlag der NSDAP, 1935), 18–19, reprinted in the German Propaganda Archive, http://www.calvin.edu/academic/cas/gpa/angrif05.htm.
19. Dean, *Robbing the Jews*, 19.
20. "Sklarek Trial Opened in Berlin," *JTA*, http://www.jta.org/1931/10/14/archive/sklarek-trial-opened-in-berlin; *Glasgow Herald*, November 13, 1929, 13; Annika Klein, *Korruption und Korruptions: Skandale in der Weimarer Republik* (Göttingen: V&R Unipress, 2014), 299–305; Donna Harsch, *German Social Democracy and the Rise of Nazism* (Chapel Hill: University of North Carolina Press, 1993), 69.
21. Harsch, *German Social Democracy*, 70–71; "Sklarek Trial."
22. The NSDAP won 13 of the 225 mandates (5.8 %). It was the first time the party gained seats in a parliament. Harsch, *German Social Democracy*, 69; "Korruption über Korruption," *Stürtz das System* (Munich: Franz Eher, 1932), 16; Drucker, *The End of Economic Man*, 201.
23. On the use of the Sklarek brothers in Nazi propaganda, see, Helmut von Wilucki, "Bewährte moderne Propagandamethoden" (Tested Methods of Modern Propaganda), *Unser Wille und Weg* 2 (1932), https://research.calvin.edu/german-propaganda-archive/wilweg02.htm; *Der Stürmer*, January 1930 and June 1931.
24. *Stürtz das System* (Munich: Franz Eher, 1932), German Propaganda Archive, Calvin University, Grand Rapids, MI, https://research.calvin.edu/german-propaganda-archive/stuerzt-das-system.htm
25. Sennholz, *Age of Inflation*, 88; *MK*, 210, 253, 696–97, 1049, 1158–59, 1264–65, 1284–85; Drucker, *The End of Economic Man*, 163; Johannes Thieme as recorded in Victor Klemperer's *I Will Bear Witness*, 7. Adolf Wagner promoted "state socialism" which was intended to prevent the chaos and instability associated with a free market economy. Barkai, *Nazi Economics*, 83–5; Drucker, *The End of Economic Man*, 80, 96, 133, 137.
26. Victor Klemperer, *I Will Bear Witness: A Diary of the Nazi Years 1933–1941* (New York: Random House, 1995), 11, 42, 45, 60, 87.
27. Sennholz, *Age of Inflation*, 92; Aly Götz, *Hitler's Beneficiaries: Plunder, Racial War, and the Nazi Welfare State* (New York: Metropolitan, 2005), 36; Barkai, *Nazi Economics*, 1, 3; Adam Tooze, *The Wages of Destruction: The Making and Breaking of the Nazi Economy* (London: Allen Lane, 2007), 186–87.
28. For example, in the case of Dr. Hugo Junkers. Tooze, *The Wages of Destruction*, 100, 126. On Nazi economic policy and the theory of underconsumption, see Drucker, *The End of Economic Man*, 131, 148–49, 157; Barkai, *Nazi Economics*, 10, 36, 37.

29. Otto Dietrich, *Das Wirtschaftsdenken im Dritten Reich* (Munich: Zentralverlag der NSDAP, 1936), 14. The idea of "the slavery of interest" by B. Köhler was the core of National Socialist economics and from *Der Aufbau* 14 (1936): 15. See, Barkai, *Nazi Economics*, 24–25, 27, 31–32, 35, 69, 169, 204, 223; Tooze, *The Wages of Destruction*, 37, 40; Götz, *Hitler's Beneficiaries*, 13; Goebbels, "Youth in the Service of German Socialism," *Der Aufbau,* January 15, 1934, 5.
30. Robert Wistrich, *Hitler's Apocalypse: Jews and the Nazi Legacy* (London: Weidenfeld & Nicolson, 1985), chap. 5; Tooze, *The Wages of Destruction*, 206, 284; *MK*, 951, 1815–18, 1932–33; Klemperer, *I Will Bear Witness*, 68–69.
31. Dean, *Robbing the Jews*, 28–29; Trude Maurer, "Part 4: From Everyday Life to a State of Emergency: Jews in Weimar and Nazi Germany," in *Jewish Daily Life in Germany*; Klemperer, *I Will Bear Witness*, 40, 68–69.
32. Tooze, *The Wages of Destruction*, 75, 89–90; Maurer, "From Everyday Life."
33. Maurer, "From Everyday Life."
34. Tooze, *The Wages of Destruction*, 81, 274–75, 277; Götz, *Hitler's Beneficiaries*, 41–45; Dean, *Robbing the Jews*, 18, 84, 89.
35. Martin Gilbert, *Kristallnacht: Prelude to Destruction* (London: HarperPress, 2006); Tooze, *The Wages of Destruction*, 278–79; Dean, *Robbing the Jews*, 54–55, 65–69, 76, 209; Götz, *Hitler's Beneficiaries*, 48.
36. Tooze, *War of Destruction*, 525; Dean, *Robbing the Jews*, 166.
37. Götz, *Hitler's Beneficiaries*, 113–16, 118, 124–25, 126, 225, 226, 265, 272.
38. Ibid., 205, 213, 217, 281–82; Edith Raim, *Nazi Crimes Against Jews and German Post-War Justice: The West German Judicial System During Allied Occupation (1945–1949)* (Oldenbourg: de Gruyter, 2013), 181.
39. Götz, *Hitler's Beneficiaries*, 285, 298.

11

"Mr. Moneybags"

The debate, in the most basic terms, over top-down regulation versus the quasi invisible hand of the marketplace continues in the present. Whether the common good is best served by government officials and bureaucracy or individuals pursuing the suited interests of themselves, their families, and their communities, divides political life into parties and parties into factions. The first harnesses the economy and directs revenue according to government policy while the second leaves economic decision-making to the laws of supply and demand, favoring the knowledge and experience of entrepreneurs, business-owners, and investors over governments, regardless of political affiliation. In today's world, the current focus of antisemitism is more often than not associated with the Muslim world and its opposition to Israel. This political conflict is, however, often intermingled with anticapitalist action and rhetoric, which still resorts to stereotypes about Jews and money. In the aftermath of World War II, as the globe split ideologically into capitalist and communist camps, Israel allied with the United States and it is in these two countries that the majority of Jews live today. It is no surprise that during the Soviet Union, Jews were associated with the capitalist West and what they termed "western imperialism." Anti-Zionism, the French historian and ex-communist Annie Kriegel observed, was as crucial to post-war communism—and therefore anticapitalism—as antisemitism was to the Nazis.

* * *

Antisemitic propaganda had been introduced into the Middle East by Nazis who had fled to the region from Europe after the war. As German towns lay in ruins and Allied soldiers liberated the death camps, shaken by the sight of the corpses and the skeletal survivors that met their eyes, military tribunals were set up to bring the perpetrators of the war crimes to justice. To escape the hangman's noose or a life in prison, former SS men and other Nazi party members tried to smuggle themselves out of Germany. The most alluring hubs for refugees were Syria and, particularly, Egypt, where Nazis often converted to Islam, taking Arabic names. Alois Brunner, who had been in command at the Drancy transit camp from where Jews were transported to death camps, chose Damascus as his safe haven from prosecution. There, he worked for the Assad regime as an intelligence agent, as well as an arms dealer, collaborating with another escaped Nazi, Major-General Otto-Ernst Remer, founder of the banned Socialist Reich Party. Dr. Hans Eisele escaped to the Cairo suburb of Maadi, an upscale part of town, and changed his name to Carl Debouche. Alfred Zingler had been one of Goebbel's chief Nazi propagandists. In Cairo, he transformed into Mahmoud Saleh and headed the Institute for the Study of Zionism, assisted by Dr. Werner Witshale and Hans Appler (who became Saleh Shafar). Another assistant was Louis Heiden who translated both the *Protocols of the Elders of Zion* and *Mein Kampf* into Arabic. Erich Altern, who changed his name to Ali Bella when he converted to Islam, had been the head of the Gestapo's Jewish section in Galicia during the war. In Egypt, he trained Palestinians in military camps, as did Ali Ben Khader, who, as *Standartenführer* Baumann, aided in the execution of Jews in the Warsaw ghetto. An early member of the NSDAP and a university professor, Johann von Leers, converted to Islam and took the name of Omar Amin. President Gamal Nasser was convinced by the *Protocols of the Elders of Zion* that three hundred Zionists controlled the destiny of Europe, and appointed Leers to head Egypt's anti-Jewish policy in Cairo. With Mahmoud Saleh (Zingler), Omar Amin Leers founded the Institute for the Study of Zionism in Cairo, the propaganda of which merged anti-Zionism with antisemitism. Under Leers' direction, hundreds of anti-Jewish pamphlets were printed, many of them associating Zionism with global imperialism, espionage, and the desire for world domination through economic means and by allying itself with the world's greatest capitalist power, the United States.[1]

In France, the Catholic Orientalist scholar Louis Massignon (1883–1962) dedicated his scholarly life to Catholic-Muslim understanding. He was fascinated with Sufism, a form of Islamic mysticism, and possessed a strong revulsion for capitalism. Like so many others, he equated capitalism with Jews and his lectures at the Collège de France at the Sorbonne often turned into diatribes against the financial world and Jewish bankers who became the stereotype for all Jews. Islam, he stated, "does not kneel down before gold . . .. Muslims have an insurmountable repugnance for banking capital, for state loans, for international cartels." In stark contrast, he portrayed Jews, from medieval Baghdad to Cairo, Amsterdam, Lisbon, and New York, to be the power behind the slave trade, the international oil trade, as well as being the controllers of Anglo-American imperialism and colonial "exploitation," including in the Middle East.[2]

In a bifurcated world dominated by two opposing economic superpowers, many Arab states fell into the Soviet camp while Israel became identified by capitalism's detractors as the US's imperialist lackey. The Soviets added appropriate "progressive" terminology that appealed to anticapitalist and, later, anti-globalization advocates, and continued to spread the image of the usurious Jew who is greedy, deceitful, and exploitative. What was different in this new construction of the Jewish financier, backed by the US, was that money was not the only object for theft, according to these propagandists. They stole the land of the Palestinians through bribery and corruption. It may be that the faceless human beings depicted in the mural by Mear One, on which the Monopoly table rests, and around which the "Jewish Mr. Moneybags" sit, are Palestinians.[3]

Since its founding, and even before, Israel struggled with its national identity. The state of Israel was born not only in political and physical conflict, as war with its Arab neighbors erupted on its founding, but with economic conflict. Many of the early settlers were imbued with ideas of a moral society, different from other, corrupt, states, where people would live in a utopian communitarian harmony, working the land, and free from their old lives in Europe. Some Eastern Europeans brought elements of socialism with them that harmonized with this vision. In creating a new land, a new Jewish people was imagined that eradicated any hint of the old land they left behind and that meant the deliberate effacing of the Jewish capitalist financier. Theirs was a socialist vision of shared wealth, shared values, and shared physical labor. In this world, there was no place for the capitalist moneylender. It was clear that the long-standing stereotype that had transformed over the centuries had endured and been absorbed by the early Zionists.

If early Zionists spoke of the new Israel as a egalitarian utopia, a cultural Zion, and a shining beacon of morality, it was always in comparison to the diaspora. The founding ethos of the New Jew jettisoned the world left behind, epitomized by the moneylender. The moneylender was not a part of Jewish life to celebrate, but something shameful to be hidden or derided. The philosopher Hannah Arendt, in her book *The Origins of Totalitarianism*, put the blame for modern antisemitism squarely on the shoulders of the "bourgeois" capitalist as, she argued, they had great wealth without political power. This was as mythical a representation as the one that evolved over the centuries, created by the legions of people who painted all moneylenders in history as standing against the common good. Opposed to the archetypal moneylender stood the "authentic" Jew who took up a "useful" occupation connected to the land. This was the vision of Zionists such as A. D. Gordon who wanted Israel to be a light among nations rather than a state like any other. Gordon considered capitalism to be an exploitative system that corroded and degraded human interaction. It was only through physical labor of the soil that a self-sufficient, equal society could be created. This new utopia was not, however, the path along which Israel, after its creation in1948, travelled.[4]

Gordon's vision was a spiritual rather than an economic one and this and other utopian ideas soon floundered as it was clear that Israel could only survive if had help from Jews living in the diaspora and became a nation like those in the West. That meant a nation with sound credit and financial institutions and an economy that was part of the global network. Without the financial aid of Jewish bankers, the land of Israel could not have been created and flourished. Indeed, much the same can be said today for it is with the financial support of the U.S. and private groups and individuals outside of the state that helps Israel's economy to boom. Israel benefits more than any other country from US economic and military aid. Since its creation in 1948, the state has received approximately $121 billion dollars in aid, with $3.1 billion in security assistance allocated in 2018. Most of the money directed to Israel from the US is, in fact, for strategic defense in the Middle East and benefits the US interests as well as Israel's security. But Israel today is far from being totally dependent upon US aid as the state has developed a highly successful capitalist economy.[5]

Israel developed into the most modern, capitalist nation in the Middle East with a dynamic high-tech industry that is exported globally (even to Arab countries). It is a path that runs counter to the "moral example" or "cultural beacon" visions. Israel's technology index is "one of the best performing areas in the world." BlueStar Israel Technology ETF rose 20 percent in the first half of 2019. The army produces engineers, intelligence analysts, coders, and technicians who create technology for these high-tech companies. As of 2017, Israel listed ninety-three companies on Nasdaq, had more than 6000 start-ups in 2016, and is a research and development base for major companies such as Google, Intel, and Apple. In 2014, Lockheed Martin opened its first office in Israel and now operates in Tel Aviv and Beersheba while other global companies have both bought out Israeli enterprises or collaborated with them.[6]

Israel's economy includes the manufacture of electronic components for computers, cell phones, software, and credit cards. The country also has a flourishing pharmaceutical, chemical, cut diamond, and aircraft industry, as well as selling many valuable medical devices. It also benefits from a thriving tourist trade which is, inevitably, affected by instability and violence in the region. While Israel lacks the oil found in other Middle Eastern countries, natural gas has been discovered off the coast of Haifa. Natural gas makes up around 60 percent of Israel's energy needs and it exports it to Jordan and, in April 2017, signed a deal with Cyprus, Greece, and Italy to pump natural gas across the Mediterranean via a pipeline.[7]

Foreign investment and trade ties beyond the Middle East also increased Israel's revenues. While the US is the biggest foreign investor in Israel, new markets have opened in Asia, particularly China and India. The pathway for Israel that Gordon and others envisioned—toward a morally righteous nation (however that is interpreted)—continues to cause conflict between those who adhere to some form of this utopia, and lament the state of Israel's commitment to capitalism and being a state like any other, and those who want Israel to be a successful part of the global economy and militarily equipped to defend itself. Although security has been, and remains, the key issue for Israeli voters, recently the economy has been a big influence on the outcome of elections.[8]

On the part of many of Israel's critics, there is a distrust of and discomfort with its economic success and its relationship with the US. Anti-Zionism often turns up at anticapitalist protests and rallies. Within twenty-five years of its founding, the Jewish state was commonly described by Palestinian leaders and the Palestinian Liberation Organization (PLO) as no different than South Africa, the country that legally separated Blacks from Whites and where the White descendants of colonists discriminated against the Black native people. By its very definition as a Jewish nation, then, Israel was accused of being an apartheid state. In the 1980s this Israel-apartheid analogy expanded into academia and then was adopted by some notable people. Most prominently, it was used by President Jimmy Carter, who had brokered the first peace agreement between Israel and an Arab country, in the title of his book *Palestine: Peace not Apartheid* (2006). In 2001, a South African professor of international law, John Dugard, was named the UN special rapporteur for human rights in the Palestinian Territories. In a report published in 2007, he described Israel as an apartheid state based on foreign occupation and colonialism. In fact, Dugard goes farther than that. Israel's "crimes" are "infinitely worse" than South Africa's during its apartheid period. It was a position he reiterated in an article he wrote for the Huffington *World Post* in 2009. Representatives of Israel and Jewish organizations have frequently complained about the anti-Israeli bias at the United Nations. Zionism has been cast not only as an "apartheid state" but also as a form of Nazism with an "expansionist nature and . . . crimes against international peace and security . . ." A 1975 resolution that equated Zionism with racism was repealed in 1991 but there are still many examples of anti-Israeli bias at the organization in New York with Israel singled out for crimes against the Palestinians without the same condemnations of Palestinian activities against Israel or egregious activity in other nations such as Saudi Arabia, China, Zimbabwe, or Venezuela.[9]

After wars in the 1960s and 1970s failed to bring about a Palestinian state and/or the eradication of Israel, pro-Palestinian activists shifted their focus and developed a strategy that rested on the disruption and destruction of Israel's economy. The movement tends towards an anti-globalist stance that views global capitalism—the internationalization of market capitalism—as an inherently corrupt and immoral Western invention that maximizes profit at the expense of the workers and the environment. Connected to that general *zeitgeist* is the Boycott, Divestment, and Sanctions movement (BDS).

On July 9, 2005, the Boycott, Divestment, and Sanctions movement (BDS) was founded by 171 Palestinian non-governmental organizations and soon was supported around the globe by a wide array of people. This includes some Jewish groups such as American Jews for a Just Peace (AJJP), Jewish Voice for Peace (JVP), and International Jewish Anti-Zionist Network (IJAN). The call was for the "international civil society organizations and people of conscience" to divest from and boycott Israel in actions reminiscent to those against South Africa. The aims were threefold: end the "occupation and colonization of all Arab lands" (including taking down the wall that runs along the Green Line, the borders of Israel, Egypt, Jordan, Syria, and Lebanon demarcated in 1949); equal rights for Arab-Palestinian citizens of Israel; and the right of return for those Palestinians who left their homes and properties during the 1948 war.[10]

This aim is not antisemitic. Protest against Israeli policy or the support for an independent Palestine is not against Jews as a collective. Boycotting a country has been a favored action in the attempt to change policy and has been used against Israel since before its creation in 1948. As far back as 1922, when Jews immigrated into Palestine, native Arabs boycotted Jewish businesses in protest. The Muslim Brotherhood, founded in Egypt in 1928, was one of many groups that protested the two-state solution and the 1917 Balfour Declaration that declared a "national home" for the Jews in Palestine to be part of British policy. In advocating the replacement of interest and profit with a "community of interests between capital and labour," its members demonstrated against "Jewish imperialism." This form of dissent continued into the 1930s and was taken up by the Arab League (founded in 1945), specifically targeting Jewish products made in Palestine. When the state of Israel was declared, the boycott focused on any Israeli export.[11]

The boycotts did not work. Instead of crippling Israel, they forced the country to become economically independent and find other markets outside of the Middle East. Even with the boycotts, Arab states at various times eluded or ignored them if it was in their economic interest to conduct trade with Israel, however limited. Of course, the primary aid that economically buoyed the Jewish state was the substantial foreign aid sent by the US government and via private donations. Nevertheless, the idea of boycotts was revived with the BDS movement, which claims some success. In his *Huffington Post* blog in June 2015, James Zogby, president of the Arab American Institute, argued that the BDS movement has been effective in its aim to make Israel a pariah state for its injustices to the Palestinians. College campuses have been the most active sites of BDS movements. In March 2015, the University of London's School of Oriental and African Studies "rocked the walls of the Student Union's bar" with chants of "BDS, yes!" In the US, a student body at the University of California, Berkeley was the first in the UC system to create a divestment campaign. Other UC campuses followed, including UCLA, UC Davis, UC Santa Barbara, and UC San Diego where students called on companies to cease profiting from attacks on Gaza. In November 2012, the student senate at UC Irvine approved a divestment resolution which recommended that UCI stop investing in firms that aided and profited from Israel's occupation of Palestinian territories. All over the United States, campuses at hundreds of universities have either a BDS movement or have endorsed the United States Campaign for the Academic and Cultural Boycott of Israel (USACBI).[12]

The number of trade unionists, political grassroots organizations, student organizations, and petitions signed by faculty supporting divestment from Israel does not indicate the success of the movement. A more telling aspect of the success of BDS is whether businesses are divesting from Israel and blacklisting their companies to significant and lasting effect. The campaign must hurt Israeli commerce to be effective. In the business world, there is ambivalence about the campaign as issues of market image compete against profit margins. In a time of appearing socially responsible in the business sphere by protesting against Israel's "oppression" of Palestinians, businesses are encouraged by BDS groups to divest from the country, either in its entirety or from the occupied territories only. While the prominent MIT professor Noam Chomsky objects to an academic boycott of Israel, he has no problem with an economic boycott. Israeli companies such as SodaStream and Mekorot water company, as well as various banks have been affected by the boycott. The British bank, HSBC announced at the end of 2018 that it had liquidated its holdings in Elbit Systems because they sold weapons to the Israeli military to be potentially used against Palestinians. Companies such as Airbnb and HP have been shamed for the business in Israel and in 2015, the head of Orange, France's telecom giant, indicated his intention to pull his company out of Israel. The uproar that followed led to the CEO Stéphane Richard traveling to Jerusalem to meet privately with Netanyahu to "clear up the confusion" and backtrack on his announcement. In January 2014 PGGM, a large Dutch pension fund, announced its intention to divest from Bank Hapoalim, Bank Leumi, the First International Bank of Israel, the Israel Discount Bank, and Mizrahi Tefahot Bank. The BDS movement has counted this as a victory for their cause but the Dutch firm insisted its exclusion of Israeli banks is not a boycott of Israel, pointing to the nearly 100 million euros it has still invested in almost one hundred Israeli companies. Instead, exclusion was based upon a multitude of circumstances including "ecological misconduct ... systematic infringement of labour laws ... bad management ...[and] [h]uman rights violations." It is difficult to know to what extent the international pressure put on businesses to relinquish ties to Israel's economy is responsible for decisions such as that taken by PGGM.[13]

In July 2015, the European Council on Foreign Relations, a think tank that influences EU policy, recommended that the EU refrain from business with Israeli banks invested in the settlement areas or, as the report calls them, Occupied Palestinian Territories (OTPs). The European Union requires that all products originating from Israel have to be specifically labeled if they come from the Occupied or Settlement area. Likewise, a Canadian judge ruled that wine made in Jewish settlements cannot bear a "Product of Israel" label. Within Israel, the Gush Shalom movement has also argued for a boycott of goods that are made in the settlement regions.[14]

The Danske Bank, the biggest bank in Denmark, blacklisted Israel's Bank Hapoalim due to its involvement in settlement construction. This was, Danske Bank said, against the rules of international humanitarian law. US investment firm MSCI-ESG removed Caterpillar from three "socially responsible" stock indices. The reason for this action was Caterpillar's sale of bulldozers to Israel that were then used in the West Bank and the Gaza Strip. Norges Bank Investment Management sold its shares in Elbit Systems, Israel's largest publicly traded arms and security firm, because of its part in building the barrier along the West Bank and its sale of drones used in surveillance and attacks in Gaza. Elbit has been blacklisted by other companies, including G4S, a British multinational security company which operates in 125 countries.[15]

By a narrow margin, in June 2014, the Presbyterian Church (USA) approved an overture calling for divestment from three US firms—Caterpillar, Hewlett-Packard, and Motorola Solutions—"doing business in Israel-Palestine." Those opposing the decision cited the "symbolic power" that divestment had to cause humiliation to Jews across the country. Those who supported the motion stressed that it was not a condemnation of Jews or Israel. In the end, an amendment to the overture was added stating that the church's action was not aligned with the "overall strategy" of the BDS initiative. While the action taken by PCUSA does not make it officially part of the BDS movement, the ideas spread by that campaign has clearly influenced a wide array of investment decisions.[16]

Another case in which BDS claimed victory was the cosmetic and beauty supply company Sephora's decision to stop selling Ahava cosmetics. The rumor was spread that LVMH-owned Sephora had taken the action because Ahava's products were made at Mitzpe Shalem, a settlement in the West Bank and used raw materials from the disputed territory. Sephora was quick to point out that they had removed Ahava from its shelves in the US only and were still selling the products at their European branches. These decisions, a company spokesman stressed, were due, not to the BDS campaign, but due to market preferences and the fact that they change their store items on a regular basis.[17]

The website for the US Campaign for Palestinian Rights claims that they have had 250 BDS victories over thirteen years. According to the *Financial Times*, there is serious cause for concern with regard to the impact of BDS on the Israeli economy. The Prime Minister Benjamin Netanyahu has talked of the dangers of this attack on Israel's economy, although some critics have accused him of cynically using the movement as a rallying cry for his leadership and party. A leaked Israeli government document claimed that the movement could cost the country's economy in the region of $1.4 billion dollar per annum due to divestment and boycott of goods. The US think tank Rand Corporation puts that deficit amount even higher, suggesting the loss of income could be $47 billion over ten years. It has been reported that foreign direct investment in Israel fell by nearly 50 percent in 2014 compared to the previous year, chiefly due to the Israeli-Gaza conflict. It rose again in 2015, especially in the fourth quarter before falling again the following year. This gloomy analysis is contested by Efraim Inbar, professor of Political Studies at Bar-Ilan University and Director of the Begin-Sadat Center for Strategic Studies, who considers the boycotts and divestments to be more an irritant than a significant threat.[18]

The BDS movement has as its primary motivation the eradication of Jewish settlements on disputed territory and the creation of a Palestinian state, neither of which is antisemitic. There is cause for concern over the increasing number of settlements in the West Bank. In 1981, there were 16,200 settlers in this region; in 2016 that number was 399,300. Neither is it antisemitic to prohibit labels that say an item is a product in Israel if it was produced in the settlements. Where the line becomes blurred between legitimate protest and antisemitism is in the singling out of Israel as a violator of human rights. There is no discussion about the role of the Palestinian Authority, the launching of missiles by Hamas into Israeli territory. Instead, Israel is treated as a pariah state. As the German Foreign Minister, Heiko Maas stated with regard to the UN, Israel is "denounced, treated in a biased manner and marginalized." While there may be no vast antisemitic conspiracy against Israel, there does appear to be some truth in Netanyahu's contention that there exists "an international campaign to blacken [Israel's] name." Due to the close relationship between Israel and the US and the success of the Israeli economy, the Palestinian cause, BDS, anti-globalism, and anticapitalist activism have combined, making Israel not only a pariah but also "a proxy for the West." It is difficult, given the wide array of participants, to know where legitimate criticism of Israel morphs into antisemitism. Leaders in Zimbabwe and Malaysia have conjured up the *Protocols of the Elders of Zion* conspiracy that Jews are plotting to control the global economy. Among the 20,000 anti-globalization protestors at the 2003 World Social Forum at Porto Alegre, Brazil held up signs denouncing "Nazis, Yankees, and Jews: No More Chosen Peoples" and wore t-shirts with the Star of David contorted into a swastika. Some of those in a Palestinian organization disparaged Israel as the power behind US capitalism. Similar visual sentiments appeared at anti-G8 meetings and other economic summits. The fact that the protesters use the term "Jews" to reflect their anticapitalism rather than "Israel" is testament to the close association that has lasted throughout the centuries of Jews and capitalism.[19]

The former French prime minister Manuel Valls criticized the boycotts of Israel products, claiming that they encourage antisemitism and foster a "nauseating climate" in France. Supporters of BDS claim that his argument is an attack on free speech and contrary to the government's support of the *Charlie Hebdo* journalists who were murdered by Al-Qaeda terrorists in January 2015. According to Khaled Abu Toameh, an Israeli-Arab journalist who is a strong supporter of StandWithUs, a pro-Israel advocacy group, it is Hamas who benefits most from the BDS movement. By weakening Israel economically and, in particular, isolating the country, Hamas has found a new ally that it hopes may "pave the way for the elimination of Israel." Whether the BDS movement will prove ineffective against global market forces and economic pragmatism, or whether it will flourish and seriously injure Israel either economically or existentially remains to be seen. At a round table discussion at the June 2015 Herzliya Conference in Israel, the former Chief Rabbi of the United Kingdom, Lord Jonathan Sacks, stated that what had once been a source of unification for Jews—Israel—was now bitterly dividing them. His portrayal of a past unity among all Jews with regards to Israel may not be accurate but there is no doubt that Israel's identity and future are now highly fractious issues both inside and outside the country. With that the case, Sacks argued that the BDS movement had been partially successful. The psychological damage caused by the BDS movement has made Israel into a pariah state deserving of divestment.[20]

The BDS movement and its supporters consist of a wide range of people who express a variety of views. The extreme point of view is not demanding the removal of settlements that are in contention or the call for an independent Palestinian state. It is the denial of Israel's right to exist as a state. In April 2017 at the University of Cork, Ireland, a conference was held called "International Law and the State of Israel: Legitimacy, Exceptionalism, and Responsibility." Among the speakers was the American Jewish emeritus professor of Bard University Joel Kovel, who held the Alger Hiss Chair for Social Studies. Kovel, an anticapitalist Marxist, believes that the world is doomed if it does not end two dangers: capitalism and Israel. He has written books entitled *The End of Nature: The End of Capitalism or the End of the World* and another on the subject of *Overcoming Zionism*, In Cork, he claimed that the world is "ecologically doomed" if Israel was not removed from the Middle East. The idea that a country in existence for seventy years can be removed without genocide is foolish at best and murderous at worst. Despite being created from a UN vote in 1947, Israel continues to be the only country in the world that has to constantly defend its right to exist.[21]

While Israel today is as far removed from the visions dreamed up by many of the early Zionists eager to shed the image of the Jewish moneylender in favor of a "New Jew," the Jewish state still is driven by a sense of moral righteousness and the specter of the moneylender. In March 2016, the Knesset, Israel's parliament, passed a new law capping the salary of bankers. Introduced by the finance minister, Moshe Kahlon, the law's intent is to narrow the gap between the employers' and workers' pay. The highest pay in a bank is not to be in excess of thirty-five times that of the lowest paid worker in the company. Passed 56–0 with no abstentions, it was not an economically-driven policy. As with any other time in history when bankers were singled out as the source of economic distress, it is a populist tactic. As Kahlon made clear, there is "moral significance" to the new legislation. It had to do with "solidarity and consideration for the weak." For the common good and as a foil to those who want to help the poor, the bankers, once again, became the quintessential image of greed and contrary to the good of society.[22]

The law was attacked by Yair Seroussi, the chairman of Israel's largest bank, Bank Hapoalim, who claimed that it would have serious ramifications for the country's economy and reverse the progress made by Israel in the global economy. As for the plan to prohibit banks from issuing credit cards, the governor of the Bank of Israel Karnit Flug has opposed this proposal suggesting that this step would lead to monopolization of the credit card industry. The battle over Israel's economic path is still ongoing but it's future as a global center for high technology seems robust, notwithstanding political uncertainties.[23]

* * *

"He who takes [usury] goes to hell and he who does not falls into poverty," wrote the fourteenth-century Italian humanist Bevenuto da Imola (c.1320–1388) in his commentary on Dante's *Divine Comedy*. Dante himself had put the usurer in the seventh circle of Hell in that book. This neatly sums up the dilemma of the spiritual ideal versus the materialist necessity. Today, credit cards are in almost everyone's wallet and mortgages are essential for most people when they purchase a home. Most countries are run on debt, which is unproblematic only if the country has the revenue to service that debt. We live in a consumerist world far removed from that of the medieval moneylender, the seventeenth-century court Jew, or even the nineteenth-century banker. But the stereotype of the greedy, capitalist, Jewish banker has managed to survive.

The belief that wealth and materialism are inherently corrupting and opposed to virtue continues to be the subject of papal sermons. In 1967, Pope Paul VI warned that "the acquisition of worldly goods can lead men to greed, to the unrelenting desire for more, to the pursuit of greater personal power. Rich and poor alike—be they individuals, families or nations—can fall prey to avarice and soulstifling materialism." And more recently, Pope Francis, in a clear departure from Pope John Paul II who had supported market capitalism, wrote that the free market and the "culture of prosperity" deadens the majority and excludes the poor. "The worship of the ancient golden calf," he noted, "has returned in a new and ruthless guise in the idolatry of money and the dictatorship of an impersonal economy lacking a truly human purpose." Only the callous would argue against helping the poor or wishing for more prosperity for more people. Very few would admire those whose only desire in life is to be rich or whose idea of success was accumulating money. But it is undeniable that capitalism—as a morally-neutral economic system—has produced the greatest prosperity for the greatest number of people compared to other systems. State control of the economy by a monarch, dictator or oligarchy—as in the Soviet Union, Zimbabwe, or Venuezuela, for example—has led to economic collapse, the reduction of available goods, and poverty. Any so-called "successes"—such as full employment or high wages—have been accomplished only through confiscation, redistribution, coercion, and the retraction of freedom.[24]

The country that has been most associated with capitalism, making money, and the unabashed celebration of the "culture of prosperity" is the United States. It is a land, the French economist and engineer Michel Chevalier wrote in the nineteenth century, in which everyone "speculates and it speculates on everything." It is also the country into which Jews have most successfully immigrated, settled, assimilated, and chosen to call their homeland. Many historians of antisemitism have shoehorned the United States into their narratives that judge every incident against or seemingly against Jews to be part of a longstanding and unrelenting antisemitism. They point to the quotas against Jews in the nineteenth and early twentieth centuries, the refusal of hotels and elite clubs to admit Jews at this time, but there was no restriction to opening their own clubs, which they did. Such quotos and social limitations were undoubtedly unpleasant but could in no way be compared to the history of Jews under Nazi control or the history of Black people in the United States until the civil rights movement. There were certain groups or individuals that openly espoused and still espouse antisemitism, such as the German American Bund in the 1930s, Gerald K. Smith, Coughlin, Long, Christian Identity groups, and, more recently, the Westboro Baptist Church, as well as individuals enamored with White supremacy or Neo-Nazism. All of these individuals spout ugly and ludicrous statements about Jewish control of the economy, but none has had a lasting effect on the nation nor have they achieved political power. Prejudice exists in every society, to varying degrees, and about all kinds of people and ways of life. The idea that you can control people's minds and erase it from the world is both naïve and disturbing. It would create a world in which freedom of speech and thought was regulated and impeded.

Jews have fared remarkably well in the US. In spite of earlier bias and ongoing but marginal hate groups, Jews have integrated and been given opportunities in the United States that have been exceeded only by the state of Israel. The U.S. was not a haven for Jews because it was a utopia free from all ills and hatred but because it was built on the Enlightenment principles that extended liberty, and, crucially, economic freedom and opportunity to them, which provided a better standard of living to more people than any other economic system so far.[25]

In the United States, criticism has not generally fallen specifically on Jews when it comes to financial scandals. Men such as John Gutfreund, the so-called "King of Wall Street," Mark Swartz of Tyco, and Bernie Madoff—all Jewish and involved in financial scandals during the 1990s— were no different to Jeffrey Skilling of Enron, Barry Minkow, Bernard Ebbers of WorldCom, and Dennis Koslowski of Tyco (infamous for his lavish million-dollar parties and the $6,000 shower curtain in his bathroom), none of whom was Jewish. The cry over "excessive" profit remains as strong as it was in the past over ostentatious lifestyles or inequalities of income. That sense of injustice is all the greater—and more legitimate—when the money that provides such lifestyles is not earned honestly. It is not "excessive" profit that is unjust. Despite the long condemnation of it, profit whatever its size is not unjust in and of itself. Profit only becomes unjust if it is attained through illegal, duplicitous, or exploitative means.

It is often argued that a bad economy leads to spikes in antisemitism. As we have seen throughout history, this is sometimes, but not always, the case. In 2008, the global economy plummeted. The investment bank, Lehman Brothers, which was the fourth largest in the US, declared bankruptcy, setting off a panic and then a crash. The firm was founded in 1850 by Henry, Emanuel, and Mayer Lehman, the sons of a Jewish cattle merchant. From 1969, there was no member of the Lehman family involved in the running of the company, which merged with Kuhn, Loeb & Co. in 1977, the firm Jacob Schiff had joined in 1875. Lehman's collapse came in the wake of the subprime mortgage crisis and the 2007–2008 recession. The ready supply of credit resulted in a higher demand for mortgages that was in excess of the quantity of prime loans available. This led to the lowering of lending standards and the high-risk mortgages was a result of government housing policies and the willingness of banks, credit agencies, and borrowers to offer and accept adjustable-rate mortgages with little or no collateral. When the interest rate rose, many homeowners were unable to pay their mortgage payments with the result of mass foreclosures and a plunge in house prices. In many cases, the houses were worth less than the loan owed to the bank. Subsequently, the US's economy went into recession and the global economy's growth slowed while unemployment rose.

People instinctively assumed the cause of the economic meltdown to be greedy bankers, the lack of regulation, and speculation. But there was no widespread accusation against Jews specifically, except among the minority antisemitic groups who spread conspiracy theories about the Federal Reserve being in the grip of the Jews on a variety of neo-Nazi websites. The general attitude towards Jews can be gauged more accurately by the treatment of one of the most scandalous schemers of that time, Bernie Madoff. In the economic turmoil, Madoff emerged as the quintessential "poster child for [financial] abuse and fraud." A stockbroker and investment advisor, Madoff concocted a Ponzi scheme that defrauded thousands of investors out of more than $20 billion dollars, becoming the largest fraud in the history of the US. As with other trading scandals at the time, Madoff lied about the rate of return that his investors would receive, continuing to lure in more clients to his "house of cards" scheme. His victims were overwhelmingly Jewish as he deliberately played on his own Jewishness to inspire trust and get them to invest their savings with him. His victims—whose money was never invested—included not only individuals but also charities such as the Elie Wiesel Foundation.[26]

During and after the 2008 economic downturn and the emergence of Madoff's crime, there were no anti-Jewish attacks and no general talk of greedy *Jewish* bankers in the US. We see similar trends in Europe, which have been steadily favorable toward Jews. Poll results in France from 1988–1991 and 1999–2000 indicate that the number of people hostile to Jews in the population was stable (about 10 percent). Anti-Jewish stereotypes have declined in the first decade of the twenty-first century not only in France and the US, but also in Germany, Austria, the UK. It was not completely absent, but there was no significant connection made between Jews and the economic crisis that reached its height in 2008.[27]

The most serious antisemitism today comes from a different sector of society. It is linked to radical Muslims and those who support their causes, especially for an independent Palestinian state. But the link forged long ago between Jews and money/usury/capitalism continues to crop up in a variety of anticapitalist movements and in politics. It is not surprising that the Corbyn-led Labour Party in Britain is both a home to antisemites and also has an extreme anticapitalist orientation politically. Perhaps the most egregious recent example of a conspiracy theory concerning Jews and capitalism was made after the attack on the Twin Towers in New York on September 11, 2001. The intent to destroy the World Trade Center was to strike at the heart of capitalism and international finance and yet the Internet was replete with conspiracy theories accusing Jews and the United States government of concocting the attack. The "proof" of the former's involvement being the alleged absence of some 4000 Jews from work that particular day. In the same conference at Cork that discussed the legitimacy of Israel's existence, Joel Kovel linked Israel to the 9/11 attack. Talking about the five Israelis (some of whom were proven to be Mossad agents) who, he said, cheered from across the river as the towers were struck, Kovel suggested the involvement of Israel with the act or terrorism. A quick check on the Internet garners a sizable number of websites dedicated to the role of Israel in the 9/11 attacks based primarily on the unsurprising information that Mossad has agents working undercover in the US. In the end, there is little, if any, difference in disseminating such accusations and propagating the *Protocols of the Elders of Zion*. Conspiracies exist, of course, but in both cases there was nothing to prove their legitimacy beyond rumor. Both imaginings emanated from the longstanding myth that capitalism was an immoral evil and that Jews were its creators.[28]

* * *

Capital was, and remains, the linchpin of innovation and economic growth. Over centuries, bankers—whether lending money from a table or bench in medieval times or from a high-rise office in New York—have been a critical element in the development of the West as it shifted from a subsistence to a surplus economy. Capitalism as a system works best when countries have deep markets, that is, markets with high trading volume and narrow bid-ask spreads that prevents the price of shares to be altered dramatically when large numbers are traded. When this is the case, a country's wealth normally grows more rapidly. Furthermore, historically, a country with a wealthier private sector is financially richer than the country with a heavily monied public sector.

The practice of interest loans aided the expansion and economic well-being of our world, but the growth of prosperity had ramifications far beyond account ledgers and bank balances. It fostered the Renaissance, privately financed playwrights and poets, funded exploration and scientific investigation. The financiers who lent money helped to build Europe's and the United States' infrastructure and great cities, as well as fund inventions that revolutionized society and enriched countless lives through labor saving devices in the workplace and at home. The time these inventions saved gave us the idea of leisure and the museums, movies, art galleries, cultural and social events, and vacations that fill it. This is not to say that there have not been, and will never be, abuses of the economic system that developed in the West over the centuries. But, to paraphrase what Churchill once said about democracy, capitalism may not be perfect, but it is the best system we have so far.[29]

Milton Friedmann wrote in his book *Capitalism and Freedom*, "the groups in our society that have the most at stake in the preservation and strengthening of competitive capitalism are those minority groups which can most easily become the object of the distrust and enmity of the majority . . . ." Developed over centuries, capitalism that is based on the free flow of money, fair competition, and open markets, is inseparable from political and personal liberty. Like all people, financiers were good, bad, honest, corrupt, mediocre, and indifferent but without the loans to provide the capital, whoever the lender, Western Europe and America would not have become the prosperous regions they are today. It is time for those who risked their capital to foster businesses, bring inventions to life, help people over hard times, buy houses, and many other things to be celebrated rather than erased from history. It is time to break the longstanding caricature of the greedy Jewish collective but that can only be successfully accomplished by also eradicating the equally mythical idea that capitalism is exploitative and immoral.[30]

Notes

1. Sayyid Qutb, "Our Struggle with the Jews," in *The Legacy of Islamic Antisemitism: From Sacred Texts to Solemn History*, ed. Andrew G. Bostom (Amherst, NY: Prometheus Books, 2008), 355–63; Jeffrey Herf, *Nazi Propaganda for the Arab World* (New Haven: Yale University Press, 2010), 260; Edwin Black, "Coke Profits Off Egyptian Jew's Seized Property," *Huffington Post*, June 7, 2012, http://www.huffingtonpost.com/edwin-black/jewish-egyptian-vs-cocacola_b_1570123.html; Albert Speer, *Inside the Third Reich* (New York: Macmillan, 1970), 96; Bat Ye'or, *Eurabia: The Euro-Arab Axis* (Madison, NJ: Fairleigh Dickinson University Press, 2005), 42–43. There were many other Nazis who fled to the Middle East. For the case of Tarek Hussein Farid, see Souad Mekhennet and Nicholas Kulish, "Uncovering Lost Past of Most Wanted Nazi," *New York Times*, February 4, 2009, http://www.nytimes.com/2009/02/05/world/africa/05nazi.html?_r=0; Martin A. Lee, *The Beast Reawakens: Fascism's Resurgence From Hitler's Spymasters to Today's Neo-Nazi Groups and Right-Wing Extremists* (New York: Routledge, 2000), 92, 97–98, 107.
2. Elie Kedourie, "Going Third World, á la Française," *Middle East Quarterly* 11.3 (2004): 65–68.

3. Gabriel Schoenfeld, *The Return of Anti-Semitism* (San Francisco: Encounter Books, 2004), 57; "Soviet Anti-Zionism or Anti-Semitism?" *Jews in Eastern Europe* 3.8 (1968).
4. Hannah Arendt, *The Origins of Totalitarianism* (New York: Harcourt Brace, 1951); Amos Perlmutter, "A.D. Gordon: A Transcendental Zionist," *Middle Eastern Studies* 7.1 (1971).
5. Foreign Aid Explorer, https://explorer.usaid.gov/cd/ISR.
6. David Rosenberg, *Israel's Technology Economy: Origins and Impact* (New York: Palgrave Macmillan, 2018); *CNBC*, https://www.cnbc.com/2019/04/05/israels-election-will-give-the-winner-control-of-a-booming-economy.html "Israel's Army, A High-Tech Powerhouse without the Sense to Cash in," *Haaretz*, August 13, 2014, http://www.haaretz.com/israel-news/business/.premium-1.610148; Naftali Bennett, "Israel's 'Secret' System of Education Drives High-Tech Powerhouse," *Wall Street Journal*, March 23, 2017; Alex Grobman, *BDS: The Movement to Destroy Israel* (Cliffs, NJ: San Remo Press, 2015), Kindle ed., chap. 6; *The Algemeiner*, April 11, 2014, http://www.algemeiner.com/2014/04/11/lockheed-martin-officially-opens-israel-office/#.
7. "Israel's Natural Gas is a Game-Changer," *The Algemeiner*, April 10, 2017, https://www.algemeiner.com/2017/04/10/israels-natural-gas-supply-is-a-game-changer/; "Israel Signs Pipeline Deal in Push to Export Gas to Europe," *Financial Times*, April 3, 2017, https://www.ft.com/content/78ff60ca-184c-11e7-a53d-df09f373be87.
8. Ministry of Economy and Industry, http://itrade.gov.il/india/israel-india/; *Times of Israel*, April 22, 2014, https://www.timesofisrael.com/asia-primed-to-beat-out-us-as-top-israel-export-market/
9. Ran Greenstein, "Israel/Palestine and the Apartheid Analogy," and "BDS Movement Call, July 9, 2005," both in *The Case for Sanctions Against Israel*, ed. Audrea Lim (London: Verso, 2012), Kindle ed.; *Democracy Now!* Online, May 6, 2015, http://www.democracynow.org/blog/2015/5/6/ex_un_official_john_dugard_israel; John Dugard, "Two States or Apartheid," *The World Post*, September 12, 2009, http://www.huffingtonpost.com/john-dugard/post_356_b_258206.html; Mr. El-Fattal, A/37/PV. 93, General Assembly, United Nations, quoted in Daniel Meron, *Anti-Semitic Rhetoric at the United Nations,* The Jacob Blaustein Institute for the Advancement of Human Rights (New York: American Jewish Committee, nd), 9; Saree Makdisi, "Does the Term 'Apartheid' Fit Israel? Of Course It Does," and Michael Oren, "Israel Isn't, and Will Never Be, an Apartheid State," *Los Angeles Times*, Op-Ed, May 17, 2014; *The Atlantic*, June 20, 2018, https://www.theatlantic.com/international/archive/2018/06/us-un-human-rights/563276/.
10. Greenstein, "BDS Movement Call."
11. Matthias Küntzel, "Hitler's Legacy: Islamic Antisemitism and the Impact of the Muslim Brotherhood," A paper presented at the international seminar series "Antisemitism in Comparative Perspective," for the Institute of Social and Policy Studies at Yale University, New Haven, 30 November, 2006, http://www.

matthiaskuentzel.de/contents/hitlers-legacy-islamic-antisemitism-in-the-middle-east; Herf, *Nazi Propaganda,* 239–40; Grobman, *BDS*, introduction.

12. Grobman, *BDS*, introduction; Fanny Malinen, "British University Votes 'Yes' to Academic Boycott of Israel," *New Internationalist*, blog; "USAC Passes Divestment Resolution with 8-2-2 Vote," *Daily Bruin*, dailybruin.com/2014/11/18/usac-passes-divestment-resolution-with-8-2-2-vote/; "Univ. of California Union Approves BDS Motion," *Jewish Telegraphic Agency*, December 11, 2014, jta.org/2014/12/11/news-opinion/united-states/union-representing-uc-academics.
13. Grobman, *BDS*, chap. 1; *Haaretz*, December 29, 2018, https://www.haaretz.com/israel-news/business/europe-s-largest-bank-hsbc-divest-israel-elbit-bds-1.6788301 "Orange's Stephane Richard Tells Israel of Regret Over Comments," *BBC Online News*, June 12, 2015, http://www.bbc.com/news/world-middle-east-33109950; BDS online at http://www.bdsmovement.net/v2/2014/giant-dutch-pension-fund-divests-from-israeli-banks-14029, January 13, 2014; PGGM website, https://www.pggm.nl/english/what-we-think/Pages/Frequently-asked-questions-about-the-exclusion-of-Israeli-banks.aspx
14. Lovatt and Toaldo, "EU Differentiation and Israeli Settlements"; James Zogby, "BDS: A Legitimate and Moral Response to Israeli Policy," *Huffington Post*, June 13, 2015, http://www.huffingtonpost.com/james-zogby/bds-a-legitimate-and-mora_b_7575794.html.
15. *Haaretz*, February 1, 2014, http://www.haaretz.com/news/diplomacy-defense/1.571849; Ibid., June 23, 2012, http://www.haaretz.com/business/decision-to-oust-caterpillar-from-influential-ethical-investing-index-linked-to-israeli-use-of-tractors-1.440509; Grobman, *BDS*, chap. 5.
16. News and Announcements, *PCUSA Website*, https://www.pcusa.org/news/2014/6/20/slim-margin-assembly-approves-divestment-three-com/; Grobman, *BDS*, chap. 3.
17. *The Electronic Intifada*, https://electronicintifada.net/content/ahava-campaign-comes-court/8881; Anti-Defamation League Website, http://www.adl.org/combating-hate/cyber-safety/c/internet-rumors/false-rumor-sephora-and-ahava.html?referrer=https://www.google.com/#.VeIZevlVhBc
18. Grobman, *BDS*, introduction and chapters 2 and 6; *The Algemeiner*, April 11, 2014, http://www.algemeiner.com/2014/04/11/lockheed-martin-officially-opens-israel-office/#; "Israel: A New Kind of War," *Financial Times Online*, June 12, 2015; *Newsweek*, June 25, 2015, http://europe.newsweek.com/foreign-investment-israel-slashed-by-half-329269; "Israel's Foreign Direct Investment," *Trading Economics*, https://tradingeconomics.com/israel/foreign-direct-investment.
19. "German Minister Condemns UN's Treatment of Israel, May 11, 2019, *DW*, https://www.dw.com/en/german-foreign-minister-condemns-uns-treatment-of-israel/a-48703040; *Washington Post*, May 4, 2019, https://www.washingtonpost.com/world/more-than-100-rockets-fired-into-israel-from-gaza-israel-responds-with-airstrikes/2019/05/04/6591a798-6e47-11e9-8f44-e8d8bb1df986_story.html?utm_term=.08551d25c299; Lars Rensmann and Julius H. Schoeps, eds., *Politics and*

Resentment: Antisemitism and Counter-Cosmopolitanism in the European Union (Leiden: Brill, 2011), 48.

20. "The Hamas Covenant," August 18, 1988, *The Avalon Project, Documents in Law, History, and Diplomacy*, Yale Law School, http://avalon.law.yale.edu/20th_century/hamas.asp; Khaled Abu Toameh, "BDS and Hamas: The New Partnership," *Gateshead Institute Website*, June 23, 2015, http://www.gatestoneinstitute.org/5940/bds-hamas; *France 24*, http://www.france24.com/en/20160120-france-boycott-israel-bds-law-free-speech-antisemitism; "Secret Sheldon Adelson Summit Raises Up To $50 M For Strident Anti-BDS Push," *The Forward*, June 9, 2015, http://forward.com/news/israel/309676/secret-sheldon-adelson-summit-raises-up-to-50m-for-strident-anti-bds-push/. The quote is from Kenneth Bob, president of Ameinu; "Lord Sacks: BDS Makes it 'Almost Impossible' for Europe's Jews to Support Israel," *The Times of Israel*, June 9, 2015, http://www.timesofisrael.com/lord-sacks-bds-makes-it-almost-impossible-for-europes-jews-to-support-israel/
21. *The Algemeiner*, April 3, 2017, https://www.algemeiner.com/2017/04/03/mossad-agents-cheered-911-claims-american-jewish-academic-at-anti-israel-conference-in-ireland/.
22. *The Independent* (UK), June 17, 2015, http://www.independent.co.uk/news/world/middle-east/controversial-citizenship-law-that-bans-palestinians-married-to-israelis-from-living-in-israel-extended-by-the-knesset-10327385.html; Benjamin Netanyahu quoted in the *New York Times*, May 31, 2015, http://www.nytimes.com/2015/06/01/world/middleeast/netanyahu-lashes-out-at-criticism-of-israel.html; *New York Times*, November 1, 2003, http://www.nytimes.com/2003/11/01/news/01iht-poll_ed1_.html; *Haaretz*, Sept. 12, 2014, http://www.haaretz.com/news/diplomacy-defense/1.615478; *Haaretz*, March 29, 2016, http://www.haaretz.com/israel-news/business/.premium-1.711553.
23. *Financial Times*, March 23, 2016, http://www.ft.com/cms/s/0/939f3172-f105-11e5-aff5-19b4e253664a.html#axzz44tndoYIW; Rosenberg, *Israel's Technology Economy*.
24. Borer, *The City of London*, 182; Muller, *The Mind and the Market*, chap. 1; Pope Paul VI, Encyclical "*Populorum Progressio*" (On the Development of Peoples), March 26, 1967, http://www.vatican.va/holy_father/paul_vi/encyclicals/documents/hf_p-vi_enc_26031967_populorum_en.html; Gregory J. Millman, "Catholics in Business Wrestle with Pope Francis' Attacks on Capitalism," *Wall Street Journal*, July 10, 2014, http://www.wsj.com/articles/catholics-in-business-wrestle-with-pope-francis-attacks-on-capitalism-1405016794; Pope Francis, *Evangelii Gaudium, Chapter 2: Some Challenges of Today's World*, 53–56, November 24, 2013, http://w2.vatican.va/content/francesco/en/apost_exhortations/documents/papa-francesco_esortazione-ap_20131124_evangelii-gaudium.html#No_to_an_economy_of_exclusion.
25. Michel Chevalier, *Lettres sur l'Amerique du Nord* (Brussels: Société belge de librairie, 1838), quoted in Kindleberger and Aliber, *Manias*, chap. 3.

26. Kindleberger and Aliber, *Manias*, chapters 1, 5, 7.
27. There were more people criticizing Jewish influence in international finance in Spain, Poland, and Hungary. Julian Kossoff, "The English-Speaking World No Longer Sees Jews as Greedy Villains: Old-Style Antisemitism is Dying," *Daily Telegraph*, 3 April 2010, http://blogs.telegraph.co.uk/news/juliankossoff/100031580/the-english-speaking-world-no-longer-sees-jews-as-greedy-villains-old-style-anti-semitism-is-dying/. Jerry Z. Muller, "Antisemitism and this Recession: The Dog That Didn't Bark," *Jewish Daily Forward*, 24 March 2010, http://forward.com/articles/126845/antisemitism-and-this-recession-the-dog-that-didn/.
28. *The Telegraph*, January 9, 2015, http://www.telegraph.co.uk/news/worldnews/europe/france/11335980/Antisemitism-in-France-the-exodus-has-begun.html; Matthias Küntzel, "National Socialism and Anti-Semitism in the Arab World," *Jewish Political Studies Review* 17.1–2 (Spring 2005): 11; On the debunking of the 9/11 myths, see Chris McGreal, "9/11 Conspiracy Theories Debunked," *The Guardian*, September 5, 2011, http://www.theguardian.com/world/2011/sep/05/9-11-conspiracy-theories-debunked; *The Algemeiner*, April 3, 2017,
29. Temin and Voth, *Prometheus Shackled*, chap. 8; Kindleberger and Aliber, *Manias*, chap. 7.
30. Milton Friedmann, *Capitalism and Freedom* (Chicago: University of Chicago Press, 2002), 21.

Index

C

D

E

J

K

L

M

N

O

P

R

V

W